A PROMISED LAND

A Promised Land

JEWISH PATRIOTS, THE AMERICAN REVOLUTION, AND THE BIRTH OF RELIGIOUS FREEDOM

Adam Jortner

OXFORD
UNIVERSITY PRESS

OXFORD
UNIVERSITY PRESS

Oxford University Press is a department of the University of Oxford. It furthers
the University's objective of excellence in research, scholarship, and education
by publishing worldwide. Oxford is a registered trade mark of Oxford University
Press in the UK and certain other countries.

Published in the United States of America by Oxford University Press
198 Madison Avenue, New York, NY 10016, United States of America.

© Adam Jortner 2024

Library of Congress Cataloging-in-Publication Data
Names: Jortner, Adam, author.
Title: A promised land : Jewish patriots, the American Revolution, and
the birth of religious freedom / Adam Jortner.
Other titles: Jewish patriots, the American Revolution,
and the birth of religious freedom
Description: New York, NY : Oxford University Press, [2024] |
Includes bibliographical references and index. |
Identifiers: LCCN 2024006503 (print) | LCCN 2024006504 (ebook) |
ISBN 9780197536865 (hardback) | ISBN 9780197536889 (epub) |
ISBN 9780197536896
Subjects: LCSH: United States—History—Revolution, 1775–1783—Participation, Jewish. |
Jews—United States—History—18th century. | United States—History—Colonial period,
ca. 1600–1775. | Jews—United States—Politics and government—18th century. |
Freedom of religion—United States—History—18th century. |
Judaism—Relations—Christianity—History—18th century. |
United States—Ethnic relations—18th century.
Classification: LCC E269.J5 J67 2024 (print) | LCC E269.J5 (ebook) |
DDC 973/.04924—dc23/eng/20240306
LC record available at https://lccn.loc.gov/2024006503
LC ebook record available at https://lccn.loc.gov/2024006504

DOI: 10.1093/oso/9780197536865.001.0001

Printed by Sheridan Books, Inc., United States of America

To Charlie and Sam: a birthright

It is not interference with things, or even with human beings, but with the development of ideas which implies the greatest potential alteration of history.

—John Brunner, *Times Without Number*

Wherever there is hope, there must necessarily be fear.

—Gershom Seixas to Sarah Kurdsheedt, 1813

CONTENTS

Author's Note: Spelling and punctation were not standardized in the eighteenth and nineteenth centuries. In general, where the differences in language and grammar in the sources were so great as to impede comprehension, I have silently corrected them.

Introduction

Rookim

JONAS PHILLIPS USED YIDDISH, ALTHOUGH he could "write my meaning better in English." But it was July 1776, and Phillips was shipping a copy of the Declaration of Independence across the seas in violation of British law. So Phillips wrote in Hebrew script to get the Declaration into the hands of his kinsman in Amsterdam and sent the letter to the Netherlands by the roundabout way of the Caribbean. Phillips was bullish on the revolution; the enclosed documents were, he wrote, "a declaration of the whole country." The war would bankrupt England and free America. "The Americans have an army of 100,000 *rookim*," he wrote, using the Yiddish term for "tough guys." The letter never made it to Holland. The British seized it and wondered if it was written in some kind of code.[1]

The Jews of the American Revolution remain similarly cryptic to us. The subject sounds more like Borscht-Belt schtick than serious history. But Phillips had plenty of company. Patriot Jews were early and unstinting in their support for the revolution, in synagogues, on the streets, and in the army. In 1770, the Pennsylvania Jew Barnard Gratz wrote to a friend, "I was going to inclose you the king's speech to parlement," but it "was such *narishkeit* [foolishness] that [it] is not worth the postage."[2] At the Battle of Beaufort in South Carolina, one of the patriot militias was nicknamed "the Jew Company" because twenty-eight of its forty members were Jewish. A memoir of the Jew Company noted that they did not use that term; they called themselves "the *Free Citizens*."[3] Solomon Bush of Philadelphia became a colonel during the war and suffered a leg wound in 1777 that, he regretted, would make him unable to "revenge the rongs [*sic*] of my injured country" soon enough. In 1774, Mordecai Sheftall was one of the few Georgians to pledge his resistance to the Coercive Acts—Britain's efforts to suspend the Massachusetts government and blockade Boston harbor. A year later, as the rebellion spread, Sheftall became chairman of the Savannah Parochial Committee—an organization that acted as a de facto government in defiance of British rule. As an extra-legal entity, the committee did not have to follow Georgia law, and therefore Sheftall as a Jew did not have to take the Christian oath of office required for all Georgians who exercised political authority in the name of the king.[4]

On May 17, 1776, Gershom Seixas, head of Shearith Israel (New York's only synagogue), organized a day of fasting and prayer, as recommended by Congress. The proclamation from Congress had been specifically drafted for Christian clergy, so Seixas was under no obligation to do anything. But he led the Jews in worship anyway, asking God to "put it in the heart of our Sovereign Lord, George the third . . . to turn away their fierce Wrath from North America." Seixas called on the "God of our Fathers Abraham Isaac and Jacob," but otherwise it was the patriot prayer suggested by the congressional proclamation. In essence, Seixas turned the synagogue into an extension of Congress—making the synagogue a patriot space. American Jews, Seixas wrote, should view themselves "as possessing equal rights & privileges, with the rest of the inhabitants."[5] Seixas soon led the patriot Jews out of New York. As the British bore down on the city, Seixas gathered up the Torah and ritual objects and crossed the East River with his fellow patriot Jews, to live in exile in Connecticut rather than worship under tory rule. In 1780, Seixas brought his followers to Philadelphia, where he became the religious leader of the first national American Jewish community. The revolution had rabbis.[6]

The revolution has long been described as a Christian or pseudo-Christian affair. Indeed, some people have dedicated themselves to the idea that American had a "Christian founding," and that therefore Christianity was and is incorporated into law and policy. This argument is more often asserted than proven. It begins with the notion that certain patriots and Founding Fathers were religious Protestants—which is true—and from there argues that Protestant interests and theologies were paramount reasons why people fought for the revolution. The argument begins with the presence of Christian patriots to assert the false conclusion that all patriots were Christians and fought for Christianity. It makes it seem as if what mattered in the revolution was religious conviction; what made a patriot was Protestant faith.[7]

It was not so.[8] The notion that Protestantism fought the revolution and that religious pluralism only developed centuries later is false. Some patriots used words like *narishkeit* and *rookim*. Isaac Franks paraded with his militia to hear "the *first* communication of the Declaration of Independence, which was read to the troops," and pledged to "defend the same with our lives and fortunes."[9] Abraham Solomon fought at Bunker Hill; Moses Myers served at Yorktown.[10] Nationally, American Jews served in the patriot army in direct proportion to their numbers in the general population (perhaps one-tenth of 1 percent).[11] Exact numbers can be difficult; an earlier generation of historians simply looked at names of enlisted men and decided whether they "sounded" Jewish.[12] This did not work in the case of Elias Pollack, who—perhaps fearful his origins would disqualify him—joined the revolution under the name "Joseph Smith."[13] Fortunately, Jewish soldiers also left direct evidence of their religion in military records—as when the New York militia exempted Hart Jacobs from military duty on Friday nights in 1776 so he could observe Shabbat.[14] The numbers, however, are not as significant as the fact that the American army did not keep data on the religious faith of its members, unlike European armies of the day. Similarly, Washington and others promoted Jews to officer status, something no Jew in Europe experienced.

Whenever and wherever American Jews petitioned for full citizenship after the war, they received it. The lack of religious restrictions on citizenship was one of the most radical results of the revolution. The rhetoric of 1776 valued autonomy over confession. The state did not derive from the church, but from the people. The Declaration of Independence itself said as much: Governments derived "their just powers from the consent of the governed; that whenever any form of government becomes destructive of these ends, it is the right of the people to alter or to abolish it, and to institute new government." The Declaration and the patriot movement made the case that "the governed," not a church or a monarch, were qualified to rule. The Jews were among the governed, and they gave their consent, joining the fight against Britain.[15]

Geography and the accidents of war gave Jewish patriots an unusual advantage. In 1776, American Jews largely lived in five cities: Charleston, New York, Philadelphia, Newport, and Savannah. By 1780, all of those cities except Philadelphia were occupied or had just been occupied by the British. Exiled Jewish patriots therefore had only one place to go to practice their faith free of tory rule. (Loyalist Jews stayed home.) By one reckoning, the number of Jews in Philadelphia tripled over the course of the war, with almost 1,000 living in America's largest city by 1783.[16] "The disturbances in this Country," wrote two Philadelphia Jews, caused "numbers of our brethren from the different Congregations in America to come with their families to reside here."[17] Philadelphia's synagogue, Mikveh Israel, inherited a Jewish community from across the new nation. These were patriot Jews, unified in political ideology more than by common religious theology or practice.

Mikveh Israel suddenly found itself with a much larger and distinctly patriot congregation. It adopted the language and style of the revolution, opening its leadership and liturgy in more democratic and egalitarian ways. In 1782, Mikveh Israel's governing board dissolved itself and created a new "constitution"—a nod to the new ideas of societies as self-created authorities structured by their members. The more traditional Talmudic term for organizing principles, "hascamoth," fell out of favor.[18] The new synagogue was to be headed by a president (parnas) and governed by an elected board (adjunta, also called a junta or junto). The elected adjunta had final say over religious matters. Mikveh Israel also carefully restricted the powers of the parnas and increased the ability of rank-and-file membership to appeal the decisions of the leadership. It was a representative synagogue for a representative democracy. The presence of an unabashedly national, patriotic congregation of Jews in the nation's capital—just a few blocks from Independence Hall—may explain why Philadelphia's Benjamin Rush later wrote that "the Jews in all the States" were Whigs.[19]

Mikveh Israel replaced its old Philadelphia-based board with a new adjunta from across the country. The synagogue of patriot Jews was run by men from Georgia, South Carolina, Pennsylvania, and even New Orleans. Gershom Seixas acted as rabbi. Rebecca Phillips of Philadelphia and Grace Nathan of New York headed up fundraising for ritual objects. Jonas Phillips served as president. Phillips had become one of the *rookim* he had written about in 1776, serving in the Pennsylvania militia and helping to organize a series of blockade runners to get crucial supplies into the colonies. Phillips invited Pennsylvania's elected leaders to the dedication of the new building in September 1782, giving "sanction to their design," the adjunta wrote, "agreeable to the Sovereignty of the United States." The new building was dedicated with a prayer for George Washington and the United States, in both Hebrew and English.[20]

So the revolution changed American Judaism as well. For the first time in centuries, Jews in the pews did not need to consult the yeshiva to determine what counted as Jewish law and practice. They would vote on it instead. The Philadelphia model adopted by patriot Jews in Mikveh Israel spread across the country. New York, Charleston, Savannah, and Richmond all founded or refounded their synagogues in the 1780s and '90s. All of them were led by patriot Jews from Mikveh Israel; all of them wrote constitutions using Mikveh Israel's 1782 constitution as a model. One of the first (if not the first) self-conscious, national congregations of religious Americans from across the country were the Jews.

When the war ended, the Jews of Mikveh Israel drafted a petition and presented it to the government of Pennsylvania.[21] They sought an end to the state's test oath—the religious requirement for office that prevented Jews from serving in elected office. They asked for this change not as Jews seeking relief from Christian authorities but as citizens who had earned their rights through their sacrifices and steadfastness. When the Jews who built the new Mikveh Israel returned to their home states, they brought this revolutionary ethos of rights with them. Every state with a synagogue abandoned its test oath by 1792. Test oaths hung around only in states where they had no practical effect. The granting of rights to non-Christians—however few in number—was an immediate result of Jewish patriot efforts during the war and its aftermath. Jewish citizenship came from the revolution.[22]

Jews were joined by thousands of Baptists, Catholics, and Quakers in seeking full religious citizenship.[23] Yet all of those confessions worshipped Jesus Christ as the Son of God. Jews did not and do not. That Jewish difference had been at the root of centuries of dispossession, repression, and violence in Europe. And then, in a revolutionary moment, those differences no longer mattered. American religious minorities consciously entered the political realm. Jewish participation mattered more than Jewish difference. As Sheftall's brother Levi wrote, "the sacred name of Citizen" was meant for those who bled for independence, and American Jews had partaken their share of "the sufferings which they and many other good Whigs [patriots] suffered." In 1779, an observer in South Carolina described America's Jews "with their brother citizens in the field, doing that which every honest American should do."[24]

Those who claim that the United States was established on specifically Christian principles or as a "Christian nation" have an obvious problem: If the United States was founded as a Christian republic, Jews (as the largest white religious minority) should have been denied citizenship.[25] The acceptance of Jews—in some cases, the very enthusiastic acceptance of Jews—indicates that the Founding Fathers and the revolutionary generation did not think of the American government as a Christian institution. Religious freedom and religious diversity were not the results of later centuries of immigration; they were present at the American Founding.

The story of the Jewish patriots also challenges the frequent claim that Jewish emancipation in the American context was automatic, that, in the words of one historian, "Jews gained their religious rights in the United States . . . as individuals along with everybody else."[26] (That view depends on whom we mean by "everyone else.") This confusion is not surprising; Americans have often ignored the way Jews obtained rights. Clergyman and Bible distributor Robert Baird observed in 1844 that "the Jew now finds an asylum, and the full enjoyment of his civil rights, in all parts of the United States. Yet I know not how it happened."[27] The idea that Jews inadvertently stumbled into civil rights echoes another anti-Semitic canard, that of Mark Twain: "In the United States he [the Jew] was created free in the beginning—he did not need to help, of course." The implication is the Jew as parasite, taking advantage rather than creating or contributing. By extension, religious freedom is fundamentally a Christian idea, to which other religions were admitted only in retrospect.[28]

The historical record shows almost exactly the opposite: Jews participated in the revolution from the beginning, and when they requested citizenship they for the most part received it.[29] Unlike in Europe, American Jews did not need a specific act of emancipation because the American Revolution had accepted them. The War of Independence itself had embraced an idea about nationhood and rights, one that was not attached to a church or religious creed. Jews became citizens because, like all patriots, they chose to.

Questions about religion, rights, and the revolution too often focus on whether the Founding Fathers went to church or were guided by religious notions. The better question is how a religiously diverse cadre of (white) patriots would get along. Patriots accepted the Jews, who pointed to that acceptance as justification for enjoying the benefits and responsibilities of full citizenship. Moses Seixas, the head of Newport's synagogue, put it bluntly in 1790: Freedom meant "every one, of whatever Nation, tongue, or language" could be "equal parts of the great governmental Machine."[30]

The presence of religious diversity in patriot ranks should turn the question from whether Christian faith animated patriot action to how patriots of all religions set aside division to establish a republic. The revolutionary settlement offered a broader and more inclusive citizenship than had existed before the war. Nowhere is this more striking than in the case of Jews, who by 1790 had achieved rights that existed nowhere else, and which had not existed in British North America before the revolution. Jews who could not have served in public offices in 1775 were elected to them in 1795.[31] The revolution engaged religious Americans of all stripes and denominations, and then reworked the relationship among those religions, both to the state and to one another. In at least this sense, the revolution transformed the idea of political rights. It is worth telling the story of the patriot Jews for this reason alone.

The story of the Jews of the revolution should prompt a reconsideration not just of a "Christian Founding," but of the Founding itself. In recent years, it has become fashionable (as historian Jane Kamensky writes) to tell the American Revolution as a story of "staggering losses, unthinkable atrocities, and uncertain victories," a world where enslavement remained, inequality grew, and freedom remained vague and unfulfilled at best. This scholarship, she writes, has been "brave and fresh and true," and necessary: "But it is not, in the end, sufficient." We need a revolution "at once faithful to the past and useful to our fragile democracy."[32]

The American Revolution is fundamental to our national consciousness, politics, culture, and style, even if Americans often know woefully little about it. The revolution was not Eden, and the new republic was no utopia. Like much of history, it stank of blood and festered with unrealized expectations. Yet we must also recognize the real and concrete ways the rhetoric and results of the American Revolution expanded freedom. The creation of American religious liberty—the story of the patriot Jews—provides a clear example of how the revolution actually created a freedom where none had previously existed. The Founding remains the bedrock of American political imagination, and religious diversity and rights were part of it from the beginning. The stories we tell about the revolution are more than history; they are a measure of our own civic capacity. Americans still need the revolution.

This is the story of *rookim*: Jewish patriots who chose to make themselves Americans. It is not the story of an American Jewish settlement in the Lower East Side or Flatbush, Brooklyn, or other obvious locations. It rises in the mountains of New Mexico, cuts through the Caribbean, and ends up in Philadelphia. It is a story of how American Jews won citizenship, and how Americans worked out broad religious rights. Gaining those rights changed American Judaism forever, linking the redemption of Exodus, the military history of Judges, the ambiguity of Ecclesiastes, and the grand narrative of Genesis to the American story. And like many American stories, it begins with a man waiting for a ship.

I

Hebrew Letters

"JEW PRIEST." THAT WAS WHAT they called him, not knowing that the Jews no longer had priests, nor that he, Moses Seixas, had not learned enough to be a rabbi. He could read a little Hebrew, enough to serve as a warden and perform the rite of circumcision (a trade he learned through a correspondence course). But a priest? No. Yet at that moment in August 1790, warden was the highest office in the Newport, Rhode Island, synagogue. Moses Seixas held it. So he stood among seven Gentile ministers—all ordained, all college men—along with a host of citizens and office-holders, watching the horizon for a sign of a ship carrying President Washington to their dock. The ministers had a letter for Washington. Seixas also had a letter for President Washington. The ministers' letter talked about providence and obedience. Seixas's letter was about survival.[1]

Perhaps he was thinking that it should have been his brother presenting the letter: Gershom, the great patriot, leader of Shearith Israel in New York, who had taken the Torah scrolls from the ark and fled with them when the British occupied Manhattan in 1776. Gershom had published a sermon for Washington's fast day, one of the only Jews to have his sermons published by his parishioners.[2] Moses was not rabbi, not a cantor—just a "Jew Priest" with a letter of his own for the new president. Washington's response would shape the course of American and Jewish history.

They were waiting at the docks of southern Rhode Island, a state that took its time joining the American republic. It failed to adopt the Constitution in 1787, and sat out the first year of the Washington administration, going

9

it alone while the other states formed a new government in New York. When Rhode Island finally joined the union in 1790, Washington headed out to visit Newport and Providence—a public relations move for an administration that had just narrowly survived a congressional vote on the assumption of state debts. When Washington arrived, Seixas, the clergy, and the town fathers formed a phalanx, guiding the president and his retinue through town. There was dinner at the state house at four, followed by the customary toasts. Washington offered, "May the last be first," a reference to Rhode Island's tardiness in ratification.[3]

It is not clear when Moses Seixas gave Washington his letter, but it was likely the following morning, after breakfast, alongside a host of others passing along their well wishes to the chief executive. The first address came from the "Citizens of Newport," a cordial welcome that praised Washington but noted Newport's distressed condition: "The present circumstances of this Town forbid some of those demonstrations of gratitude . . . our Sister States have displayed." A congressman from South Carolina, William Loughton Smith, traveled with Washington and watched as one citizen became overcome with emotion reading an address to the president and had to pass the text to a friend. After that, the clergy presented their memorial to Washington. Smith gave no indication whether Newport's "Jew Priest" presented his memorial then, too. Perhaps Smith failed to notice Seixas, or perhaps Seixas simply pressed his letter into the president's hand rather than reading it aloud.[4]

All the letters heaped praise on Washington. The citizens' letter went so far as to suggest that Washington would one day be an angel. Seixas's letter prayed that "the same Spirit who rested in the Bosom of the greatly beloved Daniel . . . ever will rest upon you."[5] What Seixas wrote, however, became a plank in the history of church and state and the history of American Jews. The Newport synagogue, he explained in the letter to Washington, having been "Deprived . . . of the invaluable rights of free Citizens," instead sought a "Government, which to bigotry gives no sanction, to persecution no assistance—but generously affording to All liberty of conscience, and immunities of Citizenship."

Washington responded in kind: "All possess alike liberty of conscience and immunities of citizenship." Indeed, he went further. Citizenship was not mere "toleration . . . as if it was by the indulgence of one class of people, that another enjoyed the exercise of their inherent natural rights," but rather something that belonged to all, so that "every one shall sit in safety under his own vine and fig tree, and there shall be none to make him afraid."[6]

The letter of the Newport Jews and Washington's response are hailed as landmarks in the history of religious freedom. In 2017, the letter was quoted on an enormous banner looking over Philadelphia's Independence Park. But there was more going on here than culture or religious rights. Newport Jews were not asking for protection of their worship; they sought protection of their *citizenship*. They wanted to know if, as Jews—members of a perennially despised nation who could not hold office in eleven of the thirteen states—they too would have the full rights of their Gentile neighbors. Would Jewish men have the same rights as other white men? Or did faith circumscribe citizenship the same way race did? Washington's generous, almost carefree affirmation of those rights has in some ways obscured just how fraught this question was.[7]

For it was not clear to the Newport Jews that full citizenship rights would be forthcoming. Rhode Island Jews had been petitioning for rights for over a century, and the colony blocked them at nearly every turn. In 1790, Rhode Island still clung to its colonial charter that pledged its residents only "liberty in the true Christian faith and worship of God."[8] Newport's Jews did not know whether their new government would protect their rights. But they imagined that it might.[9]

Of the original thirteen states, Rhode Island is perhaps the one most associated with religious freedom. It was founded by the exiled Puritan Roger Williams, who explicitly declared that religion would have no role in government: "The civil magistrate's power extends only to the bodies and goods and outward state of men."[10] The state could not touch interior belief. Williams's declarations brought plenty of settlers, and Rhode Island quickly filled with those who could not abide Massachusetts and its strictures. Rhode Island became "the receptacle of all sorts of riff-raff people," wrote a Dutch minister in 1657, calling it the *"caeca latrina"*—the outhouse—"of New England."[11] Quakers, heretics, and Baptists came flocking. In a 1665 report on the New England colonies, royal commissioners concluded that Rhode Island "is generally hated by the other Colonies."[12] By the eighteenth century, Rhode Island had acquired a reputation as the best place to find alchemists, fortune tellers, and treasure hunters.[13] Williams probably never intended for his new colony to be a haven for anyone whose behavior did not sit well in orthodox New England, but the diversity of Rhode Island was a natural consequence of his belief that civil authority could make no claim to spiritual decisions, and that each person ought to receive "free and absolute *permission* of the *consciences* of all men . . . not the very *consciences* of the *Jews*, nor the *consciences* of the *Turks* or *Papists* or *Pagans* themselves excepted."[14]

Williams did not think of Judaism as the equal of Christianity; that simply could not be. Yet he also believed the persecution of Jews (and others) hindered the Christian message. By "not permitting them [Jews] a civill life or being," Williams argued, Christian magistrates made conversion more difficult. Moreover, if the state endorsed any religious message, then it was state influence and not religious truth that determined Christian faith. Truth became an outgrowth of power. It was therefore "against the Testimony of *Christ Jesus,* for the Civill state to impose upon the Souls of the People, a *Religion,* a *Worship,* a *Ministry.*"[15] Williams repeatedly invoked Judaism when he discussed religious tolerance. On seeking the colony's first charter in 1644, he declared that "to molest any person, Jew or Gentile, for either professing doctrine, or practicing worship . . . is to persecute him." Williams called this notion "soul liberty."[16] For Williams, any state mandates regarding religious belief placed God's church under man's laws. Removing compulsion in religion would aid church and state alike. "Papists and Protestants, Jews and Turks, may be embarked upon one ship," he wrote in 1655, and if "none of the Papists, Protestants, Jews or Turks be forced to come to the ship's prayers," the ship should still arrive safe.[17]

And so Jews came to the ship of Rhode Island, formalizing themselves into a community in Newport, and building a synagogue by 1763. The daily life of Newport Jews was well documented by Ezra Stiles, Calvinist minister of Newport and future president of Yale University. At first glance, Stiles seems an odd ally for the tiny Newport community. Ordained in 1749, Stiles revered the punishing standard of his Puritan forefathers. He believed himself "predestined to misery" which could only be lessened "the more earnestly I sought the divine Favour."[18] His diary is a major source for eighteenth-century American intellectual history, a magpie's nest of details and tidbits about all sorts of subjects. One of his favorite topics was the Old Testament, and that led him to Newport Jewry. Stiles learned Hebrew, studied Talmud and Zohar (meaning "radiance," and a text of what is known as the Kabbalah), and became profoundly interested in Jewish mysticism.[19]

Stiles never considered Jews spiritual equals; he described New York's Jewish population as the "Open & professed enemies to a crucified Jesus."[20]

Jews were not the only ones he found wanting. When his blood was up, Stiles lashed out at other sects, particularly small ones. He believed the pacifist Shakers were secret saboteurs, "sent over into America by Ministerial Connexions, to excite Confusion & religious Disturbance."[21] When the deist patriot and hero of the revolution Ethan Allen died in 1789, Stiles noted with satisfaction that the man was finally in hell.[22]

Yet Stiles became a good friend to the Jews of Newport. He attended the opening of their synagogue, recording the details of its liturgy and architecture (Corinthian columns, wainscotting, and a 200-year-old Torah). In 1770, he attended Newport's first bar mitzvah. A year later he was a guest for Passover.[23] He was apparently a great fan of Purim, noting the holiday several times in his diary and attending synagogue at least once to hear the reading of the Book of Esther. (No word on whether he joined in the shouting down of Haman.) He attended Jewish preaching, and especially respected a 1773 sermon on "the divine Benevolence, Mercy, and Love."[24]

That sermon was delivered in Spanish, and Stiles admitted he only understood parts of it. The first Jews of Newport were Sephardim—the descendants of Jews of Spain and Portugal, who since 1492 had faced a royal ultimatum of conversion or exile. From this edict emerged a class of *conversos*—Jews who adopted Christianity. Some *conversos* continued to practice Judaism secretly. That in turn led to centuries of violent repression, even of those *conversos* who had become devout Catholics for generations.

At least one *converso* made it to New England, and on his arrival in Newport in 1752 he immediately underwent the rite of circumcision. That *converso* was Aaron Lopez, a leading merchant. His father and other male relatives arriving with him also chose to become circumcised. Such mid-life operations strongly suggest the family had kept its Jewish faith hidden for generations. Circumcision was necessary, Lopez later wrote, for it represented "the covenant which happily characterize[s] us a peculiar flock."[25] Circumcision was one of the few things that connected Ashkenazic Jews—of Central European origin—and Sephardic Jews in America. By the end of the eighteenth century, Ashkenazim probably comprised a majority of the Jewish population in Rhode Island and America, but to the wider public the Jewish community seemed to speak with a Spanish accent. The first synagogue in New York used Sephardic services, as did the first synagogue in South Carolina. Those differences, however, might have been a blessing in disguise. The problems of communication among Jews who spoke Spanish, Dutch, and German as native tongues encouraged the rise of English in Jewish communities. When the first Jewish prayerbook was published in 1826, it taught the Sephardic rite—though it was written in Hebrew and English, not Spanish.[26]

Languages were not the only difficulty for colonial Jews. The Newport synagogue confronted a very modern problem: how to keep a good rabbi in a small town. At least six rabbis passed through between 1759 and 1775.[27] Just before the revolution, the Jews of Newport settled on Isaac Touro, a Sephardic Jew from Amsterdam, as the leader of the community. Technically Touro was a hazan, not a rabbi. The distinction was fuzzy in the early republic. "Hazan" meant the cantor, the person who chanted the services, but who also might circumcise, teach Hebrew, and perform other functions. "Rabbi" was a term of respect for a Jewish scholar, but given that the nearest rabbinical academies were thousands of miles away, the term was deployed flexibly. Manis Jacobs, a nineteenth-century New Orleans merchant, was eulogized after death as "the rabbi of New Orleans," though he had no formal religious education.[28] Gershom Seixas was called "rabbi" and recognized as such by the New York state legislature in 1784, but he had never been to yeshiva and sometimes dropped Christian idioms into his sermons. (He once described Moses as "directed by the holy Spirit.")[29] When a yeshiva-educated clergyman came through Newport, Stiles noted with satisfaction, "He is really a rabbi."[30]

In many ways, however, the Dutch-educated Touro was not the leader of the community. That distinction belonged to the ex-*converso* Lopez. Having survived his mid-life circumcision, Lopez adapted to the commercial life of Newport, and by the eve of the revolution he had become one of its wealthiest citizens.[31] Stiles classed Lopez with Socrates as one of the righteous men who did not perceive "the Truth as it is in Jesus Christ" but who "would almost persuade us to hope that their Excellency was infused by Heaven, and that the virtuous & good of all Nations & religions, notwithstanding their Delusions, may be bro't together in Paradise."[32] Not all of Lopez's trading ventures were strictly legal. His sterling reputation was firmly grounded in part because the white merchant class of Newport looked the other way when it came to contraband. (Lopez smuggled Dutch tea to the British colonies in the 1750s.)[33]

Moreover, Lopez engaged in slave trading—a greater blow against claims of his "Excellency" and another way in which he mimicked the Newport elite. Rhode Island was a center of the Atlantic slave trade.[34] Not all of those enslaved left Newport; southern Rhode Island developed a plantation economy that farmed beef, sheep, and dairy products for export to the American South and the Caribbean.[35] Stiles owned slaves, and by 1776 so did Lopez. When the revolution broke out, Lopez ceased commerce in human beings, though the trade continued for years in Newport. Although Lopez claimed in 1772 to have "no opinion" of the slave trade, his investments financed the forcible transport of over a thousand Africans to the Americas—most of whom were sold in Jamaica and other loathsome sugar colonies. Lopez's contribution to the slave trade perhaps helped secure the conviction in his own mind that he was like the other Newport merchants, virtually all of whom participated in and profited by the sale of African peoples. Lopez primarily traded in other goods, and the grisly numbers above still did not make Lopez a major slave trader, but these are excuses.[36]

Other whites did not share the conviction that Jews were like them. From the 1680s to the 1780s, the status of Jews in Newport was an open question. Were they citizens, entitled to all the rights and privileges of their (white) Christian neighbors? Or were they merely residents—permitted to live in the town but no more?

Rhode Island's royal charter of 1663 seemed to want it both ways. The document differed slightly from Roger Williams's original 1644 charter. The 1663 revision came when Charles II reclaimed power from Parliament in England, but the new charter still contained landmark language of religious freedom, declaring that "no person within the said colony, at any time hereafter, shall be any wise molested, punished, disquieted, or called in question, for any differences in opinion in matters of religion." Instead, all "persons may . . . at all times hereafter, freely and fully have and enjoy his and their own judgments and consciences." The charter validated Roger Williams's concept of soul liberty and promised that Rhode Island would be "a lively experiment, that a most flourishing civil state may stand and best be maintained" with a "full libertie in religious concernments."[37]

Yet this charter also had some Christian assumptions the 1644 version did not have. King Charles II declared his intention to secure the Rhode Islanders' "liberty, in the true Christian faith." The charter also insisted that all royal subjects of Rhode Island must be prepared to defend "their just rights and liberties against all the enemies of the Christian faith."[38] Where did that leave the Jews? Subject to the political winds, at the very least. In 1684—not long after Roger Williams died—Rhode Island's governor William Coddington attempted to seize Jewish goods, arguing that no formal right to trade had been granted to the Jews. Any rights or privileges Jews might enjoy must come from a specific request given by king or parliament—for Jews and other non-Christians ought to have no expectation of free action in a government that was, after all, an extension of the will of Christ. The kingdom was a Christian kingdom. What mattered was not presence or allegiance, but religious doctrine. The legislature overruled the governor by defining the Jews as "strangers being not of our nation." The distinction meant they were not subjects but nevertheless were entitled to legal protection as long as they remained "obedient to his Majesty's laws."[39] A year later, Coddington made another attempt, this time spurred on by William Dyre, Rhode Island's surveyor general. In March 1685, Dyre insisted that Jews were aliens with no rights to conduct trade, and moved to seize "the said Jews goods or estates . . . as Aliens." The attempt to grab Jewish property in Rhode Island failed a second time. A jury held Dyre at fault, returned the property to the accused, and made Dyre pay the court costs.[40]

It was a victory, but a narrow one. The Jews of Newport avoided being defined as a completely subordinate group in a Christian state and instead would be defined by their allegiance to the Crown. Yet the Jews remained "strangers"—protected, but not actual English subjects, and certainly not full citizens. They were still legally different—not truly the king's people nor anyone else's. Similar designations arose throughout the next century. In 1719, the state republished the statutes granting "all men of competante estates" the right to vote and hold office, but then rewrote the clause to read "all men *professing Christianity* of competante estates."[41] Congregationalist divines perpetually reminded readers of Jewish perfidy in published sermons that circulated throughout New England. Jonathan Edwards, the foremost theologian of his day, expected Jews to become Christians one day, but in the meantime, he denounced them as an international bloodsucking cabal, writing that Jews secretly dreamed "of being masters of the whole world and expect actually to be made such when their master comes."[42] Increase Mather, of Salem witch trials fame, saw Jews as "guilty of the most hideous and horrid blasphemy against the Son of God." Mather assured Christians that even the Jews could be saved, although he chose to do so by evoking some of the greatest hits of medieval anti-Semitism. He alleged that Jews poisoned wells and repeated the myth of the blood libel: Jews, he told listeners, "have been wont once a year to steal Christian babies, and to put them to death by crucifying out of scorn and hatred against Christians." Mather himself expressed mild skepticism on these latter points, though held to his firm belief that "the guilt . . . lyeth on the Jewish Nation to this day, even the guilt of the bloud of the Savior of the world."[43]

It was Aaron Lopez and his associate Isaac Elizer who made the first push for full Jewish civic membership. In 1761, Lopez and Elizer, as leading merchants of the town, applied for naturalization as "freemen" of Rhode Island. Their legal claim was based on the 1753 British naturalization of Jews—a short-lived statute that provoked an anti-Semitic backlash in England. The Superior Court of Rhode Island turned the petition over to the legislature, and the legislature denied it: As "the said Aaron Lopez hath declared himself to be a Jew, this Assembly doth not admit him nor any other of that religion to the full freedom of the colony." Jews were not to be permitted to vote or hold public office. Less than fifteen years before the revolution, the Jews in America had achieved toleration, but not "full freedom."[44]

Lopez and Elizer tried again in 1762 and were again denied. This time the court cited the Christian language of the colony's 1663 charter: "The free and quiet enjoyment of the Christian religion and the desire of propagating the same were the principal views with which this colony was settled." To allow Jews to be naturalized, therefore, was "inconsistent with the first principles on which the colony was founded." This was nonsense. Roger Williams had believed the gospel *only* spread when no civil penalties existed for non-believers. But the colony's officials were explicit that because Rhode Island had a Christian charter, no non-Christians could join.[45]

Undaunted, Lopez went to Massachusetts, where the Gentile merchants Henry Lloyd and Samuel Fitch helped him receive naturalization. Lopez needed only to obtain a certificate of residence in Rhode Island and take an oath of loyalty to England's royal house of Hanover, and "declare, that no foreign prince, person, state or potentate hath or ought to have any jurisdiction . . . or authority ecclesiastical or spiritual within the realm of Great Britain."[46] The *converso* Jew took the oath to keep Britain Protestant, and on October 15, ten years after arriving in Newport, he became a naturalized subject of George III. The Jews were having better luck with the hardliners of Congregationalist Massachusetts than with the supposed religious radicals of Rhode Island. Stiles wrote in response, "Providence seems to make everything work for the mortification of the Jews, and to prevent their incorporating into any nation"—likely embracing the double meaning of "providence" as the mysterious ways of God and the capital of Rhode Island.[47]

Thus, when Seixas described the Jews of 1790 to George Washington as "deprived as we heretofore have been of the invaluable rights of free citizens," he was likely thinking of Newport's own story and not a generalized history of the Jews. The questions of Jewish citizenship and the American Revolution bound themselves together as the colonies slithered through the imperial crisis of the 1770s. As Britain tightened its grip on the colonies, and as the drumbeat for independence grew throughout New England, Newport Jewry undoubtedly pondered which of the two sides might give them their "full freedom." There was hope in patriot rhetoric; John Adams, for one, called for "unlimited freedom of religion . . . essential to the progress of society." Yet in Rhode Island, the patriots were the elected assemblymen who had denied Lopez naturalization. Meanwhile, the Massachusetts officials who arranged Lopez's naturalization were tories.[48]

Lopez began as a tepid patriot. In 1775, he assured the Massachusetts authorities that he backed their cause—and told the British authorities much the same. (He needed both royal and patriot authorization for a whaling expedition he wanted to fund.) In 1779, however, Lopez sent help to Connecticut's patriots. The British had sacked the town of Norwalk, and they had done it on Tish B'Av, the Jewish commemoration of the destruction of the Jerusalem temple. Lopez responded to the tragedy by donating money to the "relief of the unhappy suffer[er]s of Norwalk."[49]

The Newport synagogue seems to have shared Lopez's wariness, at least at the war's outset. They selected a visiting rabbi, the Jerusalem-born Samuel Cohen, to give a sermon for a declared patriot fast day in July 1775, in the wake of Bunker Hill. Stiles attended but did not mark it as a "Liberty sermon," as he had previously done a Baptist homily in the preceding weeks.[50] In 1773, the presiding hazan, Isaac Karigel, addressed a host of luminaries in the synagogue, including Rhode Island governor Joseph Wanton and Massachusetts judges Peter Oliver and Robert Auchmuty. All three men were key loyalists. Karigel's sermon on that day came in the wake of the burning of the HMS *Gaspee* in Narragansett in June 1772. The *Gaspee* had been tasked with hunting pirates, but when it ran aground on the colony's shore in June 1772, enterprising continentals boarded and set her on fire.[51]

The *Gaspee* affair had patriots and royalists fuming at one another in colonial Rhode Island; Karigel's 1773 sermon was intended to lower the temperature. It defended traditional Jewish law against the notion that human reason could ever justify the cessation of "conforming ourselves" to traditional institutions. "It is incumbent upon us," Karigel explained, "to observe even those precepts we do not comprehend . . . because they are given to us by the great sovereign monarch." The Temple was destroyed in ancient days, he declared, because "the small and poor aspired to be in everything on a level with the great and powerful, all order and regulation being lost." The allusion to the patriot uprising was unmistakable: Virtue "must consist in not considering the least upon an even parallel with the greatest."[52]

Karigel's sermon targeted deist notions of natural reason, but the political undertones were surely intended to salve wounds and assert monarchical rule in a colony unsure of what that rule might require of its inhabitants. It likely pleased the beleaguered Governor Wanton, and the very presence of such officials at the synagogue suggests in turn that Jewish loyalism in Newport would have had a welcome audience among royal appointees. Isaac Touro would remain loyal to the Crown throughout the war. Perhaps Touro and Karigel hoped for better protection of their rights under royal rule than Lopez had received in 1762.

They would be disappointed. Newport's Jewry sided with the patriots when the fighting broke out. In the meantime, however, Karigel's equivocating and Touro's toryism painted the entire community with the brush of loyalism. In 1773, glass was broken in the synagogue. The Massachusetts patriot agitator James Otis branded Rhode Island tories as "Turks, Jews, and other Infidels, with a few renegade Christians and Catholics." Once again, the Jewish position in Newport was under siege.[53]

Indeed, one of the first things the Rhode Island government did upon declaring independence was to make certain kinds of prayers illegal. Once the assembly received the Declaration of Independence in July 1776, they first voted to approve the document and then banned any "*Preaching or praying*" that the "*King* (of G. Brit.) to be our rightful Lord & Sovereign, or shall pray for the Success of his Arms." The penalty included prison time. In other words, the state of Rhode Island simultaneously declared independence and restricted religious practice. Anglican churches across the state closed. The state that began as a "lively experiment" of religious liberty in 1636 intended to police religion in 1776 to obtain political uniformity.[54]

At least eleven ministers objected, and when some "principal Gentlemen" of Rhode Island petitioned on their behalf, "representing that they were peaceable," the legislature turned on the petitioners and "ordered them before them, & tendered the Test." Rhode Island's prayer ban was not a mild corrective; it was an active program of religious conformism. One Baptist minister refused to take the oath; the legislature applied pressure and had him praying "heartily for the Congress & our Army" by the following Sunday.

Only a handful of clergy were excused: an aged Baptist, a Moravian, and Isaac Touro, "the Jew Priest excused because a Foreigner."[55] Whether the legislature meant Touro was foreign because he was Dutch or because he was Jewish is unclear. Whatever the case, Touro certainly was a loyalist; perhaps the legislature knew that Jewish prayers were not given in English at the time and so did not worry too much about what the "foreigners" were saying.

Yet the Jews did not think of themselves as foreigners; they were ready to become Americans. Newport's Jews supported independence by 1776. When the British occupied the city that year, the Jews of Newport overwhelmingly abandoned their reticence and embraced the patriot cause. Almost all the Jews left the city and went to patriot-controlled territory. Even Stiles could list only six or seven Jewish loyalists who remained. Lopez led the way, moving to the town of Leicester in Massachusetts, where he bemoaned "the melancholy situation of that happy country [America]."[56] The war left his home in shambles, "a collection of straw, dirt, and nastiness."[57] From his redoubt in southern Massachusetts, Lopez funneled money to the cash-strapped United States—a "loan" that he must have known was functionally a gift. At least two Newport Jews—Moses and Abraham Isaacs—enlisted in the revolutionary army.[58]

The Jews who remained in Newport, including Moses Seixas, fared poorly. The synagogue was turned into a British field hospital.[59] Patriot partisans made life difficult; Touro admitted he was "reduced in his circumstances" due to the stress he "suffer[e]d from persecution for his attachment to [the British] government." Newport was wracked by shortages, "much distress'd," wrote Lopez in 1779, "for want of fewell and provisions, those individuals of my society [Jews] in particular."[60] Rachel Myers, a member of the community, "struggled with many difficulties" and found herself unable to afford "her children . . . the necessaries of life."[61] According to Seixas's records of circumcision, four out of the five baby boys who underwent the procedure during the occupation did not survive to see the British leave.[62] Isaac Hart, a loyalist associate of Lopez, fled to Long Island after the war. There a mob shot and bayoneted him, then beat him to death with muskets. No one was ever held accountable.[63]

Stiles—despite his long association with the synagogue—blamed the British occupation on Newport's handful of remaining Hebrews: "Jews are very officious as Informing against the Inhabitants . . . So that the Inhab. are cautious & fearful of one another." Stiles frequently nursed suspicions of world Jewry. In 1770, he accused a nameless international Jewish cabal of acting against America's interests. He believed there was "a secret *Intelligence office* in London . . . where the Jews live." This nameless organization was "supported by the Ministry" but was "intirely a Jew Affair" and "boasted of having Intelligence of every Occurrence of any consequence in America."[64] Stiles's friend and delegate to the Continental Congress, Henry Marchant, gently wrote back to him, "I think you must be mistaken about the ministerial Jew-store."[65]

Elsewhere, however, Jews were earning a reputation for revolutionary enthusiasm. In Charleston, South Carolina, Richard Lushington's "Jew Company" fought under General William Moultrie to repel British troops landing on Beaufort Island, and then again in the assault on Savannah in 1779.[66] Over a dozen Jews gave their lives there for the cause. A list of the members includes one reference to "Solomon—the Chosan." That was probably a nickname, since Charleston's hazan at the time was Abraham Alexander—who instead enlisted in Wade Hampton's 2nd South Carolina dragoons.[67]

Some Jews won acclaim early on in the fight for liberty. Francis Salvador lived in the South Carolina backcountry and was an early convert to the revolution. Salvador's uncle had urged passage of the Jewish Naturalization Bill in England that failed so spectacularly in 1753, so Francis knew where Jews stood in the Old Country. Although South Carolina barred non-Christians from holding office, Salvador was nevertheless twice elected to the South Carolina Provincial Congress. He was killed in action while investigating military alliances with Native American nations in 1776.[68] Haym Salomon of Philadelphia partnered with Robert Morris, a delegate of the Continental Congress and signer of the Declaration of Independence, to secure funding for the government in Philadelphia throughout the revolution (although Salomon's posthumous promotion to "financier of the Revolution" has been somewhat mythologized.)[69] In New York, Gershom

Seixas turned his *bimah* into a bully pulpit, praying for Washington, Congress, and "the Men of these United States . . . may thy Angels have them in Charge, and save them from Death, and all manner of distress."[70] Reuben Etting was captured by the British after the fall of Charleston. One legend has it that when the British learned Etting was Jewish, they chose to offer him pork as his provisions. Etting refused to violate the kosher laws and went without rations—which surely contributed to his subsequent death from tuberculosis.[71]

Aaron Lopez never saw the end of the war; he drowned in May 1782. Isaac Touro fled Newport, first to New York and then to Jamaica. That left Newport Jewry without leadership at the very moment when patriots took control. The Rhode Island Jews who had remained loyalists had no reason to anticipate that they would receive equal treatment under American law. The Articles of Confederation did not stipulate it, and Rhode Island patriots showed a willingness to demand religious obligations and to qualify citizenship based on religion. And of course, when the Constitution arrived with the promise of a Bill of Rights, Rhode Island declined to join. In the 1780s, the Jews of Newport were a community balanced on a knife's edge. They lived in an age of rights and an age of rebellion, surrounded by the rhetoric of religious freedom but always aware that the taint of Touro's toryism might bring another round of exclusions.

So to lead them the congregation picked Moses Seixas, a man whose life embodied the ambiguities of American Judaism in the Age of Revolutions. He was of both Sephardic and Ashkenazic descent. Family legend later claimed that his *converso* ancestors escaped the Portuguese Inquisition by hiding in a laundry basket that was carried to the river under the nose of the visiting Inquisitors—which perhaps explains why the first Seixas born in New York was named "Moses."[72] That was in 1744, with his brother Gershom and other siblings arriving soon after. Moses went to Newport in 1770 to marry and found the city to his liking.

Between then and Washington's arrival in 1790, Seixas served various roles for Newport's Jewish community, but although he was their chief religious authority, it is not clear how much Jewish law he understood. He wrote to other Jews seeking answers to questions—could the person who read from the Torah scroll read from a printed book instead? How was mourning to be handled? Could a person read rather than chant from the Torah during services?[73] In February 1790, Philadelphia's hazan had to explain to Moses the difference between written and oral Torah—a fairly basic distinction for a rabbi, more obscure to the laity.[74] Seixas possessed neither rabbinical training nor a rabbinical mind; he had access to Jewish traditions but lacked a deep understanding of them.

His social connections, on the other hand, represented a more significant asset to the Jewish community after the war. He was a merchant and investor, and later became cashier and one of the principals of the newly established Bank of Rhode Island. His brother-in-law was the kosher butcher, and Seixas had acted as an intermediary for his patriot friend Lopez during the war. Seixas had a patriot family, particularly Gershom (the "rabbi") and their younger brother Abraham, a veteran of Washington's army.[75] Seixas had other revolutionary "brothers" as well—the Freemasons. Masonry had long been open to Jews, and Jewish names appeared in the lists of the London lodge as early as 1740. Seixas joined after the British left Newport, and he rose to prominence. Indeed, he presented a masonic appeal to Washington at the same time he delivered the synagogue's letter.[76] In the absence of a trained rabbi, a prominent merchant Mason with patriot connections was perhaps the best choice for leadership.

Seixas himself was a reformed tory. Early in the war, he and several others wrote to General Henry Clinton, who had fought the patriots at Bunker Hill, professing their "Allegiance to our most gracious Sovereign." Seixas explained that he and other Jews had not signed the "general address of support" from Newport because of property interests in patriot-held Nantucket, "which they greatly fear would be immediately seiz'd on by the Provincials" if they openly professed loyalty to the Crown. This might have been a ruse, although Moses certainly could have joined his patriot brother in Connecticut if he had wished. He never did. British occupation, however, seems to have soured Seixas on the empire. In 1780, when the British army withdrew, Seixas signed a pledge to defend Newport "to the utmost of our Power and Ability . . against the King of Britain."[77]

Seixas chose to remain in America at war's end, affirming his loyalty to the American experiment. As the warden of the synagogue, he immediately faced a challenge from Newport's Jews, a "capricious and whimsical" bunch. Jewish leaders urged Seixas to alter the worship services. Seixas replied that he lacked the authority or influence to do so. There were problems relating to the strictness of kosher laws. Seixas's brother-in-law the butcher was accused of subverting order in the pews over an issue regarding his role as *shohet* (kosher butcher).[78] When the synagogue's shofar (the ram's horn trumpet) broke, the community failed to obtain a new one from Europe, and plans to borrow one from New York fizzled. Worse, the man assigned to sound the shofar had been caught in a scandal. He was "a profligate," according to Seixas and made the community "ashamed for the *Goyim*." Rather than have "a Stigma cast on us"—and unable to find another *baal tekiah*—it appears that Seixas simply shelved the ceremony altogether for some time.[79]

It was therefore a community fraught with anxiety that addressed Washington in 1790 during his visit to Newport—tarnished by toryism, treated as foreigners, stuck in a town ravaged by occupation, squabbling among themselves, and bereft of the sound of the shofar. Their joy at having "the invaluable rights of free citizens" referred not to the deep Jewish past but to immediate hopes in the wake of American strife. Their awe and gratitude at the construction of a "Government, which to bigotry gives no sanction, to persecution no assistance," was not a statement of fact. It was a hope and an aspiration. The Jews were not telling Washington what they already knew; they were asking him to affirm that the government of America would—as Rhode Island had not—afford "to All liberty of conscience, and immunities of Citizenship."

The Newporters were not the only Jews to write to Washington. Georgia's Mickve Israel congratulated Washington in May 1790, and a joint letter from the congregations of New York, Philadelphia, Charleston, and Richmond arrived in December. These missives referenced citizenship as well, but with greater circumspection than did Seixas. In Georgia, where the Jewish Sheftall family had been leaders of the revolution, the Savannah synagogue told Washington, "Your unexampled liberality and extensive philanthropy have . . . enfranchised us with all the privileges and immunities of free citizens, and initiated us into the grand mass of legislative mechanism." The combined address of the other four synagogues—a missive Seixas refused to join—praised Washington, lauding the president as the man whose sword "opened the way to the reign of Freedom" and whose hand "gave birth to the Federal Constitution." It emphasized that "every political and religious denomination" ought to demonstrate affection to Washington, and "in this, will the Hebrew Congregations . . . yield to no class of their Fellow Citizens." Jews would act with other Americans, because Jews were the same as other Americans.[80] These letters bore the imprint of patriot Jews who had secured liberty in states that had adopted the Constitution; they were enfranchised, Fellow Citizens. It was a done deal. Newport's Jews had no such assurances.

For all the praise the letter-writers heaped on Washington, they likely knew little about Washington's true religious affiliations. Indeed, Americans still know little about Washington's own religious faith. That was probably the way Washington wanted it. Given multiple opportunities to state his religious faith for the record during his presidency, Washington passed every time.[81]

Washington was born into the Anglican (Episcopal) church, and remained a member all his life. Yet the Father of his Country kept the specifics of his religious beliefs to himself; there are few indications about religion in his private letters. Historians must therefore examine Washington's religion through his church attendance and public pronouncements.[82] Washington while president usually attended church, but he declined to kneel for prayer, and he refused to take communion. When a minister at Philadelphia's Christ Church called him out—denouncing "those in elevated stations who invariably turned their backs on the celebration of the Lord's Supper"—Washington ceased attending on the Sundays when the eucharist was offered. "If he were alive today," writes the journalist Stephen Waldman, "[Washington] would absolutely head to church, unless there was a really good football game on."[83]

His public pronouncements were similarly indefinite. He referred to "Jesus Christ" only once in his thousands of pages of writing—in a letter to the Delaware Indians. Much of his correspondence was written by underlings and aides-de-camp; Washington had approval over the final drafts, of course, but it would be difficult to consider these writings as direct statements of his religious views.[84] Washington clearly believed God acted in the affairs of humanity, and he consistently urged prayer and acts of goodwill in the belief that such things could sway God's actions. He condemned swearing among his soldiers because armies "could little hope for the blessing of heaven" by engaging in "impiety and folly."[85] When the American forces won at Saratoga, Washington offered thanks to "the supreme disposer of events." He credited "the miraculous care of Providence" when he survived an early military encounter. He proclaimed national fast days. His letters demonstrate a thorough familiarity with the Bible; he employed biblical allusions as central metaphors and as throwaway references, as when he wished that war profiteers would be hung "five times as high" as Haman.[86] Yet his public statements also tended toward a certain vagueness regarding the name or identity of God, deploying terms such as "Providence," "the Deity," or "the Grand Architect," rather than "Father,"

"Redeemer," or "Christ." He credited the fog that covered his escape from New York in 1777 to "Providence or some unaccountable something." It is hard to imagine a vaguer term for God.[87]

Ministers attempted to get Washington, once president, to commit to an open, public declaration of Christian faith. He never made one. In 1789, the minister and former Harvard president Samuel Langdon directly requested Washington to declare himself a "disciple of the Lord Jesus Christ." Washington wrote a letter back referring to "the Great Author of the Universe." In 1796, a collection of ministers repeated Langdon's request. Washington replied referencing only "the Divine Author of life and felicity."[88]

Washington was not hiding some secret infidelity, for he constantly reminded Americans of the duty of praising "that great and glorious Being" for "His kind care and protection of the people of this country." Nor is it likely that he was a closet agnostic; he became a godfather eight times, each time affirming in church his belief in the Trinity (an oath Thomas Jefferson, for example, refused to take). Washington did not sign James Madison's 1785 memorial advocating an end to Anglican establishment in Virginia.[89] He was certainly a devout Christian (by the standards of the eighteenth century, if not the twenty-first), although a quiet and perhaps an idiosyncratic one.[90]

Possibly Washington was simply a latitudinarian—an Enlightenment movement that sought to emphasize ecumenism over theological differences. Latitudinarians cared more for Christian unity than for squabbles over what kinds of vestments clergy should wear or what exactly happened to the bread and wine during communion. Yet latitudinarianism was primarily confined to Protestants; Catholics, Jews, and other religious traditions were still beyond the pale. Not so to Washington: He made repeated efforts throughout his career to include such groups in the American experiment. His latitudinarianism—if that is what it was—was a national affair.

Washington seemed to have a genuine care and concern for the rights and liberties of small religious groups with more enemies than adherents in America—Catholics, Swedenborgians, Jews, Muslims. Admittedly, there were strong political reasons for some of Washington's directives, as when he forbade his soldiers from burning the pope in effigy when he was trying to woo Catholic Quebec to join the revolution in 1775.[91] He told his Baltimore agent that he did not care if the tradesmen working on his house were "Mahometans, Jews, or Christian of any Sect—or they may be Atheists," as long as they were of good character.[92]

Indeed, Washington seemed to go out of his way to deny any specifically Christian objectives in his administration. When the Presbyterians of Massachusetts and New Hampshire expressed their regret that there was no "explicit acknowledgement of the *only true God and Jesus Christ, whom he hath sent* inserted some where in the *Magna Charta* of our country," Washington accepted their congratulations and replied with a typically polite rebuttal: "The path of true piety is so plain as to require but little political direction. To this consideration we ought to ascribe the absence of any regulation, respecting religion, from the Magna-Charta of our country. To the guidance of the ministers of the gospel this important object is, perhaps, more properly committed."[93] The president wanted public virtue, but would not commit his state to any religion.

However, when he received thanks from more marginal religious groups, Washington repeatedly and unabashedly discussed rights. In 1793, he echoed his response to Newport when he told Baltimore's Swedenborgian church, "We have abundant reason to rejoice, that in this land the light of truth and reason have triumphed over the power of bigotry and superstition." In America, every person may "worship God according to the dictates of his own heart. . . . [I]t is our boast, that a man's religious tenets will not forfeit the protection of the laws, nor deprive him of the right of attaining and holding the highest offices that are known in the United States."[94] In 1790 he wrote to the Universalists that "however different are the sentiments of citizens on religious doctrines," still, "their political professions and practices are almost universally friendly to the order and happiness of our civil institutions."[95] A week later, he was writing to the Newport Jews that "every one shall sit under the safety of his own vine and fig tree, and there shall be none to make him afraid."[96]

Several other religious groups expressed their fears to Washington even as they praised his ascension to the presidency. The Catholics—a handful of Americans in 1790— lauded Washington for "extend[ing] the influence of laws on the manners of our fellow citizens" and encouraging "respect for religion." But they insisted on their claim, as revolutionary Americans, to "equal rights of citizenship, as the price of our blood spilt under your eyes." Washington concurred: "All those who conduct themselves as worthy members of the Community are equally entitled to the protection of civil Government." It surely pleased the Catholics, who concluded their letter with a direct appeal for civil rights: "We pray for the preservation of them, where they have been granted; and expect the full extension of them from the justice of those States, which still restrict them."[97]

The Virginia Baptists—still a minority among Protestants—were similarly frank about their concerns: "When the constitution first made its appearance in Virginia, we, as a Society, had unusual strugglings of mind; fearing that *the liberty of conscience,* dearer to us than property or life, was not sufficiently secured." They remembered "when Mobs, Bonds, Fines, and Prisons were our frequent attendants."

Washington's response to the Baptists brimmed with the same full-throated defense of religious liberty he offered to the Newport Jews: "If I could have entertained the slightest apprehension that the Constitution framed in the Convention, where I had the honor to preside, might possibly endanger the religious rights of any ecclesiastical Society, certainly I would never have placed my signature to it." As for future events, "no one would be more zealous than myself to establish effectual barriers against the horrors of spiritual tyranny, and every species of religious persecution. . . . [E]very man, conducting himself as a good citizen, and being accountable to God alone for his religious opinions, ought to be protected in worshipping the Deity according to the dictates of his own conscience."[98]

The letter from Newport Jews was thus part of a much broader effort by marginal religious groups in the United States to wring promises from Washington. If, as the Baptists said, they were truly reliant on Washington's goodwill and protection rather than law for the support of religious liberty, then it appears that Catholics, Swedenborgians, and Jews felt similarly— and that all of them wanted something in writing. The letter Seixas handed to Washington was a call for religious freedom in America. "We now . . . behold," Seixas wrote, "A Government, which to bigotry gives no sanction, to persecution no assistance." Behold, and not possess: The Bill of Rights had not passed yet. The promise was there, and the Newport Jews were pressing for acknowledgment.

They got it. Washington's response has become a classic defense of American religious freedom. He opened the letter by referring to the welcome he received "from all classes of citizens," thereby assuring Newport Jews that they, too, were citizens and part of the government. Washington then addressed both the spoken and unspoken concerns of the Newport letter. He unequivocally included the Jews as protected citizens in the republic: "All possess alike liberty of conscience and immunities of citizenship." In choosing this phrase, he repeated the phrasing of the synagogue back to them (as Washington so often did in his correspondence). The same was true of his assurance that "the United States ... gives to bigotry no sanction, to persecution no assistance, requires only that they who live under its protection should demean themselves as good citizens."[99]

Washington added a few insightful phrases of his own. It was Washington, and not Seixas, who brought up the issue of toleration—"no more ... spoken of, as if it was by the indulgence of one class of people, that another enjoyed the exercise of their inherent natural rights." It was only "good citizens"—no matter their faith—who empowered the government, and hence, there was no more need for mere "tolerance." There were only natural rights. And it was Washington who introduced the motif of the vine and fig tree, a biblical phrase he employed over fifty times in his letters, and one he sometimes used to describe Mount Vernon.[100] In a sense, Washington was handing a response to Seixas that affirmed the Jews' common standing as white citizens of the republic: a kind of covenant between the Jews and their president.

It was all symbolism, of course. Washington's letter changed no laws and it did not alter the 1663 Rhode Island charter. The state stubbornly kept the charter, which promised liberty only to "true Christian faith and worship," as its governing law until 1842. The Newport community instead withered in the wake of the revolution. Seixas certainly succeeded; he would have been right to see the letter as a victory, and he went on became Grand Master of Rhode Island's masons. His death in 1809 prompted universal mourning, but tellingly, few public responses came from the synagogue. The Jewish community continued to shrink. By 1820, the community had vanished, and the synagogue later became a way for Henry Wadsworth Longfellow to imagine that *all* Jews had similarly vanished: "Dead nations never rise again."

The winnowing of Newport's Jews has been read as an omen for modern American Judaism's difficulty in maintaining the faith of new generations. In Newport, however, it seemed that patriot Jews had not all returned at war's end. Many had gone to New York and Philadelphia, where legal protections for non-Christians were being hashed out. Newport Jewry had Washington's word—but they had only Washington's word. Their disappearance suggests that religious freedom in America was a patchwork affair. Religious liberty did not arise naturally with the revolution. It was not the automatic result of "Enlightenment thinkers and Protestant dissenters" in which "Jews played no significant role," as one scholar summarized the era.[101] Nor did religious rights naturally grow out of the British colonial era; they came with the revolution. Religious liberty was a religious choice and a political change. Understanding the legacy and the origins of revolutionary religious freedom therefore requires a deep look into the entire colonial world. For there were places known for Jewish neighborhoods then that are less well-known for Jewish neighborhoods today—including Spain, Brazil, New Mexico, and others.

2

All Over the Map

COLONIAL AMERICA WAS NOT FOREORDAINED to be a place of religious freedom. The grants of residency allowed to Jews in 1654 New York did not "develop" into the religious freedom Americans enjoy today. Indeed, most of the twenty-three Sephardic Jews who arrived in New York in that year were not seeking refuge from Europe. They came from Brazil, where the Jewish community was being dismantled.

American Jewish history usually focuses on the British North American colonies, but before 1776 those places were imperial afterthoughts. They mainly supported the Caribbean sugar trade, to which the British were latecomers. Spain invaded Mexico and the Caribbean almost a century before Jamestown was founded in 1607. Spain, not England, hosted the first Jews in the Americas, despite the fact that it also banned Jews from its territories.

For centuries in the medieval world, Judaism had flourished in Muslim Spain. Under Islamic law, Jews and Christians held equal legal status on the Iberian Peninsula. Such a position did not offer full equality—Muslims outranked both Jews and Christians—but it represented an improvement over much of Christian Europe. The Jews of Spain eventually took the name of the peninsula—Sefarad—as their designation: Sephardim. In the century before Columbus, however, Islamic rule crumbled. Reinvigorated Catholic powers pushed into Islamic Spain, forcing Muslims south. As Muslim rule receded, so too did traditional Islamic protections of Jews. In 1391, anti-Jewish riots broke out along the Spanish coast. Thousands were massacred; thousands more were forced to convert to Catholicism. One *converso* was Rabbi Salomón Ha-Leví, whose descendant, Juan de Oñate, first led the Spanish into New Mexico.

But conversion did not end anti-Semitism. Baptism in Spain did not grant a person equality with other Christians, especially if the baptized had Jewish or Muslim blood. At some point, the epithet *marrano* came to be applied to these converts—"swine."[1] In 1492, King Ferdinand and Queen Isabella unified the kingdoms of Spain under a single monarchy, pushing Spain's last Muslims out of Granada. The victory was followed by an imperial ethnic cleansing: Granada's fall inspired inquisitors and royals to convert the Jews once and for all.[2]

Ferdinand and Isabella thought it was a great idea. They ordered the Jews of Spain to convert or leave. This choice was even less palatable in the fifteenth century than it sounds today. Exile from Spain was not simply a matter of crossing the border. For many Jews, it was impossible. To the west, Portugal required a fee to enter. To the east, France banned Jews, as did England. If Jews made it to the few towns in Western Europe where they were permitted, they would be forced to wear badges, or "Jew-caps." Spanish Jews who could not arrange transport would be compelled to accept baptism.[3]

The very fact that the conversions had come under threat of violence became a reason for some Christians to hate *conversos*. If these Jews had only converted to save their skins, they wondered, how could they and their descendants ever be trusted? Bernard Gui, author of an influential inquisitorial text, sneered, "Jews try, whenever and wherever they can, secretly to pervert Christians and bring them to the Jewish perfidy, especially those who previously were Jews but converted and received baptism."[4] Rumors circulated that Jewish converts were trying to convert "cradle Christians" to Judaism. Spain forced Jews into the Catholic Church, then persecuted the converts for being Jewish.

Some *conversos* adopted Catholic Christianity and raised their children as faithful Catholics. Others maintained Jewish practices, passing down traditions across the generations. "All lived as observant Catholics," as one historian notes, but "some were clandestine Jews."[5] Such "crypto-Jews" were not numerous, yet their very presence made all *conversos* suspect in the eyes of the law. When the ruling powers needed a scapegoat, *conversos* always remained an option.

For Ferdinand and Isabella, 1492 was a year of religious cleansing. The monarchs would not learn what Christopher Columbus found in the western Atlantic until 1493. As Columbus fumbled his way across the ocean, King Ferdinand expelled the Jews and authorized the Spanish Inquisition to begin its infamous work of policing the faith. Crypto-Judaism was a crime, a defamation of the true faith and the state that defended it. The first offense meant torture; the second offense meant death—unless a *converso* protested innocence, in which case even a first offense warranted execution. Those condemned died by fire in the public square in a ceremony called the *auto-da-fé*—"act of faith."[6]

And then Columbus returned, and it soon became clear that he had discovered an entire hemisphere unknown to Europe, and not just a shortcut to India. Jews and *conversos* in Spain discovered a potential Atlantic escape route. Both devout *conversos* and crypto-Jews made their way to Mexico and the Caribbean. As early as 1501 the Spanish crown banned *conversos* in the colonies; a decade later the decree was extended to prohibit even the Christian children and grandchildren of condemned and executed Jews from occupying public office in the New World. By 1525 the *limpieza de sangre* ("purity of blood") had been declared throughout Spain. Christianity could now be measured by ancestry as well as faith; anyone with one Jewish grandparent was a *converso* and subject to different laws—those pertaining to impure blood. Spanish Christianity now had a genetic component. The *limpieza de sangre* extended to the colonies. Only those whose Christianity stretched back four generations could be permitted to enter the New World.[7]

On October 17, 1528, the Mexican Inquisition enforced this law to the letter. They burned a man named Hernando Alonso alive for the crime of Judaism in the Aztec capital, now known as Mexico City. Alonso had served as a carpenter in the army of Cortes. He parlayed his service into acquiring extensive tracts of land that had once belonged to Native Americans. Alonso had apparently been spotted trying to wash off his child's baptism. Convicted of crypto-Judaism, Alonso was set ablaze in front of the great pyramids of Tenochtitlan—the first Jewish martyr in the New World.[8]

Alonso was not alone. One Diego Morales survived six episodes of torture in Mexico over the next twenty years on suspicions of Judaism.[9] Marina Gutiérrez Flores de la Caballeria and her families reached Mexico through bureaucratic maneuvering and a forged document claiming a pure Christian heritage; they were in fact *conversos* (and devout Catholics).[10] The Inquisition caught Vera Moxica before he left Europe; Moxica had applied for a license to travel to New Spain and sworn his ancestry was "without stain or descent of Moors or Jews." Unfortunately for him, the Inquisition already knew of other Jewish Moxicas, and put Vera on trial for lying.[11] The bishop of Havana complained in 1508 that "practically every ship is filled with Hebrews and New Christians."[12]

By one estimate, the Inquisition prosecuted as many as 5,000 *conversos* in Mexico through the 1630s; it seems likely that at least some of them were crypto-Jews.[13] On the other hand, inquisitors often extracted confessions of Judaizers through torture, so it is difficult to have any certain knowledge of how many people who confessed to crypto-Judaism actually practiced it. In Oaxaca in 1739, a woman confessed to joining orgies attended by many "Jews and heretics." She also confessed to flying in the sky with devils and committing acts of sexual lewdness while airborne, so it seems unlikely her confession represents evidence of Judaism in the New World.[14] Since the charge of crypto-Jewry became a useful way to silence ecclesiastical or political rivals, many of those prosecuted as Judaizers likely had no Jewish ancestry at all. Much of the evidence of purported crypto-Judaism of Mexico emerged from the torture chamber.[15]

A few historical fragments suggest that some form of Judaism did arrive in Mexico, however, and traveled from there to the American Southwest. The town of Santa Fe had been occupied by indigenous nations for thousands of years; though nominally Spanish, its population was overwhelmingly Native American. Here was a place with few Europeans and where mumbled Hebrew prayers or fasting on High Holy Days might go unnoticed.[16]

In 1589, the Inquisition arrested Luis de Carvajal, governor of Nuevo Leon, a region that then comprised much of today's Arizona, Colorado, New Mexico, and California. The Inquisition charged de Carvajal (a *converso*) with practicing Judaism, and indeed, de Carvajal had brought numerous relatives with him to the New World without the usual religious documentation required by the Spanish crown. His nephew (also named Luis) told the Inquisition in Mexico that he still followed the Law of Moses, though he had never had a day of formal Jewish instruction. The younger Luis had even attempted to circumcise himself. His uncle died in prison, and the younger Luis was executed in Mexico City in 1596 after years of teaching what he called "the Law of Moses." In Spain, Phillip II despaired that North America "has become contaminated with Jews and heretics."[17]

Mostly, however, convictions for *judiazante* ("Judaizing") relied on confessions suborned by torture. Some of the investigations into New Mexico's crypto-Jews veered into the absurd, as in the case of Gómez Robeldo, who endured multiple inquisitorial investigations of his penis to determine if the scars on it came from circumcision or genital ulcers. Cristóbal de Herrera, a Santa Fe soldier, was accused of teaching Judaism to Native Americans in Mexico's Oaxaca; part of his trial turned on whether or not he had once said that Jews were intelligent.[18]

Yet some crypto-Jews did survive in the lands of the Apaches and Comanches. Their echoes resonate in cultural practices still performed in the twenty-first century. Some Hispanic families of New Mexico light candles in the bottom of deep jars on Friday nights, or play a game with a four-sided top on Christmas. Others celebrate an event called "the Feast of St. Esther" around Passover. The Catholic Church has no recognized St. Esther, and the practice is likely a residue of a long-forgotten Passover ritual. Non-Jewish men interviewed about their childhoods in New Mexico have acknowledged the practice of circumcision in their families.[19] As late as the 1960s, the Catholic bishop of Santa Fe banned a local practice of building outdoor shelters and eating a harvest meal on the days before the first frost—clearly a memory of a crypto-Jewish Sukkot.[20]

A similar exodus of crypto-Jews occurred in Brazil. Portugal's King Manuel originally accepted Jewish refugees from 1492 Spain, but when he married Ferdinand and Isabella's daughter in 1497, his in-laws insisted that expulsion of the Jews accompany the dowry. (Ferdinand and Isabella really, *really* hated Jews.) The Jews of Portugal faced conversion or expulsion; once again, some escaped to the New World. A group of *conversos* landed in Portuguese Brazil as early as 1502; indeed, Portugal deliberately banished to Brazil some *conversos* convicted of crypto-Judaism.[21] As with all *conversos*, most had become practicing Catholics, but in places like Baía and Recife, clandestine efforts at kosher law and male circumcision continued *sotto voce*.[22]

For *conversos* in Portugal, Brazil offered some of the same attractions as New Mexico had held for their Spanish counterparts. It was far from Europe, and primarily a Native American space. Then in 1630, the town of Recife was conquered by the Netherlands. The new rulers issued an edict promising "the liberty of Spanish, Portuguese, and natives, whether they be Roman Catholics or Jews." A number of *converso* families openly declared their Judaism—the first to do so in the New World.[23]

Dutch Protestant Reformers had become chummier with local Jews. This was not true of *all* Protestant reformers, of course. Martin Luther's 1543 book *On the Jews and Their Lies* historically has been unhelpful in improving Jewish-Christian relations. Dutch Protestants did not extend their protection out of any modern sense of equality. A small state with few natural resources, the Netherlands needed all the talent and soldiers it could get. It worked: By 1645, an entire company of Jews fought against the Portuguese to keep Brazilian cities Dutch.[24] A number of Recife *conversos* came out of the closet and began openly practicing. One man traveled to Europe and back to receive the rite of circumcision. Recife built the New World's first synagogue and hired the first transatlantic rabbi, situating both on the Rua dos Judeos—Jew Street.[25]

The toleration of Dutch Brazil was still a far cry from religious freedom. Jews could worship and practice business, but that was about it. They could not proselytize or marry Christians; no Jew could have a Christian servant (or visit a Christian prostitute). Protestant clergy attempted to shutter the synagogue on Rua dos Judeos. Jews who argued theology with Christians could be convicted of heresy. Christian merchants constantly complained about competition with Jews, or requested that Jews wear badges. Jewish existence in Recife owed more to the support and goodwill of the Estates-General in Amsterdam than to local powers. It was the Estates-General's edict in 1645 that required the Jews in Recife to be treated "in the same way as the other inhabitants of the United Netherlands." Religious protection was a tenet of a ruling junta, not an established social principle.[26]

In 1654, the Dutch lost control of Recife. The Portuguese navy retook the city after a decade of siege warfare and guerilla combat. The Portuguese commander offered generous terms (for the seventeenth century): Protestants and Jews had three months to clear out, taking what they could carry.[27] Most of Recife's Jews headed back to Amsterdam, or to other Dutch ports of call in the Caribbean. Of the hundreds of Jews in Recife, only twenty-three decided to make their way north to New Amsterdam— a fur-trading fort that would, one day, hold more Jews than any city in the world.

Those twenty-three *refuseniks* from Brazil did not intend to sail for Dutch New York at all. They boarded the *Valck* in Brazil intending to head for New England or Martinique. Storms pushed the ship to Jamaica, then Cuba. In Havana, the captain of the *St. Catrina* offered to take them to New Amsterdam for triple the normal price (or they could remain in

Spanish Cuba, where Judaism was illegal). With little choice, the Jews of the expedition agreed to his terms. When they arrived in New Amsterdam, several of the Jewish refugees (both men and women) were imprisoned for the debt they incurred during the crossing. The Dutch governor, Peter Stuyvesant, thought of Jews as "hateful enemies and blasphemers of the name of Christ" who should "be not allowed further to infect and trouble this new colony." Stuyvesant wanted them shipped back to Portugal where they would surely be arrested and possibly killed.[28]

It was not a great start.

The story of the "original twenty-three" has become valorized in American Jewish history. The 350th anniversary in 2004 occasioned a series of exhibits, websites, and festivals praising 1654 as emblematic of the "integral relationship between American freedom and Jewish continuity."[29] But the original twenty-three could not have been the original twenty-three because they were greeted by Jews already in the city. Solomon Pietersen, a Dutch Jew in New Amsterdam, acted as a lawyer for the refugees. It is from his account that we know of twenty-three Jews, "big as well as little," showing up at the docks (that is, both adults and children). Otherwise, the exact number of refugees was unclear. Pietersen and two other Jewish merchants arrived in New Amsterdam months before the *St. Catrina*, making them the first Jews in New Amsterdam.[30]

Peter Stuyvesant either did not care or did not notice Pietersen, but he wanted the Recife Jews expelled. Luckily for the refugees, New Amsterdam still had to answer to Old Amsterdam. Stuyvesant served as the agent of the directors of the Dutch West India Company. The directors denied the governor's request to expel the Jews. The Jews could stay, the directors decided, and they lectured Stuyvesant that what mattered was not confession but loyalty. They were specifically thinking about Recife: "The Jewish nation in Brazil have at all times been faithful and have striven to guard and maintain that place, risking for that purpose their possessions and their blood."

New Amsterdam's Jews did not become citizens nor receive full rights. They could not build a public synagogue or serve on guard duty, nor would the colony support any of the Jews who might fall into poverty. Stuyvesant howled. So did others. Christian pastor Johannes Megapolensis, a Dutch Reformed church official in the city, thought the Jews were "godless rascals, who are of no benefit to the country," and that "still more of this lot would follow and then build here a synagogue." The Jews had "no other god but the unrighteous mammon and no other aim than to get possession of Christian property." Megapolensis begged the authorities to get rid of them.[31]

In a sense, Megapolensis got his wish. Within a few years, most of this transient Jewish community had left the colony. Abraham de Lucena and several other Jews arrived from the Netherlands in 1655 with instructions to support the original twenty-three. De Lucena brought the first Torah scroll in the mainland colonies with him, but soon he and his Torah had left. By the time the English seized the city in 1664, most of the Jews who had arrived in the previous decade chose to go elsewhere. Perhaps only one remained to watch the transfer of power. Jews would not open a synagogue or worship openly in New York for almost eighty more years.[32]

The real center of Jewish life in the Americas was the Caribbean, the nexus through which all imperial worlds passed. By 1700, the sugar islands conquered by Spain, France, Britain, and other European nations had become the dark heart of a system of human misery. People kidnapped in Africa and sold into slavery at the Gold Coast slave depots were shipped there, then worked to death on sugar plantations. An enslaved person brought to the Caribbean could expect to live only five years under the regime.[33] Human beings were the commodity; sugar was the product. The Caribbean islands—even smudges of land like Nevis or St. Croix—generated untold sums for trade magnates and imperial crowns back in Europe. To a great extent, by 1700 most of the New World colonies in North America existed primarily to service the sugar islands; in 1763, France chose to surrender all of Canada to Britain rather than lose the island of Guadeloupe (all of twenty-five miles across).[34]

Such European outposts also formed Jewish communities. The Dutch West India Company arranged for a small number of Jews to settle at Curaçao, a semi-arid island forty miles north of Venezuela. Curaçao's anti-Semitic governor at the time did not favor the idea. The governor was—you guessed it!—Peter Stuyvesant. Stuyvesant left Curaçao to take the gig in New York in 1650; after that, the Jews arrived.[35] By 1688, they had a synagogue, and by the middle of the eighteenth century, the colony had around 2,000 Jewish residents.[36] In 1652, David Nassy, an Amsterdam Jew who had lived in Dutch Brazil, received permission from the company to settle fifty Jews in the colony of Cayenne (now French Guiana). Nassy called his settlement Jodensavanne—"Jew's savannah." The Jews received permission to build a synagogue. Like other Europeans, the Jews of Jodensavanne built slave plantations. This enslaved outpost had a synagogue and a rabbi long before New York.[37]

Other Caribbean islands also built synagogues before any rose on the North American mainland. Bridgetown, Barbados, had a Jewish population well before Manhattan, and built a synagogue by 1664. The Jews of Jamaica raised a house of worship called Neve Zedek; an earthquake destroyed it in 1692. The tiny island of Nevis built a synagogue in the 1680s; Dutch Martinique built one in 1667. Indeed, a synagogue rose in Madras—the British colonial zone in India—before one appeared in New York.[38]

The Jewish world of the British Caribbean, in fact, gave rise to one of the most iconic Founding Fathers—the only one to have his own hip-hop musical. Alexander Hamilton grew up in the Jewish neighborhood of Nevis and attended the island's Jewish school. No records remain from that institution, though Hamilton's son recalled that on one of the few occasions his father mentioned his childhood, he smiled and recalled "having been taught to repeat the Decalogue in Hebrew, at the school of a Jewess." In his late teens, Hamilton admitted he "had not yet received communion."[39]

Was Hamilton Jewish? A 2021 investigation into Hamilton's origins suggested that he was. Hamilton's mother, Rachel Faucette, married Johan Michael Levine on the island of St. Croix years before Hamilton's birth. Levine had a typical Jewish name and worked as a merchant on an island with an established Jewish population. If Levine was Jewish—and that is a big if—then it is also possible that Rachel Faucette converted to Judaism in order to marry him. Their son, Peter, was not baptized until he was an adult. That in itself does not prove that Johan and Rachel were Jewish, but they were certainly not faithful Anglicans.[40]

Five years after the wedding, Levine had Faucette imprisoned for adultery. Faucette sat in a cell for months, a punishment Levine believed would "change her unholy way of life." It did, in fact, change her life: She got out of the marriage and moved to St. Kitts. There she met James Hamilton. James and Rachel relocated to Nevis, where they had two sons out of wedlock. These were the scandalous circumstances of birth that haunted their younger son, Alexander, all his life.[41] So, if Levine was Jewish and if Faucette converted to marry him and if she did not get re-baptized after leaving him, then when Alexander Hamilton was born in 1754, his mother would have been legally Jewish, thus making Hamilton legally Jewish as well, since Jewish descent is traditionally traced through the mother.

That is a lot of ifs. While there's no evidence for Hamilton's infant baptism, there is also no evidence he had a *bris* (ritual circumcision), or a bar mitzvah, or even that the family were members of the Nevis synagogue. The swirling number of ifs seems to indicate that his mother probably wasn't Jewish when Hamilton was born, but it also indicates how closely linked Hamilton's family was to the Caribbean Jewish community. Hamilton grew up in a town with a sizable Jewish neighborhood, went to a Jewish school, and learned Hebrew as a kid. Hamilton certainly understood Judaism better than any other Founder. But when he arrived in New York in the early 1770s, he unequivocally lived as an Anglican (although he famously ignored Christian injunctions about adultery).

New York's "original twenty-three" of 1654 were therefore part of a broad array of Jews moving around in tiny numbers in the colonial world. The half-measures pursued by Dutch officials in Manhattan and Amsterdam were par for the course for Jews across the colonial world. Conditions and laws were spotty. In 1654, Jews received better legal treatment and greater freedom elsewhere in the New World. Any of those places—Bridgetown in Barbados, Paramaribo in Suriname, Port Royal in Jamaica—might have developed into a Jewish haven. When New York Jews built their synagogue Shearith Israel in 1730, it was the eighth synagogue in the English colonial world. (If we include the Dutch colonial world, Shearith Israel becomes the seventeenth synagogue founded.)[42] In other words, the progress of religious freedom and the rights of religious minorities did not develop in any kind of progressive or linear fashion. Grants of residency, military alliances, and acts of toleration did not lay a foundation for rights. Opportunities to create religious freedom will not always lead to freedom. The Jewish communities of British North America ended up in a fight for freedom not because they had already been granted liberty, but because they knew from experience how it could be taken away.

In some ways, this is good news for anyone who loves religious liberty: It means that occasions for establishing religious freedom can occur in numerous contexts, and that religious liberty can be constructed. It is no simple accident of law; it can be built and rebuilt. There is also bad news, however. Once created, religious liberty does not always endure. Jewish rights in the New World, made in the 1600s, became shaky in the 1700s. Reliance on individual rulers and local traditions proved an ephemeral strategy.

For example, Jewish rights in Suriname, located on the northern coast of South America, came under attack by a new governor in 1685 (almost at the same time the Rhode Island government sought to seize the property of its Jews). In Suriname, a new leadership tried repeatedly to ban Jews from working on the Christian Sabbath, and called Jewish marriages legally questionable. By the 1710s, some of these efforts succeeded.[43] In Virginia, a 1705 law declared that "Jews, Moors, Mahometans, or other infidels" could not "purchase any christian white servant," and that if such a transaction took place, the servant was immediately free. The law was primarily aimed at policing the color line, since it prohibited anyone of African or Native American descent—even if they were Christian—from owning a white servant or slave. Nevertheless, the law now made clear that "christian whites" made up a superior class of person. Indeed, if any white Christian decided to "intermarry with any such negro, mulatto, or Indian, Jew, Moor, Mahometan, or other infidel, every christian white servant of every such person so intermarrying, shall, *ipso facto*, become free."[44] In 1704, less than ten years after three Jews became naturalized, South Carolina explicitly limited the vote to Christians. In 1759 the colonial legislature revised the ban—tightening it so that only Protestants could vote.[45] Religious divisions hardened in the eighteenth century. Delaware formally seceded from Pennsylvania in 1682 rather than be ruled by Quakers.[46]

It was not always an existing government but fear of a coming regime that changed Jewish status. Forty-two Jews arrived in Georgia aboard the *William and Sarah* in 1732. This Hebraic influx bolstered the (white) population of 120, provoking howls from the trustees that Georgia "would soon become a Jewish colony." Georgia was indeed now a quarter Jewish. In 1734, the trustees ordered the Jews to leave, but the colony's non-Jewish settlers in Georgia disagreed. One white Christian wrote that these new arrivals "behaved so well as to their morals, peaceableness, and charity that they were a reproach to Christian inhabitants." The nascent colony did not accord the Jews full membership, however. In 1738 the settlers petitioned Britain for the right to enact slavery in the colony, which was founded to be abolitionist. The petition included this note: "The *Jews* applied for Liberty to sign with us; but we did not think it proper to join them in any of our Measures." Jews might have morals and charity, but under Georgian colonial rule they were still Jews, not people. When war broke out two years later between Spain and England, Jewish colonists in Georgia recognized that if the tiny colony fell to Spain, the Inquisition would follow. Jewish

Georgians such as Samuel Nunes knew that Spanish rule meant an *auto-da-fé*, and "fear of the Spaniards drove [them] to Charleston." By 1741, all but two Jewish families had fled Georgia. In 1762, the legislature denied even those Jews the right to build a cemetery.[47] Mordecai Sheftall, then a twenty-something slaveholder from one of the remaining Jewish families, must have wondered about this restriction. Within twelve years, he would be the de facto leader of revolutionary Savannah.

The real move against New World Jews came from France. The French crown controlled several Caribbean islands with a handful of Jewish residents. A series of royal officials gave tacit approval of the Jews and ignored Jesuit efforts to expel the Jews for killing Christian babies (which the priests assured the officials was commonplace). In Quebec, however, a ban against Jews went into place, and the Jews were forbidden to settle.[48]

Then in 1685, Louis XIV banished *all* Jews from French colonies, as they were "declared enemies of the Christian name." Louis called it the *Code Noir*, and officially it simply standardized French colonial law. One of those standardizations, however, forbade all non-Catholics from living under the king's domains in the New World. Jews and Protestants had three months to leave. Colonial French Jews fled to Dutch and British Caribbean islands in search of refuge—rather than to any mainland British colony. Jews were banned in all territories that flew the French flag until the 1770s.[49] When the French seized St. Eustatius in 1709, the island's Jews were expelled for the length of the occupation.[50] Canada had no Jews until the British seized control. In 1720 the Code Noir was explicitly invoked to expel Jews from Louisiana.[51] In 1738, one "Jacques Lafargue" arrived in Quebec; it turned out that he was actually a Jewish woman named Esther Brandeau in disguise. The governor sent Brandeau to the nuns of Quebec in the hopes she would convert; when she did not, officials shipped her back to France.[52]

The inconsistent and fluctuating nature of the Jewish experience in the Americas reminds us that the colonial world was a hive of laws and requirements based on birth. There were important advances in the idea of self-government and human liberty in the colonial Americas: the Mayflower Compact, Williams's Rhode Island, the Zenger case (involving freedom of the press). But these freshwater streams fought a rising salt tide of restrictions, controls, forced migrations, and slavery. Expansive European colonies met resistance from indigenous Native American nations, sometimes prompting massacres of Indians (as in the Pequot War, 1637) or of white colonists (King William's War, 1689). Contact with the

Spanish annihilated the Taino civilization. (Epidemics played a role, but Columbus and the conquistadors also enslaved entire nations.) Alliances between British colonists and Native American nations reworked the political geography of North America from the moment John Smith founded Jamestown. By 1730, treaties such as the infamous Walking Purchase were turning Native American land into colonial possessions. During the Seven Years War, the British forcibly relocated over 10,000 Acadians from Canada to Louisiana, where they became the Cajuns. Thousands died in the forced relocation. Massachusetts executed Quakers, homosexuals, and people suspected of witchcraft—not as frequently as mythology might claim, but often enough to remind New Englanders that independent religious thought was not tolerated. Restrictions on freedom were the norm in the colonial world.

Slavery ran through all of it. The enslavement of Africans in the New World from the 1500s until abolition in Brazil in 1888 was the largest forced migration and the greatest reversal of freedom in the history of the world. Slavery was, as we've seen, most brutal in the sugar islands of Haiti, Jamaica, and Cuba, but it found its way into every European territory. A fifth of all residents of New York were enslaved Africans, and a planned uprising of 1711 was put down with extreme cruelty. Executions of supposed perpetrators took place on Wall Street; the condemned were burned over fires kept low so they would not die quickly.

Enslavement shaped the colonial world, in places where Jews gathered in large numbers (Suriname, Barbados), in places where they gathered in small numbers (New York, Charleston), and in places where the law prevented them from settling at all (Louisiana, Haiti). The presence or absence of Jews did not affect the slave system, but the slave system affected Jewish life. Some Jewish merchants became rich off the slave trade and the plantation system. Aaron Lopez profited from the forced labor of his fellow humans. Jodensavanne exploited slaves for labor, along with all other plantations in Suriname.[53] A few Jews opposed it. In New York, Moses Judah became a member and then an officer in the Society for Promoting the Manumission of Slaves. Over fifty years, he became involved in the liberation of about fifty people.[54] Still other Jews were born from it. Biracial Jews born of enslaved African or Native American mothers and Jewish fathers lived across the colonies. Some of these partnerships were consensual; others were forced. The personhood of the children of these unions shifted across the various Jewish communities of the Americas. In Suriname, male children of such unions could be circumcised and attend the yeshiva; in other colonies such recognition of the personhood and Jewishness of such children was rare. David Nassy in the Caribbean freed three slaves who bore his name—they were very likely his children, and they went on to establish a prayer group for Jews of Afro-Jewish ancestry. Most enslaved Jews had no such luck.[55]

Though Jews did not have legal equality with Christians, that did not make all of them advocates for freedom. Indeed, individual Jews participated in the slave system at roughly the same rates as did their far-more-populous white Christian neighbors. Yet false mythology has held and continues to hold that Jews in particular fostered and developed the slave trade. Claims that Jews created the slave trade have been frequently debunked. It is not difficult to demonstrate that the vast majority of those involved with the slave trade were not Jewish. Nevertheless, the myth lives on. In 1913, the German historian Werner Sombart described New World Jews as an "ant-heap," feverishly building the slave system. The idea has stuck.[56] The colonial Jews lived in a world of slavery, and some of them profited from it. The Jews did not create the slave trade, but neither could it be said that Jews formed any kind of "benevolent masters." Neither fact exculpates those Jews who practiced slavery or those Jews who stood by—nor does the fact that Barbados restricted the number of slaves Jews could own.[57]

The colonial world was built around hierarchies and restrictions to freedom. It was not a republic or a democracy *in utero*; it was an empire. The powers of the colonial world could simply forbid the open practice of Judaism, and when they did not ban it, Jews had no security for their freedom.[58] Their rights were always contingent upon the communities they lived in, the whims of the ruling class, and the decrees of monarchs. To an extent, this was simply anti-Semitism and anti-Judaism, and to an extent it was true of virtually every group living in the European colonies. Even whiteness could not protect a people who had become inconvenient for the ruling class (as Acadians and Quakers discovered). The colonial world was a world of gradations and discriminations.

That was the case in New York after the English seized power, when Jewish life and liberty depended on imperial currents as much as local conditions. The English king who turned New Amsterdam into New York was Charles II, whose navy took the city in 1666. Charles hated the Puritans but enjoyed sleeping with women who were not his wife, so he took a fairly lax view of religious conformity. In 1674, he extended an open religious policy to New York, ordering the royal governor to "permit all persons of what Religion so ever, quietly to inhabit within ye precincts of your jurisdiction."[59] Perhaps because of this policy, a new influx of Jews arrived in New York in the 1680s. Still, the edict went only so far: Jews were "denizens" rather than subjects. In 1685, Jews petitioned New York's common council for public worship, and the council turned them down. For good measure, the Jews lost their previous right to engage in retail trade.[60]

In 1685, Charles died and the throne passed to his Catholic brother, James II. A tense few years followed as England's Protestant Parliament squared off against a monarch who, it appeared, planned to return his country to the Catholic fold. In 1688–89, rebellions broke out across England and her colonies. Parliament ousted James; New England overthrew its royal governor. In New York, royal officials were pushed out and Jacob Leisler, a rigorous Calvinist holdover from the days of Dutch rule, assumed control. Leisler required all inhabitants to swear an oath to the Protestant religion. In 1691, his junta forbade all Jewish and Catholic worship. New York seemed to be on its way to its own *Code Noir*.

But the overthrow of James in England brought very different monarchs to the throne—the Dutch King William III, who ruled as co-regent with his English wife, Queen Mary II. (A college in Virginia is named for them.) William and Mary undertook a policy of toleration to integrate Puritans and Anglicans in England and Wales with Presbyterians in Scotland. It would not do to have a Calvinist faction restricting worship in New York, especially without the king's say so. In 1692, Leisler was put to death and his cohort defeated. William and Mary's choice for governor, Henry Sloughter—who had put down what was called Leisler's Rebellion—restored Jewish rights to worship as part of the cleanup effort in Manhattan.[61]

Still, New York never attracted many Jews in the eighteenth century. Even by 1770, only about 300 lived there. It was not as large as Barbados, not as prominent as Suriname, not as rich as Jamaica. Jews in British North America muddled through. They did not seem destined for greatness or even significant growth. The Caribbean outposts had more Jews, more synagogues, and a more vibrant Jewish life.[62]

Nor was religious liberty growing in the 1700s. If anything, it shrank. Eighteenth-century Virginia required an Anglican oath from all who entered.[63] Maryland established the Church of England as a state church in 1692. New York state began paying Protestant ministers to preach a year later. North and South Carolina strengthened their establishments, and transatlantic missionary societies strengthened the ties of all the colonial establishments with the Protestant homeland in England.[64] Neither demographics nor economics favored the mainland British colonies as a haven for Judaism or religious liberty.

But the Jews of New York and other British North American colonial enclaves that emerged after 1700 had one significant difference from their Caribbean brethren: Their synagogues were weaker. In larger colonial Jewish communities, the synagogue acted much like those in Protestant Europe, where the state delegated control of the Jews to them. They wielded both religious and political authority over their congregations. The *mahamad*—the governing board of the synagogue—dominated Jewish life. In Europe, "the individual Jew could belong only to the organized Jewish community, which consequently exercised hegemony over all members of the Jewish faith."[65] So too in the Dutch island of Curaçao, where the synagogue regulated Jewish "dress, morals, reading matter, attendance at plays and operas, and sexual conduct."[66] The synagogue "was essentially a partially self-governing enclave" with control over the Jews. In Suriname, island authorities granted the *mahamad* the right to ensure the "good government and tranquility" of Jodensavanne.[67] In 1764, the Comte d'Estaing simply picked one of the illegal Jews living in Haiti and made him the leader and tax collector for the informal community.[68] When Jewish Purim celebrations became too raucous on St. Eustatius, the island's colonial government alerted the *mahamad*, who then cracked down on those who "beat, or make a noise in Synagogue with a hammer, or any other instrument" during the Feast of Esther.[69] The state said Jews could not shout down Haman, the *mahamad* complied, and a Jewish practice ended.

Mainland synagogues had no such authority or clout. Unlike Curaçao and Barbados, Jews arrived piecemeal in New York after 1654, and they had not been permitted to build a house of worship—so through neglect, the synagogue lacked the legal authority over Jews of its cousin institutions in Europe and the Caribbean. When Shearith Israel finally became New York's first synagogue in 1730, it was a humble affair (more cottage than church) and its influence over the Jewish community by necessity would be by moral suasion rather than legal action—a feature that would serve it well in the years to come.[70]

Something remarkable but little noticed happened as Shearith Israel stumbled toward existence. Due in part to the new regime and a revision to naturalization laws, it appears that a number of New York Jews applied for and became freemen in the years following 1692. That meant that a few Jews—a very few—might qualify to vote.[71]

At least, that was the allegation in an electoral crisis in 1737. A close election for a seat in the colonial assembly roiled the city. One Cornelius Van Horne narrowly lost to the former assembly speaker Adolphe Philipse. Van Horne challenged the outcome by attacking the legality of the vote. Nonresidents, soldiers, and Jews, Van Horne claimed, had no right to vote in English territory. Van Horne's claim went before the colonial assembly, and both Van Horne and Philipse submitted "Lists of those Persons they have any Exceptions to"—that is, their purported lists of illegal voters. After much legislative rambling, Philipse's side offered "some of the *Jewish* profession to be admitted as evidence"—that is, to bring forth some Jewish witnesses. The speaker, however, announced "it was the Opinion of the House, that none of the *Jewish* profession could be admitted as evidence." Jews could not testify before the legislature, not even in their own defense.[72]

The real blow came the next day, when the legislature unanimously decided "it not appearing to this House, That Persons of the *Jewish* re-ligion have a Right to be admitted to vote for Parliament Men in *Great Britain*, it is the unanimous Opinion of this House, That they ought not to be admitted to vote for Representatives in this Province." Apparently one legislator, William Smith Sr., gave a roaringly anti-Semitic speech on Van Horne's behalf, and "so pathetically described the bloody tragedy at Mount Calvary" that "the unfortunate Israelites were content to lose their votes, could they escape with their lives." Smith's son credited timely inter-vention by some Philipse supporters for preventing New York Jews from being "massacred, that very day, for the sin of their ancestors in crucifying Jesus."[73]

To add insult to injury, the assembly then voted that "Non-Resident freeholders"—those men who owned land but did not live in the district—*could* vote, and the next day began going through the lists presented by Philipse and Van Horne. In other words, the colonial legislature banned Jewish voting first, and then started to go through the evidence.[74]

It is possible that the assembly chose to scapegoat the Jews as part of a political ploy. Excluding Jewish votes while keeping non-resident freeholders and soldiers enfranchised left Philipse with enough votes to win the election. It is also possible, however, that the assembly was genuinely shocked to discover—as readers and historians might be—that Jews were voting in New York in 1737. Not *all* Jews, of course—just the ones who owned sufficient property, likely the ones with whom Abigaill Franks shared "the faire Character" she thought her own wealthy family exhibited. Jews had never formally been granted this right under the monarchical rule of colonial New York. A very few of them had slipped into this right, and these few Jews may have been voting for years until a political crisis emerged and they became an easy target for political schemes. All law came from Parliament and the Crown. The Jews had no rights not specifically given by that government.[75]

So the assembly revoked the Jewish vote. It had applied to a handful of men for years, and then it was simply gone, swept away overnight in a burst of anti-Semitism and political opportunism. Philipse kept his seat. Van Horne went away, and there was now legal precedent for keeping Jews under the monarchy out of colonial elections. As so often happens in history, being Jewish did not matter until it did.

Jewish rights—like all rights—did not progress naturally. They could be gained and they could be lost. They are secured by political guarantees and security concerns. By the 1750s, New York's Jewish men had lost significant rights. The city was marginal in the Jewish Atlantic world, and there was no reason to think it would be a haven of freedom, or that its 300-odd Jews would become citizens along with their Christian neighbors by 1789. Nearly a thousand Jews lived on Curaçao by 1789. While tolerated, they did not receive full rights until an act of emancipation in 1825. The smaller, less organized, less wealthy Jewish communities in the States beat them to it by decades.[76]

Religious freedom was not foreordained, and it did not come from a long colonial tradition of toleration and freedom. There was no clear, consistent movement toward it in the colonies prior to the American Revolution. By extension, there was no clear colonial era move toward Jewish rights or emancipation. What freedoms there were existed by chance and were dependent on ruling regimes and individual rulers. There was therefore no general hope or expectation of Jewish citizenship in the colonial era, certainly not when considered in the broad European imperial system.

And then the revolution came.

3

The Rabbi of the Revolution

LIKE THE REVOLUTION ITSELF, THE rabbinate of Gershom Seixas was spackled together with whatever materials were at hand. Gershom didn't mind a bit. He had no yeshiva training because there were no yeshivas on his side of the Atlantic. He dressed like an Episcopal minister because that was what was available. And he took whatever salary he could. Manhattan's Shearith Israel synagogue was neither large nor important enough to merit (or afford) a fully trained rabbi. Caribbean communities could tempt ordained men from Europe. Mainland British colonies relied on laymen with a working knowledge of Hebrew to do the job of rabbis. Shearith Israel asked Gershom Seixas to do just that in 1768, when he was just twenty-two years old.

But what to call him? Officially Seixas was a hazan, a position combining aspects of a modern Jewish cantor, Sunday school teacher, and community secretary. The name didn't catch on, so Jews borrowed Christian terms for their clergy. Isaac Bangs referred to Seixas as "The Priest." The Charleston hazan David Nunes Carvalho called him "reverend" and "pastor." Even his home synagogue referred to Seixas as "Reverend Mister." Only when the community addressed the Council of Censors in 1783 did his fellows Jews refer to him as *Rabbi* Seixas.[1]

Seixas never worried much about the terms people used to describe him. He called himself *"home-born"* which he also chose to render *"Native."*[2] In Seixas's mind, Jews and Americans overlapped. He could dress like a minister, he could be called reverend or priest or rabbi. Even he could come up with no better title for his fellow hazans than "Revd-Jew-Clergymen."[3] But that was all window dressing. "Obey the law of God handed down to us by our divine Legislator," he declared in 1805. "We shall then be better men & better Citizens."[4] When it came right down to it, Gershom Seixas believed that the heart of the republic and of his faith was moral virtue and practice—so not only could a Jew be an American, a Jew ought to be an American.

Seixas became the Rabbi of the Revolution. He forged his place in the country and the movement through position, circumstance, and a fierce patriotic theology. Alone among the patriot Jews, he had sermons published in his lifetime. He served on the board of Columbia University, and he acted as an ambassador of Judaism to civil leaders and Christian clergy. In part that was due to his patriot bona fides, and in part, it was due to the very confusion over whether he was hazan or rabbi or "Revd-Jew-Clergyman." When American Jews requested recognition by the public and the state, the state saw them as if they were a Christian denomination. They expected an ordained minister, even though Judaism had no ministers, and American Judaism no ordained clergy of any kind. But Seixas was ready to assume the role. When he did, he secured a foothold for Jewish rights, and began the long transformation of the American synagogue into a distinct institution in Jewish life.

Gershom was New York's first hazan born in the New World, son of an Ashkenazi mother and a Sephardic father. Through his father, Gershom was connected to the Seixas clan of Portugal—the ones whose ancestors had supposedly escaped the Inquisition by hiding in a basket. Through his mother, he was connected by blood or marriage to the Levy, Franks, and Hays families of the British Atlantic. Gershom conducted services in Spanish style but peppered his letters with Yiddish terms not used by Sephardic communities—*tauliss* for a prayer shawl, *hatiss* for sinner, *koogle* for . . . well, kugle.[5]

Gershom and Moses's father, Isaac, arrived in the Americas in 1738, and he established a commercial practice. He had some success, despite the Anglo-Spanish war that broke out just after he arrived and must have made his Sephardic name a source of some tension to neighbors in New York. Pronounced "Say-Shuss," it led to multiple misspellings, including at one point, "Mr. Sexies."[6]

Isaac married Rachel Levy in May 1740 and therefore into the Levy-Franks clan, New York's most successful Jewish family. This did not cause great celebration in the Franks household. Abigaill Franks, the materfamilias of Jewish New York, felt "displeased" with Rachel's choice. Isaac, she knew, had a temper.[7] Abigaill also seemed shocked at Isaac's easy rapport with his customers. He managed to deal with "Triffling People with Soe much patience." How could Isaac be a grocer "in the Jerseys with a Contented mind"? Abigaill, presumably, could not.[8] Other members of the Franks family thought he was too poor. But it was the Sephardim who were really angry, Abigaill noted: "The Portuguese here were in A Violent Uproar about it, for he did not invite any of them to ye Wedding."[9]

Isaac and Rachel got married at a low point for Manhattan's Jewry. Religious restrictions were becoming harsher in the British colonies. The electoral crisis of 1737 involving Cornelius Van Horne and Adolphe Philipse specifically restricted Jewish rights and codified any misunderstandings about whether Jews were members of the body politic of New York. (Answer: They were not.) In 1740, Oliver Delancey, a merchant who sided with the British in the revolution, led a mob that attacked a Jewish home, broke the windows, "tore everything to pieces and swore they would lie with the woman." In 1743, a mob attacked a Jewish funeral in New York, waving "an image" (possibly a crucifix) over the corpse and uttering their own prayers over the dead "in such a vile manner that, to mention all would Shock a human ear," according to the newspaper account.[10]

State churches were becoming stronger. Battles between Puritans and Presbyterians (Dissenters) and the Church of England (Anglicans) marked most of the 1600s, but the 1700s found these groups united against Catholic Europe. The British empire adopted a kind of triple establishment—Anglicanism in Britain, Presbyterianism in Scotland, Congregationalism in New England. This was not toleration or religious freedom in any sense—just ask the Virginia Baptists who were arrested for performing marriages or jailed for preaching without a license.

Imperial governments of the 1700s embraced the power and privileges of state churches. An interlocking system of Protestant networks, societies, and communities appeared across the empire with broad government support, linking British Protestants across oceans. These state churches and organizations in turn supported imperial objectives in the name of keeping the empire Protestant. Denominational fussing took a back seat to broader religious objectives. The salient religious organizations of the eighteenth century were the alphabet soup of organizations and missionary societies— SPG, NEC, SPRKP, SPCK, and others—which connected distant

Anglicans, Presbyterians, and Congregationalists in a firm Protestant union dedicated to "ideas and projects that were in line with imperatives" of the empire, as historian Katherine Carté writes.[11] Imperial support of this kind of Protestant establishment also meant that the eighteenth-century churches of the British empire joined in the support of many of its most heinous aspects—enslavement, expropriation of indigenous lands—as part of the supposed cost of "stability and expansion of the empire as the best vessel through which to ensure a thriving protestant world." Not all Protestants, of course. Baptists in New England and Massachusetts faced legal and social disruptions to their preaching, worship, and ceremonies.[12]

The British state made an abortive effort to offer Jews something like recognition, too. It did not go well. In June 1753, Parliament passed the infamous "Jew Bill," which intended to extend state sanction to a thin wedge of non-Christian religious belief. The Bill made it possible for foreign-born Jews to be naturalized into Britain without receiving the Lord's Supper (i.e., Christian communion), as was required by law. The Bill would affect only a handful of Jews; functionally it gave them the right own property, not the right to vote or hold office.

But passage of the Jew Bill sparked anti-Semitic furor in Britain. Public prints showed Jews taking over London, Jews carrying off bags of money, Jews allied with the devil. The London *Evening Post* suggested that an army of Jews would circumcise every British male. British merchant Jonas Hanway and others saw the Jew Bill as an existential political crisis, since the nation had to be founded on Christianity; the eucharist was a "*badge of honor* as a Christian and a Protestant" but also "*a token of fidelity to the state.*" Hanway explicitly declared that Christianity was the glue keeping the state together. And if Christianity kept the state together, the people of the state could have no religious freedom.

Mobs attacked Jewish peddlers in the street. One of them—Jonas Levi—was murdered. Parliament repealed the Jew Bill in November 1753; the effort to expand Jewish rights to hold property had been measured in months.[13] At almost the same time, other Jewish rights contracted. An older 1740 law allowed naturalization for foreign-born Jews in the colonies, but when two Rhode Island Jews attempted to invoke the law in 1762, the state legislature refused to enforce it.[14]

The anti-Jewish outburst in Britain came among a series of tightening restrictions for Jews and religious minorities in the colonies. New York's Jewish cemetery was desecrated in 1746 and again in 1751.[15] Georgia's legislature refused to permit a Jewish cemetery in 1762, despite thirty years of Jewish presence in the colony.[16] Even Ben Franklin engaged in anti-Semitic canards in a 1764 campaign against the Quaker party, where he described his opponents as Jews out to defraud renters.[17] Nonetheless, the mainland North American colonies under Britain never expelled the Jews, as happened in French and Spanish colonies. On occasion, Jews even found paths to legal recognition; Mordecai Sheftall secured his right to land in 1755 as a native-born resident of Georgia, even in the wake of the Jew Bill.[18] Still, the overall state of religious rights for those outside the triple Anglican-Presbyterian-Congregationalist establishment was shaky. As one American Jew in 1758 suggested about a European relative, "I would not advise him to come here."[19]

The rise of yet another Protestant innovation in the 1730s did little to change the situation for Jews. The New Light movement—known today as the Great Awakening—generated even more splits and church divisions among Protestants in the eighteenth century. Led by colonials like Jonathan Edwards and Britons like George Whitefield and John Wesley, the New Lights proclaimed that a Christian could *feel* salvation—believers could actually know (more or less) whether they had been saved. These ideas were radical among Calvinists, who denied that any human being could ever presume to know what God had decided. ("The heart," wrote Calvin, "is an idol factory.") Over the next decades, churches would split over these doctrines, spurring Baptist growth and eventually giving rise to the Methodists.

The Awakening did not, however, fundamentally alter the empire or its new establishment. The followers of Whitefield and Wesley showcased themselves through noteworthy revivals, but they functioned through the existing imperial Protestant networks. New Lights did split churches, but those churches remained Anglican, Presbyterian, and Congregationalist, and so freely accessed imperial support and connection. New Light churches largely remained within imperial Protestantism. Long-standing historical claims that the Great Awakening inspired the American Revolution have little merit. The Old Light-New Light divide did not map on to patriot-loyalist splits, and of course the revolution took place forty-odd years after the New Light revivals. New Lights wanted preachers who could feel God's grace, and they wanted the British empire to support their churches. They got both. The Awakening made British Protestantism stronger, not weaker.[20]

Similarly, the Awakening reflected the general imperial ambivalence about Jews and affirmed their second-class legal status. Edwards, for example, was profoundly interested in biblical Jews but almost never considered the place of Jews in the contemporary British empire. Edwards once had a Jewish neighbor, "who appeared to me the devoutest person that ever I saw in my life; great part of his time being spent in the acts of devotion, at his eastern window, which opened next to mine." Not that Christians should emulate this pious Jew: Edwards took Jewish devotion as evidence that "to be zealously engaged in the external exercises of religion, and to spend much time in them, is no sure evidence of grace; because such a disposition is found in many that have no grace." Jews mattered to Edwards only as a warning to Christians.[21]

Not all Jews of the 1750s shared the devotion of Edwards's neighbor. Numerous members of New York's Shearith Israel, for example, turned the synagogue into a forum for defamation, ridicule, and open combat. In 1755, Solomon Hays and David Gomez got into an argument about whether to shut the window in the women's gallery. Hays had to be physically thrown out. (This happened on Yom Kippur.) He filed assault charges. Then a whistleblower accused synagogue leadership of passing off *traif* meat as kosher: that "your Hazan neither sees the meat nor knows whether it has been properly or improperly killed" and the butcher only "pretends that said Hazan has duly signed the certificates."[22] Abraham Abrahams hit a fellow Jew in the synagogue. In 1768, Manuel Josephson and Judah Hays ridiculed an octogenarian called to the Torah because his *talis* dragged on the ground; they made faces "at the Elders and at the persons who give out the Honors of the Synagogue." Samson Simson in response called Josephson a "dirty dog."[23]

One scandal dwarfed the others. Phila Franks—daughter of Abigaill—married Oliver Delancey, the same Oliver Delancey who once killed a man in a tavern brawl and was New York's best-known anti-Semite to boot. It was Delancey who raised the 1737 mob that attacked immigrant Jews from Holland and broke up a Jewish funeral with "a Rabble . . . got together."[24] Phila kept her marriage a secret for sixth months.[25]

The synagogue of New York was not going to be an easy assignment. Shearith Israel didn't even bother looking for a rabbi. They simply wrote to other communities seeking an unmarried "Young Man, of good Morals & strictly religious." Joseph Jeshurun Pinto—unordained, Amsterdam-born, literate in Hebrew and English—took the job and sailed from London in

1759. The job defeated him. Almost immediately after arriving, Pinto was accused of scandal, so that one of his first tasks as hazan was to compose a long letter to the synagogue defending himself. "I searched my inmost soul," he wrote, "and examined my actions from my earliest childhood." However, "I found nothing sinful clinging to my hands, but nevertheless my heart found no rest."[26]

It is unclear exactly what anyone had complained about, but Pinto helpfully listed several iniquities of which he was guilty, including skipping several ritual fasts and having evil thoughts. Citing Torah, Talmud, and prophets, he praised the power of forgiveness and promised to behave better. He also promised to serve without pay through Rosh Hashanah, so the congregation might try him out. The board relented and Pinto stayed on, but it was an inauspicious start.[27]

Pinto lasted six years. By 1765, he had a wife and two children, and even with extra cash from teaching, the salary at Shearith Israel wasn't enough. When a chance inheritance arrived in Europe, Pinto left. "This is the only Instinct That forces him to leave," he insisted, but given the trouble New Yorkers gave their hazan, he might have chosen politesse over frankness. Shearith Israel immediately began looking for a replacement, and Pinto was soon back in Europe.[28]

And that's where Gershom Seixas comes in, possibly as Pinto's protégé. As noted, he had no formal training, was unmarried, and only twenty-two years old.[29] Nevertheless, according to a scrawled note in Portuguese among the records, on July 3, 1768, the adjunta elected Seixas over the caretaker hazan, Isaac Da Silva. The adjunta left little evidence as to why Gershom got the job, although when a candidate from Curaçao applied, the adjunta informed him that he would have to pay his own way to New York before they decided to hire him.[30] Seixas had the advantage of proximity.

Gershom inherited Pinto's old troubles. In 1770, an unknown group of Jews sat in certain synagogue seats and said they would not move "unless it be by force." The other Jews accepted the offer and threw the men out. The synagogue consulted the mayor of New York, Whitehead Hicks, who informed the congregation that constantly taking the wrong seats disrupted worship, and that the city could arrest them for it.[31]

Problems continued. Barack Hays and Manuel Josephson—who had mocked the old man's talis while in the synagogue—publicly claimed they had been defamed in the synagogue. In 1772 Hays was expelled for disruptive behavior. That same year, a Shearith Israel parishioner called his own brother a bastard during a baby-naming ceremony. Barack Hays sued the synagogue, complaining that the Simson and Myers families had too much influence, and even declared that New York Jews "would kill many" if not "for the Christian law." Solomon Simson countersued.[32]

It was a difficult calling for a hazan in his twenties. Seixas, however, seemed to have a quick smile and sense of humor. He positively glowed when his letters made others laugh.[33] Once, an anxious and depressed parishioner wandered New York streets all night long. Seixas found him, brought him to his own home, gave him a place on the couch, and counseled him. Perhaps his large family provided some negotiating experience for dealing with the feuding clans of New York Jewry—he eventually fathered sixteen children.[34]

Seixas also found a new way to deal with the complaining, rivalries, and violence in the synagogue: He involved the state. When Hays sued the synagogue for defamation, Seixas and the adjunta felt no compunction about going to the legal system of New York. In Christian Europe, rabbis had political as well as religious suzerainty over their communities. That was not true in a British colony without rabbis, so Seixas could reverse the arrangement. As the leader of a faith community, he contacted the state when there was trouble or violence. The synagogue in New York operated like any other civic group in the colony.

Seixas may have felt more comfortable reverting to state rather than religious law in 1772 because of his own lack of experience. By all accounts, he was a voracious reader and insatiably curious about history, philosophy, and chemistry, among other things, but in the early 1770s there were gaps in his knowledge. So he "informed himself of those subjects" needed to administer law and Jewish tradition.[35] Pinto had likely trained Seixas in Hebrew but not in Talmud or Mishnah. Like many Enlightenment autodidacts, Seixas made do with whatever came to hand. Both his limited learning and his position as hazan (again, not rabbi) may explain why he allowed Shearith Israel to bring an internal Jewish issue to the attention of the (nominally) Christian state.

The patchwork nature of Seixas's training was always apparent. He sometimes confused rabbinical authorities in his writing. His Mishnah was limited to a single tractate that had been published with the prayerbook used at Shearith Israel, and he probably owned a copy of the Sephardic *Shulkhan Arukh*, a sixteenth-century Jewish law code.[36] He knew the Hebrew Bible well; family legend had it that he read prayers at Shearith

Israel by the time he was five.[37] Seixas occasionally tried his hand at gematria, Jewish numerology.[38] He also read Gentile tracts and arguments and corresponded with Christian theologian George Bethune English. Seixas read Voltaire, Rousseau, and Joseph Priestly. He had deep appreciation for the rationality of the Enlightenment, though he refused to deny the divine nature of the Sacred Scriptures, a term he abbreviated "S.S." (In retrospect, maybe not the best shorthand for a Jew to use.)[39]

At times, he sounded downright Protestant. In 1805 he told listeners that "from the first transgression of Adam all Men became sinners," and thus began the "consequence of original sin."[40] Grace and salvation were frequent themes in his sermons, although he seems to have defined them a little differently than did his Christian neighbors. These Protestant turns of phrase were not just for show, or an effort to make New York Christians more comfortable. In letters to his daughter Sarah, Seixas wrote of the "kind interposition of Grace" and thanked God for mercy "to us poor miserable sinners."[41] He also read the deist writers, which he blended with his Judaism. All people, he wrote, had to obey "the moral and social law" but only Jews have "the religious law" and "from our law many others have been founded."[42]

This idea was a significant development, both for Seixas and for how Jews conceived of their relationship to the state. Jews *and* Gentiles followed the moral and social law. Since it was moral virtue that mattered, Seixas was suggesting (among other things) that religions aside from Christianity possessed morality—one of the classical keys to citizenship in a republic. Israelites had their own religious tenets—from which, he implied, Christianity, Islam, and others had borrowed—but the same moral law as everyone else. In terms of a social contract, a kind of sameness characterized both Jews and Gentiles. This idea did not originate with Seixas. Indeed, Jefferson wrote something similar in 1781: "The legitimate powers of government extend to such acts only as are injurious to others. But it does me no injury for my neighbour to say there are twenty gods, or no god. It neither picks my pocket nor breaks my leg."[43] If so, then the courts of New York were the correct forum for resolving struggles within the synagogue. And, of course, going to the courts supplemented the authority and respectability of a (then) young "rabbi" with patchwork education—something else Seixas probably knew.

In 1770 these notions about religious and social law were just ideas in the minds of Seixas, Jefferson, and others. Like Jefferson, Seixas was reading Enlightenment writers who thought much the same thing, including Matthew Tindal, John Toland, and the radical writer Bolingbroke from whom Jefferson borrowed some of his ideas. In 1814, Seixas wrote that he read these deists "50 years ago," which would have meant he had been deeply versed in them in the 1760s and 1770s, when he began as hazan.[44]

By education and temperament, Seixas had versed himself in the rights of man, and had been willing to take risks to see if the government would live up to those ideals. He was a patriot reader before he was a patriot leader.

These ideas percolated throughout 1770s New York, although not universally accepted. Indeed, New York saw some of the harshest clashes between those who favored independence and those unwilling to break with Britain. Patriots in New York had a special fondness for congregating at taverns. That encouraged broad participation from people of different religious backgrounds. (Jews would have been unlikely to join in if patriots had gathered to organize in churches, for example.) Organizing in taverns also fueled protest with alcohol. So marches became brawls, and brawls became riots. Stamp Act protests in 1765, for example, began at the Merchant Coffee House and Burns's Tavern, where patriots pledged not to import goods until Parliament repealed the act. Fortified with a few drinks, patriots led a mock funeral procession through the streets to "bury Liberty." They smashed lamps and windows along the way, and ended up sacking the house of a British military official, burning his furniture, and drinking over 250 gallons of his wine.[45]

Gershom's brother Benjamin, along with fifteen other militia men, publicly warned New York that the militia groups of various neighborhoods needed to coordinate their training. Given "the present critical situation of the public affairs of the Colonies and the Mother Country," they wrote, it was "a matter of the utmost consequence to the liberties of America that every member of the Community capable of bearing arms should acquaint himself with military discipline."[46] Benjamin joined the patriot protest formed in a civic space—taverns—where he did not need a special exemption as a Jew. He was just another patriot. In 1770, the "Battle of Golden Hill" broke out in lower Manhattan—a scuffle between patriots and British soldiers posting handbills.[47] The battle took place in Eden Alley—one street over from Shearith Israel.

As the imperial crisis intensified, the churches got involved. Indeed, Congress asked them to get involved. In the wake of Lexington and Concord in 1775, the Continental Congress became an ad hoc government

of the not-yet-declared-as-independent United States. The months between Lexington and Concord in April 1775 and July 1776 saw intensified
violence and mobilization without providing any clarification. Congress
put an army in the field, but it also fitfully sought reconciliation with
Parliament. Leaders in Congress mostly commanded local followings
back at home; few patriots commanded national attention, and therefore,
Congress's legitimacy as a national decision-making body had not been
established.

So Congress turned to the churches. In March 1776, in the midst of
conflict and confused diplomacy, Congress called for a day of fasting, humiliation, and prayer, to "supplicate the mercy of Almighty God, that it
would please him to pardon all our manifold sins and transgressions, and
to prosper the Arms of the United Colonies, and finally, establish the peace
and freedom of America, upon a solid and lasting foundation."[48] Congress
was essentially calling upon patriot ministers to speak on its behalf. If the
churches could be convinced to respond to Congress's call, they would le-
gitimize both Congress and the revolution. Clergymen were local leaders
par excellence who could speak for the (inchoate) national government
of May 1776. Subsequent generations have seen in this move a desperate
call for divine aid (which it was) or a cynical ploy to force institutional
churches to take sides (which it also was). Either way, "clergymen became
essential intermediaries between would-be national leaders and average
Americans."[49]

Clergymen. Not pastors. Not ministers. Seixas saw to that. The original
call by Congress asked for "people of all ranks and degrees" to fast in acknowledgment of "god's superintending providence," as a form of repentance to "frustrate the designs of our unnatural enemies; and by inclining
their hearts to justice and benevolence, prevent the further effusion of
blood." If that proved impossible, then people should ask the Almighty "to
crown the Continental arms by sea and land with victory and success." All
this was to be done "through the merits and mediations of Jesus Christ."[50]
It was one of the rare specific mentions of Christ by Congress (and a reference which General Washington expunged from his general orders for the
fast day). Congress was not too concerned about sidelining Jews—if indeed
they were even aware that 0.1 percent of their countrymen were Jewish. The
prayer was not mandated, only "earnestly recommend[ed]," despite what
some twenty-first-century authors have suggested. Shearith Israel simply
could have gone on its way, assuming that the "merits and mediations of

Jesus Christ" were not its business. Perhaps if they had, Jewish participation and Jewish status in the country would have continued as it was, in a kind of twilight between foreigner and citizen.

It did not happen that way because Gershom Seixas took a risk. He held services on May 17, 1776, and the Jews of Shearith Israel joined in what Congress deemed "a day of fasting, humiliation, and prayer." In so doing, Seixas became an extension of Congress—he validated and justified its call, and acted in its name. In turn, he offered up a prayer in line with their request. He asked God to "put it in the heart of our Sovereign Lord, George the third . . . to turn away their fierce Wrath from North America" and to "send the Angels of mercy to proclaim Peace to all America," more or less directly worshipping in the form recommended by Congress. Seixas called on the "God of our Fathers Abraham Isaac and Jacob," but otherwise it was the patriot prayer.[51]

Seixas's full sermon has not survived, but at some later point in the war, he gave a "Prayer for Peace" that echoed the same sentiments, asking that "the Lord of Hosts be the shield of those who are Arm'd for war by Land, and for those who are gone in ships to war on seas."[52] Given Seixas's lifelong interest in moral virtue, he connected political change to civic virtue, as he did in 1805 when considering the 613 commandments of the Torah: In "the revolutionary affairs of Man . . . nothing is durable except goodness & Virtue, accompanied by faith hope & charity."[53] John Witherspoon, the Princeton Presbyterian and only clergyman to sign the Declaration of Independence, preached a similar message on the 1776 fast day: "Nothing is more certain than that a general profligacy and corruption of manners make a people ripe for destruction." By contrast, when virtue and manners prevail, "the attempts of the most powerful enemies to oppress them, are commonly baffled."[54]

It is easy to miss Gershom Seixas and the Jewish fast of 1776. Contemporary historians and pundits certainly have; they assume that preachers wanted a Christian state. Indeed, Witherspoon's 1776 sermon has been cited as evidence that, as one historian puts it, "morality could only arise out of authentic Christian faith."[55] Witherspoon said something rather different. Witherspoon did make a pitch for Christian salvation, noting that even in the midst of war and political fracture, salvation was a separate and more important question than "whether you and your children shall be . . . at liberty or in bonds." Yet having said that, he immediately declared that the issue of Christian salvation was *not* at stake in the battle for political liberty; the revolution was "a commotion, from which religious differences have been so entirely excluded." "I have already endeavored to exhort sinners to repentance." He wished to "point out to you the concern which every good man ought to take in the national character and manners." Indeed, Witherspoon concluded by saying, "True religion is nothing else but an inward temper and outward conduct suited to your state and circumstances," and therefore, "God grant that in America true religion and civil liberty may be inseparable." Moral and civic virtue were something distinct from Christianity: "I do not wish you to oppose any body's religion, but every body's wickedness."[56]

Witherspoon did not know it, but a few miles north of his New Jersey pulpit the Jews of Shearith Israel were praying for the same thing. Indeed, both Witherspoon and Shearith Israel quoted Micah 4:3 on that 1776 fast day: "They shall beat their swords into ploughshares, and their spears into pruning-hooks."[57] Seixas and Shearith Israel were entering a space Congress and preachers like Witherspoon had opened. Much of the rhetoric surrounding the call for a fast used explicit Christian language, yet it was not limited to Christian congregations. All "sects" were asked to preach, and Witherspoon (among others) declared that the issue of salvation was separate from the moral virtue needed to succeed as a republic. And so Seixas and the Jews simply joined the fast—and thus the revolution, aligning their synagogue with Congress and the patriot cause.

The Founders and Gentile patriots likely did not know on May 17 that the New York synagogue had thrown in with the patriot churches—but when they did learn of Jewish support, there was no uproar, no backlash. Jews joined the revolution by assuming they could. They stepped toward citizenship by acting like citizens, gained rights by acting like rights-bearing people. Judaism as an institution and as a religion did not require the special dispensations that it did in Britain, France, or Germany because the idea of civic virtue was broad enough to include them. If morality and "religion," not doctrine, made citizens, Judaism could join without having to ask and get an exception. No exceptions were required for virtue.

The fast did not bring peace. On July 3, General Howe landed British troops on Staten Island and began constructing trenchworks. On July 4, Congress declared independence. On July 9, Washington had the Declaration read to all the troops on Long Island. Isaac Franks was present and remembered how "we *all* with One Voice, Declared that we would support and defend the same with our lives and fortunes."[58] Despite their resolve, Washington's troops were outnumbered and undersupplied. When Washington had his men practice shooting, they could only fire twice to conserve gunpowder. Patriots stripped houses of lead for bullets and built trenches across Brooklyn Heights. The war was coming to New York.[59]

Seixas knew the town would soon come under British military rule. Should the Jews remain? Or should they head elsewhere to live by their principles? It is a dilemma Jews and other religious minorities have faced all too often in history. Seixas and the synagogue had aligned with Congress. There would be repercussions. Jews in particular faced religious complications if they chose to flee. Jewish life and practice require certain ritual objects. A Torah, a *yad*, a mezuzah, a shofar: These are part of Jewish life. One could be a Jew without them, but Judaism as a way of life, as a community, requires them. There is no analogue for a Torah scroll in Protestant Christianity. The Calvinist disdain for ritual objects makes their religious practice more portable than Judaism. Although the sacred scrolls are not an essential part of Judaism, the Torah is nevertheless a living thing—not so much an object used in worship as a participant in worship. When nine Jews gather for prayers at synagogue, the Ark can be opened and the Torah scrolls counted as the tenth member for minyan. When a scroll is damaged, or torn, or simply worn down by time, it is buried rather than discarded. A Presbyterian or Congregationalist could leave occupied New York and pick up their ritual and religious life. Jonas Phillips wondered if, when the patriot Jews left, "the abandonment of the Synagogue property might be the final dissolution of the Congregation."[60]

Gershom Seixas rose to the occasion. The Jews *and* the Torah would flee New York. Seixas was a patriot, and like his beloved Enlightenment authors, he believed that consent was intrinsic to government. He therefore suggested, as his descendant later wrote, "closing the synagogue rather than continue it as a Tory organization." However, Shearith Israel had both patriot and loyalist members; praying for peace in May was not the same as escaping to liberty in August. Seixas apparently took it upon himself to address every member of the synagogue on the importance of leaving. As they prepared to go, just days before Howe landed in Brooklyn, he gave yet another sermon on patriot themes. Seixas's actual words on the eve of invasion have been lost to time, but according to local legend there was not a dry eye in the house. Perhaps he preached then as he did many years later: a lesson on Abraham who "quit the place of his nativity, his kindred and the house of his father . . . and at every place where he arrived and pitched his tent; he built an altar unto the Lord."[61] What mattered was that Seixas and the patriot Jews solved the problem of keeping their religious community intact even as they escaped British control. They took their Torah with them.

Like Moses crossing the Sea of Reeds, Seixas led his community out of Tory bondage to a new land of freedom, bearing the Torah scrolls with them as they passed over the East River and headed into Connecticut. The great chronicler of American Jewish history, Jonathan Sarna, described the experience as "freighted with deep symbolic significance. . . . Over the opposition of the congregation's Tories, Seixas took with him the Torah scrolls and other religious 'sundries.'" In orchestrating the move, Seixas created a patriot Jewish community, carrying its own implements to practice their faith, and therefore "Seixas and his followers felt secure that God accompanied them in their wanderings."[62] N. Taylor Phillips, a Seixas descendant, wrote at the turn of the twentieth century that once Seixas had left, the synagogue was an empty shell: "No serious effort . . . was made to re-open the synagogue with any regularity until about the time of the declaration of peace."[63]

Heartwarming and uplifting as the story of the patriot Torah is, it is also a little schmaltzy. Seixas was no Charlton Heston in *The Ten Commandments*. He did not heft the scrolls and march out of the synagogue like it was Simchas Torah. Given the proximity of enemy troops, he and the rest of the congregation likely stole away unnoticed. Seixas almost certainly shipped the Torah and other goods to Stratford, where they planned to set up a synagogue in exile. Indeed, the only source material for the story of the patriot Torah is a receipt from Seixas to Shearith Israel for expenses incurred "in removing the Scrolls and other Synagogue property to Stratford, Conn," and for mending the box the Torah came in.[64] The comparison of Seixas and the East River to Moses and the Sea of Reeds originated with Phillips, who was eager to burnish the family's patriotic credentials.[65] However, not all Jews left New York. Shearith Israel was not an empty storefront. The synagogue had *two* Torahs.[66] One headed to Connecticut, the other stayed in New York: a patriot Torah and a tory Torah. Some Jews chose to struggle on under British occupation.

The existing divisions in Shearith Israel did not map onto loyalist or patriot response. Discontents like Manuel Josephson fled to Connecticut with Seixas, while troublemakers like Barack Hays and Abraham Abrahams stayed on.[67] Lyon Jonas served as the nominal head of a reduced congregation, but New York's population swelled as loyalists arrived from New England and New Jersey for safety. Shearith Israel soon included loyalists like Rachel Pinto from Connecticut and the Hart family from Newport.[68] Isaac Touro came to New York when the Patriots recaptured Rhode Island, briefly serving as hazan. Most significantly, a German Jew named Alexander Zuntz arrived in Gotham as a commissary with the Hessian forces and became an informal intermediary between the loyalist Jews and the occupying armies. Zuntz chose to stay in America after the war, mending fences with patriots and becoming a pillar of New York Jewry.[69]

Somewhere between Seixas's flight in 1776 and the British evacuation in 1783, someone tried to burn the loyalists' Torah. According to Phillips, two British soldiers broke into Shearith Israel, stole the Torah ornaments, and desecrated the sanctuary. One of them apparently tried to torch the scrolls, but failed. The incident may have been premeditated anti-Semitism, or just the vandalism that usually accompanies occupation. You can still see the Torah scrolls with their burn marks at the New York Historical Society.[70] British officials tasked with law and order in the city responded by flogging the soldiers.

General Howe and his lieutenants made efforts to recognize and defend religious minorities during the occupation. Immediately after hostilities broke out in 1775, British officials agreed to end the Anglican monopoly on a state church. They added the Presbyterian and the Dutch Reformed churches to the list, creating a triangle of state religions. This move likely came too late. Royal officials had put off recognizing dissenting churches for years. Still, the British regime needed all the support it could muster, and protecting religious practice in New York—which had numerous Presbyterian and Calvinist adherents from its Dutch New Amsterdam days—was a way to protect the status quo. If religious tolerance could build loyalty, so be it. Jews were not specifically included, of course, but the punishment of the synagogue's vandals suggest some effort by the officers to accommodate Jews loyal to George III. And occupied New York had plenty of love for the king. In June 1777, the city celebrated George III's birthday "very magnificently and with great solemnity," wrote a Hessian soldier in his diary, adding that "at twelve o'clock noon all the cannon were fired three times on the water by the men-of-war, frigates, and schooners. . . . [T]here must have been over three or four thousand cannon shots."[71]

Escaping New York did not reflect a stark choice between religious freedom and enforced conformity. Jews who stayed seem to have kept their amorphous legal status. The choice was therefore not between exile and *auto-da-fé*, but between the chance for a more assured liberty and a hazy status quo. That in itself made the choice unusual in Jewish history. New York's Jews had already achieved some degree of toleration in the century since their arrival; at points they had even possessed some rights. But it had never been a sure thing. Under Seixas's leadership, they took the first steps toward an Enlightenment relationship with the state.

The Jews of 1776 had a choice few Jews had ever had in Christendom: They left *for* something. The relatively mild treatment of Jews in pre- and post-occupation New York suggests that we should take their patriot language seriously. Seixas believed that government existed through the consent of the governed. Knowing that such a thing could be realized, he chose not to live under a government that refused to realize it. The Jews of Shearith Israel were not bargaining for religious rights in exchange for their support (as their Baptist brethren did elsewhere in the nation). They left without any guarantees of religious liberty, into harsher conditions and an ad hoc synagogue. They had little to lose by staying. Yet Seixas and his followers believed in the revolution, and so they walked away from New York— literally, in the case of Isaac Moses, who refused to ride on Shabbat and therefore set off on foot, heading north from Wall Street.[72]

But why Connecticut? Hartford's "Jew Street" was about the extent of Jewish presence there before the war. Founded as a religious alternative for those Puritans who felt Massachusetts Bay lacked sufficient piety, Connecticut was stalwart in its orthodoxy. Its few Jews were mostly famous for not being Jewish. The Pinto family of New Haven had Christian sons who attended Yale. Michael Judah maintained a Jewish life and identity, though his wife and children adopted Christianity. One "Mordecai Marks, Jew," was baptized at Stratford in 1729.[73] Before the revolution, the Seixas family bookended the state, with Gershom in New York and Moses and Isaac in Newport, almost as if they were deliberately avoiding Connecticut.

In the revolution, however, Seixas family geography favored Stratford as a refuge. The town was accessible by sea and land for both halves of the clan. Gershom and the Shearith Israel patriots arrived first, in August 1776.[74] Isaac came with a handful of Newport's Jewish patriots in December.[75] Isaac's patriotism predated Gershom's; he had joined the radical merchants of 1770 who insisted on a non-importation policy in the face of British recalcitrance. Isaac's feelings may have influenced Gershom, but they did not extend to his son Moses, who remained under British rule in Newport.[76] Still, Connecticut was such an odd choice that as late as 1779, Isaac Seixas's sister Rebecca had no clue where he was: "I could not learn where the troubles of America had carried you," she wrote. She sent the message to Moses in Rhode Island, hoping it would somehow reach her brother.[77]

Stratford had other advantages. The town had a reputation for tolerance of those who opted out of Congregationalism, the official state church of Connecticut. In 1722, Timothy Cutler and Samuel Johnson, a rector and tutor at Yale, converted to Anglicanism. They were both immediately dismissed. Undaunted, Cutler and Johnson opened Connecticut's first non-Congregational church in Stratford in 1724. Five years later, Mordecai Marks was baptized there. When the revolution ended, Stratford became the home of Connecticut's first Methodist Society. Stratford's religious culture seemed to offer haven to religious dissidents, and Seixas might have considered that sufficient reason to establish a refuge there.[78]

Other Connecticut towns hosted patriot Jews. Joseph Simson, the parnas of Shearith Israel, settled in Wilton. He became a correspondent of Connecticut's patriot governor, Jonathan Trumbull, who shared Simson's love of Hebrew.[79] Patriot Jews settled in Norwalk, Danbury, and Stamford.[80] The scattered Shearith Israel refugees apparently gathered in Stratford for Jewish festivals and holidays in what was likely Connecticut's first minyan. Gershom's wife gave birth to their daughter Sally; his brother Benjamin joined them.[81] At one point, Seixas felt comfortable enough in his safety to sneak back into New York to perform a wedding—Abraham Zuntz apparently wanted the regular hazan to do the job.[82] In 1799, Seixas remembered the patriot Jews worshipping in Connecticut "agreeably to the rites & ceremonies of our forefathers."[83]

That may have been a rose-colored memory. In almost the same breath, he described the Jews in Connecticut as "driven from our public place of worship and dispersed in various parts of the Country."[84] Coastal Connecticut was soon a seat of war. Samson Mears went from Shearith Israel to the town of Norwalk, in part because of its obscurity. The British, Mears wrote to Aaron Lopez, "will have greater objects to attend to than this insignificant place. . . . I don't apprehend much danger here from the enemy."[85] Isaac Seixas knew better: "This State will be very soon invested by a very Strong force." British transport ships had been spotted outside New

London, Isaac wrote, so may "the Lord for his mercy's Sake keep us all from so much danger & grant us his holy protection."[86]

The war came to the coast in 1779. Isaac wrote in March of that year that God had answered his prayer and "blocked up" New Haven's harbor with ice to prevent a British attack.[87] In summer, God's ice melted, and British warships escalated their raids on Connecticut. On July 5, naval forces invaded New Haven. British forces plundered the town and burned American ships at harbor. Two days later, the British hit the town of Fairfield. When the local American commander—Samuel Whiting, in Stratford—refused to submit, the British burned 190 buildings. Whiting had too many miles of coastline to defend with too few troops. He despaired that he could not "prevent their Ravaging, plundering, & burning all the Towns upon the coast."[88]

Several Americans in Norwalk—including its Jewish citizens—petitioned for naval support as early as 1777.[89] That support did not materialize, and on July 11, Norwalk paid the price. Mears wrote to Lopez of "the approach of the savage enemy." Norwalk became a scene of cannon bombardment, musket shots, and "vast columns of smoak ascending from the conflagrated buildings." British forces burned 292 buildings in Norwalk, including 100 homes. Mears and his family abandoned their house and goods and headed upcountry. On learning of the attack on Norwalk, General Washington wrote that "the depredations and ravages of the Enemy upon your coast, give me great concern." Yet he had to acknowledge that "the means of protection in my power, are not equal to my wishes." He sent a detachment of troops, but both the commander-in-chief and the general citizenry knew that American forces could do little to stop "the horrors and the distress" of the Connecticut coast.[90]

The attack coincided with Tish B'Av, the Jewish commemoration of the destruction of the Temple. That year, Mears understood its meaning: "We truly celebrated the Anniversary season with all its gloom that our predecessors experienced." Mears and twenty others huddled in a single room while the British bombarded the town, "incessant firing of cannon and musquetry." Mears wrote that the "women and the children . . . precipitately set off" in the sheeting rain from fear that their redoubt would not hold. They were right, and Mears and the men followed soon after.[91] Judith Myers in later years recalled how they were "obliged (by the approach of the British army) to fly with such things only as were of the first necessity." Mears and her family expected to return for the rest of their belongings later, only to find that the British "burned the town and with it whatever the inhabitants had left behind them."[92]

The seeming weakness of the American forces on the Connecticut coast bred a political reaction that sent the Jews out of Stratford. Their town lay between New Haven and Fairfield. On July 9, 1779, in the midst of the attacks, several of the town's citizens asked William Samuel Johnson—future framer of the Constitution—to negotiate some kind of settlement with the British. Johnson requested that townsfolk sign an agreement with him that "his person and property might be secure from insult or injury" if he tried such a thing. Johnson never put the plan into operation, and the British sailed off soon afterward.[93] But word got out to the patriots that Stratford had attempted to negotiate a separate peace with the British. Johnson was arrested. Stratford was placed under martial law, and a series of loyalty trials commenced.[94]

Just about everyone in Stratford faced questioning about their fealty. Coastal Connecticut had acquired a reputation for loyalist sympathies. Revolutionary soldier Joseph Plumb Martin spent part of the war in Norwalk, where he found the inhabitants "almost exclusively what were in those days termed tories. An old lady, of whom I often procured milk, used always . . . to give me a lecture in my opposition to our good king George." When he told his fellow patriots, they decided "not use any of the milk I had of her, for fear, as they said, of poison."[95] Norwalk rioted in 1778 when Connecticut's own militia requisitioned grain.[96] In 1776 the loyalist Christopher French sought "Protection from the Fury of Populace" in consequence of "the Behavior of the Mobb."[97] The groundwork for trouble was already present before the British attacks destabilized the region.

Consequences for loyalism could be severe. Connecticut converted the Simsbury Mines to hold ordinary criminals as well as suspected loyalists. Ceilings in the former copper mine were barely five feet high. They had no natural light; moss and mold grew on the decaying woodwork, and the copper impregnations gave a green cast to what light there was. Over a hundred prisoners used a communal tub for a latrine. Edward Huntington, a prisoner there, called it a "dark abyss." Tory clergyman Samuel Peters called it the "catacomb of Loyalty." Locals called it simply "Hell."[98]

The Jews must have been on their guard. None of the known Jewish residents of Stratford joined in the 1779 trials, though the Jewish refugees had previously lent their names to such efforts. Jews joined Gentiles in calling for increased naval patrols, and Myer Myers partnered with the Gentile Peter Betts to report on a suspected loyalist in 1776, a man they discovered "disputing about the times" in a public house and claiming that Continental soldiers would "always give backs" (i.e., run) from the British.[99] But in 1779, the Jews did not join in.

The trials began on July 17, seeking to establish what had been done "of a treasonable nature." Patriot officials spent much time investigating the actual scrip of paper promising Johnson protection in exchange for negotiating with the British. But while many locals acknowledged having seen it, few admitted to signing it. Even a man who had circulated the sub-scription for signatures denied signing it. The officials pressed on. Had there been any conversations "about relinquishing independency?" No, it had never been considered "*by any means*," replied the defendant. When the accused at Stratford were asked whether they were aware that the pa-triot forces might order the population to flee the town rather than sur-render, one citizen answered tersely, "I am not going to be driven out of Town. I believe I can raise as much force as you." Connecticut in 1779 faced a "want of spirit to support government," wrote merchant Simeon Newell about his native state. "My country seems like a person bleeding at both jugulars." Isaac Seixas echoed his Gentile neighbor: "God send us better times."[100]

Stratford was undergoing loyalty trials in a state with deep divisions. Emotions ran high. In Darien, the brother of a Tory soldier was strapped to a log headed to the sawmill in the hopes of making him talk.[101] The trials, perhaps more than the naval raids, must have triggered cultural and personal memories. Isaac Seixas had *converso* origins in Portugal and remembered the Inquisition. Questioning loyalty and discussing removal raised worrisome questions for these men and their families. Mordecai Michael Hays wrote to Aaron Lopez about the "Art & dissimulation" of New England, and recommended "a very Watchful eye."[102] In 1780, Connecticut reopened the Simsbury mines for prisoners. That same year, the Shearith Israel patriots headed south to Philadelphia.[103]

The revolution was in trouble. Savannah and Charleston had fallen to the enemy. Jews could stay in Connecticut and weather an atmosphere of suspicion and questioning, or they could try and build an American insti-tution. It would be something new—a national religious organization of citizens, uncreated by the state. Nothing like it had been attempted by Jews in centuries. Philadelphia was calling.

4

Jews at War

SOLOMON BUSH JOINED THE FIGHT in the winter of 1776, when the odds of beating Britain looked bleak, and "distinguished himself . . . when the Service was Critical and Hazardous." So decreed Pennsylvania's Supreme Executive council in 1777, when they promoted Bush to the post of deputy adjutant general in the Pennsylvania militia. By September, he was fighting at the Battle of Brandywine with Washington.[1] The British eventually captured him. They would come to wish they had not.

The British hammered the rebels at Brandywine. Howe smashed the American flanks; a bullet did the same to Bush's leg. The doctors sent him to Philadelphia to die or recover. Bush survived, but in the meantime the British captured Philadelphia. Bush hid at his father's house in Chestnut Hill, nursing his shattered thigh. He planned to make his way back to the American forces as soon as his legs could carry him. "My wishes," he wrote to his friend Henry Lazarus, "are to be able to get Satisfaction and revenge the Rongs of my injured Country." After twenty-two days of hiding, someone ratted Bush out. He "fell into the hands of the British army," as he wrote. The British allowed him to remain at his father's and required him to report regularly to a British officer to confirm that he was no longer a combatant.[2]

Bush still found ways to serve the cause of independence. In December 1777, Bush spotted "a plain Dress'd Man with a flap'd Hat" who passed a letter to a redcoat. Bush then saw the soldier vanish into an occupied house held by British officers. Bush kept watch and soon a Hessian officer emerged, praised the spy as a "damn'd clever little fellow, his intelligence from time to time had been of great use to us." The officer then blurted out that the letter had come from Washington's headquarters.

Bush used back channels to get the information to General John Armstrong of the Pennsylvania militia. The general passed "the examination of young Bush" on to George Washington, emphasizing that the intelligence be kept secret so that Bush was not exposed. Bush kept watch in Philadelphia. Though "incapable of performing any military duty" because of his injury, Bush continued his fight for his "injured Country."[3] In 1779 he was made a lieutenant colonel in Washington's army, the highest federal military rank achieved by an American Jew in the war.

Bush's patriotism was never in doubt. As he listened to the cannonading against Fort Mitchell from his father's house, he wrote Lazarus that he "hope[d] to tell you New York is ours before long." Nor was his Judaism in doubt. In 1782, he contributed funds for the new synagogue at Mikveh Israel.[4]

Bush was one of at least fifteen Jews to attain officer's rank in the revolution. When compared to the total number of revolutionary officers— 14,000—the number seems small. Jews, however, represented only one-tenth of 1 percent of the overall American population. They therefore served as officers in the same proportion as their percentage of the population. The new patriot armies recruited and promoted Jews without regard to religious profession. Given the chance to fight, Jews signed up, and the patriots accepted them. At war's end, Haym Salomon responded to anti-Semitism at the statehouse by writing that Jews "have in general been early uniform, decisive whigs, and we were second to none in our patriotism and attachment to our country!" Jews could therefore "assert [their] own share in the public consequence."[5] They claimed citizenship.

Jews made this claim based on military service. While patriot zeal mattered, the patriot Jews believed their contribution on the battlefield made the difference. As the Mikveh Israel patriots wrote, Jews "can count with any religious society whatsoever, the whigs among either of them; they have served some of them in the continental army; some went out in the militia to fight the common enemy."[6] How Jews became citizens therefore in some ways depended on wartime service.

Investigating Jewish service in the revolution requires smashing some stereotypes. Nobel Prize–winning physicist Arno Penzias once complained that American Jewish schoolchildren got Haym Salomon as the "consolation prize" of revolutionary war heroes. Of course the *banker* was Jewish, Penzias explained, because "it was taken for granted by everybody (including us, I'm afraid) that Jews just didn't make good soldiers."[7] Eighteenth-century European armies kept Jews away from fighting forces, especially the officer class. This exclusion both created and reinforced classic anti-Semitic ideas about Jewish men, including notions that Jews had no loyalty to anyone but themselves, would never risk their lives for Gentiles, and were cowardly and physically weak.[8] These kinds of issues never seemed to bother Washington and his commanders. Even more surprising, lack of military experience did not stop American Jews without family traditions of military service from joining the campaign.

Estimating Jewish participation in the revolution is tricky. Earlier historians sometimes scanned enlistment rosters for "Jewish" names, a highly dubious method in any age, but markedly so in an era when Old Testament names were standard for Gentiles as well as Jews. In 1975, historian Samuel Rezneck shifted his focus to officers—men like Bush, Francis Salvador, and Isaac and David Franks, who by nature of their position left a more significant paper trail.[9]

Practicing Jews in the American forces left their own marks—sometimes literally. Abraham Solomon signed the muster roll at Bunker Hill in Hebrew. Solomon's origins are unknown, but his unit nicknamed him "Solomon the Jew."[10] Elias Pollock signed on to a militia unit as "Joseph Smith," perhaps trying to hide his Jewish origins.[11] Philip Moses Russell served with Bush at Brandywine and then became a surgeon's mate for the long winter at Valley Forge. There he survived "an attack of the prevailing campfever, the result of his incessant attention to the wounded and sick, which impaired his vision as well as his hearing."[12] Moses Myers became a major in the Virginia militia and finished the war at Yorktown.[13]

Common soldiers of all faiths in the revolution left little in the historical record, given the short enlistments and irregular record-keeping of certain units. But some names still emerge from the patchwork. Manuel Noah's revolutionary credentials are only known because his son became a playwright.[14] The service of "Old Mordecai," an Alabama Jew, comes from an 1847 interview with him as a nonagenarian.[15] Moses Levy left a record of his service in the form of letters from his father, in which the two shared gossip about the conflict and hoped Spain would join the fight.[16]

Sometimes a soldier's Judaism found its way into the record. Reuben Etting was captured by the British after the fall of Charleston. When the British learned Etting was Jewish, they chose to offer him pork as provisions. Etting refused to violate kosher law and eventually perished. The same story is told about Mordecai Sheftall's experience on a prison ship as well. (He survived.)[17] In 1776, Hart Jacobs informed the New York Committee of Safety "that it is inconsistent with his religious profession to perform military duty on Friday nights, being part of the Jewish Sabbath." The committee exempted Jacobs from duty on Shabbat, and Jacobs stood guard the rest of the days of the week.[18]

The most Jewish militia company—the "Jew Company" of Charleston, South Carolina—saw action at the Battle of Beaufort, but several members stayed with patriot forces across the country. Though the unit was originally raised in Charleston's King Street (and was, Jacob I. Cohen recalled, "composed mostly of Israelites"), Jewish soldiers like Marks Lazarus and David Cardozo went on to fight at Ft. Moultrie, Savannah, and Charleston.[19] Cardozo survived the fighting, and 150 years later, his descendant Benjamin was named to the Supreme Court. Justice Cardozo may not have known that his ancestor fought in a mostly Jewish unit that called themselves "the *Free Citizens*," suggesting the full meaning the Jews of the regiment attached to the revolution. This was not a fight for Judaism but for citizenship—legal recognition for membership in the body politic, as was denied them in Europe. Nor were the Free Citizens the only Jews to see multiple engagements. So did Moses Cohen—who was at Ft. Moultrie in 1776 and Yorktown in 1781 and therefore served one of the longest enlistments of any soldier in the revolution.[20]

For the most part, military service in Europe had been closed to Jews since the end of the Roman empire. A Christianized Rome banned Jewish service as offensive to God, and subsequent kingdoms and potentates had largely followed suit. These strictures were violated on occasion—as when Polish Jews joined the fight against Tartar forces in 1589, or when the Jews of Mainz organized a unit to fight a Crusades-inspired pogrom in 1096. In general, however, seventeenth- and eighteenth-century armies did not want Jews. All the major powers discouraged or outright banned their service. Revolutionary France finally accepted Jewish soldiers in the 1789 French Revolution but did not include Jews in conscription lists for another twenty years. Russia began Jewish conscription in 1827 by setting the draft age for Jews at twelve. (For all others, it was eighteen.) Over half of the Jews in nineteenth-century Russian armies were children. In Britain,

Jews could join the military but, until 1829, were forbidden from being officers.[21]

New World Jews therefore had neither the family traditions nor professional training to encourage them to service. But then, plenty of colonials were new to professional soldiering. Reports from the first months of war revealed a host of gung-ho volunteers who looked nothing like an army. As one diarist noted, "Plain Countrymen have now clothed themselves in martial forms."[22]

Those green volunteers—Gentile and Jewish—bungled the first encounters of the war. Patriots claimed that freemen volunteers would fight better than a European army. This was not true. By 1777, Washington was upbraiding Virginia's Patrick Henry for sending him volunteers and not enlisted men: "The *Volunteer kind* are uneasy, impatient of Command, ungovernable" and preferred "to do as they please" rather than take orders. Washington needed enlisted men signed to long periods of service. Getting men into the Continental Army was the priority, and so intentionally or not (most likely not), the American government took men where they could find them. Washington and the army even ignored their own ban on African American troops to recruit soldiers. Washington had found several Black soldiers ready to fight for independence when he took over the Continental Army in 1775. He imposed a ban on Black soldiers, but that policy in the words of one historian, "nearly resulted in the demise of the American cause." By war's end, over 5,000 Black soldiers served in Washington's army.[23]

The revolutionary army was not a place of full equality. Black and (hidden) female soldiers did not get the same opportunities that white men did. But the need for soldiers and officers outweighed other concerns. And at least in the field of religious belief, the army did not make distinctions. Washington did not hesitate to promote capable men. Perhaps he felt about them the way he felt about workers in general—they could "be Mahometans, Jews, or Christians of any Sect—or they may be Atheists," as long as they had "good characters."[24]

Isaac Franks was just the sort of man Washington needed. Born in 1759, Franks signed up before independence was declared, and cheered the reading of the Declaration of Independence as a soldier in Washington's forces.[25] Franks's sentiment would be tested. His unit found itself at the Battle of Long Island, "in the head of the Battle, and in the retreat to New York," as he wrote in an 1818 memoir about his service. Washington stationed Franks's unit on the East River at the Fly Market (later home of the Fulton Fish Market). Franks was there when Cornwallis invaded. The American army escaped, but Franks's unit was captured. Franks "continewed [*sic*] steadily and actively in the army of the United States." After three month's confinement, he escaped, crossing the Hudson River "in a small leaky skiff with one single paddle to the Jersey shore."[26]

From New Jersey, Franks worked his way back to the Continental Army at Peekskill, New York, where he joined the Quartermaster Department. Within a year, he became the Forage Master at West Point.[27] In 1780 Franks was named lieutenant colonel for the 7th Massachusetts regiment, which remained posted near New York waiting for Washington to order the retaking of the city. Washington never gave that order, but Franks apparently came to know Washington well enough to offer the president his family home in 1793, when the yellow fever broke out in Philadelphia. Washington acccpted, and the president lived in a Jew's home for a few months. By that time, Franks had become a Quaker, so there was no mezuzah on the lintel. Washington clearly did not care about the religious proclivities of the citizens, and neither did Franks. In 1818 he described himself as "a Native Born Citizen," and "never absent from the United States."[28]

Francis Salvador's revolution in South Carolina was shorter but more celebrated. In 1773, Salvador left England to settle in the Carolina backcountry. Even though South Carolina barred non-Christians from holding office, Salvador was twice elected to the South Carolina Provincial Congress. Back in England, Salvador's uncle had urged passage of the Jewish Naturalization Bill in 1753, so Francis surely knew where Jews stood in the Old Country.[29] Salvador allied with William Tennant, a prominent Christian evangelist in the provincial Congress. Tennant and Salvador apparently had no trouble accepting one another as patriots; they both sat on a committee judging the case of one John Dunn, accused of speaking ill of the American cause. (Among Dunn's crimes was apparently naming his dog "Tory," but Salvador and Tennant recommended that the patriots overlook that.)[30] Salvador also worked with Whigs and loyalists seeking to calm tensions in 1775.[31]

But once "the whole country was flying," as he wrote in a letter, Salvador lost patience with the tories and partisans he called "Scopholites" ("Scoff-a-lites").[32] Salvador's impetuousness led him into a skirmish that secured his reputation as a martyr but did little to advance the cause. On hearing two loyalists claiming the British had allied with a nearby Cherokee settlement, Salvador headed off with forty men and directly into an ambush. Salvador was shot three times. He lived for forty-five minutes, shook hands, and, according to Andrew Williamson, the militia commander, asked, "whether I had beat the enemy?" Williamson told him yes. "He said he was glad of it . . . and said, he would die in a few minutes." In retaliation, Williamson burnt the Native American town of Seneca "entirely to ashes."[33]

This pattern of assault, ambush, and retribution became a feature of military engagements between white and Native American forces in revolutionary campaigns. It culminated in Washington's scorched-earth campaign against the Iroquois nations in 1779 that ended in the torching of Indian towns and thousands of casualties. In this outburst of violence and confusion, Salvador became a casualty of war. Arthur Middleton—a signer of the Declaration of Independence—wrote, "I bewail for my heart the fate of that poor fellow Salvador; what I feel for him gives me some idea of what I must experience should my dear connection or intimate friend receive an untimely stroke."[34]

Mordecai Sheftall also earned some share of fame. His parents had arrived along with the klatch of Sephardim in 1733; Mordecai was born two years later. After most of the Jews of Georgia left, it took forty years for the community to get a minyan of ten men. When they did, the congregation worshipped at Sheftall's house in Savannah.[35]

A year after the Jews began meeting at his house to pray, Sheftall became the chairman of the patriots' "Parochial Committee." Such committees were spontaneous patriot organizations that began acting like governments in defiance of the British. As the Georgia patriot William Few wrote in his memoirs, legitimate power had been misused by imperial officials, and therefore power "had dissolved in Committees of public safety, appointed by the people."[36] In other words, the patriots had enough popular support to defy the existing law and did so.

The Parochial Committee ran the Georgia committees, and Sheftall ran the Parochial Committee. The committee enforced patriot embargoes; at times, the committee became a de facto local government, doing "whatever it thought needed doing for Savannah," including appointing a local Anglican priest when the assigned pastor (a loyalist) fled town.[37] Royal governor James Wright noted the rise of "one Sheftall, a Jew" as a particularly ominous development in the colony. Nor was Mordecai alone. David Nunes Carvalho seized a British ship in 1776, and David Sarzedas became a lieutenant in the war. Indeed, Georgia's Jews overwhelmingly favored the Revolution.[38] When the British occupied Savannah in 1778, numerous Jews were specifically banned from political action, including Mordecai Sheftall, Mordecai's son Sheftall (yes, Sheftall Sheftall), Mordecai's brother Levi, Philip Minis, Cushman Pollack, and Philip Jacob Cohen—almost the entire male Jewish community.[39]

Governor Wright described the patriots of Georgia as "of the Inferior Class," including "a Parcel of the Lowest People, chiefly Carpenters, Shoemakers, Blacksmiths, etc. with a Jew at their head." Wright meant the accusation as an insult, but he actually pointed to one of the effects of the break with Britain. Prior to the revolution, both Jews and "the lower sort" had little to no access to political power. When the colonial political class was overthrown, and the "inferior Class" took over, Jews came with them. As the patriots took control, those who had been on the outside were now holding the reins of power. Royal government required a pledge of belief in Christianity. The informal Parochial Committee had no such pledge. Sheftall became head of the de facto Savannah government out of his patriot credentials, not his declaration of faith. It made Wright heartsick: "It is really terrible my Lord that such people should be suffered to overturn the Civil Government."[40]

By 1777, Mordecai Sheftall had joined Georgia's military staff in the Commissary Department. His job was to ensure that the American troops got the supplies they needed. This was a famously unpleasant task, given the cash-strapped government and not-yet-professionalized soldiers of revolutionary America. Sheftall attempted to get specifics on what was needed from Henry Laurens, the rice planter from South Carolina who had replaced John Hancock as president of Congress; none was forthcoming. He therefore spent his own money to supply and outfit the Georgia troops. He was never repaid.[41]

When the British attacked Savannah in December 1778 Mordecai remained at his post for as long as possible. Only when British forces were actually in the city did the family try to retreat across the Musgrove River. But the creek was at high water, and Mordecai's son did not know how to swim. Penned in, the Sheftalls and over 100 troops were captured by Scottish and loyalist regiments. The prisoners were then marched into a yard formerly owned by Moses Nunes, another Savannah Jew.[42]

The British held Mordecai Sheftall as "a very great rebel." Sheftall's recalcitrance did not help. He contradicted the British regarding the victualling of prisoners and tricked a colonel into confusion over the state of the battle plans for Charleston. He was almost " 'skivered' by one of the New York [loyalist] volunteers" as a result. Instead, the British imprisoned Sheftall "amongst the drunken soldiers and negroes" where he "suffered a great deal of abuse." If Sheftall, who was himself a slaveholder, learned anything about the justice of human bondage by being on the receiving end of punishment, he never said so.[43]

The British eventually locked both father and son Sheftall aboard a prison ship in Charleston Harbor. These ships—sometimes called "prison hulks"—had already earned a grim reputation in New York harbor, where the British built slapdash prisons from cattle ships, transports, and fire ships. Hulks like the infamous *Jersey* became known for sparse rations, brutal oversight, lack of clothing, and appalling hygiene. It surely represented a severe change for Mordecai Sheftall, whose children "never knew what want was" prior to the war.[44] A doctor visiting one prison ship in Charleston declared that only death could improve conditions there. Another ship had such appalling smells that when a handful of captives went ashore to bury dead comrades, they brought back graveyard dirt simply so the other prisoners could have something else to smell.[45] Ebenezer Fox, imprisoned on the *Jersey*, called the ships a "floating Pandemonium."[46]

Mordecai began his imprisonment on the *Raven*, where he received no rations his first two days. The British then transferred father and son to the hulk *Nancy*, where Mordecai used his status as an officer to finagle better conditions. In April, the British deposited father but not son at Sunbury, Georgia. As an officer, Mordecai had the right to know about the men under his charge, and when he got no information about his son, he claimed those rights, and informed Samuel Elbert, his superior officer, that he "would hardly refuse him the indulgence granted to every other Continental officer." Sheftall used his post to the fullest. "Whatever may be said of me," wrote Mordecai, he saw to it that his son "was taken in the line of duty as every other officer was." Sheftall did not expect the rules to be any different for Jewish officers than for anyone else. Sheftall was released from the *Nancy* in the early summer of 1779, and both Sheftalls remained in Sunbury on parole (a kind of "good behavior" system used by both sides in the war, where prisoners lived outside jail and swore not to leave a certain area).[47]

Sunbury soon fell into chaos. The failure of French and American forces to retake Savannah scattered military units across Georgia, and Sunbury was turned inside-out. Tory irregulars, Mordecai wrote, "fled at the approach of the American army" but when American forces faltered, the loyalists came back, "threatening vengeance on all those who should fall into their hands." One particular "Tory armed party" was "hovering around the country" and "threatened to kill American officers." The Sheftalls and other American officers got word to General Benjamin Lincoln of Massachusetts, who told them to flee but also "to consider themselves still on parole." The Sheftalls and company pursued a very loose interpretation of that rule. They somehow found their way onto the *Betsey*, a British brig captured by an American privateer, and set sail for Charleston. En route they were captured by the HMS *Guadalupe* and taken to Antigua, where the governor placed them back on parole.[48] By 1780, the Sheftalls were finally exchanged and sent to Philadelphia, where Mordecai helped build Mikveh Israel, and Sheftall continued serving the army by delivering supplies to American prisoners of war.

Meanwhile, the British were clearing the rebels from Savannah. That meant a ban on Jews. Governor Wright was clear on this point: "I judged it also necessary to prevent the Jews who formerly reside[d] here from returning, or others from coming to settle here." Jews were the problem, as he wrote to his superiors in London: "These people, my Lord, were found to a man to be violent rebels and persecutors of the King's loyal subjects." It was not cruelty, Wright assured British officials, for "however this law may appear at first sight . . . the times require these exertions." In Wright's words are the echoes of anti-Semites across time: it isn't our fault the Jews are trouble. Times require these exertions.[49]

Wright's campaign against the Jews foreshadowed that of Sir George Rodney in the Caribbean. Rodney outdid Wright; he expelled the Jews from the island of St. Eustatius. St. Eustatius (also called "Statia") was a scrap of rock under Dutch control. Too small and arid for widespread sugar cultivation, the island was nevertheless heavily enslaved. Its only town was half reclaimed from the sea with dykes, and half "dug out of an immense mountain of sand and rock." Of all the Caribbean islands, wrote the traveler Janet Schaw in 1776, it was "the only ugly one I have seen." Still, the place had a harbor, so the Dutch made all seven square miles of the island a commercial center. "Never did I meet with such variety," wrote Schaw; "here was a mercht. vending his goods in Dutch, another in French, a third in Spanish, etc. etc. . . . [O]ne end of the town of Eustatia to the other is a continued mart."[50] The island hosted a community of Jews, as well as

Swedes, Danes, Russians, Irish—and an unknown number of African peoples, nations, and traditions.[51]

This unlikely locale became the first place where the United States was recognized by a foreign power. On November 16, 1776, the American brig *Andrew Doria* arrived at the port to purchase weapons and present a copy of the Declaration of Independence to Statia's Dutch governor. Officials at the harbor likely did not recognize the flag the *Andrew Doria* flew—the American stars and stripes—but they fired the customary nine-gun salute for foreign vessels. Governor Johannes de Graff seemed pleased to see the Americans and their Declaration. He later gave a party for the ship's commander.[52]

The island also provided black-market supplies for the American rebels. Washington's army ran out of powder reserves within the first nine months, so enterprising American sailors and merchants slipped past British blockades to Statia. They divided up the powder shipments among smaller pilot boats to evade British warships.[53] Statia could charge nearly seven times the going rate for gunpowder in Europe, and its proximity still made the deal worthwhile for the Americans. "Tories sneak and shrink in front of Americans here," noted a Maryland merchant in Statia in 1776.[54]

Support for the American cause was strong among the Jews of St. Eustatius as well. In 1777, the British seized an illegal cargo off the coast of Maryland. Paperwork aboard indicated that the suppliers were all Jews from Statia. By 1781, Statia's local congregation included Samson Mears— one of the Shearith Israel patriots who had taken flight to Norwalk.[55] Mears had lived in Statia as recently as 1775.[56] When patriot Jews of Philadelphia wrote for legal recognition of their rights, they specifically mentioned the Jews of British North America as well as "their brethren at St. Eustatius"— the only Jewish community outside the thirteen states they chose to include in the patriot fold.

Statia's good times ended when Britain found proof of American plans to ally with the Netherlands. Henry Laurens, now the American ambassador to the Netherlands, headed across the Atlantic in 1780 with a draft copy of a treaty of amity and commerce between the Dutch and "the persons calling themselves the United States of America." A British schooner spotted Laurens's packet ship and gave chase. Laurens tried to get rid of the evidence by throwing the treaty overboard. But he failed to weigh down the bag properly, so it floated in the water and the British fished it out. The British now had the draft treaty and a *causus belli* to expand the war to include the Dutch—and those troublesome islands supplying the Americans.[57]

The man tasked with shutting down Statia was Rodney, an admiral with a sterling career and notable naval victories in previous imperial conflicts. With France now in the war, the British Caribbean was reeling; the Bourbon kingdom had seized the islands of Dominica, St. Vincent, and Grenada. When Britain declared war against the Netherlands, Rodney moved to even the score. His fleet seized Statia in February 1781 before the islanders even knew war had been declared. St. Eustatius had sixty soldiers; Rodney arrived with 3,000 across fifteen warships. Rodney took the island without a fight. He needed to sabotage the black-market trade in supplies to the Americans, so Rodney dubbed the capture of the island and all its people an action against "piracy." As outlaws, "pirates" were not covered by the rules of war. Rodney took full advantage of this; he continued to fly the Dutch flag over the island to lure American and French ships into the harbor. The British ransacked the island, ordered the confiscation of all private property, and even dug up graves in search of treasure. The islanders, Rodney explained, were all "Traitors to their King, and Parricides to their Country . . . mixed with Jews, and Dutch."[58]

The Jews in particular became Rodney's obsession. On taking control of the island, Rodney ordered the Jews of Statia rounded up and expelled. He later explained that they "cannot be too soon taken care of—they are notorious in the cause of America and France." Statia's Jewish men were informed they had one day to prepare for exile, and could not take any goods or family members with them. Troops collected men in a weighing house; they stripped them of their clothing, and then cut up their clothes, so "that every shilling of money which they might attempt to conceal and carry off should be discovered and taken from them," as the British statesman Edmund Burke declared on the floor of Parliament. They held the Jews for three days, "unheard of, and unknown." Thirty of the men were deported to St. Kitts; the rest were released from the warehouse to find their personal goods being auctioned by the British forces. The British statesman Edmund Burke condemned Rodney's sack of Statia on the floor of Parliament, especially Rodney's "aggravated cruelty inflicted on the Jews while they remained in the weigh-house."[59]

The Jews of Statia petitioned all the British commanders. "For what reason or from what motive we are to be BANISHED from the island, we are at a loss to account. If any of us have committed a crime for which they are punishable, we humbly beg those crimes may be pointed out." All that "can be alledged [*sic*] against us," they wrote, was "the religion of our forefathers." Some of the island's Jews were British subjects, and they begged the particular right of "those who live under the British constitution, to be indulged with their own sentiments in matters of religion."[60] Instead, they had been forced "to give up the keys of our stores, with an inventory thereof, and of our household plate and furniture, and to hold ourselves in readiness to depart this island, ignorant of our destination, leaving our beloved wives and helpless families behind us."[61]

Their petition did no good. Rodney was already treating the islanders as pirates, and if he had little patience for pirates, he had even less for Jewish pirates. Even a loyalist Jew, Burke noted, who had arrived in Statia after Newport fell to the patriots, was "ruined, by the commanders of a British force, to whose cause he was so attached." Jewish homes were looted and valuables seized; Jewish graves were opened and ransacked.[62]

Rodney's actions in Statia (including but not limited to the expulsion of the Jews) roused the ire of Parliament, and Rodney decided to return to London to exonerate himself in the fall of 1781. As a consequence, he was not available to intercept the French fleet under the command of Francois-Joseph de Grasse in September. A less-seasoned captain led the British response, and was routed. De Grasse then sailed on to blockade Cornwallis's army at Yorktown, which allowed George Washington to trap the British army against the sea. The future British prime minister Lord Shelburne complained at the time that "he solemnly believed that the capture of Lord Cornwallis was owing to the capture of St. Eustatius." One facet of the American victory at Yorktown could be traced to an anti-Semitic outburst by Britain.[63] Rodney's actions against the Jews and the general public of Statia were conveniently forgotten when the admiral defeated the French navy in April 1782 at the Battle of the Saintes—where he did defeat de Grasse. Rodney became a hero in London at the same moment Washington became an icon in America. Their differences on the Jewish question were not determinative, but they are instructive. In the American War of Independence, religious inclusion worked out better for the Americans than anti-Semitism did for the British.[64]

This was not the only public attack on religious minorities in wartime Britain. As English Catholics attempted to prove their loyalty in the face of American rebellion, Parliament passed a Catholic Relief Act, which made minor efforts at ending Catholic disabilities in Great Britain. (The act allowed them to inherit land, though it did not provide freedom of worship.) The act led to a Protestant uprising in the Gordon Riots of 1780. Hundreds were killed, Catholic chapels destroyed, and Newgate and other prisons opened and prisoners released. Meanwhile, Jews and Catholics were serving as officers and soldiers in Washington's army.[65]

Back in Georgia, two such Jews—Levi Sheftall and Philip Minis— agreed to act as guides for the 1779 Franco-American effort to retake Savannah. Minis said he could "guide any party, even through the woods" within fifteen miles of the town. France's Comte D'Estaing took their suggestions and their intelligence. He even set up a unit of reserves "at the Jew's burying ground," the tiny Jewish cemetery donated to the community by Mordecai Sheftall, and set out to besiege Savannah.[66]

The battle was a disaster. The British ambushed the French forces before the trenchworks were finished.[67] Despite superior numbers the Franco-American forces failed. D'Estaing blamed the overconfidence of "the Americans, who are doubtful of nothing even when they have not the most elementary resources."[68] The blame filtered down to Sheftall and Minis. For Levi Sheftall, it began a lifetime of rumors of loyalism. In 1780, the British listed Levi in the disqualifying act as someone who had set up "a pretended independent State" in Georgia. In 1782, the restored patriot government listed his name in the confiscation act leveled against those "traiterously [sic] Adhering to the King of Great Britain."[69] Levi Sheftall did return to occupied Savannah, where the British again brought him up on charges of rebel activity, this time for passing food and information to suspected American soldiers, and promising them "what intelligence he could."[70] Levi went back to Savannah, but he still aided the patriots. Nevertheless, in the immediate postwar some patriots wanted him punished: "I hope that . . . I may not be kept from the country which I drew my first Breath in on the Report of some Villion [sic] whose name is buried in Oblivion." Levi got his wish; in 1787 he was restored to full citizenship, but rumors of loyalism and his part in the disaster of 1779 followed him for the rest of his life.[71]

Similar accusations dogged David Salisbury Franks, who served in the army and later worked as a diplomat and amanuensis for Thomas Jefferson. He had the bad luck, however, to serve under Benedict Arnold, and the general's betrayal hounded Franks for his entire career. Of course, Franks had his own problems; Jefferson found Franks honest but "light, indiscreet."[72]

Nevertheless, Franks believed in the cause. Born in Philadelphia, he settled in 1774 in Montreal, where he became one of the few supporters of independence in the Francophone colony. Indeed, the British jailed him in the spring of 1775, a "short tho' rigorous imprisonment," as he later remembered, "on account of my attachment to the cause of America." Some pro-American graffiti had marred Montreal's statue of George III, and Franks had mouthed off in favor of the sentiment. When the Americans invaded, Franks was elated. When the Americans left in defeat, he followed.[73]

Franks served at the Battle of Saratoga and soon found himself "in Arnold's military family at West Point until his desertion to the enemy," as he rather delicately put it after the war.[74] Arnold's treason blindsided Franks. Arnold actually wrote to Washington to absolve Franks and another subordinate of any guilt. Franks still requested a court of inquiry into his own behavior—a privilege of rank for the lieutenant colonel— and General Washington agreed. The court fully exonerated Franks, but he was nevertheless "deranged from the army." Oddly enough, Franks then escorted Arnold's wife to Philadelphia—but Peggy Shippen Arnold was also a spy, and later expelled from the city. Franks was then appointed to serve as part of the American diplomatic corps, but having already flubbed two efforts to spot enemy agents in his midst, he did not have much luck as a diplomat. By 1786 he had been recalled, and his public service ended.[75]

The point of all this is not to lionize the Jewish patriots, but to point to their presence and their service. Most Jewish patriot soldiers were not heroes. (The Sheftall brothers would later play ignominious roles in legally defining Jews as "white" to justify their slaveholding practices.) The question is not whether to treat them as heroes, but whether their fellow patriots treated them as common soldiers. Jewish wartime military service was real and, as noted, in keeping with the size of the American Jewish population. When Jews pointed to their Whiggish bona fides, they did not exaggerate or prevaricate. They were not slipping into their rights and citizenship unnoticed, as Mark Twain later suggested. They did "have to help"—and they made their mark.

Even Haym Salomon. The Polish-born Jew who became Arno Penzias's twentieth-century consolation prize joined the fight to establish the new nation. But as Penzias noted, the popular legends of Salomon do not exactly help counter anti-Semitic stereotypes. Salomon became one of the country's financiers in 1778, scraping together funds to keep the Continental Army in the field and the government afloat. He worked closely with Robert Morris, the superintendent of finance, on this gargantuan task. Yet the myths told about Salomon are even more gargantuan. Among them: that he paid all the French soldiers on American soil himself. That the king of France only agreed to a loan when he knew Salomon backed it. And that when George Washington needed funds, the general contacted Salomon during Yom Kippur services, and that very night in the temple, Salomon was able to donate $240,000 and got the other Jews to contribute $160,000.[76] These are all myths, and they lean into the mythology of Jews as moneylenders whose cash represents the sum total of their worth as allies. Yet confusion remains over Salomon even when the myths are discounted. Some of the trouble is there were between five and seven other Jews in British North America called Haym, Hyam, or Hiam Solomon.[77] Moreover, Salomon's son—also named Haym—deliberately exaggerated the financial contributions and acumen of his father in the 1800s.

The so-called financier of the revolution was born Moses Hayyim son of Solomon in Poland and arrived in North America in 1772.[78] In June 1776, a New York patriot recommended Salomon as "warmly attached to America" and hence a safe choice to provision American troops north of New York City at Lake George.[79] While at Lake George, Salomon apparently accepted a much more significant role: spy. New York City fell to the British in August. Salomon returned there in September and was almost immediately captured, as was noted in his posthumous memorial in Congress.[80]

It is possible that getting caught was his plan all along. He spoke French, German, Polish, Russian, and Italian, and he quickly became assigned by the British as a purveyor to the Hessian troops of New York. The British needed him as a go-between; perhaps Salomon's origins as a Polish Jew blinded the officers to the depth of his patriotic loyalties. Once in place, however, Salomon played the long game, using his time with the Hessians to encourage them to resign. He was also "of great Service to the French and American prisoners and has assisted them with Money and helped them off to make their Escape." His marriage into a known Tory family may have helped his cover. After two years of this undercover work, the British got wise, and "pursued by guards," he made his escape from New York on August 11, 1778.[81] Salomon's intelligence career remains hazy. Rather than being captured intentionally he might have bungled the job, and ended up in a position to aid escapees by sheer luck. He himself wrote only a few paragraphs about his life after being "taken up as a spy." However, his sacrifice was real: His wife and son remained in occupied New York. All his finances were wiped out, and though he petitioned Congress in 1778 for redress, none was forthcoming. In any case, three years later, Robert Morris came looking for Salomon. Morris, a signer of the Declaration of Independence, had been made superintendent of finance for the United States by Congress in 1781. He particularly needed money for "a vigorous prosecution of the present Campaigne"—that is, the assault on Yorktown. Salomon was an ideal choice for a broker. He had by then rebuilt his financial operation and was acting as broker for the French army in America and extending loans to several cash-poor members of Congress (yet another career move that did not exactly smash stereotypes).[82] James Madison was among his customers. Although later legend claimed Salomon was financing these loans exclusively with his own money, that appears not to be the case.[83]

Both Morris and Madison began by referring to Salomon as the "Jew broker" in their notes and diaries. Over time, Morris switched to "Mr. Salomon" and Madison to "little friend."[84] The shift was small but significant (even if patronizing on Madison's part). Morris and Madison did not invite Salomon in because of their religious tolerance but because of his skill. Like Washington and the army, they needed men. Salomon's presence in turn helped validate the place and presence of Jews in the new American experience. He eventually turned the sobriquet "Jew broker" on its head in 1784. When the ex-tory Philadelphian Miers Fisher—who had been imprisoned during the revolution in part for his Quaker beliefs—blasted "Jew brokers" at the Pennsylvania legislature, Salomon replied that Jews "have in general been early uniform, decisive whigs, and we were second to none in our patriotism and attachment to our country!" This sacrifice, he wrote, allowed him "to assert his own share in the public consequence."[85]

If the legend of Salomon is overblown, his Judaism was not in question. He was the largest contributor to the building fund of Mikveh Israel in 1782. He assisted the Jewish refugees of Charleston when they resettled in Philadelphia. He served in various positions at the synagogue and signed the 1783 letter to Pennsylvania's Council of Censors. He did not work on Shabbat. His commitment to Judaism was far clearer than that of Isaac Franks or Solomon Bush, both of whom married outside the faith and drifted from Judaism after the revolution.[86]

Other Jewish patriots who could not fight backed the American government in other ways. Isaac Moses also assisted Morris on America's behalf. Aaron Lopez provided relief to the Americans at Norwalk after the British attacked the town. When the British seized David Hays's farm in 1779, his son Jacob managed to escape, driving their head of cattle to patriot lines to feed the American army.[87] Simon Nathan provided financing for George Rogers Clark's extension of the war into the Northwest (as Kentucky and Illinois were then known).[88] When Morris considered moving the government to Baltimore in 1776 as the British headed to Philadelphia, Benjamin Levy told him to make free use of his house and home: "These are not times for compliment and ceremony."[89]

Although barred from active service, Jewish women found ways to win the war for America. Abigail Minis and her five daughters signed a petition to British governor Wright after the conquest of Savannah, announcing their intention to go to Charleston rather than remain under British rule. Wright agreed; he was planning to exile Jews anyway.[90] Charleston was not much better. Frances Sheftall saw "no less than six Jew children buried since the sige [sic]" of 1780, when the city fell. She endured the British cannonades there, as "the balls flew like haile."[91] Hannah Erwin Israel married into a Jewish family and rescued a herd of Wilmington cattle from seizure by the British.[92]

Not all Jews were patriots. When nearly a thousand New Yorkers greeted Britain's General Howe with a "Declaration of Dependence"— loudly announcing their loyalty to the crown—at least fifteen Jewish names were on the list.[93] Seven Jews signed a loyalty oath when Charleston capitulated in 1780.[94] Britain's Edmund Burke praised the Jewish Pollack family for their loyalty and for "import[ing] tea contrary to the command of the Americans."[95] Barack Hays, who had given Shearith Israel such fits in the 1760s, began as a Whig, then joined the British service as a guide for General Clinton's forces.[96] Rebecca Franks—cousin to David Salisbury and Isaac Franks—became the talk of loyalist Philadelphia while the British held the town. "You can have no idea of the life of continued amusement I live in," she wrote in 1778, as Washington and the army shivered miles away at Valley Forge. "I can scarce have a moment to myself." A socialite with a Jewish father and Christian mother who participated widely and actively in Howe's fetes, Rebecca does not seem to have practiced Judaism— at the very least, she wrote enthusiastically of her love of ham—but given that she was the known by the sobriquet "The Jewess," most Philadelphians probably missed the distinction.[97] At one loyalist fete, British soldiers participated in a faux joust. Each team of knights chose a lady as their special favorite. The Knights of the Burning Mountain chose "The Jewess."[98] Franks's reputation did not endear her to Philly's patriots or Jews. Her father faced three trials for treason after the British left Philadelphia. The third one stuck and he and Rebecca were expelled from the city in 1780.[99] "The danger of the war I have in measure reconcil'd myself to," she wrote in 1781, but she feared "being sent the L'd knows where."[100]

The point is not whether Jews "were" tories or patriots, but whether they could make a legitimate claim (as they later did) to have fought for and believed in the "sacred cause of liberty." When Jewish patriots in the immediate wake of the war and in the years to come pointed to their service as a basis of their citizenship, it was no trick or exaggeration. And when Jewish patriots wrote of their experiences in wartime, they simply assumed they were citizens, that they already had full membership in the struggle against Britain and the colonial apparatus. When patriot merchant Michael Gratz wrote to his wife about Howe's evacuation from Philadelphia, he called it "the good news of our city being again in our possession."[101] "Our" meaning *American*, not Jewish—two Jews talking to one another about their country, with no politicians, generals, or officials listening.

Jewish patriotism and Jewish service were real. They assumed their place in the movement; the movement accepted them and was better for it, as it was with every new patriot who swelled the ranks. Jews—like Baptists, Catholics, Anglicans, deists, and all religious groups—had been divided by the war and had served in the war, and its patriot victors were now ready to build a new world. As Mordecai Sheftall wrote to his son at war's end, "Every real well wisher to his Country must feel himself happy, to have lived to see this longe and bloody Contest, brot to so happy an houre more Especially as we have obtained our independence. . . . But thanks to the almighty it is now at an end."[102]

There was, however, one difference between the Jews and the Baptist, Catholic, deist, and other patriots. As the country moved to rebuild itself in the wake of the war, the Jewish patriots had all ended up in the town of Philadelphia. They had already begun the process of building a national religious organization and consciousness, but events of the war and the trials of British invasion also brought these patriots Jews together physically, in the same city. It gave them a chance to forge both their own community and institution—Mikveh Israel.

5

The Synagogue of the Revolution

THE WAR WAS GOING BADLY for the patriots in 1780. The French alliance had not delivered the knockout blow patriots hoped for. The British had hunkered down in New York and unleashed new forces in the American South. Savannah surrendered in 1778. Charleston fell in May 1780. These British victories secured the loyalty of numerous former slaves for the British cause, including Harry Washington, the former property of George Washington. Meanwhile, the general faced his own setbacks. The largest Continental offensive of 1779 was the scorched-earth campaign carried out against the Iroquois nations. That strategy boomeranged and brought Native American reprisals on the Pennsylvania-New York frontier. Everywhere, it seemed as if the loyalist and British forces were surging and the patriots falling back.[1]

Refugees from Savannah, Charleston, New York, and other British-held areas poured into patriot country. For American Jews, Philadelphia was the last place standing. Only Philadelphia had any kind of established Jewish presence and so became "a magnet for political refugees," in the words of one modern historian. It was not that Jewish life was impossible in occupied towns. Newport and New York continued to hold services under British rule. The decision to relocate was a political as well as a religious decision, the choice of Jews who wanted to live as Jews but who could not countenance British tyranny. Those of "our brethren who have during this Calamitous war fled," Philadelphia Jews later wrote, arrived in the city "from different parts for refuge . . . that we might meet to offer up our Prayers to the Holy God of Israel."[2] And so they came: Gershom Seixas and Haym Salomon from New York, Mordecai and Sheftall Sheftall from Savannah, Benjamin Nones from Charleston, Simon Nathan from New Orleans by way of Havana. Another Seixas brother, Abraham, came north after a stint in the South Carolina regiments.[3] Isaac Franks escaped from a British prison and came to Philadelphia after his discharge.[4] Manuel Josephson came from Germany by way of New York and provided *halakhic* advice for the new community.[5] Daniel Gomez, a Jewish Indian trader, came to Philadelphia to enlist. He was eighty years old, but he informed a skeptic that he could stop a bullet as well as a younger man.[6] Having met the Jewish community of Philadelphia, the patriot physician Benjamin Rush concluded "The Jews in all the states" were Whigs.[7]

Philadelphia would not have been the first choice for such a diverse cast of revolutionary Jews when the crisis began. New York was older, Charleston larger, Savannah more enthusiastically anti-British. The fortunes of war, however, dictated that Philadelphia was to become the last redoubt. America's Jewish patriot partisans now lived and worshipped in the same place, forging a common American Jewish identity firmly grounded in the revolutionary ethos.

Philadelphia was not much of a Jewish center in 1780. Despite Pennsylvania's vaunted founding as a haven for religious dissent, Jews had no citizenship rights when the colony was founded. "Penn's Woods" were named for William Penn, a Quaker who had served prison time for his beliefs. To Penn, religious freedom was a prerequisite for authentic Christian life. If one form of belief had civil advantages and another had restrictions, no one could know who the real believers were. Pennsylvania's founding document declared that all those who believed in one God "and that hold themselves obliged in conscience to live peaceably and justly in civil society, shall, in no ways, be molested or prejudiced for their religious persuasion, or practice, in matters of faith and worship."[8]

But while Penn allowed broad freedom of practice, he did not want religious equality. The new colony of Pennsylvania instead practiced a "soft establishment." Church and state were not united, but the political order had religious requirements. Penn believed the Quakers possessed a distinct authority to rule, as they were the "only truly regenerate [people] of their time."[9] His 1701 Charter of Liberties allowed all believers in one God the freedom to "live quietly under the Civil Government," but all Pennsylvania voters and officeholders had to "profess faith in Jesus Christ."[10] Penn believed that true faith could not survive when it was compelled. However, he also believed that society depended on the true faith occupying the seat of government. These were not easy imperatives to square, and Penn never resolved them.

Then Nathan Levy arrived, bringing beer. Born in New York, the Jewish Levy had come to Philadelphia in 1735 shipping a local brew, and he settled permanently in 1737. By the 1750s, Philadelphia's Jewish community consisted of a few interrelated households. The Levy, Franks, Bush, Etting, and Gratz families formed the heart of a mostly German- and Yiddish-speaking Jewish community, perhaps twenty-five families. They did not get along. On Rosh Hashanah 1768, Philadelphia's tiny Jewish community had rival minyans meeting in different private homes.[11]

But then, Philadelphia was already a riot of competing and complaining religious sects. It may have been easier to be a Jew in a place where many other white residents were also "minorities." In 1744, a visitor named Alexander Hamilton (not that Alexander Hamilton) experienced the shock of finding one tavern filled with "Roman Catholicks, Church [of England] men, Presbyterians, Quakers, Newlightmen, Methodists, Seventh day men, Moravians, Anabaptists, and one Jew."[12] By mid-century, Philadelphia was easily the most religiously diverse city in North America. The Christian mystic and alchemist Johannes Kelpius established a commune on Wissahickon Creek, north of the city. Philadelphia had a growing number of deists, Benjamin Franklin among them. Some of these groups had arrived in search of religious toleration; others ended up in the colony during the wars between France and Britain that engulfed the Atlantic in the eighteenth century. In addition, there were Native American religions crisscrossing the city and its trade routes into the interior. And among the 10 percent of Philadelphia's population who were enslaved were Christians, Muslims, and practitioners of a variety of traditional African religions.[13]

Philadelphia's Jewish community finally established a house of worship in 1771. It was named Mikveh Israel, and like all colonial synagogues, it was often abbreviated with "KK" for *kahol kadosh*—"the holy congregation." Kahol Kadosh Mikveh Israel (KKMI) was a humble affair. Barnard Gratz called it "a Synagogue Altho' in Miniature"—a single room in a private house.[14] Prewar Philadelphia's Jewry was a tiny group; when Gratz asked his brother Michael to give his compliments to "all the Jews in Philadelphia," he could very well have meant it literally.[15] They borrowed a Torah scroll and a *yad* from New York and opened their doors.[16]

The spirit of the revolution ran deep in Philadelphia Jewry. In 1765, the Non-Importation Agreement circulated in Philadelphia in response to the Stamp Act. The Agreement amounted to a boycott on British goods until the act was repealed. Of 375 signatories, nine were Jews—not a huge number, but well over their proportion in the general population. The Gratzes, the Levys, and others signed on.[17]

Mordecai Levy wavered on the question of breaking from England, but Lexington and Concord decided him. In 1775, the Jewish merchant embraced Jefferson's logic of revolution: "I believe that Kings are no longer to be feared or obeyed, than while they execute their just laws," and the "corrupted British Ministry with a venal Parliament at their heels" failed that test. In 1776, Thomas Jefferson explained the same idea—that kings existed to serve the people. For the people had inalienable rights, and "to secure these rights, governments are instituted among men, deriving their just powers from the consent of the governed." Jefferson too wrote that George III had failed: "a prince whose character is . . . marked by every act that may define a tyrant" aided by a legislature seeking "UNWARRANTABLE jurisdiction over US." Jefferson did not crib from Gratz, but both men shared a common outlook that kings did not rule by divine right but with limited powers granted by the people. And as Jefferson put it, "Whenever any form of government becomes destructive of these ends, it is the right of the people to alter or abolish it, and to institute new government." Gratz had known that a year earlier. He wrote, "I now believe all Assemblies to be legal and constitutional, which are formed by the united suffrages of a free people; and am convinced that no soldiers are so respectable, as those citizens who take up arms in defence of liberty."[18] The Pennsylvania merchant and the Virginia philosopher agreed that political legitimacy did not come from God or a church, but from the consent of the governed. This radical idea would spread among Jews and Gentiles alike.

It was at this point that Jonas Phillips bought his copy of the Declaration and sent it off to Amsterdam to share the good news. "The Americans have already made themselves like the states of Holland [a republic]," he wrote confidently.[19] He added a word of caution: "How it will all end, the blessed God knows." He was right to be worried, both for the uncertain state of American liberty and the place of Jews in it. Not everyone in Pennsylvania believed that its religious diversity—especially its Jewish diversity—was a good thing. In 1776, the state of Pennsylvania rewrote its constitution, and when they did, they wrote the Jews out of it.

The Quaker commonwealth revoked the powers of the king in 1776. A new government was needed, so a state constitutional convention met in the middle of wartime. The convention initially proposed changes that would have broadened religious freedom. The only religious oath required for officeholders was the pledge "I do believe in one God, the Creator and Governor of the Universe."

The lenient test oath had its defenders and opponents. The latter were led by Henry Melchior Muhlenberg, an evangelical Lutheran minister of Pennsylvania, an immigrant, and a self-described "old fogy." In his early days in Germany, Muhlenberg explored efforts at Jewish conversion, but his letters and journals showed a fairly static belief in the bloodguilt of Jews for the death of Christ. A parishioner once asked him whether Jews could be saved, as they were the brethren of Jesus. Muhlenberg replied, "God had made a decision to stop preaching to Jews when they rejected his apostles." Indeed, if God "had continued to send one apostle and servant after another, how many thousands of righteous souls would not the Jews have killed up to this present day?"[20]

Jews were not the only focus of his animus. Muhlenberg had no doubt that Christianity was destined by God for conquest: "Why did the Christian nations vanquish the heathen in the East and West, the Moors in Africa, and the Jews scattered everywhere if it was not to establish the rule of the Christian religion?" In the same breath, Muhlenberg further explained that every defeat of Christians by non-Christians did not count, since "in every instance this happened by divine permission and in accordance with the just judgment of God because God's people broke faith." To Muhlenberg, Christianity alone produced political prosperity: "If we repudiate the Christian religion, we shall most surely lose the riches, liberties, and privileges connected with it."[21]

When Muhlenberg heard that Jews and other non-Christians might therefore receive fuller civil rights, he was livid. He met with the president of the University of Pennsylvania and leading ecclesiastical authorities, arguing for the impossibility of a "Christian people" ruled by "Jews, Turks, Spinozists, Deists." The men drafted a longer test oath and presented it to Benjamin Franklin, president of the convention. Muhlenberg then began circulating a petition which claimed that "in Struggling for the common cause of civil and religious Liberty," Christians must "keep fast the sacred religious Privileges and Immunities heretofore possessed."[22]

Perhaps Muhlenberg protested too much. His own patriot credentials were specious. While his English letters were carefully neutral, his private letters in German expressed clear loyalist views.[23] But Muhlenberg's opposition to toleration in all forms was genuine; even after the revolution, he argued that toleration and independence would bring forth "damnable inclinations, passions, lusts." He believed the whole notion of toleration was not a Christian principle but the invention of his enemies, who "wish to have ... unbridled liberty for themselves but are unwilling to grant them to the true Christian."[24] Newspapers published letters arguing that American officeholders needed to acknowledge the revealed will of God "in the Old and *New Testament*." The correspondent named "R" wrote that if "Jews or Turks" entered government, the land would be "unsafe for Christians."[25] Even Franklin found himself on his back foot. Though he preferred the looser oath, and though he believed parts of the Old Testament "impossible to be given by divine Inspiration," on this issue he found himself "overpower'd by Numbers," as he wrote later in life.[26]

Franklin caved. On September 25, 1776, the convention strengthened the test oaths, making it state policy that no one could hold office unless they also pledged their belief in God as "the rewarder of the good and punisher of the wicked" and acknowledged "the Scriptures of the Old and New Testament to be given by Divine Inspiration." It was a shocking reversal; historian William Pencak called it the "first significant triumph for anti-Semitism in the new nation."[27]

It was not an auspicious beginning for Jewish freedom at the dawn of the Revolution. Perhaps it was especially galling that Muhlenberg himself avoided taking a test oath to the patriot government in 1777. When the British occupied Philadelphia, he was back to his loyalist habits: "I have had the good fortune to be a subject," he wrote a friend in New York, "of George III, and up to this time I have neither broken nor transferred my oath of fealty."[28] General Howe's occupation of the city in 1777—a result of patriot defeats at Brandywine and Germantown—was intended to reinforce loyalism like Muhlenberg's. Had Howe succeeded in his objective, religious freedom for all might have gone down as a war casualty, with the test-oath zealotry of Muhlenberg and his allies triumphant.

Howe failed, however. Loyalists hailed him when he entered the city, but Howe's condescending treatment of the locals "makes Whigs wherever he marches," wrote American general Jedidiah Huntington.[29] From his sickbed, Solomon Bush wrote: "Howe's march this way has made many

Whigs."[30] Howe spent lavishly on balls and refined amusements. Most significantly, when Howe left the city in May 1778—with no significant military gains and a fresh French alliance squeezing the British cause—he threw an elaborate festival dubbed the "Meschianza." The celebration included fireworks, jousting, a regatta on the Delaware, and feasting. It was at this party that Rebecca Franks was chosen as "the Jewess" for a team of pretended knights. Elizabeth Drinker, who kept a diary during the occupation of Philadelphia, noted the "Scenes of Folly and Vanity" seemed ashen to the patriots: "How insensible do these people appear, while our Land is so greatly desolated, and Death and sore destruction has overtaken and impends over so many." Even loyalists thought it was a bad idea, "ill-timed" wrote one, given "our Country . . . being involved in a French War."[31] The patriots had a field day with Howe's extravagance, though it is not clear whether Howe played into the stereotype of an effete, foppish aristocrat or actually helped create it.

Eventually the British left Philadelphia in order to attack elsewhere. That military decision would change American Jewry. "The disturbances in this Country," wrote two leaders of Mikveh Israel, "cause numbers of our brethren from the different Congregations in America to come with their families to reside here."[32] Most of that influx came after the British had evacuated Philadelphia and turned their attention to the South. The British officers who attacked Georgia, South Carolina, and the Connecticut coast did not know they were about to create a patriot Jewish community.

When Savannah fell in December 1778, Georgia's patriot families began to leave, and many headed to South Carolina. Savannah's small Jewish population added only about ten people to the minyan at Charleston, including at least three Jewish defectors from British and Hessian forces.[33] They joined a community that openly espoused the patriot cause and had given rise to the "Jew Company" at the Battle of Beaufort. Benjamin Nones arrived in America from France in 1778 and joined the Continental Army at the siege of Savannah and the Battle of Camden. (Later stories that he carried General Johann De Kalb personally off the battlefield are exaggerations.)[34] Indeed, at war's end, a "WELLWISHER TO THE STATE" wrote in a newspaper that Carolina's Jews had "considerable share in our late Revolution" and thought the state ought to invite more of them to settle there.[35]

As so often happens, however, a refugee crisis sparked the embers of anti-Semitism. As the redcoats marched north from Florida to Georgia, a

South Carolina paper complained that refugees pouring into Charleston were "of the *Tribe of Israel* who, after taking every advantage in trade the times admitted of in the State of Georgia, as soon as it was attacked by an enemy, fled here for an asylum with their ill-got wealth, dastardly turning their backs upon the country, when in danger, which gave them bread and protection." The letter was signed, "An American."[36]

The writer may have encountered some fleeing Jews, though it is just as likely that "An American" was venting spleen and standard anti-Semitic slurs: Jews didn't fight, Jews sapped strength, Jews were only in it for the money. The patriot Jews of Savannah must have been heartened by the response in the paper's next issue. A letter from a "real AMERICAN and a True hearted ISRAELITE" informed readers that Georgia Jews trading in Carolina had actually left town, "and are now with their brother citizens in the field, doing that which every honest American should do."[37]

"An American" and "A real AMERICAN" presented the question as the war sputtered in 1779: Were Jews parasites or citizens? Did they have some inherent trait that weakened the young nation, or were they "brother citizens"—adding their strength to everyone else's and pulling together? It was a different kind of Jewish Question, although unlike Pennsylvania's test oath debate it had nothing to do with religion. God went unmentioned. The "American" claimed to see the Jewishness "on inspection of their faces." The Jewish response from "real AMERICAN" called that idea "blind." Jews were fighting Britain and fleeing tyranny. Soon everyone could see the Jews fighting for the cause. The "ISRAELITE" believed that once the patriots had a chance to see Jewish citizenship for themselves, the question would solve itself. Everyone would soon see Georgia Jews fighting and Charleston's Jews "as staunch as any other citizens of this state." Or as Mordecai Sheftall put it at war's end, "An intier [entire] new scene will open it self and we have the world to begin againe." Fighting was what made Americans. Citizenship was a choice backed by service."[38]

These questions prefigured later debates over the emancipation of European Jewry, but with a key difference: The American state had never explicitly declared itself a Christian organization, and therefore, a Jew could choose to join. The question was whether the republic would accept them when they did. In some European countries, Jews had received privileges from various royal houses. Nonetheless privileges are not rights, and therefore, Jews had to receive specific acts in order to make themselves citizens in France, Holland, and England. Among American patriots, however, every doctrinaire Christian, every conscientious Jew, every backsliding Catholic or deist found himself in the same relationship to the Crown—they had all chosen to reject it. What would that mean for religion and the republic?[39]

In March 1780 the British placed Charleston under siege and captured it weeks later. Once again, the patriot Jews chose to be citizens rather than subjects. Of fifty-six Jewish men in Charleston, forty-two left the city when it fell. The British occupiers made it a point to force the Jews who remained to sign a loyalty oath—yet even two of those who signed eventually fled north to Philadelphia. When they arrived in 1780, they were just in time to meet up with the Stratford-New York refugees.[40] By one estimation, the city's Jewish population tripled during the war. Philadelphia's old synagogue was going to be too small—physically and ideologically. Once gathered, the patriot Jews began thinking nationally, not unlike the creation of national thinking among the collected soldiers of Washington's army. Jews from different cities who had thought in terms of local regions or Atlantic trade now formed a different, national unit. In the words of two Philadelphians, American Jews, having "fled here from different parts for refuge," reconstituted Mikveh Israel on March 24, 1782. They created a far more democratic synagogue than any yet known.[41]

The minutes of the first meeting of the new Mikveh Israel declared independence for American Jews in much the way Jefferson had declared independence for the colonies. The previous Philadelphia congregation, the assembled American Jews declared, had possessed "no right or legal power" to establish rules for the community, since it was formed only "according to the custom of other congregations," not as a united group and not under the conditions of free men. Now, however, the subscribers swore to "bind ourselves one to the other that we will assist . . . to form a constitution and rules for the good government of the congregation" in order to "promote our holy religion and establish a proper congregation in this city."[42] It was the same idea Jefferson had cribbed from Locke in 1776—a contract theory of government. Only free and independent men could form a government of their own choosing. The old congregation had been formed under the leadership of only a few families, and under the aegis of monarchical edict. That no longer sufficed; free men created their own institutions. The collected patriot American Jews were simply declaring themselves, as Jews, free men. In recognition of this fact, the old hazan, Isaac Moses of Pennsylvania, voluntarily stepped down, and a new chairman was elected in his place—Isaac DaCosta of South Carolina.

American Judaism began that day. The new Mikveh Israel constitution made significant democratic changes to its old version. They elected five "adjunta men"—board members—who in turn selected a parnas (president). These six would then draw up a code of laws, which was then "laid before the Congregation for their Approbation." Furthermore, each member had the "right to give unto the said Parnas & Adjunta in writing, such rules or regulations as he thinks proper to present." For good measure, the synagogue constitution was to be read aloud at Passover, so everyone had a chance to hear it.[43]

It was a marked change from the 1770 constitution, which required all members to "submit to any orders of the president of the synagogue." The 1770 constitution allowed the president to withhold all religious courtesies from a member if he decided that the said member had insulted the synagogue. This decision could be appealed—but only to the next president.[44] By contrast, the constitution of 1782 allowed individuals to appeal the president's decision to the adjunta and even to the congregation itself. The new Mikveh Israel strengthened the position of the members—those free men who comprised it. By 1824, KKMI's revised constitution made it perfectly clear who was in charge: "The members of this congregation shall have power to pass all rules, regulations and bye-laws necessary for their government, provided the same be not repugnant to the constitution and laws of the United States" or the "established principles and practice of the Jewish religion."[45] Membership would also be voluntary—another change for Jewish congregations. In monarchical Europe, being Jewish was a matter of birth and legal status. The Christian state determined who was a Jew and placed the Jews under the authority of the synagogues. The state gave the rabbis authority over Jews, and individual Jews could not question that decision. They might convert, of course, but they could not choose to be Jewish and not live under rabbinic writ.

In wartime Philadelphia, that changed. All those present at the March re-founding of Mikveh Israel agreed to the authority of the elected junta; those not present had fifteen days to consent to join. A week after writing the draft, the members of the junta sent DaCosta and Sheftall around town to circulate the rules to known Jews. The new congregation wanted to be sure that all Jews had a chance to accept the compact. Later arrivals could request to join—and by May 1782, applicants had already lined up. In September, someone suggested that any Jew should have the right to speak in a meeting, even if he was not a member and had no right to vote. The motion was voted down. The synagogue and the Jewish community were different things.[46] This synagogue would be a community of choice—a contract.[47]

Elsewhere in the British colonies, the synagogue and the Jewish community remained identical. Montreal's synagogue of 1768 made "membership practically compulsory," and when they changed their laws during wartime (in 1778), they declared that "any Israelite that will not sign these our laws and regulations" within twenty days would be forever barred from any privilege or honor in the congregation.[48] In Curaçao, the synagogue bylaws maintained social order and obedience through centralized authority. The bylaws banned all other synagogues, kosher butchers, or reading of prayers outside synagogue jurisdiction. The *mahamad* exercised control over personal life and had final approval over Jewish marriages. The protocols of the synagogue on the island of St. Thomas similarly listed punitive measures of control and forbade the Jews to form any other synagogue on the island.[49]

The changes in Philadelphia 1782 were the beginning of a new kind of democratized American Judaism. The synagogues of the United States would follow Philadelphia's model—with good reason, since virtually all synagogues in America came under the leadership of patriot Jews who had served at Mikveh Israel. In 1790, the new constitution of New York's Shearith Israel described itself as a "compact" for those living in "a state happily constituted upon the principles of equal liberty." Jews of the city were "entitled to every right and privilege belonging to this community," but they had to subscribe to the constitution itself to join. Anyone "professing to live as a Jew" could join but did not have to. The synagogue community and the Jewish community were not the same thing.[50] The 1791 constitution of Savannah's new synagogue went into effect on a vote of three-fourths of its members, and new Jews wishing to join could apply and be admitted on a majority vote of the adjunta.[51] When Charleston's synagogue applied for incorporation from the state in 1790, they claimed only the desire to worship publicly and help the poor, not any jurisdiction over the Jewish community.

Mikveh Israel's approach laid out a new American model for religion, something scholars now call "voluntarism": religion as a matter of choice. It is so familiar to twenty-first-century Americans that few notice it. "The synagogue" is not the same thing as "the Jews," just as any particular church does not correspond to "the Christians." In most of Europe, religious institutions presupposed allegiance of subjects and received state sanction.

Europe's Jews were born into synagogues simply by being Jews born in a Christian state. In the United States, American Jews would choose allegiance—as would members of other faiths. Voluntarism dovetailed with the revolutionary idea that the state needed moral virtue but not theological uniformity. The American Revolution did not begin as an effort to remove religion from the state, but that is where it ended. The patriot Jews of 1782 were on the vanguard of the transformation.

Mikveh Israel built its voluntarism in an American rather than regional character. The March meeting of 1782 saw the entire, all-Philadelphian adjunta resign. They were replaced with a national group: Benjamin Seixas of South Carolina, Hayman Levy of New York, Jonas Phillips from Philadelphia and New York, Simon Nathan from French North America, and Bernard Gratz of Philadelphia and the western frontier. All of them, in one way or another, were refugees from the war.[52] Gershom Seixas of New York became hazan. Mordecai Mordecai of Easton, Pennsylvania, assumed the task of soliciting donations from synagogues in London and Amsterdam. The voting members of the March 17 meeting made sure their leadership represented a national organization. Later subscribers—over one hundred Jewish men—confirmed the choice.

Benjamin Franklin approved. Along with a number of other Gentiles, Franklin contributed funds to the new synagogue, as they prepared to purchase a building to accommodate the expanded congregation. Franklin did not give this money out of any deep philosemitism. Like many Founders, he had mixed feelings about Jews; he assiduously defended religious freedom and also freely traded in stereotypes. (When the French creditor Jean de Neufville demanded payment from the Americans in 1781, Franklin called him "as much a Jew as any in Jerusalem." Neufville was not Jewish, and Franklin did not intend it as a compliment.)[53] Franklin's contribution, therefore, had nothing to do with his love of Jews in particular. Yet when Mikveh Israel put out a call for "worthy fellow Citizens of every religious Denomination" for donations to a synagogue—when they explained that Jews "had been exiled from & obliged to leave" their homes "on account of their Attachment to American measures"—the first name on the subscriber list was Benjamin Franklin. Other notables followed, including a signer of the Declaration (Thomas McKean) and a drafter of the Constitution (Thomas Fitzsimmons). A significant number of revolutionary leaders subscribed as well.[54]

The contribution of Franklin and others to the patriot synagogue matters in considering the question of a "Christian nation." If the Founders, as some historians and pundits have argued, believed that only Christianity produced the kind of civic virtue that the nation required, why would they support a Jewish congregation?[55] If, however, the Founders sought moral virtue—not necessarily connected with any particular religion—then Franklin's contribution not only makes sense but reflects the conviction that the morality that good government requires is based not on confession but on action.

Such was the unique situation of the American Jews and the nature of American citizenship: If morality rather than doctrine built the republic, then Judaism "counted" in the state. It would not need to seek a special exemption from the state—as it did in Europe, where state churches and long tradition limited membership in the state to particular Christian confessions. In America, God was often invoked in the fight to make the nation. Citizenship, however, seems to have been deliberately constructed in a religiously diverse sense.

Simply because Jews had become accepted did not mean they were liked. By late April 1782, the synagogue found a site for their new building in Sterling Alley.[56] Then the German Reformed church complained. It sat next to the proposed synagogue site and objected to Jews worshipping nearby. As Isaac Moses explained, the Jews did not think it "should in the least disturb You, but to our great Surprise we are told it will."[57] It is not clear what the Reformed church—an old Calvinist branch of Protestantism—meant by "disturb." The Jews of 1782 were facing a problem that Mormon meetinghouses, Muslim mosques, and Sikh temples face in the twenty-first century: Christian citizens may not want a strange or unfamiliar religion in their neighborhood.

Mikveh Israel had two choices: They could enter a legal battle or they could find somewhere else. The synagogue had the support of leading citizens and strong patriot credentials, but their legal status was unclear. Pennsylvania's test oath was still in operation and no First Amendment yet existed. So Isaac Moses opted to defuse the situation. He gave in.

Moses wrote to the German Reformed church that in order to "understand each other" and "prevent any future disputes," the Jews would relocate. There was, after all, "another piece of ground, not so convenient for our purposes," and more expensive. If the German Reformed church was willing to buy the lot on Sterling Alley where the synagogue was to have been built, Mikveh Israel would find another place, even at an increased cost to themselves.[58]

The German Reformed congregation did not respond, despite pleas from Moses that the "season of the year advances, the Tradesmen are waiting to begin . . . and we are in want of our Synagogue." On May 9, Benjamin Seixas called a general meeting of the synagogue. According to the minutes, it "seemed to be the General Sense of the Gentlemen belonging to our Congregation, that we should not Build" on Sterling "if another proper Lott could be procured." A site on Cherry Street was available. Mikveh Israel bought it. They now had two sites. In consequence, they immediately were short on funds. Jonas Phillips tried to raise an additional 300 pounds sterling but only came up with half. They sought funds from Caribbean synagogues.[59] The junta auctioned off the rights to lay the cornerstones of the new synagogue. Those who offered the highest pledge were entitled to have a *misheberach* (blessing) in the new Synagogue, and a memorial on every Yom Kippur in perpetuity. Moses and Phillips both won an auction.[60] They are mentioned at Mikveh Israel services to this day.[61]

Jacob Rader Marcus, the great historian of American Judaism, accused the synagogue of cowardice. In his 1955 collection, *Early American Jewry*, he wondered, "Did they not have the courage, in a free country, to build a house of worship on a lawfully acquired piece of ground? Were their leaders afraid to insist on their rights?"[62] Yet in 1782, it was not clear what rights they truly had. Promises of free worship for monotheists had long been the rule in Pennsylvania—but it was not clear how far that right went. Moses and the adjunta were making the case that they were citizens by asserting their rights; these were not reflected rights already established, and therefore, they were unwilling to submit them to a court decision. They chose to make peace rather than push for immediate rights. It was not the most satisfyingly dramatic response, but it may have been the wisest.

Mikveh Israel did not have the apparatus of religious freedom; its members were still constructing it. Religious liberty was a byproduct of independence and fighting the revolution—a consequence of citizenship. Those who fought, who grappled with the responsibility and consequences of independence, eventually settled on religious liberty as part of the practicalities of American citizenship. Nonetheless, the patriots did not know in 1782 that the revolutionary victory would last. Barnard Gratz wrote in 1781 of Philadelphia in "Confusion within these few days past, owing to the Pennsylvania Line, having mutinied." The Pennsylvanians had, in fact mutinied and marched, and "we dreaded the consequences of such a procedure." Gratz then relayed that Congress eventually placated the mutineers. Still, it had been a near thing. Freedom was fragile.

Mikveh Israel's concession in 1782 demonstrates that rights were very much in flux in the wake of the revolution. Avoiding open conflict with the German Reformed church allowed Mikveh Israel to continue its campaign for rights they had not established in 1782—which may be why they invited the entire executive council of Pennsylvania to the synagogue's dedication. The invitation asked the council to join them, so their presence would "give Sanction to their design" to consecrate the synagogue "to the service of Almighty God."[63]

The new place was a nearly square, two-story brick building, with separate entrances for men and women. Here the refugee community gathered together those sacred objects of worship that had compelled them to seek out one another in the crisis of war. Jonas Phillips provided a Torah scroll. Abraham Seixas provided the Havdalah cup, and Solomon Myers Cohen of Charleston gave the cloth for the reader's desk. The assembled Jewish women from across the states raised a subscription for the curtains for the ark and covers for the Torahs.[64]

Gershom Seixas stepped easily into the role of hazan, as both patriot leader and Jewish authority. The American hazan was less a formal rabbi and more of a synagogue functionary, subject to the adjunta in an arrangement quite different from that in Europe. ("Most preachers" in America "are hired . . . like cowherds in Germany," wrote one immigrant clergyman, who faced so much hostility from his congregation that he found he would "rather perform the meanest herdman's duties in Germany than be a preacher in Pennsylvania.")[65] In a world where no hazan needed formal training, the synagogue community had a great deal of leverage in appointing them. Still, in Philadelphia, there was really only one choice. Seixas combined Hebrew knowledge with patriot experience and had already led one flock through a dangerous exile in Connecticut.

Seixas led the afternoon services for the rededication of 1782, adding prayers in Hebrew and English for General Washington and the United States. The ceremony was possibly the site when Seixas gave his "Prayer for Peace in the American Revolution," which years later Gershom gave to his brother Moses to be copied for posterity. Seixas asked God to "bless, guard, preserve, assist, shield, save, supremely exalt, and aggrandize to a high degree, His Excellency the President & the Honorable Delegates of the United States of America in Congress assembled, His Excellency George Washington, Capt. Genl. & Commander in Chief of the Federal Army of these States," as well as the government of Pennsylvania, "and all Kings & Potentates, in Alliance with North America." He also asked God to "save and prosper the Men of these United States, who are gone forth to War. . . . May the Lord fight for them."[66] The format of the prayer followed a traditional Hanoten Teshu'ah, the Jewish prayer for the governments under which they live. Nothing required Seixas to expand it to include French and Spanish allies, or the armed forces. It was Jewish, patriotic, and new—a creation of the revolution. The assembled Jews perhaps thought of themselves the same way as they assembled at the Cherry Street synagogue, marched the Torahs around the building six times, and set them in the ark. They had a home.

A series of marriages cemented the national character of the patriot Jewish community. The size of Jewish enclaves in colonial British North America made finding partners challenging for those who wanted to marry within the faith. With so many Jews from across the country now gathered in one place, romance blossomed like a summer camp in the 1980s. American Judaism's new national synagogue turned patriot connections into family connections. Philip Moses of South Carolina wed Philadelphia's Sarah Machado. Simon Nathan married New York's Grace Seixas (sister to Moses and Gershom). Ephraim Hart of New York was joined to Frances Noah of Philadelphia. Jacob Mordecai returned from the West Indies to marry Judy Myers of New York. Jewish women of Philadelphia chose husbands from Baltimore, Charleston, and Easton, Pennsylvania.[67]

Those were the high points. The disagreements began almost immediately. The congregation supported the move to Cherry Street, but the synagogue's design rankled Jonas Phillips. On May 28, Phillips cast the lone dissent in a 3-1 adjunta vote approving a plan to set the building seventy-five feet back from the road. Phillips was livid. Such decisions were erroneous, "not sufficient . . . for the benefit of the Congregation."[68] He wanted more space behind the building for the hazan's house, a Hebrew school, and an outhouse. If the synagogue sold the proposed space fronting Cherry Street, it could perhaps pay off its extra expenses from the move. Phillips feared that once the front lot was sold, the space would be used to build houses, and who knew what kind of Sabbath-breakers might live there, ready to "Disturb us in our Worship, and Lumber up the yard of the Synagogue with filth, and nastiness."[69]

Phillips also complained about the placement of the door, claiming that Jewish law prevented it from being located on the west side of the building. Without a rabbi handy to answer the question, the adjunta called together an impromptu group of leading Jews from around the nation: Seixas, Manuel Josephson, and Isaac DaCosta (from New York, Philadelphia, and Charleston, respectively). They asked this group of laymen to seek a *dinim* (Jewish legal ruling) on the subject.[70]

The synagogue was operating without a map. There was no real precedent for the laity to offer up learned opinions on Jewish law. The usual route had been to contact rabbis in London or Amsterdam, but the patriot Jews needed to handle this question internally—perhaps because in the heat of revolution they had decided that their own consent mattered more than clerical expertise. Or perhaps because the continuing European naval war (which stretched into 1783) made trans-Atlantic mail problematic. Phillips was not an *alter kaker* railing at the institution; he had devoted himself to the synagogue and to the revolution. He had arrived from Europe as an indentured servant and eventually entered trade, becoming one of the wealthiest Jews in Philadelphia—with some assistance from his wife, Rebecca, daughter of the Nunes and Machado clans of Savannah. Both Phillipses were friends with Benjamin Rush, and like him, ardent patriots; Jonas was the man with the copy of the Declaration of Independence who had talked about American *rookim*.[71]

Seixas and the others ruled nonetheless against Phillips: "A door of a Synagogue (in places where our prayers are said to the Eastward) ought to be in the West, and that it is not to be deviated from where there's Sufficiency of Ground for that Purpose."[72] Phillips found another problem: The salary of the *shammash* (a synagogue functionary who lit the candles and locked the doors) was too high. Phillips wanted to cut it by two-thirds.[73] Phillips and the adjunta argued over whether and how to place the name of the synagogue over the lintel. The argument got so heated that the junta had to adopt a rule that "no person be suffered to speak to each other, but to address the Parnas, only under the penalty of half a crown for each offense." (The money went to the poor box.)[74]

In September 1782, Jonas Phillips was elected parnas of Mikveh Israel. He would prove a polarizing leader. On September 25, the congregation met to complain about seat assignments and "arbitrary proceedings in the Junta" just two weeks into the new term. At that meeting, Phillips's behavior was so maddening to the congregation that they required him to stand down as chair and let Mordecai Sheftall run the meeting instead. They spent much time trying to establish the rules for the proceeding, and there was "considerable time . . . taken in a debate by the accusers and the accused." Benjamin Seixas, Simon Nathan, and others were fined for speaking out of turn.[75] The meeting ended with no resolution. It was picked up at the next gathering of the congregation, when Cushman Pollack finally came up with a workable solution: "It appears that nothing criminal has been done," he said, but "many irregularities have been committed from a misconstruction of the Constitution since their election. Therefore recommended that any thing that has happened, be buried in oblivion." The motion passed.[76]

The meeting's minutes ended with clues suggesting just how bitter the arguments had been. The congregation unanimously accepted Moses's proposal "that we do now bind ourselves, by the Strictest ties of honour to behave with decency and decorum, in the time of worship." Anyone acting out of turn was to be stopped by the parnas—that is, Phillips—"and we will support him in his office." Those orders specifically referenced hazan Gershom Seixas: "The Hazan shall obey all orders given him, by the Parnas in writing or in the Synagogue at the usual time of service. He shall not judge if they are right or wrong, but shall enter his Complaint . . . to the adjunto."[77]

By October, most of the junto tried to resign. Two members tried to quit at once, and the junto called a meeting of the whole congregation to see if this was legal.[78] By the time they met, a third member had quit. The congregation agreed to accept fines from those who left before their term was up, but forbade more than two members to leave at one time.[79] That proved tricky a few months later, when three newly elected members of the junto all chose to pay a fine rather than serve.[80] In the middle of this debacle, Benjamin Seixas was still trying to get the adjunta to name a total cost for the new synagogue so he could find ways to pay for it, but "a dispute arose . . . and the adjunta adjourned," without giving Seixas a final number.[81]

Rivalries in synagogues were not new. New York's Shearith Israel needed to consult the mayor in 1770 when two members identified only as "C & D" broke the rules and "seated themselves in Vacant seats in Defiance to the Rulers, & will not move." In 1779, Montreal's synagogue admitted "the brethren of this congregation have . . . most shamefully, maliciously, and wickedly aspersed the characters of each other."[82] But Philadelphia's disagreements transcended name-calling and mudslinging. A patriot congregation needed procedure; it could not operate on arbitrary rules or even on deference to authority. The problem had emerged at South Carolina's Beth Elohim in early 1775, when Isaac DaCosta and others accused their junto of "arrogat[ing] to themselves, rights of their own creation of an arbitrary nature, which are inconsistent for the ruling of a congregation, justly & equitably." The dispute arose over whether the synagogue rules had been precisely followed. DaCosta undoubtedly brought the memory of this crisis to Philadelphia and the creation of Mikveh Israel.[83]

Some readers may think that simmering arguments within synagogue leadership are also an aspect of American Judaism—and in a sense, they are. The post-revolutionary Jewish community was based on choice as much as on ethnicity or belief. Jews had to choose to join, and the synagogue stood for those who joined. Questions of religious warrant therefore ran into questions of popular authority. Methodists and other American Protestants faced similar issues. American churches split if the impasse became serious enough. Mikveh Israel had been intended as a national, unifying Jewish group. Would they split as well?

Seixas, Phillips, and the entire Mikveh Israel community had to deal with questions of religious law along with questions of democracy, community, and procedure. In May 1782, Jacob I. Cohen had presented himself for membership. One of the few Jews of Virginia, he had done business with the frontiersman Daniel Boone, and when the war came volunteered in the "Jew Company" of the South Carolina militia. Cohen had been captured by the British and agreed not to return to South Carolina as a condition of release. As a patriot Jew, he headed to Philadelphia.[84] There he met Esther Mordecai, the widow of Moses Mordecai, and the two were soon engaged. The problem lay in their last names. Esther's maiden name had been Whitlock; she had converted to marry Mordecai. Jacob's last name suggested he was a *kohen*, a member of the priestly line descended from Aaron. And according to Jewish tradition—at least in the *Shulkhan Arukh*—a *kohen* could not marry a convert.[85]

Did that ruling apply in Philadelphia? Mikveh Israel had no rabbi. It was self-created and self-ruled. When Cohen approached the parnas in June, announcing his intention to marry Esther, the adjunta did not immediately rule against him. They clearly knew this marriage might violate Jewish law, but they did not feel they could rule on it. On a 3–1 vote, they requested three men—Mordecai Mordecai, DaCosta, and Josephson— "to know their sentiments and the denim [*dinim*, ruling], respecting the same." It was the same procedure the synagogue followed to solve the question of where to put the door.[86] Nearly two months passed before DaCosta and Josephson wrote back. They said no: "No Cohen, can marry a woman, Situate[d] as the Widow Mordecai is." The congregation was not to "Take any notice . . . respecting the said marriage," unless Jacob Cohen would write to the parnas and junta, "agreeing therein to abide by their Directions or decision."[87]

Jewish learning and tradition were being consulted, but it was still catch-as-catch-can. And it was unclear just how this junta-appointed band of knowledgeable laymen had gained the power to make binding decisions over synagogue members. Did Cohen have to obey? Did anyone? As the Virginian Jew Rebecca Samuel later wrote, in this country, "anyone can do what he wants. There is no rabbi in all of America to excommunicate anyone." It was, Samuel wrote, both a headache and "a blessing."[88]

Cohen rejected the ruling, and other Jews agreed with him. On August 25, the junta debated the ruling, then brought Mordecai, DaCosta, and Cohen into the discussion as well, and "a great while was Spent in debating." According to the minutes, DaCosta "proved by our Laws that they were quite Contrary or Exactly in opposition to such Marriage," and yet the junta did not forbid Cohen to marry. Instead, they gave Gershom Seixas instructions not to perform the ceremony, forbidding him "to marry Mr. Cohen to Mrs. Mordecai & not to mention his name in Synagogue."[89]

It appears that Seixas as hazan supported the marriage; the minutes refer to a letter he wrote, now lost: "In answer to your Letter of the 24th of August," the junta wrote to Seixas, "we now inform you that you are not to marry Mrs. Mordecai neither are you to be present at the Wedding." The intensity of the response suggests that Seixas had been in favor of it—but just as the hazan had to be ordered to follow the directions of the parnas, so, too, he was ordered here not to perform the ceremony. The hazan was not the voice of the synagogue; he was the servant of the synagogue.[90]

Jonas Phillips, for one, wanted to emphasize the point. He sought a subsequent motion to inform the entire congregation "that the Parnas & Junta, have forbid the Hazan to mention the name of Jacob Cohen & wife in Shull." The wedding violated Jewish law, and therefore, "all who were present at the same are Liable to the same punishment." This motion, however, failed, 3–2. Instead, the junta adopted a motion declaring that "as a full and decided opinion was this day given respecting the din on the marriage now in question," and, further, that the junta would later inform the congregation "what Punishment will be incurr'd by those, that marry the parties or attend the same, and that the said Law be published on Tuesday next." In other words, they knew the marriage would happen anyway, and attached no clear punishments. That motion passed, 3–2, with Isaac Moses the swing vote.

Jacob Cohen and Esther got married as scheduled. After all, two members of the junta—Simon Nathan and Bernard Gratz—voted no to both proposals, suggesting that they thought the marriage was fine.[91] Other Jews showed their approval by attending the wedding— including Haym Salomon and Mordecai Sheftall. Sheftall even signed the ketubah. Nothing could stop Cohen from marrying in the company of those who consented. If Mikveh Israel refused, Cohen could form his own synagogue.

He did just that. In 1789, Cohen became one of the founders of Richmond's Beth Shalome. Their synagogue constitution made clear where the power lay in republican Virginia: Any rule or regulation that a member objected to must be reviewed by "a meeting of all the members," with at least two-thirds of all members present, and any resolution needed to pass by a majority vote of that meeting. Only then could the regulation take effect. Rules would be established by a majority, not by tradition or rabbinical edicts. Cohen was not having another debacle like the one in 1782. Neither, frankly, was Philadelphia: In 1806, Cohen returned to Philadelphia, and Mikveh Israel elected him parnas.[92]

In September 1783, the abrasive Phillips was reelected president of the synagogue and refused the honor. Nevertheless, he agreed to stand for a second vote, between himself and Simon Nathan. That vote ended in a tie. They drew lots; Nathan won.

For a man who didn't want to be president, Phillips had a hard time going. In October, he refused to hand over the congregation's deeds. These legal documents were generally "given up from one P[arnas] to the other, which Mr. Phillips refused, As Some Books, papers, deeds, etc. had been detained from him during his administration."[93] Phillips essentially decided to hold the deeds hostage. By mid-November, the issue had still not been resolved. Phillips demanded a return of the money he had advanced the congregation. The junta refused on a 4–1 vote—only Phillips himself voted in favor. "I will deliver the deeds of the Shool to the Parnas on Condition that the Parnas repays me the money I am in advance for the Congregation," he insisted. Haym Salomon threatened legal action, warning Phillips that he could either "lend us the Deed or go in prison & carry it."[94]

The standoff dragged on. The back pages of the minutes were pockmarked with references to the drama: "Should any ind[ividual] refuse to deliver up those papers as are customary from one Parnas to the other, what you will do with him?"[95] The synagogue records as late as 1789 make reference to "all papers belonging to the Congregation, except deeds of lots of Synagogue, which Mr. Phillips has."[96] At times, Phillips's behavior resembled the old joke about the Jewish man on a desert island who builds three synagogues (the one he goes to, the one he used to go to, and the one he wouldn't be caught dead in). It would have been easier simply to quit. It would have been just as easy for Mikveh Israel to quit him.

But Phillips and Mikveh Israel stuck with each other. They held together because they were bound up in a revolutionary search for rights. At the November meeting where Phillips refused to surrender the deeds, he also reported on the progress of a synagogue committee working to "alter the Clause respecting the Jews"—that is, to ask the state government to amend Pennsylvania's 1776 restriction of public office to Christians only. Phillips made several motions regarding the effort, and he and all other junta members agreed "that we get it done immediately" and send a notarized petition to the state.[97] They were ready to take a stand as patriot Jews.

The immediate problem was test oaths. In the 1780s, they existed in most states. Maryland's 1776 constitution was direct about it, claiming that "all persons, professing the Christian religion, are equally entitled to protection in their religious liberty" unless that religion disturbed "the good order, peace or safety of the State, or shall infringe the laws of morality, or injure others, in their natural, civil, or religious rights." It was a cumbersome way of declaring that religion ought to be a bulwark of morality and civil rights, and that Christianity should do the job but sometimes did not. (It also creatively allowed for a declaration of religious liberty while also allowing support for Maryland's state church.)[98] North Carolina also tried to define the notion that religion would be a sufficient glue for the state, except when it wasn't. Its 1776 constitution stipulated that "no person ... who shall hold religious principles incompatible with the freedom and safety of the state shall be capable of holding any office," which could mean almost anything. And again: The state declared that "all persons shall be at liberty to exercise their own mode of worship," except for "preachers of treasonable or seditious discourses." North Carolina then included a test oath in the negative: No one who denied "the truth of the Protestant religion" could hold office.[99]

Muhlenberg and others wanted to enshrine Christianity as a kind of legal requirement. They claimed Christian confession would create trust and ensure loyalty. On that count, test oaths failed. Jacob Duché, chaplain for the Continental Congress in 1774, defected to the British in 1776. His 1774 prayer is widely circulated among religious Americans today: "O Lord our Heavenly Father . . . look down in mercy, we beseech Thee, on these our American States, who have fled to Thee from the rod of the oppressor." Less well known is his 1777 assessment of the revolution: "Independency was the idol which they had long wished to set up, and . . . rather than sacrifice this, they would deluge their Country in Blood."[100] Georgia's John Zubly began as a delegate to the Continental Congress, but ultimately decided that rebellion was not justified by scripture. He began writing religious tracts encouraging Americans to return to the king. Patriots, he warned, "loved rebellion more than the gospel." In 1787, James Madison complained of test-oath proponents, "The inefficacy of this restraint on individuals is well known." It might even be worse among legislatures than elsewhere. The "conduct of every popular assembly," wrote Madison, "acting on oath, the strongest of religious ties, shews that individuals join without remorse in acts against which their consciences would revolt." Test oaths were "much oftener a motive to oppression that a restraint from it."[101]

Jews were not alone in their fear of test oaths. In 1783, Baptists in Virginia watched in shock as the legislature prepared to reinstate an official church. Baptists had transformed their status in Virginia during the war. Colonial Virginia had established Anglicanism as the official state church, and the small but growing Baptist faith of the 1750s faced official opprobrium. Baptists paid fines if their clergy performed religious functions and often were denied official government license to preach. Mobs and vigilantes had free rein to harass and intimidate them. Baptist minister Samuel Harriss was dragged by his hair by a thug breaking up his sermon. When Baptist James Ireland had the audacity to preach to African Americans, slave patrollers rushed the meeting, seized the enslaved, beat them, and forced them away from the preaching. Ireland was arrested for giving a sermon without permission. While in jail, Ireland preached through his prison window until some of his opponents stood on a table and urinated on him through the bars.[102] Other Virginia mobs threw live snakes or hornets' nests into Baptist meetings, and sometimes broke up worship with gunfire.

State officials looked the other way; in at least one case, local magistrates led the mobs. Pre-Independence Baptists were simply not worshipping in the true church and Virginian officials owed them nothing.[103]

When the revolution broke out, Ireland and other Baptists successfully parlayed their support for the rebellion into legal relief from unequal treatment under Virginia's Anglican establishment. Virginia's wartime government suspended some of the more odious restrictions, and Virginia's non-Anglican clergy agreed to support the revolution. Indeed, Baptist preachers became some of the best recruiters for the fight. At least nine Baptist ministers who had personally been jailed or beaten for preaching served in a military capacity—not just as chaplains—during the war.[104]

In 1786, however, Virginia reconsidered instituting a state church. The Baptists erupted. They had not fought in a war for the government to tell them what Christianity was or was not. Amelia County Baptists wrote a letter to the legislature, explaining that they couldn't believe that they had risked so much in the revolution, only "to forfeit the Confidence of our Countrymen, or that the Church-of-England Men have rendered such . . . meritorious Services to the State, as to make it necessary to continue the invidious Distinctions which still subsist."[105]

There was a spiritual issue as well. As Baptist preacher John Leland noted, "If government can answer for individuals at the day of judgment, let men be controlled by it in religious matters; otherwise let men be free."[106] For Leland and Baptists, faith given under governmental duress was not given with free will and was therefore no faith at all. True religion could not exist without the separation of church and state.

Baptist petitions flooded Virginia at almost the same time Mikveh Israel's petition went to the government of Pennsylvania. Like the Baptists, the Jews were going to have to defend their claims to full citizenship. As Phillips wrote in 1776, "How it will all end, the blessed God knows." Seixas took the lead in Mikveh Israel's petition. In January 1783, he purchased a small leather-bound volume entitled *The Constitutions of the Several Independent States of America*, which also contained the Declaration of Independence and the Articles of Confederation. Seixas began going through each of the state constitutions, making careful notes on every state's laws concerning religion, and specifically, the rules concerning election to public office. (This book and its marginalia still survive as part of the Rosenbach Collection in Philadelphia; the notes are in Seixas's handwriting.) The hazan then chaired a committee tasked with responding to

Pennsylvania's test oath. The committee included Haym Salomon, Simon Nathan, Bernard Gratz—and Phillips.[107] The committee put aside their differences and began their work. Perhaps they knew that the patriot Jews would soon be heading back across the new nation, and they would bring the case for religious freedom with them when they did.

The notes exclusively concerned religion and elections. At the end of New York's constitution, Seixas wrote "By the Above Constitution of New York there is no impediment for a Jew being Elected into any post of Honor Trust or Proffit."[108] So, too, for New Hampshire: "There is no impediment in the above constitution of a Jew, becoming an officer thereof either in the Legislative, Judicial, Executive or Military Departments."[109]

For states with test oaths in 1783, the notes were more complex. Regarding Pennsylvania's 1776 constitution, the committee put a marginal line next to the document's declaration of religious freedom: "All men have a natural and unalienable right to worship Almighty God according to the dictates of their own consciences and understanding. . . . Nor can any man, who acknowledges the being of a God, be justly deprived or abridged of any civil right as a citizen." A similar marginal line occurs at the text in the same document requiring an oath for officeholders attesting to the truth of the New Testament. Their conclusion is written at the end of the document: "No Jew can be a member of the General Assembly, (of the Representatives of the Freemen) of Pensilvania [sic] as appears by the 10th Sect, of the Above Constitution on Acct of the Declaration that it requires should be made."[110] The same was true with Maryland—"By the above Constitution, No Jew can hold any post of Trust or profit, see Art. 35." Here Seixas recorded the article that cited the need for a religious oath, not the longer discussion about which religions did or did not promote morality. Seixas and the committee were interested in legal forms, not theoretical justifications.[111] Seixas made a marginal scribble (in the form of a pointing hand) next to Virginia's clause that "the right of suffrage in the election of members for both houses, shall remain as exercised at present," and then he concluded at the document's end, "I do not find any impediment of holding any office of Trust or proffit, unless in the former Laws of Virginia, there was an impediment. See that part in the Constitution marked"—then he drew a second pointing hand. (Someone will surely note this as an eighteenth-century emoji.)[112]

Seixas underlined the wording of the test oath in South Carolina's constitution: "No person shall be eligible to sit in the house of representatives unless he be of the Protestant religion." The notetakers at Mikveh Israel took the brightest view of this restriction, noting that if Jews were banned from the South Carolina House of Representatives, then all the other state offices must be open to them: "By this constitution a Jew may be Elected either Govr, Lieut. Governr. [or] Member of Privy Council."[113] For Georgia and New Jersey, despite having constitutional clauses limiting elected office to Protestants, they were exuberant beyond measure. The committee wrote, "By the Above Constitution of Georgia there is no impediment of a Jew being either Govr, Councellor or Representative in Assembly or any other office of Trust or proffit either Civil or Military." They justified that claim in an odd way: "Altho in Article 6 the Representatives must be protestant, a Jew being a protestant is not incapacitated."[114] And where New Jersey's constitution allowed "all persons, professing the belief in the faith of any protestant sect, who shall demean themselves peaceably under the government as hereby established, shall be capable of being elected into any office of profit or trust," Seixas and his team wrote, "a Jew is a Protestant, & therefore is Entitled to Enjoy all offices."[115]

What was going on? The logic for assuming Jews to be "Protestant" may refer to New York's constitution, which allowed all believers in God to serve in office—unless they were Catholics. In that sense, New York's Jews were "Protestants"—that is, non-Catholics. If that was the logic at play in the committee's response to Georgia's constitution, then they were indeed looking very hard for ways to work around their exclusion from full citizenship. There can be no doubt that the Jews of Philadelphia knew about these legal restrictions, and that they were taking dead aim at them, even unto absurdity. The effort may seem far-fetched—but these Jews were living in a world where America had just thrown off the British yoke. Who could say what was and was not far-fetched?

So in November 1783, while Phillips and the junta were bickering over deeds, the committee of which they were a part drafted a petition and presented it to the general membership of Mikveh Israel.[116] The congregation voted to send it on to the Pennsylvania Council of Censors—a branch of the Pennsylvania government "whose duty it shall be to enquire whether the constitution has been preserved inviolate in every part; and whether the legislative and executive branches of government have performed their duty." According to Pennsylvania's 1776 constitution, the council would not be elected until October of 1783 "and every seventh year thereafter." In other words, as soon as the government office tasked with preserving the rights of the people was in office, the patriot Jews of Mikveh Israel took action to press for legal recognition of their full citizenship.[117]

The committee adapted the petition directly from Seixas's notes: "The tenth section of the frame of this [Pennsylvania] government deprives the Jews of the most eminent rights of freemen, by disabling them to be elected by their fellow-citizens to represent them in the General Assembly." The synagogue then requested that if and when a convention would be called to revise the 1776 constitution, the assembled delegates would consider amending the test oath. It was a quiet document, perhaps consistent with the claim it made that "in the religious books of the Jews . . . there are no such doctrines or principles as are inconsistent with the safety and happiness of the people of Pennsylvania." Jews were loyal, Jews were moral, and they were patriots—made of the same ideological stuff as their Christian fellow-citizens. If, the petition asked, the constitution of Pennsylvania stated that "no man who acknowledges the being of a God can be justly deprived or abridged of any civil rights as a citizen on account of his religious sentiments," then the religious oath "deprives the Jews of the most eminent rights of freemen."[118]

Not that the Jews wanted to run for office—Gershom wrote that he "cannot say that Jews are particularly fond of being representatives of the people in assembly"—but the restriction was "a stigma upon their nation and their religion." It was "inconsistent with . . . the said bill of rights." Pennsylvania's Jews, Seixas wrote, "can count with any religious society whatsoever the Whigs among either of them." They had joined the army and supported the militia. "The conduct and behaviour of the Jews in this and the neighboring states, has always tallied with the great design of the Revolution." He mentioned specifically the cities under British siege whose patriots had fled to Philadelphia: Newport, Charleston, New York, "and their brethren at St. Eustatius"—the tiny island whose Jewish community defied the British and faced exile as a result.

The petition was a message to the censors that Jews possessed moral virtue, and therefore that the test oaths were enforcing only confession, not morality. Jews believed in liberty, Jews were moral, and therefore they had already made themselves citizens. The Jews of Philadelphia had absorbed the dictates of the city's guardian angel, Ben Franklin, who argued that Americans ought to "judge of the present character of sects or churches by their present conduct only."[119] The Jewish experience of fighting for the revolution—their "attachment to the Revolution principles" and their accordance with the "great design of the Revolution"—made them into free men, and free men were equal before the law.

The 1783 request was a milestone in American and Jewish history. As Marcus noted in 1970, Seixas's memorial "reflects almost every nuance of apologetics which the modern Jew has employed in his search for a fuller life." But it was also unlike the arguments of European Jewry in that it was a fully democratic argument at heart: Power emerges from the people, who contribute as a whole in making the state. Therefore, sacrifice for that cause—as soldiers, refugees, and wartime supporters—was evidence that they were part of the state. Perhaps even more significantly, although the legal difference between Jewish and Christian citizens was small in 1782, the Jewish patriots knew that there was a difference, and they would not be silent. Their knowledge of their own rights—and the knowledge that they must request those rights when withheld—had come to them through the revolution. They were prepared to pursue full citizenship; it was not a given, and it was not an accident.

The Pennsylvania Council of Censors considered the request on December 23, 1783. They referred to Seixas as "Rabbi," and read the letter aloud, with particular attention to Seixas's wording about the tenth section. In the end, however, the censors tabled the petition.[120] Nevertheless, the petition received wider notice than its consideration by the Council of Censors. It appeared in three newspapers, where it received generally positive notice. The *Freeman's Journal* argued that the religious test should be revised to simple belief in God; such a change would bring Jews to the state whose "attachment to the cause of liberty, might be of extensive and permanent service." The writer also promoted Jewish stereotypes. He thought Jews would bring wealth, and that the best part of having them in America was that they might convert. The *Independent Gazetteer* kept to a strictly political line. The Jews "have been peculiarly firm and united in the great cause of America," and "therefore are, of right, entitled to all the privileges and immunities of her mild and equal government." That meant no test acts: "It is an absurdity" to say "a man, or a Society is Free, without possessing and exercising a right to elect and to be elected."[121]

Four years later, Phillips (once again a board member at Mikveh Israel) tried again. He wrote to the 1787 Constitutional Convention, citing the Pennsylvania test oath and claiming his rights based on Jewish service in the revolution: "It is well known among the citizens of the thirteen United States that the Jews have been true and faithful Whigs, and during the late contest with England they have been foremost in aiding and assisting the states with their lives and fortunes, they supported the Cause, have bravely fought and bled for liberty which they cannot enjoy." Should the Convention remove the oath, "the Israelites will think them self [*sic*] happy to live under a government where all Religious societies are on an Equal footing—I solicit this favor for myself, my Children and posterity and for the benefit of all the Israelites through the 13 United States of America." The letter was dated in both the Jewish and Christian calendar.[122]

Other synagogues followed suit. New York's Shearith Israel wrote to Governor DeWitt Clinton, congratulating him on "a constitution wisely framed to preserve the inestimable blessings of civil and religious liberty." The "members of our congregation" planned to "render themselves worthy of these blessings by discharging the duties of good citizens." Their token was their wartime conduct: "Though the society we belong to is but small when compared with other religious societies, yet we flatter ourselves that none has manifested a more zealous attachment to the sacred cause of America in the late war." All three signatories were New York Jews "lately returned from exile"—that is, former members of the Philadelphia patriot community. The activism of Mikveh Israel had spread.[123]

As the Treaty of Paris brought the war to an official end in September 1783, the patriot Jews of Mikveh Israel began to head home, and Mikveh Israel found itself "few in Numbers, and some of them agoing away."[124] This reverse exodus further worsened the financial woes of Mikveh Israel, as dues-paying members left town but bills for the new property did not. Nonetheless the passage home for people like DaCosta, Sheftall, and Cohen also brought the activism of Mikveh Israel to the rest of the country. And it made a difference.

Test oaths fell as Jews returned home with the experience of the patriot synagogue and the argumentation of Seixas and Phillips. Georgia got rid of its test act in 1789. South Carolina—the most restrictive state—lost its test act in 1790. Pennsylvania's fell in 1790, Delaware's in 1792. Georgia, South Carolina, New York, and Pennsylvania all had Jewish communities, and all of them lost their test oaths. There were few Jews in Virginia prior to the revolution, but after the war, Jacob Cohen and other Mikveh Israel dissidents established the first synagogue in Virginia, and of course Virginia's test oath vanished in 1786.[125] States without significant Jewish populations in the 1790s—Connecticut, Massachusetts, North Carolina— retained their oaths simply because they weren't challenged. It seems that when non-Christian religions asked whether religious freedom applied to them in the new republic, the answer was yes.

In an organizational sense, at least, American Judaism owes its origin to the revolution: The patriot Jews worked and lived together in a single community, founded a synagogue, then returned home and remade their own synagogues in the image of Mikveh Israel. Every American synagogue of 1789 was led by someone who had spent time at Mikveh Israel. Structurally, therefore, the American revolution likely had a greater immediate effect on Judaism than on any other religious group in America. Judaism may well have been the first truly national American religion.[126]

The project to create religious rights was bound to the project to create rights for Jews. If Judaism was to be a national religion with full rights, Protestants would have to prepare for what the Reverend David Caldwell of North Carolina called "an invitation for Jews and Pagans of every kind to come among us." As the refugees from Philadelphia returned to their liberated cities, Americans began to realize that some of their patriot citizens were already Jews.

6

A Possibility of Jews

ON JULY 30, 1788, AS North Carolina stumbled through the effort of ratifying the US Constitution, she remained stuck on the issue of "Jews, Mahometans, pagans, &c." Eleven other states had ratified the document and brought the federal government into being. North Carolina was struggling to follow. The absence of a federal test oath was the problem. The minister David Caldwell called it "an invitation for Jews and pagans of every kind to come among us" which would "endanger the character of the United States." No one, he insisted, supported the "emigration of those people."

Former governor Samuel Johnston conceded that religious freedom required "a possibility of Jews, pagans, &c. emigrating to the United States." That was the cost, he maintained, for a government that could not "intermeddle on the subject of religion." He added, "When any attempt is made by any government, to restrain men's consciences, no good consequence can possibly follow." If some future American Muslim should "acquire the confidence and esteem of the people of America by their good conduct and practice of virtue, they may be chosen" for public office. Religious freedom protected the right of voters to choose whom they wanted along with the rights of everyone to worship according to conscience. Johnston was certain the Christian majority would undoubtedly bring "those people" into the churches. "The children even of such people would be Christians," he said, and would "add to the progress of the Christian religion."[1]

Religious freedom won signal victories in 1786 and 1788, with the Virginia Declaration of Religious Freedom and the Constitution's provision that "no religious test" ever be required of officeholders. But these victories were not coterminous with the revolution. The debates of 1788 came years after the guns fell silent at Yorktown and the peace treaty was signed in Paris. Religious freedom accelerated after the revolution, as American citizens puzzled over the "possibility of Jews" among them and in their halls of government. Jewish freedom was a test case—and across the new nation, the patriot Jews from Mikveh Israel raised their voices to remind fellow Americans of their service in the war and the freedoms they had won. Jews were imagining themselves as citizens within a revolutionary generation that was re-imagining what it meant to be a citizen. The return of the Jewish patriots from Philadelphia shaped this first era of American religious freedom.

To this generation of Jews, all of America seemed wide open. Samuel and Moses Myers discussed their options in the postwar world: New York had "considerable good business," while Georgia was "a young country and promises success." Or "Wou'd you prefer Philadelphia," Moses asked, with its contacts to London and Amsterdam? Should they "embark in the spring for Maryland"? In the end, Moses picked none of those places; he ended up in Norfolk, Virginia, where eight years later he was elected president of the city council.[2]

Still, the 1780s was not a decade of sweetness and light. Even as Myers marveled at American possibilities, he knew nothing was settled. He for one "should not be surpris'd at a civil war taking place on this continent."[3] When "regulators" in western Massachusetts tried to seize a federal armory to protest taxes, in an uprising called Shay's Rebellion, it shook Myers badly. "The strides taken to overset government in eastern states," he wrote, "by and by will be a general case." The war was over, but the new states had just thrown off one government and there was no guarantee they would not throw off another.

Peace meant work for American Jews—work in formalizing and defining freedoms, shoring up revolutionary credentials, and building a republican government. The British evacuated New York in November 1783; by February 1784, Gershom Seixas had returned to Gotham. Seixas seemed at first unsure about going back. In November, he negotiated with Mikveh Israel over a new contract. But his salary came from the community *tzedakah*, and he wrote that several members were settling accounts for money loaned to build the new synagogue (*binyan abait*) and counting it as *tzedakah*—which left Seixas unpaid. He urged the synagogue "to provide accordingly" for him and his enormous family.[4]

It was at this point that Hayman Levy, the new parnas of New York's Shearith Israel, made a bid for America's most prominent Jewish "minister." Seixas liked Levy, whom he described as "capable of demanding a proper Respect in the Office of Parnas." Levy had held the job for only a few weeks. The former Hessian parnas, Alexander Zuntz, publicly resigned in the synagogue on December 6, in keeping with an agreement only to serve until the British evacuated the city. Levy was named as temporary successor at a meeting of nine Jews a few days later. Two weeks after that, they made the choice permanent. Those gathered requested Levy to write Seixas, to inquire as to "whether he looks upon himself as hazan to this KK [Kahol Kadosh] or not."[5]

Seixas did not know what to think, given how, as he put it, "Shearith Israel is now situated." (Levy had called a meeting for all Jewish men over twenty years old to confirm his status as parnas; only eighteen people showed up.) Seixas asked for a salary equivalent to what Philadelphia had promised. But his real concern was synagogue politics.[6] New York had the same problems as Philadelphia. Two weeks after Levy wrote to Seixas, KKSI had a row over intermarriage, just as KKMI had had, with the acting junta refusing to allow Benjamin Jacob to marry a Gentile despite his "intent to make her a Proselite." Seixas wrote to Levy that he required "the Zeal to have the same Mode of carrying on Public Worship as <u>We</u> unanimously agreed to and established in this city." Seixas wanted the same style that Mikveh Israel had made for itself. He wanted New York to adopt Philadelphia's unanimous vote to "bind ourselves, by the Strictest ties of honour to behave with decency and decorum, in the time of worship."[7] That vote had come in the wake of September's furious arguments over how the junta ought to work. Seixas worried that "Parties are formed (and forming) to create divisions" in the New York synagogue "by which means a general Disunion seems to prevail" among "the reputable members of the Congregation."[8]

Levy managed to convince Seixas that New York would come up with the salary and that he could command "Decency and Decorum in time of Public Service." By February 1784, Seixas informed Philadelphia's junta that he would finish his contract and then depart for New York, being "called to my former place of Residence (& the place of my Nativity)."[9] He described the move as a "call"—a term usually used to describe a Protestant minister's shift in position. By mid-March, things at Mikveh Israel had soured, and Seixas received "several letters" condemning him.[10] Seixas might have stayed on in Philadelphia had they had worked out a clear system of democratized governance. But under Phillips, and with its unstable junta membership, Mikveh Israel could not. In the end, Seixas headed back to New York and left conflicts over deeds and jurisdictions behind.

When Seixas again stood before New York's congregation, he announced a new regime of "stricter attention . . . paid to the Rules of Decency & Decorum," especially during the service. People should not simply leave in the middle of the service, or talk and laugh during prayers. Seixas had particular words for parents who let children "commit those Misdemeanors which are so highly reprehensible." (Some readers may have encountered decorum issues in modern synagogues that match those of Shearith Israel's in 1784.) It needed to stop, Seixas declared, because it brought contempt upon the community and because such things prevented the community from worshipping God, "to glorify his holy Name."[11]

Seixas had to patch together Shearith Israel's Connecticut refugees with the Jewish loyalists who had remained. Fortunately he was on good terms with the parnas of the occupation. Alexander Zuntz, a Hessian Jew, had arrived with the British and become the leader at Shearith Israel. Seixas had crossed enemy lines to perform Zuntz's marriage in 1779. The loyalist hazan of Shearith Israel—Jacob Raphael Cohen, from North Africa by way of Montreal—actually switched pulpits with Seixas so that the loyalist New York rabbi went to the patriot congregation of Philadelphia when the patriot hazan of Philadelphia went to New York. (New York probably got the better deal; Samuel Hays complained that Cohen "gives precepts they don't mean to follow.")[12]

Some loyalist Jews did not stick around in the new republic. The quarrelsome Barack Hays ended up in Montreal, where he begged the local royalists for employment "to allow his pay to continue." Jacob and Esther Hart found their circumstances severely reduced when they fled from the patriot reoccupation of Newport in 1780. They lived in New York until 1783, then headed to London, where neither survived long. Their relative Isaac Hart was lynched on Long Island for his tory beliefs.[13]

Jews who had supported the Crown and wished to stay in Shearith Israel simply remained, however. Abraham Abrahams and Uriah Hendricks submitted to British rule in 1776 but voted along with everyone else in December 1783 to invest Hayman Levy with the powers of parnas. Rachel

Pinto sided with the British after the sack of New Haven; she remained a dues-paying member of KKSI for the rest of her life. And in a gesture of reconciliation, Zuntz was made a member of the junta after resigning as the loyalist parnas.[14]

The problems of Mikveh Israel followed Seixas back to New York. As in Philadelphia, there was a crisis over money. The New York synagogue never paid him his full salary in the financial crunch of the mid-1780s. Only a few months into his new term at KKSI, Seixas petitioned for additional resources, which the junta denied. In 1785, the congregation briefly let Seixas go for want of funds, and two years after that Seixas had to resign briefly before he could get the board to promise to pay him "whenever the funds of the Synagogue were adequate." In 1792, Seixas again complained that he had already accepted one decrease in his rent allowance and could not afford another.[15]

The ongoing crisis of funding and leadership was exacerbated by the democratization and legal equality Seixas helped create. When the British left New York, the state got rid of its piecemeal establishment and in 1784, simply chose to recognize any religious society that applied for incorporation. Shearith Israel incorporated that same year, and received the same legal status as Christian churches. The 1784 law, however, required any incorporated religious community to have a board of trustees. Shearith Israel named a slate of trustees distinct from the adjunta. Within a year, however, the adjunta and the trustees had fallen out, each claiming that it had the right to make decisions for the synagogue. Greater lay control led to struggles within the congregation over how a synagogue should be run, and even over what Judaism meant. An addition to the Shearith Israel constitution in 1790 gave the trustees control of "all the temporalities of religion." In practice, that meant the trustees had undisputed control over, for example, synagogue seating—another issue in which American Jews challenged traditional conceptions.[16]

In 1785, the three Judah sisters—Abigail, Becky, and Sally—refused to accept their assigned seats. "When the gentlemen trustees can convince us that we are subject to any laws they choose to make," they wrote, then the trustees "may endeavor to exercise their authority." KKSI sat women and men separately, as was traditional, but the Judah sisters insisted that regulations putting married women in the front of their gallery "hinder us from attending Divine Worship." So the sisters simply took the seats they wanted.[17] Seixas sided with the sisters. He wrote to the board in an official capacity, explaining that the materfamilias of the Judah clan was willing to pay the increased charge for the women's seats. Seixas's response, though procedural, nevertheless represented an extraordinary move toward democratization: synagogues had long been divided by gender, part of an enduring rabbinical tradition that women bore a different relationship to God. The Judah sisters, in the wake of independence, asserted their rights as Jews to make decisions about worship. Governments (in the form of state-mandated trustees) could not make those decisions. Women had a role to play in worship as Jews. And Seixas backed their revolt—tossing out generations of practice.

The Judah sisters' gambit did not work. The trustees reprimanded Seixas and took the Judah sisters to court. The sisters were convicted of trespass. Their mother left KKSI, but all three sisters eventually rejoined. Issues involving seating continued. In 1786 the congregation tried to rewrite the rules for High Holy Day seating; Manuel Myers put a lock on his seat because a fellow congregate named Lion Hart kept taking it. Despite the "decorum" he sought, Seixas could not make New York Jews obey him.[18]

That was how it seemed to go. Philadelphia's Mikveh Israel had further commotion over intermarriage. Mordecai Mordecai had been selected as an expert to rule on the Cohen-Whitlock marriage in 1782, but did not sign the *dinim* forbidding the match. By 1785, Mordecai actually officiated at a wedding ceremony for a mixed marriage. Born the son of a rabbi in Telz, Lithuania, Mordecai had served as Philadelphia's *mohel* and knew more than his share of Jewish law. When his niece married a Gentile in 1785, Mordecai approved. He headed to Easton, Pennsylvania, and performed a second marriage ceremony for the couple, this time according to Jewish law. He even wrote out a ketubah and read it aloud in English so the Gentile groom could assent.[19]

The junta condemned the action and Mordecai wrote a fierce reply, claiming that their lack of knowledge of the law was the issue: "If you have parused my Latters wright with all the partikeles of the Law that I Laid daun Before you, you Caud Nauer Came to a Such Conclusin." Mordecai claimed that the junta had no basis for action because only one witness had spoken up, and, therefore, no ruling could be made. Mordecai did not specifically deny that he had performed the wedding, only that the junta could not hold him accountable under Jewish law. The junta either "did not paruse wright, or Eles I Canat halp saying you did not understand it."[20] He denied that any elected leadership of the community could rule on

Jewish law. Only those who knew the law (and he included himself in this group) could offer opinions on it. For good measure, he signed his communication, "Mordecai, son of the Rabbi Moses of Tels."[21]

It was another classic problem of democratization. Marriage had become a civil ceremony in a state without a church, and any Jew (not just a rabbi) could declare a marriage valid. In another example, in 1804 Solomon Levy married his late brother's widow in South Carolina—a match forbidden by Jewish law. The synagogue could not stop the marriage. Instead, other Jews of Charleston satisfied themselves by taking out a notice in the local paper "to make known to the public that the said marriage is incestuous, illegal, unconstitutional, unprecedented, improper, inconsistent, absurd, nugatory and contrary to all the Jewish laws." Two days later, a response in the same paper asked, "If Mr. LEVY has committed an act contrary to divine law, he will be punished by that divine law:—Shall mortals take cognizance of the breach of divine law, unless that divine law has been adopted as the municipal law?"[22]

Back in Philadelphia in 1785, the junta had no means of enforcement to make Mordecai obey its dictates. The same process had Protestant Christian groups breaking away from one another to form new churches across the nation. Unlike Protestants, Jews prized communal harmony— and given their small numbers, could ill afford to split. Philadelphia's junta tried to refer the matter to a Dutch rabbi. The letter conveyed their frustration: "The matter touches the very roots of our faith, particularly in this country where each acts according to his own desire. . . . The congregation has no power to discipline or punish anyone." Even banning people from synagogue for infractions did no good, since "these evil people pay no heed and come to the synagogue . . . it is impossible to restrain them from doing so because of the usage of the land."[23] If the community was forged by belief and practice, and not enforced by rabbinical decree, essentially anyone could become a nominal Jew. They could not physically force Mordecai out. Juntas, and trustees, and individuals, and hazans were all making religious decisions, and all of those decisions could be religiously valid.

Another intermarried Jew died in Philadelphia that same year, and a junta-appointed committee ruled the body could be buried in a corner of the Jewish ceremony, but without the customary ritual washing and shrouds. Mordecai Mordecai intervened again; he and several others disobeyed the edict and washed and shrouded the corpse. The parnas actually caught Mordecai in the act of preparing the body, and Mordecai "paid no attention to his words and on the contrary quoted laws against him." Mordecai insisted both on his right to interpret Jewish law to his satisfaction and on the right to membership in Mikveh Israel. In the end, Mordecai headed off to join other Mikveh Israel dissidents in Richmond, where he would share a synagogue with Jacob Cohen.[24]

Other troublemakers stayed in Philadelphia. Jonas Phillips continued to withhold the deeds after Seixas left in 1784, despite letters begging him to sign them over. Mikveh Israel nonetheless continued to rely on Phillips, who continued to kvetch.[25] They had little choice as the patriot Jews returned home after the war had ended in 1783. Even a year later, Michael Gratz found it impossible to calculate how many Jews would belong to Philadelphia's synagogue in the coming months, "as Sundry members of them are going out of town."[26] During most of the 1780s and until 1792, the work of making KKMI solvent fell to Benjamin Nones, the French Jew from Charleston who became parnas for much of the period. Mikveh Israel applied for the right hold a lottery to make up the shortfall in finances. The Pennsylvania legislature agreed to the 1790 lottery, without which, Nones wrote, "we should in all probability have had our House of Worship torn from us and converted to profanation."[27] The legislature offered more reassurance than the Jews had received from the Council of Censors, anyway.[28]

After Seixas's departure, the new hazan of Philadelphia was Jacob Raphael Cohen, Seixas's predecessor in loyalist New York who opted to stay in the new nation after the war. In Philadelphia, over the next twenty years, Cohen worked as hazan, Hebrew teacher, and shochet simultaneously, sometimes without a contract.[29] Cohen's compensation for his labor was episodic, as evidenced by the curious incident of the dead dog in the cistern. Cohen wrote a furious letter to his parnas, refusing to live in the house the synagogue had provided for him unless something was done with the "Dangerous, Unwholesome and offensive" cistern. The bricks had deteriorated so badly that a neighbor's dog had fallen in and drowned, and remained there so long it began to stink.[30] Cohen's tenure survived this disaster, but was indicative of the shoddy conditions under which he lived.

Sometimes it was not about money. Cohen played a critical role in the symbolism of religious equality in the new nation. As states began ratifying the new Constitution in 1788, the Framers and their Federalist allies began throwing "federal processions"—lavish parades intended to impress and sway voters. When New Hampshire and Virginia narrowly voted to approve the document in late June, Philadelphia's Federalists threw together a massive celebration on July 4, 1788. They made a point of inviting Cohen. Like all such fetes, the 1788 procession was awash in symbolism. One float featured a giant ship dubbed "Union"; an actor portraying George Washington served as commander.[31] A giant "federal edifice"— thirteen stories high—was carted through the streets. Tradesmen of all sorts walked in the parade: cabinetmakers, bricklayers, glovers, butchers, printers, brewers, barbers, stationers, tailors, and others. The blacksmiths marched with a portable forge where they literally hammered swords into plowshares.[32]

The city's clergy marched, too—and here Cohen played his role: "The Rabbi of the Jews, locked in the arms of two ministers of the gospel, was a most delightful sight," wrote Benjamin Rush. "There could not have been a more happy emblem contrived, of that section of the new constitution, which opens all its power and offices alike, not only to every sect of christians, but to worthy men of *every* religion." The parade ended at "long tables of provisions," one of which had been set aside for Cohen and other Jews—a kosher table, with "a full supply of soused salmon, bread and crackers, almonds, raisins, etc." set up by the city's former hazan, Isaac Moses.[33]

The kosher table of 1788 is one of the most remarkable things in the remarkable history of the patriot Jews and the revolutionary moment. The Federalists who planned the procession had only a few days to put it together, and yet somehow they ensured that Cohen would join with Christian ministers and that he and the other Jews in the parade and in the city would be able to join in the feasting afterward.

Kenneth Silverman wrote that these processions showed Americans "observing themselves in the process of defining themselves." If so, then Jews had been observed and defined within the body politic. Rush saw the meaning of the clergy at the parade, marching with linked arms in groups of four and five: "Pains were taken to connect Ministers of the most dissimilar religious principles together." It was, Rush wrote, indicative of how "free government" could promote "christian charity" by opening the way to government service "to worthy men of *every* religion." To Rush, Christian charity required a prohibition on test oaths. The Constitution was not just meant to be inclusive, but *radically* inclusive. Even with so few Jews around, the federal parade not only brought them in but made possible their full participation with the kosher table. And as Rush noted, "rabbi" Cohen was standing in for all other faiths. If Rush needed a divine symbol to approve this interpretation, he got it; the sky that night shone with the aurora borealis.[34]

Cohen's inclusion capped several uncertain years for American Jews. In 1784, while speaking against Robert Morris's Bank of the United States, Miers Fisher warned legislators that the bank had Jewish backing, and was therefore a security threat because it involved "foreign" elements. Jews would by nature charge "high and unusual interest," Fisher explained. He wanted the state to charter another bank (his own) to protect the citizens against the Jews.[35] A few days later, Haym Salomon took up the response, publishing his reply in the *Independent Gazetteer* under the name "A Jew Broker."

Salomon did not try to answer the tangled specifics of the nebulous Shylock stereotype. He instead pointed to Jewish support for the revolution as evidence of the Jews' virtue, and Fisher's cruelty and toryism as evidence of his perfidy. Those who made such attacks had no virtue, and this was a republic of virtue. It was not a question of faith, Salomon wrote, but of "political *heresy*," and Fisher's "character, *fetid* and *infamous*," disqualified him from casting shade on any patriot.[36] The issue was not avenging "the injuries of particular societies and sectaries," Salomon argued, but protecting the state. Rights were for those who served the public. Therefore, Jews were safe and tories were not. Jews were "early uniform, decisive whigs, and we were second to none in our patriotism and attachment to our country!" Indeed, to attack Jews was to attack the very idea of virtue that made self-government possible. Such attacks "seemed wanton, and could only have been premeditated by . . . a base and degenerate mind."

Salomon had good reason to make this accusation, for Fisher had indeed sided with the British in the war. "Your conspicuous *Toryism* and *disaffection* long since buried you in the silent grave of *popular* oblivion." Salomon turned the language of religious intolerance back on Fisher, who had been "exiled and excommunicated by the state, *as a sly, insidious enemy; severed and detached from the generous bosom of patriotism* and *public virtue*." Who was Fisher "to approach *our political vineyard,* and blast the fruits of those labors for which you neither *toiled nor spun*"? Salomon mirrored the Passover liturgy's story of the wicked son—this revolution is for *us* and not for *you*; Fisher was "a meer *tenant at sufferance*." "Who were the spies and pilots to the British? Who prolonged the war? Who was the cause of so many valuable men losing their lives in the field?" Tories, not

Jews. Case closed. Religion did not make citizens; loyalty to country did. Anti-Semitism was anti-revolutionary. It was anti-American.[37]

Different languages about Judaism circulated as the United States drifted through the postwar haze—an older language that classified Christianity as the cause of the state, and the newer language letting virtue and service create citizens. The languages overlapped because the political system was in flux. New ideas had won a war, and yet because those ideas had never quite addressed religion, Pennsylvania (and the country) was left with what historian Nicole Eustace called a "combustible mix of aristocratic and democratic models of society and politics." The Americans did not really have a consensus on which of multiple ideas to listen to, "much less agreement about the kind of society they hoped to create."[38]

Jews were an anomaly, yet they were not an anomaly, depending on the language encountered. They symbolized difference; they symbolized the sameness of the patriot cause. The revolution had left questions of citizens open; as American governments were rejected, revised, and reestablished from 1783 to 1800, those questions took on sharper definition. Such questions could be *wide* open, in a way most twenty-first-century Americans are unaware of. New Jersey left a loophole in its constitution that allowed women who owned property to vote. When a special convention was called to close the loophole, the representatives refused. So for a decade, women cast votes in at least one state. As a Trenton newspaper put it, "Every free person who pays a tax should have the vote." A Morristown voter also linked female suffrage to the ideals of the revolution: "The prevailing theory is that taxation and representation should go together." Possibilities of radically inclusive citizenship rang out in revolutionary tones in the aftermath of the war. Patriot women had, after all, shown their virtue in the imperial crisis and revolution by organizing and promoting the boycotts of Britain. But by 1807, the tide shifted, and the language of women as ruled by passions rather than virtues had seeped into the political conversation. Women, argued a male voter, "do not even pretend to any judgment." If women could not possess virtue, they could not vote. New Jersey revoked their right, and female enfranchisement ended.[39]

Similarly, religious rights for non-Protestants (and Baptists) were sometimes praised as the essence of the revolution and sometimes denied as a plot to ruin the state. American Jews actively pursued the language and ideology of radical inclusion enshrined in Philadelphia's federal parade. They fought to make themselves citizens.

In Charleston, for example, Jewish difference became a sticking point in the only divorce granted by state courts between the revolution and Reconstruction. Mordecai Lyon accused his wife, Elizabeth Chapman, of "scandalous behavior." Chapman must have felt similarly because she "cordially consented" to the divorce. The two Jews called on the Charleston synagogue to provide a *get* (divorce papers) in accordance with Jewish law. Beth Elohim gathered an ad hoc committee of members who (in theory) knew the *halakha*. They granted the divorce, and then enacted a venerable Jewish ritual: Lyon threw the document at Chapman and she caught it, demonstrating that he was willing to give it, and she was willing to accept. Both partners became free to marry again.[40]

That decision only held among Jews, however, and Lyon soon wanted to remarry. South Carolina had some of the most restrictive divorce laws in the state; the practice was banned until 1868.[41] And yet in 1789, South Carolina's secretary of state duly recorded the divorce, and Lyon remarried a year later. Clearly, the state felt that if divorce was part of Jewish custom, then why should the state get involved? Yet it also demonstrated a clear double standard: state laws could bind Christians in one way, and non-Christians in another way. In 1801, Carolina courts similarly limited the fines against Solomon Moses—who had punched a fellow Jew in the face—by noting the synagogue had also made Moses pay restitution.[42]

Also in 1791, Charleston saw an outpouring of general enthusiasm in praise of American institutions and religious freedom when the local synagogue patched up an internal rift. The South Carolina *Gazette* cried that the "shackles of religious distinction are no more."[43] The natural scientist John Shecut wrote that the "salutary effects of tolerance in points of religious faith" gave the United States "the respectable footing on which this nation stands." Shecut cited an unnamed Jewish friend who fully believed the revolution had been fought for "religious and political freedom" and delivered Jews "from religious thralldom under British rule." What was good for the goose was good for the gander: "What surer pledge can any government possess for the fidelity of any portion of its citizens, than the claim it has on their gratitude, for the protection afforded to their dearest rights?"[44] Jews could exemplify the revolutionary settlement, and Jews could be outside the laws of the state, sometimes at the same time.

This dynamic assumed sharpest relief in Georgia. The Sheftall clan returned home, and soon found their political enemies claiming that Jews could not be Americans. In 1784 there appeared an anonymous pamphlet entitled *Cursory Remarks on Men and Measures in Georgia*, written by "A Citizen." The pamphlet was less a coherent argument than a series of political complaints packaged around a candy center of anti-Semitism. The Citizen's nominal goal was to protest a court case that had declared that Jews but not Native Americans had standing to sue in Georgia courts. Sheftall was the plaintiff. The Citizen howled. Jews were "at all times, and upon all occasions, to be esteemed as being precisely upon the same footing with Mulattoes or Meztizoes."[45] Jews could not be tolerated or allowed political power; it violated all codes of law. *Men and Measures* traced the authority of American courts back to English precedents, and since no English law ever allowed Jews to claim civil rights, those rights *could not* now exist in Georgia. Jews carried only the rights they had when Georgia had been founded by Englishmen in 1732. The revolution changed nothing; a Jew was always a Jew, and no Jews could "become citizens but by the aid of the Legislature" in this "Christian Country." The common law forbade it.[46]

Out came all the old classics of anti-Semitism. Jews, the Citizen wrote, "enter very little into politicks further than to favour that system which is most promotive of their pecuniary interest, the principle of lucre being the life and soul of all their actions."[47] Jews preferred monarchy and arbitrary government because biblical Hebrews had preferred rule by judges, sanhedrins, and King Herod, all "despotic as dictators." Blood libel got a mention; the Citizen apparently believed the legends that Jews of England would "on a Good Friday . . . steal a Christian child, and privately to crucify him in derision of his religion." Jews had only snuck back into England in the seventeenth century "with the help of long purses." Yes, the Citizen admitted, Jews could worship under Georgia's law, but that "says no more for them than it does for the Bramins of China [India], or the Mussulmen of Turkey." Geographic errors aside, the Citizen was adamant. Jews, Muslims, and Hindus had no "grant of any civil right whatever."[48]

Even worse, the Jews of Georgia were uppity: "We see these people eternally obtruding themselves as volunteers upon every publick occasion, one day assuming the lead at an election, the next taking upon them to direct the police of the town, and the third daring to pass as jurors." Here and elsewhere, the pamphlet alluded to Mordecai Sheftall, who had dared to lead Savannah's revolutionary movement and had the audacity to involve himself in Georgia's postwar politics. If Jews could do that, then "what are we to expect but to have Christianity *enacted into* a capitol heresy." Then came the kicker, the thing that makes *Men and Measures* sound like it was written yesterday on an alt-right site: The author claimed he was not prejudiced. "I am as far removed from being a votary or friend of persecution as any man on earth. Had the Jews in this state but conducted themselves with common modesty and decorum, I should have been the last person to point out their disabilities." He even told readers about his Jewish friends: "one whole family . . . of upright demeanor."[49]

The pamphlet was printed anonymously and circulated in the Georgia capitol among the legislators as the 1784–85 session got under way. The intent was clear: The legislature, if not the people of Georgia itself, had to do something. Jews had no more rights, the Citizen warned, than escaped African American slaves. Freedom could only go so far.

Sheftall's half-brother Levi wrote the response to *Men and Measures* and published it in the Georgia *Gazette* in January 1785. Levi wrote only a paragraph, but it was enough. The author of *Men and Measures* "subscribes himself a Citizen" but Levi asked, "What had the Jew particularly alluded to [Mordecai] . . . done that he should not also be entitled to the rights of citizenship"? Then Levi listed the patriotic services Mordecai had rendered Georgia in the revolution—including having his property seized, imprisonment for refusing to reveal the location of patriot gunpowder, and "as became a faithful citizen, discharge[ing] the several trusts reposed in him." Whether or not such a man "and the rest of his profession in this state" should have the same rights as a slave, "I leave to the Whigs to judge." Levi signed his response, "A Real Citizen."

Levi's original draft was even more specific about Jewish patriotism. Referring to "A Citizen" as "a pretended Citizen," Sheftall wrote, "He says he has traveled with the Jews through a wilderness of History. It had been much better for him, had he traveled as far to the Northward, as some of them had done and partook his share of the sufferings which they and many other good Whigs suffered." Here, it is the journey north—a journey *to Philadelphia*—and enduring privation during the war that entitled people to "the sacred name of Citizen." Of course, Levi hadn't gone to Philadelphia; Mordecai had. Levi may have been arguing that the Jewish exile into Philadelphia had extended citizenship to *all Jews*, even those Jews who stayed loyal or neutral.[50]

Levi did not attempt a point-by-point rebuttal of *Men and Measures*. Instead, he made one point that cut through everything else: Citizenship comes from service. It is an action and not a status. Jews answered the call;

therefore, they are citizens, and nothing else matters in a government ruled by the consent of the governed, not the dictates of history or a monarch.

It is unclear whether *Men and Measures* or Levi Sheftall's response had greater purchase on Georgia's government. Months after the exchange, the Georgia legislature mildly altered its religious establishment, granting "equal liberty and Toleration" to "all the different sects and denominations of the Christian religion," and permitting public money to be spent on Christian churches. Georgia's Baptists objected: "Religion does not need such carnal weapons as acts of assembly and civil sanctions, nor can they be applied to it without destroying it," they wrote. Only one county ever sought public funds for its churches. The law was certainly not invoked in 1788, when Mordecai Sheftall was elected as warden for Oglethorpe ward.[51] At the 1790 convention to draw up a new state constitution, Georgia abandoned its test oath altogether.

Levi Sheftall's response seems to have scuttled *Men and Measures*—but it was not just Sheftall's eloquence that did the job. Sheftall and the patriot Jews who left records in Georgia were also *white* Jews, and it was unquestionably easier for white Jews to act like rights-bearing people in the 1780s when whiteness was a virtual prerequisite for citizenship. This aspect of the effort for Jewish citizenship was usually unspoken, but it was at the very heart of the case that prompted *Men and Measures*. Sheftall in 1784 had "forcibly detained" an enslaved man named Trimmer, claimed by a Creek man named Samuel Nunez. Nunez wanted his property back.[52] According to Samuel's father Moses, Sheftall planned to sell Trimmer unless the court intervened.[53] The court's ruling determined that Nunez could not sue for damages, because as a non-white person, he had no legal standing in Georgia courts. Jews counted, Native Americans did not.

Except Nunez was *also* Jewish, son of a woman of the Creek nation and Moses Nunez. Moses Nunez was a Jewish trader and translator among the Creeks at Tuckabatchee for decades. Moses lived among and married into Native American family networks.[54] Samuel was therefore both Jewish *and* Creek, and related through his father to Mikveh Israel's Jonas Phillips. Samuel Nunez may not have practiced the Jewish faith among his Creek relatives in Tuckabatchee, but given that his Jewish father testified on his behalf, both he and Sheftall certainly knew about the Nunez family's Jewish heritage.[55] "The Citizen" knew it too, referring to Samuel as "descended of a white father (who is also supposed to be of the race of Jacob) and a free Indian mother."[56] Given that the "property" in question was a Black man, Mordecai must have understood his citizenship as connected to his whiteness when he argued that loyalty and not religion mattered in the new American state. And religion did not matter: Nunez could not claim citizenship by his family faith.

Race, however, did matter. In the 1784 Sheftall-Nunez case, the court ruled 2–1 that Sheftall had a right to sue and Nunez, "a Coloured Man," did not.[57] As "either Indian or otherwise," it was Nunez and not Sheftall who needed to show "that he is a Naturalized Citizen of this State under the said Act, so as to enjoy the Priviledges of a Free Citizen." Race as well as religion had been on the docket, which in turn had angered the author of *Men and Measures*, who felt that Jews should be accorded some status between African Americans and Native Americans. ("A Citizen" believed that Native nations should be treated as citizens, and in this way, "rise above the Jew.")[58] The court ruled instead that in 1784, race came first: "the Act of Assembly makes a distinction between White and Coloured People."[59]

White Jews rarely extended their case for religious citizenship outward to include any other disenfranchised groups. There were exceptions—Moses Nunez insisted on legal recognition of his three biracial children in his 1785 will—but in general Jews of European descent thought of themselves as white and sought legal definition of the fact.[60] Given the circumstances of the early republic, this motive is perhaps understandable—but it was not accidental. When the opportunity arose, American Jews struggling for civic rights often identified themselves as white and against non-whites engaged in similar efforts for legal recognition. Haym Salomon, for example, advertised in a Philadelphia newspapers for Joe, an enslaved man who "RAN AWAY." Salomon went so far as to warn that Joe "will endeavour to pass as a free man," which in a sense was what Salomon did in his 1784 letter to Fisher.[61] In the case of Sheftall, the long road to citizenship also involved a denial of citizenship to a fellow Jew. The Sheftalls' Jewishness did not stop them from becoming citizens, and Samuel Nunez's Jewishness did not save him from being cast out of citizenship.[62] Whiteness, like religious freedom, did not simply happen. Legally and culturally, religious freedom and racial unfreedom were constructed.

Jewish citizenship in the revolution's wake was not therefore a rising tide of freedom for all, nor did American Jews create religious freedom on their own. There were many forces leading to the decline of test oaths. But the work done by Jews made them look like rights-bearing citizens, and that work and that status was in turn recognized by the state in a transformative revolutionary moment. And that made a difference in practical religious freedom in the United States. Virtually every state with a significant revolutionary Jewish population lost its test oath before 1796. Almost every state without a sizable Jewish population in 1790 waited much longer before jettisoning its test oath, and often only after a subsequent political and religious battle.

Then and now, of course, state constitutions are small potatoes. (Sorry, Delaware.) Those who claim Christian origins for America reference the test oaths in the early state constitutions, but not their elimination a decade later. Meanwhile, many more people call the US Constitution a Christian document, which it does not claim to be—and some patriots of the Founding Era worried about that. Jews and Judaism were front and center as the debate over the federal Constitution stirred the nation.

7

"Congress Shall Make No Law . . ."

THERE WERE THOSE IN THE American Revolution who wanted to make the United States a Christian nation. Some of them tried to place Christian language in the nation's founding document. These efforts failed. Americans in the revolutionary period specifically considered a religious definition of the state and an explicit acknowledgment of Christianity by the government—and they said no.

It began with Virginia. In 1786, the state considered a general Christian establishment, and instead chose Jefferson's Statute on Religious Freedom. Virginia legislators turned down the idea of a Christian nation on political and religious grounds as representing the interference of government in matters exceeding its mandate. "If the Assembly have a right to determine the preference between Christianity, and other Systems of Religion that prevail in the world," noted one church meeting, "they may also, at a convenient time, give a preference to some favored sect among Christians."[1] Virginia Baptists knew which "favored sect" would get picked, and it was not theirs.

The first full disestablishment in the United States therefore came as a response to the effort to impose a state church. Virginia's Baptists had been able to swap support for the revolution in exchange for a weakening of the Christian establishment in 1776. But when the war ended, the Virginia legislature prepared to make the Anglicans once again the state form of religion (with the possible narrow addition of Presbyterians). The cry of "public virtue" came from Virginia's Anglican clergy. They maintained that morals were necessary for a republic, and Christianity was necessary for morals, so all Virginians ought to be taxed for the support of a general Christian establishment. Patrick Henry and John Marshall supported the idea. George Washington equivocated; he thought support for religious institutions was important, but he insisted that people only be required to support their own religion, and he specifically included both Christians and non-Christians. People ought to "support . . . that which they profess, if of the denominations of Christians; or declare themselves Jews, Mahometans or otherwise."[2]

Baptists and others said no. They looked to Jews and Muslims as examples of why a union of church and state hurt *Christianity*. A group of Virginians in the town of Chesterfield explained that establishing religion would force out all kinds of new allies just at the moment the state needed them: "Let Jews Mehomatans and Christians of every denomination enjoy religious liberty. . . . Thrust them not out now by establishing the Christian religion lest thereby we become our own enemies and weaken this infant State."[3]

James Madison did not much care for Baptist faith—he found it "obnoxious to sober opinion"—but he and Jefferson saw a deist-Baptist alliance as an opportunity to end Virginia's establishment.[4] Madison joined the Baptist groundswell and succeeded in delaying the establishment bill so that legislators could get a sense of public opinion—which turned the legislators decisively against a general Christian establishment. With Madison leading the opposition, the bill for a general establishment went down to defeat. There were not even enough votes to get it out of committee. Madison then guided Jefferson's Statute for Establishing Religious Freedom through the legislature. The Statute declared religious freedom and conscience to be "the natural rights of mankind," and that "our civil rights have no dependence on our religious opinions." The statute got rid of assessments for churches, state establishments, and test oaths; no one could be "compelled to frequent or support any religious worship" or "suffer on account of his religious opinions or beliefs." Matters of religion "shall in no wise diminish, enlarge, or affect their civil capacities." Madison did not even tolerate a late effort to at least mention Christianity in the bill. Opponents sought to insert the words "Jesus Christ" into the bill instead of the far more generic "the holy author of our religion." The legislature rejected that amendment almost 2 to 1. In January 1786, the unaltered statute became law by an even wider margin.[5]

Average Virginia Protestants seemed in favor of a full disestablishment. Prince Edward County Presbyterians asked for disestablishment to "relieve us from a long Night of ecclesiastical bondage."[6] Madison found his "table was loaded with petitions & remonstrances from all parts against the interposition of the Legislature in matters of Religion."[7] Baptist stalwart John Leland said, "The notion of a Christian commonwealth should be exploded forever." If Christians received any worldly aid or emolument, then it would be impossible to tell who was a Christian by faith and who was a Christian for profit. Better, Leland said, "If a man merits the confidence of his neighbors, in Virginia, let him worship one God, twenty Gods, or no God—be Jew, Turk, Pagan, or infidel, he is eligible to any office in the state."[8] Leland was likely echoing Thomas Jefferson's published quip that "it does me no injury for my neighbour to say there are twenty gods, or no god. It neither picks my pocket nor breaks my leg."

Leland's Jews, Muslims, and pagans were largely theoretical. Few Jews resided in Virginia before 1769, when Jacob I. Cohen arrived—the same Cohen who joined South Carolina's Jew Company, helped refound Philadelphia's synagogue in 1782, and whose marriage to a convert caused an uproar over authority in Mikveh Israel.[9] So there was at least one patriot Jew in Virginia when Madison fought for disestablishment, and the question is whether that affected the debate. What were the odds that Cohen and Madison actually knew each other?

They knew each other. In 1782, Edmund Randolph had written to Madison about a mutual business deal facilitated by "Mr. Coan, the Jew in this town."[10] Cohen met Madison in Philadelphia, where Cohen had joined the Patriot synagogue and where Madison was serving in Congress. In August 1782—at the exact moment Cohen was struggling with the synagogue junta as to whether they could bless his marriage—Cohen made a loan of fifty pounds sterling to Madison to keep him afloat during American peace negotiations.[11] At the same time, Madison also noted he had taken out a loan from "Haym Solomon, a Jew Broker"—that is, Haym Salomon, another Philadelphia Jew involved in Mikveh Israel.[12] Such loans had kept the government in operation; runaway wartime inflation made boarding in Philadelphia more and more expensive.[13] Madison later noted that "other members of Cong[res]s from Virginia whose resources public & private had been cut off" received financial help from Salomon, "on a small scale for current wants. We regarded him as upright, intelligent, and friendly in his transactions with us."[14]

The point is not whether Cohen or Salomon spoke in favor of religious freedom with Madison or whether they convinced him that Jewish rights were worth protecting. The point is that Madison knew and worked with at least two Jewish patriots during his time in Congress. Cohen had even served in uniform. When Madison advocated religious disestablishment in 1786, he knew full well that America had more religions than just the diverse sects of Christianity—and that patriot sentiment extended beyond the bounds of Christian churches.

As a political idea, disestablishment had Jewish supporters in Philadelphia and Richmond, and powerful Baptist advocates in Virginia. Yet the rest of the country was a hodgepodge of regulations and restrictions. In 1787, the Articles of Confederation had no state arrangements with the church and so had nothing to disestablish; the words "God" and "church" do not appear in the Articles, and "religion" occurs only in reference to a mutual defense pact. Moreover, disestablishment was not the same thing as religious freedom; New Jersey's 1776 constitution cut all taxes for support of religious establishment at the same time it declared that only Protestants could hold public office. North Carolina made the same restriction, and also granted all church lands the colony had possessed to the Anglicans.[15] Such "glebe lands" as they were called, could be lucrative. In South Carolina, monies generated from glebe lands probably gave the Anglican church greater authority in the early republic than it would otherwise have had—power coupled with its de facto position as the state's Protestant church.[16] South Carolina's 1778 constitution made "Christian Protestantism . . . the established religion of the state." In order to define what "Protestantism" was, the state constitution listed five separate theological articles to which all elected officials had to swear. The articles were taken from the Anglican Book of Common Prayer.[17] In other words, the law defined "Christian Protestantism" as Anglicanism and went from there.

In the wake of the revolution, disestablishment and religious freedom existed alongside state churches and test acts. Jews, Baptists, and other Americans were petitioning to change that. But there was no religious crisis in the 1780s that mandated a broad shift in favor of religious freedom. Instead, the shift came as part of wholly different upheaval—the Constitutional Convention.

Religious pressure did not provoke the Constitution. Textbooks are correct in noting that concerns over the weakness of the Articles had Franklin, Washington, Madison, and others worried about runaway democracy. State legislatures were making things easy for debtors and hard for creditors, leading to a credit crunch that the haves disliked and the have-nots loved. Daniel Shays's 1786 attempt to prevent the state of Massachusetts from collecting his taxes ended particularly badly. Yet a weak central government that could not collect taxes was precisely what Americans had fought the revolution to get, so Shays's Rebellion did not provoke a universal call for a new system of government. That explains in part why the Constitutional Convention kept its meetings secret in 1787, with notes forbidden and windows latched.[18]

Independence Hall was full of Framers, but a religious establishment and religious freedom both went almost unmentioned. Religion almost never came up during the long summer of drafting the document. The text of the Constitution itself shows this lack of interest. The First Amendment's broad protections were (naturally) an *amendment*—not in the original draft of 1787. The lack of protections for religious liberty did not seem to bother the delegates to the convention, who were far more concerned about preventing state governments from printing money. (That's Article 1, Section 10, which one Framer called "a great favorite of mine.")[19] Madison's secret notes recorded much rhetoric concerning the slave trade, the powers of the legislature, and representation for small and large states, but little about religious liberty.

In fact, the convention actually decided not to pray. On June 28, in the middle of a cantankerous debate over representation in Congress, Benjamin Franklin rose and declared that "God Governs in the affairs of men" and "without his concurring aid we shall succeed in this political building no better, than the Builders of Babel." It was an extraordinarily move for the old sage. Franklin rarely made direct calls for prayer. Now he moved that "henceforth prayers imploring the assistance of Heaven, and its blessings on our deliberations, be held in this Assembly every morning before we proceed to business, and that one or more of the Clergy of this City be requested to officiate in that Service." Alexander Hamilton objected. If they brought in a minister to start praying for them, it would "lead the public to believe that the embarrassments and dissensions within the convention, had suggested this measure," and would destroy public faith in the convention. (Madison noted that "several others" objected as well, but he did not record their thoughts.) Edmund Randolph (another friend of Cohen's) suggested a compromise—invite a preacher for July 4, presumably to obscure their difficulties, and "thenceforward prayers be used in the Convention every morning."[20]

But the call for daily prayers did not pass. After a brief debate, the convention simply adjourned "without any vote on the motion." There were no daily official prayers at the Constitutional Convention—which stands in marked contrast to the assumption of public religiosity many modern observers ascribe to these men. Perhaps that is to be expected. John Rutledge, for example, openly declared "Religion & humanity had nothing to do with this question. Interest alone is the governing principle with nations." He was defending his support for the slave trade.[21]

The text of the Constitution itself contains only one reference to religion: Article 6 declares that members of the federal government must uphold the Constitution, "but no religious test shall ever be required as a qualification to any office or public trust under the authority of the U. States." It essentially swept away all test oaths for the future federal government, and it passed overwhelmingly, with little debate. Only the delegations from Maryland and North Carolina voted no. Perhaps not coincidentally, both states would be the settings for public efforts to prevent Jews from holding office—Carolina in 1808, and Maryland 1818–1823.

Indeed, the most public religious event surrounding the convention might have been a literal witch hunt. On May 5—the day Madison arrived—public suspicion fell on a woman known as "Korbmacher" in South Philadelphia. Several street preachers blamed her for the death of an infant, and soon a mob attacked her "upon the supposition that she was a witch." Korbmacher survived, but in July, the mob came for her again. This time, the mob carried her through the streets, hooting and pelting her with stones. Korbmacher died of her injuries. The same newspapers that carried rumors about the secret proceedings at Independence Hall also carried the story of Korbmacher's lynching and death.[22]

None of the delegates recorded a response to the witch hunt of 1787. But at least one patriot did. In November 1787, a writer known only as "Old Whig" wondered how far the people could be trusted to run a government if they were out in the streets lynching women for witchcraft? An attack against a suspected witch was "an example to warn us how little we ought to trust the unrestrained discretion of human nature," he wrote. It was a good reason, Old Whig warned, to demand a Bill of Rights be attached to the Constitution.

Old Whig had seized upon one of the great controversies of the Constitution in its own day. It was meant to be a document of "We the

People." Indeed, the Framers went to some length arguing that only "the people," not state legislatures, could ratify the document. But questions about religious freedom underlined the tricky part of the question: Who *were* "the people"? Was it God's law or natural law that made this commonwealth? The process of ratification embodied this strange reverence for and ambivalence about "the people" as the source of authority. Madison told the convention "the new national constitution ought to have the highest source of authority," yet Madison did not favor a direct popular vote on the Constitution.[23] The Convention declared that the Constitution would become law only through a series of dedicated ratifying conventions. Such a move allowed for popular choice but fixed the actual final ratification vote in the hands of a discrete number of men whom Madison and his allies could lobby.

At the same time, however, the vote for ratifying conventions was opened up to a broader array of Americans than before. Nathaniel Gorham of New Hampshire noted that ratification conventions were superior to state legislatures: "In the States, many of the ablest men are excluded from the Legislatures, but may be elected into a Convention." Gorham was specifically talking about the clergy, but he could well have meant Jews, Baptists, Catholics, or any other religious minority.[24]

Federalists knew that the voting public in 1787 was something quite different from the public at large. Voting for the "ablest men" almost always excluded women as well as nonwhites and the poor. Revolutionary lawmaker David Ramsay simply declared African Americans "inhabitants, not citizens"—expected to live "agreeably to the fixed laws, without any participation in government." A thin trickle of manumission after the revolution slightly reduced slavery in Virginia and led to its abolition in Pennsylvania. But it did not change ex-slaves into full citizens. Meanwhile, John Adams dismissed women's claims to citizenship by writing that women were "designed for domestic concerns," despite his wife Abigail's plea that he should "remember the ladies."[25]

Yet borders between the public and the voting public remained permeable. The excuses offered by Ramsay, Adams, and others did not engage the essential nature of what a citizen was, and the very notion of African American and female citizenship did get a hearing in the early republic. Property-owning women in New Jersey actually voted in the 1790s, as we've seen. In 1790, the state legislature confirmed women's suffrage when passing an election statute referring to voters as "he or she." African

Americans, meanwhile, rarely received the vote, but depending on the state they lived in, they achieved what one historian calls an "approximation of citizenship" in the immediate wake of the revolution.[26] Piecemeal emancipation in Pennsylvania and New York occasionally allowed free Black men to vote. In slaveholding Maryland in the post-revolutionary era, free Blacks emancipated before 1783 retained their right to vote; those freed afterward gained no such right. Even this "approximation of citizenship" closed in 1802, when the state limited the right to vote to "free white male citizens, and no other." For a short while, however, the possibilities for voting expanded. The idea of "the people" was inchoate and slippery in the early republic. Freedom might be contagious, but plenty of Founders wanted to inoculate the nation.[27]

So did the Founders mean to include Jews as "ablest men" or even as "the people"? No Jews were elected to the ratifying conventions, but several close allies of Jewish patriots were. In South Carolina, Samuel Lushington (Gentile commander of the "Jew Company") served in the ratifying convention, and joined the majority in voting for the Constitution. Lushington likely counted actual Jewish votes in his column in 1787; poll lists for Charleston in 1787 are spotty, but one election list included Isaac DaCosta revolutionary patriot from Mikveh Israel, as well as Philip Hart, who signed the synagogue's letter to President Washington in 1790.[28] John Wereat and George Walton, Mordecai Sheftall's friends and allies from the patriot cause, both won election to the Georgia ratifying convention, and Wereat served as its president. He voted yes, as did the convention.[29]

But that was not the case everywhere. Pennsylvania's ratifying convention picked as its president Frederick Muhlenberg, son of the pastor Henry Muhlenberg, who directly opposed non-Christians in government. Pennsylvania ratified. In New York, John Jay prominently defended the Constitution, and (secretly) wrote some of the *Federalist Papers*; he was also on the record as opposing Jewish rights. New York also ratified.

This kind of ambivalence suggests the obvious: Jewish rights were an issue in ratification, but they were certainly not *the* issue. Religious liberty as a whole took on an amorphous shape in the ratification debates. Neither Federalists nor Anti-Federalists had a coherent plan for it. It was not clear in 1787 what the Constitution would do with religious freedom. After all the Constitution *as originally drafted* that year had no First Amendment, though it did insist that "no religious test" ever be asked of federal officeholders. That was precisely what worried some people. "An

Enquirer" in Montgomery County, Pennsylvania, noted that his traveling companions all condemned the proposed government "as a vile system of tyranny." Their objections included the complaint that "a Roman Catholic and a Jew stood as good a chance of being President of the United States as a Christian." But that was only part of the worry. "An Enquirer" also noted complaints about a lack of hunting and fishing rights, an absence of a ban on theater, and reported one man who "had lately broken a new wagon in driving it over a piece of bad road, [and] complained that it contained nothing in favor of repairing our road."[30]

In other words, the Constitution held in such reverence in the twenty-first century was not well-loved in the eighteenth. It seemingly had something in it for everyone to hate. The voting public was going to critique every part of the proposed new government rather than separately vote on religious disestablishment and the end of federal test oaths. Once again, Jewish rights were present in the entire revolutionary question in the United States, not in a separate act.

The deliberations to create the US Constitution were kept secret. The argument over whether to accept it, on the other hand, was public. Those in favor (Federalists) wrote an array of essays, including the *Federalist Papers*, which were reprinted across the young nation. (When asked about the Constitution's chances for ratification, Washington wrote that "much will depend on . . . the recommendation of it by good pens.") Anti-Federalists wrote "hundreds of essays and short squibs," some of which had wide circulation but which more often were published only once.[31]

This public debate in many ways justified the Constitution, especially when Anti-Federalists succeeded in adding a Bill of Rights. The Constitution gained legitimacy in part from the public it created through the print debate over it. Americans, as the saying goes, put up their constitutional roof before they built their national walls. Arguing over what comprised the highest law bridged significant gaps in a fairly heterogeneous (if white and male) citizenry. Federalists and Anti-Federalists both claimed to speak for "the people," and, in the process, they began the long process of defining what and who the American people were. Jews were explicitly part of this process; religious freedom for non-Christians was considered and accepted not only by the Constitution but through the debates.

Federalists sought to confirm the Constitution. Anti-Federalists sought to block it. Each side pointed to aspects of religious liberty in ways that favored their own positions. In North Carolina, Anti-Federalist Henry Abbott denounced the absence of religious tests in the Constitution; the majority of his district was Presbyterian, Abbott argued, but, with no religious test, "Pagans, Deists, and Mahometans might obtain offices among us." Federalist James Iredell countered: "America has set an example to mankind to think more modestly and reasonably; that a man may be of different religious sentiments from our own, without being a bad member of society."[32] Both men thought the national character necessitated their position.

Speeches and essays often referred to Jews as hypothetical Americans. One writer simply listed Jews along with Quakers, Muslims, Deists, beggars, and Blacks—he used more derogatory terms—and lambasted the Constitution for failing to ban any of those "abominable wretches."[33] New Hampshire Federalist John Sullivan listed religion as chief among the objections of the Constitution's opponents, "blinded through excess of zeal for the Cause of Religion." Anti-Federalists, Sullivan wrote, thought the "Security of our having the holy Scriptures" was at stake if "a Turk, a Jew, a Roman Catholic and what is worse than all a universalist may be president of the United States."[34]

Of course, Jews, Muslims, and Universalists were in short supply as candidates for office in New Hampshire during ratification. As Sullivan intimated, the real concern was not that any particular Jew would become president but rather a belief that Protestant Christianity could not survive without test oaths and state sanction. If no oaths were required, was *any* religion acceptable? Did patriot feeling or religious confession make an American? To drive the point home, Anti-Federalists frequently invoked the specter of Jews, Muslims, and Catholics as potential threats. If the Constitution "gives the command of the whole militia to the President," wrote one New York essayist, then "should he hereafter be a Jew, our dear posterity may be ordered to rebuild Jerusalem."[35]

The most famous author in the debate mostly dodged the question of religious freedom. "Publius," the pen name for the combined efforts of Alexander Hamilton, James Madison, and John Jay (authors of the *Federalist Papers*), never mentioned Jews at all and barely mentioned religion. It bears repeating that the writings most obsessively connected to constitutional interpretation in the twenty-first century have nothing to say on the topic of religious freedom. Federalist 19 briefly discusses religion in Switzerland, but as part of a discussion on the importance of a unified foreign policy, not religious freedom and the state. The *Papers* contain no references to Christ or Christianity, and it contains only a single sidelong reference to rights of self-preservation as decreed by "nature's God."[36]

Federalists did not want to talk about religion. Anti-Federalists did. While Publius lectured New Yorkers on the philosophical benefits of the Constitution, Pennsylvania's Anti-Federalists issued their objections to the document. Number one was the need for "the right of conscience to be held inviolate" and a clause guaranteeing the federal government could not alter any law that "provide[s] for the preservation of liberty in matters of religion."[37] Publius might have been avoiding a wedge issue by skipping over religion. John Jay in particular would have wanted to avoid the issue, since he was clearly not an advocate for full religious freedom—he had, as noted, complained about Jewish rights and blocked Catholic liberty in New York's constitution.

Under pressure, Federalists turned to Jewish citizenship as an argument *for* the Constitution. John Leland asked, "Why should a man be proscribed, or any wife disgraced, for being a Jew, a Turk, a Pagan, or a Christian of any denomination, when his talents and veracity as a civilian entitles him to the confidence of the public?"[38] Weighing citizens by talent and truthfulness aided the Christian cause, as Samuel Spencer told North Carolina's ratifying convention: "As there is not a religious test required, it leaves religion on the solid foundation of its own inherent validity" rather than propped up by state favors. "Gentlemen urge that the want of a test admits the most vicious characters to offices," he continued. "I desire to know what test could bind them. If they were of such principles, it would not keep them from enjoying those offices. On the other hand, it would exclude from offices conscientious and truly religious people."[39] As one historian has put it about the debate over religious tests, "If Muslims, Jews, and Catholics . . . embodied all that was alien and menacing to the American status quo, they also became simultaneously emblematic of the principles of universal religious freedom and political equality enshrined in the Constitution."[40]

Anti-Federalists seemed divided over hypothetical Jews. Unified in opposition to the proposed federal government, Anti-Federalists could not agree on an alternative. The movement therefore included both those who thought the Constitution needed an explicit religious warrant or test oath to limit religious freedom and those who thought the Constitution needed an explicit declaration of religious liberty. The Anti-Federalist known as

"M" opposed the Constitution because he feared "Jews, infidels, papists, deists, or atheists" in government.[41] Abraham Yates, however, declared that "rather than to Adopt the Constitution I would *Risk* a government of Jew, turk or Infidel"[42]

Anti-Federalist voices therefore advocated all sorts of relationships between church and state. The writer Centinel said the Constitution needed a "declaration, that all men have a natural and unalienable right to worship Almighty God, according to the dictates of their own conscience and understanding."[43] One Virginia Baptist wrote on behalf of his brethren that "What is dearest of all—*Religious Liberty*, is not Sufficiently Secured," and that as a result if a president and a majority of Congress favored one religion over another, "they may oblige all others to pay to the Support of their System as Much as they please." He would not accept assurances otherwise: "If Oppression does not ensue, it will be owing to the Mildness of Administration & not to any Constitutional defense."[44]

Spencer had good reason to fear, for other Americans wanted church and state connected directly. The citizens of Townshend, Massachusetts, held a town meeting on the last day of 1787 and declared, "We think it necessary that our Civil rulers be professors of the true religion." Therefore, they could not agree "to a Constitution which will admit into governt. Atheists Deists Papists or abettors of any false religion, tho we would not Exclude any Denomination of Protestants." If "True religion" was the foundation of good government, the people had a right to require the Constitution to include a provision about the "public worship of God" and require others to follow it. The Massachusetts state constitution allowed such things, after all.[45]

Townsend's citizens put the question directly: Was it enough for those who served to merely be good men, or did they need to be Christian? Could anything other than Christianity secure morality? Others wondered whether insisting on Christianity actually harmed morality, by keeping those who would not take false oaths out of office while doing nothing to prevent oath-breakers from getting in. One Massachusetts writer warned against the "the cloak of religion" that promoted plans "detrimental to the peace and happiness of mankind."[46] John Sullivan described his Anti-Federalist opponents as wearing "the masque of sanctity."[47] In South Carolina, Presbyterian minister Francis Cummins vacillated on the "no religious test" clause at the ratifying convention. He ultimately supported the Constitution, since to compel worship was "to take it away from him by force."[48] William Vans Murray, an American in London, echoed those comments in his book *Political Sketches*: "If there be a man in the empire excluded from the fullest rights of citizenship, mere[ly] on account of his religion, the law which excludes him is founded on force, and is a violation of the laws of nature." He praised the ban on test oaths: "Christians are not the only people there. There are men, besides Christians, who while they discharge every social duty are shut from the rights of citizenship."[49]

Another pseudonymous pamphleteer assumed that any morality grounded in nature would fail. Christianity being supernatural did not have this flaw.[50] Preacher David Tappan wrote, "Virtue enlightened and invigorated by political and christian knowledge, is eminently the soul of the republic." An October essay in Virginia called for more explicit connections between church and state: "The native charms of moral rectitude... are too feeble to ensure the requisite practice of virtue when opposed to the allurements of self-interest and self-gratification." Only Christianity could check "the want of virtue, public and private" which were "one principal source of our distresses." The writer proposed providing state money to churches to ensure Christian morality.[51]

These views—that Christianity had a special place in American law and American civic life, and non-Christians had no place in the republic—were discussed and debated in the early republic. Yet, once again, those ideas went down to defeat. Oliver Ellsworth ("A Landholder," in the Connecticut newspapers) explained that Christianity was not the basis of the law, because "I am accountable, not to man, but to God, for the religious opinions which I embrace." Governments needed only "to protect the citizens in his rights, to defend the community from hostile powers, and to promote the general welfare." That required no particular religious affiliation. Making officeholders assent to a creed of any sort made them "either a saint by law, or a hypocrite by practice." Madison agreed in *Federalist* 10: "We well know that neither moral nor religious motives can be relied on as an adequate control."[52] This was the view of the Constitution even before the Anti-Federalists added the Bill of Rights. The pleas of Townsend and the notion that Christianity was inherent in the law were considered and rejected.

American Jews of 1787 understood the stakes and generally supported the Federalists. One Pennsylvania observer described the pro-Constitution faction as consisting of former soldiers, shopkeepers, "attorneys-at-law, public defaulters, and Jews." He did not mean it as a compliment.[53] The Savannah synagogue wrote to Washington in 1789 with specific praise for "the energy of federal influence" that has "enfranchised us with all the privileges and immunities of free citizens, and initiated us into the grand mass of legislative mechanism."[54] As the new federal government got under way in New York, Gershom Seixas led Shearith Israel in thanksgiving for the "conclusion of the late war," the "establishment of public liberty," and "the new constitution."[55]

A new constitution—not just a new set of rules but a break with older British ideas of liberty as a collection of traditions, instead of as a birthright: Seixas, like other Federalists, noted how the US Constitution marked a *discontinuity* with British and European law. Common law and precedent from Britain did not apply—which was how a Jew like Mordecai Sheftall came to run the wartime patriot committee of Savannah. Madison and other Federalists saw the Constitution as a written declaration of the grounds and power of government; it was not an outgrowth of British tradition. Letting common law stand, Madison pointed out, would have "brought over from G. B. a thousand heterogeneous & antirepublican doctrines." Indeed, the anti-Semitic (and anti-Black) arguments Sheftall encountered in the 1784 *Men and Measures* pamphlet had relied on British common law as *the* law: "The Jews in Georgia at present stand upon the same footing they did in England in the year 1732," when Georgia was founded. To the pamphleteer, people carried the law with them: "When a free people . . . migrate to a new soil, with intent to settle the same, they carry with them as their birthright all the laws of their mother country then in force." Jews had not been made citizens by Parliament; they were aliens then and so aliens now.[56]

Madison and the Federalists said otherwise: The American people had broken with Britain as a people and had established a new government on their own authority—and that government, codified in the Constitution, began with the people and not with a specific act of God or grant from a church. It was a new social compact. The lack of precedent resulted in the creation of new freedoms. American Jews helped create, in their own small way, that discontinuity.[57]

A little-noticed aspect of American life is the irony that "the best-loved portions of the Constitution appear in the first ten amendments," as historian Woody Holton notes. Americans tend to identify the Bill of Rights with the Constitution and the Constitution with the "Founding Fathers." But of course, the Framers of the Constitution never intended to have a Bill of Rights; their opponents foisted it onto the Constitution as the price of acquiescence. Anti-Federalists failed to block the Constitution, but they squeezed concessions from several ratifying conventions. If the Federalists wanted to codify the power of government, they also had to codify the rights of citizens. The Bill of Rights was a gift of the Anti-Federalists, and a challenge the Federalists accepted. Adding a Bill of Rights could bridge the gap; it could give both Federalists and Anti-Federalists a stake in the amended Constitution as the basis of government.[58] In terms of Jewish rights, the acceptance of the Constitution (with a Bill of Rights) by both Federalists and Anti-Federalists assured that the idea of a self-created people without specific religious warrant—with Jews in—would become the basis of American law and government.[59]

Anti-Federalists in seven states attached or published proposed amendments along with their official notice of ratification. (North Carolina and Rhode Island did as well, but they initially rejected the Constitution.) All told, the conventions proposed over 100 possible amendments for a Bill of Rights. The proposals ranged widely. They included guarantees for familiar rights (trial by jury, freedom of speech), and other recommendations that waited until the twentieth century for ratification (term limits for the president, a ban on poll taxes). There were a few oddball amendments too. Virginia wanted an amendment mandating that Congress publish its proceedings once a year. However, virtually all the states who insisted on a Bill of Rights included religious freedom as a proposed amendment. Maryland requested an amendment declaring "no national religion established by law, but that all Persons be equally entitled to Protection in their religious liberty." New Hampshire was blunt: "Congress shall make no laws touching religion." Virginia included two proposed amendments on religion: one protecting the rights of religious pacifists, and the other declaring that "no particular sect or society ought to [be] favored or established by law." The use of "society" as well as "sect" indicated these Anti-Federalists were thinking beyond Christianity.[60]

None of the proposals suggested adding a religious test. Some Anti-Federalists groused that "a Christian country" should "hold out some distinction between the professors of Christianity and downright infidelity or paganism."[61] But when it came down to it, not a single convention proposed a new test oath. None sought to add a word about America as a Christian nation. South Carolina did mention that the phrase "no religious test" should read "no other religious test," as taking any oath was by definition religious. But it did not claim that any particular religion or any form of Christianity needed to be added to the document. Anti-Federalists argued for religious liberty and for test oaths at the same time, but when it came to codifying their concerns, the former won out.

Whittling dozens of amendments down to a workable list became Madison's job at the first Congress in 1789. Madison drew up a summary list of twenty amendments, despite protests from Anti-Federalists seeking a vote on *every* proposed amendment one by one. Madison originally wanted the amendments inserted into the text of the Constitution itself, so that Article 1, Section 9 would include the phrase "the civil rights of none shall be abridged on account of religious belief or worship, nor shall any national religion be established, nor shall the full and equal rights of conscience be in any manner or on any pretext infringed." That mouthful more or less combined most of the proposed religious freedom amendments. But the word "national" worried Elbridge Gerry of Massachusetts (who made it a habit to object to virtually everything Madison proposed in those days). Surely, Gerry argued, the government was meant to be federal and not national? Gerry also attempted to specify the sects who would be granted rights of conscience—to argue that only Quakers and Moravians, with long-standing pacifist principles, could argue for a religious exemption to military service. Thomas Scott of Pennsylvania then mentioned the danger of freethinkers as a class of Americans to whom he did not want to give the rights of conscience. In other words, the First Congress debated whether to specify particular Christian sects and no other religions in its guarantees of religious freedom. They voted no. The House of Representatives opted for Samuel Livermore's generic "Congress shall make no laws touching on religion or the rights of conscience" which avoided the troublesome word "national."[62]

The First Amendment still had not reached its final form. Roger Sherman, who had served at the Constitutional Convention and now sat in the House of Representatives, succeeded after several votes in having the amendments attached *after* the Constitution's text rather than inserted within it. The Senate, taking up Madison and Livermore's phrasing, reshuffled some of the amendments, got rid of others, and made minor wording changes. The House and Senate held a conference committee, and the phrase "Congress shall make no law respecting an establishment of Religion, or prohibiting the free exercise thereof" entered American social and legal vocabulary.

That language passed Congress as the third amendment. The original first amendment concerned apportionment of seats in Congress, and the second forbade Congress to raise its own pay. Those two never got ratified by enough states, and so what would have been the third became the First Amendment, enshrining freedom of religion, speech, the press, petition, and assembly. That put the language and location of the First Amendment in its familiar location: broadly writ, focused on individual liberties, and separate from the main body of the Constitution.

Congressman Aedenus Burke thought the new amendments were "frothy and full of wind, formed only to please the palate." Burke and his allies had pushed hard for more substantial structural changes to the Constitution, but Madison and the First Congress left those aside and instead shored up individual rights. The debates on amending the Constitution ended up collecting a series of rights that "Federalist and Anti-Federalists alike claimed to cherish," as one historian puts it, formulating them into a broadly acceptable list, while simultaneously avoiding the structural changes men like Burke had wanted.[63] The amendments therefore "read like instructive guidelines rather than definitive compilations or explicit legal commands."[64]

Madison loved the amendments for that very reason. They were not just law, he wrote, but a guide for future generations. Madison wrote that they could "serve as public markers, signals that could activate and sharpen public awareness, especially over time."[65] He did not intend these rights merely to exist as artifacts, but as aspirations. Madison's final wording of the First Amendment perfectly fit that purpose: They did not mention specific religions, nor specific rights of religion. Neither Jews nor Quakers received a specific "emancipation" because the existence of citizenship preceded any confessional association. The Amendments confirmed what the revolution created: a broad religious citizenship that did not belong to any particular church or tradition. Congress was not to touch "religion." And that liberty was written into a separate list of discrete amendments that probably helped the language serve as Madison hoped—as "public markers . . . over time."

American Jews rejoiced. Gershom Seixas praised the Constitution in front of his congregation and later sermonized about the divine blessings of living in a country "where no exception is taken from following the principles of our religion" and "a Magistracy, who are disposed to sanction every religious model of worship."[66] Richmond's tiny but growing

Jewish community held a banquet to celebrate the Constitution's ratification in 1788 and gave this toast: "May the Israelites throughout the world enjoy the same religious rights and political advantages as their American brethren."[67]

What is more, the Federalists—the supporters and drafters of the Constitution—knew of Jewish support and responded to it. The strongest evidence of the mutual respect comes from yet another "federal parade" organized by Hamilton and Federalist allies in New York in July 1788. Virginia had narrowly approved the Constitution, but New York's Federalists still had to face their ratifying convention. In order to demonstrate public support for the new government, Hamilton arranged for a massive parade to show public support.

In a small but important move, the organizers delayed the parade from July 22 to July 23, specifically "in order to give the Jews an opportunity to Join in the festivals, the 22nd being one of their holidays." Tish B'Av that year fell on July 22, and although there were not many Jews in the city, New York Federalists wanted them in the parade. So the Federalists moved the parade back a day. "I think it a great Compliment paid the Jews," wrote Federalist Adrian Bancker. The parade featured clergy of all different denominations, including Seixas representing the Jews. At the banquet afterward, "the members of the Clergy from the City, Anglicans, Presbyterians, Catholics, Lutherans, Calvinists, Jews, all indiscriminately seated"—all made citizens. Federalists did not merely accept or tolerate Jews; they actively sought them out and supported them.[68]

The federal Constitution was not written for Jews, and it was not written with much Jewish-American input. Yet the theoretical question of Jews and the actual presence of Jewish Americans found its way into the debate, and that debate concluded with a constitution that, at least on paper, included Jews and other religions as full citizens at the federal level. Moreover, the process deliberately scrubbed pre-existing European common law and its anti-Jewish artifacts, while legitimating through ratification and debate the idea of people self-created.

So American Jews began to pursue the logical conclusion of living in a state without Protestant scaffolding. If, as Seixas taught, Jews followed the same moral requirements as everyone else, and if moral virtue rather than creedal statements comprised the body politic, and if Jews gave "strength and stability to the laws entered into by our representatives," then Jews were members of the body politic and needed no particular legislative act to achieve citizenship. If the United States was "the only place where the Jews have not suffered persecution," as Seixas wrote in 1810, then they could and should help build the republic. They began that work right away.

8

<hr>

Alien and Sedition

JEWS LOVED GEORGE WASHINGTON. In Richmond, Beth Shalome synagogue wrote out a new prayer for the federal government. In translation, the 1789 prayer thanked God for placing "the President of the United States to act as our leader," and asking for "Common sense, knowledge and insight upon the head of our state, May he act justly towards us, gladden and bring joy to our hearts." But the real veneration for the president was more apparent in the Hebrew—the first letter of each line of the prayer spelled out *vav aleph shin yod nun gimel tet aleph nun*—"VASHINGTON." (There is no "W" sound in Hebrew.) The prayer was an acrostic for the name of the American president.[1]

The Jewish enthusiasm for Washington extended to the president's allies, at least in the early days of his administration. "Federalists" was a nickname applied both to supporters of the Constitution and to the Washington administration. Historians often refer to them as a "political party," but they had little of the organizational or financial apparatus of modern Republicans and Democrats. Federalist leaders tended to be those who had served in the Confederation Congress or in Washington's army, with reputations built across state lines. They also tended to be those who suffered most from the economic depression that hit the nation at the war's end. In those first few years, Federalists also tended to support broad religious freedoms.

Jews made for natural Federalists in 1790. The wartime experience of Mikveh Israel had forged them as a national group; the Jewish leadership of New York, South Carolina, and Georgia had worked together to build a patriot synagogue in Pennsylvania. Jews had been soldiers in Washington's army and allies of the Confederation Congress. Jews thought and pressed for rights on a national scale. While not all synagogues faced the credit crunch of the mid-1780s, Mikveh Israel did. As patriot Jews headed home, Mikveh Israel was left with nation-sized bills and only a local membership to pay them. ("Continental Mon'y it will not purchas[e] straw with us," grumbled Moses Gomez.)[2]

South Carolina's Jews took advantage of their voting rights to back Federalists and religious liberty, particularly in the 1790 election for delegates to revise the state constitution. "As none of our brethren were delegates," wrote Nathan Levin, "they determined to support such persons" as would uphold the rights of the Jews. Their preferred candidate was Charles Cotesworth Pinckney (Federalist nominee for president in 1804). Others who received the "undivided support" of Charleston's Jews included Edward Rutledge, David Ramsay, William Drayton—all pro-Constitution men. Richard Lushington, the Gentile commander of the Revolution's "Jew Company," served as a delegate as well.[3] The 1790 convention and its new constitution dumped the 1778 state establishment and its five theological requirements for official religion, leaving only a guarantee for religious liberty.[4] Delegate Christopher Knight wrote to the synagogue to express thanks for "the assistance I received from you and the members of the congregation at the late election." Knight also thought he should offer the Jews some money, "to serve the poor or be of any use in any respect to the congregation." Hazan Jacob Cohen wisely returned the funds. Though certain of Knight's "good intention," Cohen and Beth Elohim refused the money lest "it may be suggested . . . that the members of our community were to be bought."[5]

Other prominent Jews gravitated around Washington and his allies. Solomon Simson worked on plans for a mint with John Jay; Simson and Isaac Moses were clients of Alexander Hamilton.[6] Pinckney recommended Abraham Seixas to Washington for a federal post.[7] Solomon Bush made repeated applications to the president for a diplomatic office, highlighting his work for American shipping in London.[8] Meanwhile, opposition to the Washington administration began to dabble in anti-Semitism. Alexander Hamilton's plans to assume state debts and charter a national bank became one of the first targets. One newspaper included this bit of doggerel:

A public debt's, a public blessing,
Which 'tis of course a crime to lessen.
Each day a fresh report he broaches,
That Spies and Jews may ride in coach[es].

The reference to the public debt was an unmistakable jab at Hamilton, who had declared "A national debt, if it is not excessive, will be to us a national blessing." Hamilton—who attended a Jewish school in the Caribbean—was not branded as a Jew, but his economic plans received their share of anti-Semitic slurs. One newspaper said that the beneficiaries of Hamilton's plan would be "Jews, members of Congress, and foreigners." The *New York Journal* refused to print the word "penis," but left little doubt to readers when it referred to Hamilton and his cronies: "The ***** of these people may be unmutilated, and may be in the original Christian state, but their minds are far gone in Israelitish avarice."[9]

Federalists seemed to have a lock on Jewish support in 1790. It was not a critical alliance for Washington—American Jews were a tiny sliver of the voting population—but Jewish devotion to Washington, the president's support for religious freedom, and the opposition's flirtation with anti-Semitism brought the two together.

Yet just ten years later, most Jews would identify with the opposition Jeffersonians, and it would be the Federalists dallying in anti-Semitic attacks. The Sheftall clan made the move. In 1792, Sheftall Sheftall critiqued the French Revolution, a sure sign of Federalism: "Our friends the French I am afraid Are Going down hill—a mob Rules."[10] Yet by 1796 Mordecai Sheftall had been elected to the state legislature as a Jeffersonian and was exchanging political gossip with James Jackson, Georgia's senator and a Jefferson elector.[11] After Mordecai's death in 1797, his widow, Frances, sought to obtain a revolutionary pension. She added this plea: "I am told there is a decided Majority of Republicans [Jeffersonians], and who if not from them are the Distrest families of old patriots to look for justice?"[12] Mordecai Myers joined the Jeffersonians as well, seeking to end the "despotic reign" of John Adams, Washington's successor. Myers thought the Federalists were old tories and pompous merchants, intent on "abridging the public rights."[13] Naphtali Judah inscribed a giant image of Tom Paine's head on the sign for his bookshop—a sure indication he was ready to sell Jeffersonian books like Paine's *Age of Reason*.[14]

The shift was mutual. Federalist and future president John Quincy Adams habitually referred to Jews in derogatory terms, calling one Gentile congressman a "squat little Jew-faced rotundity," and complaining about "Jew-brokering tricks." While serving as an American diplomat, Adams passed through a Jewish ghetto in Germany and took the time to describe it as "A Nasty, dirty, Place indeed, and fit only for Jews to live in."[15] ("The word *filth*," wrote Adams, "conveys an idea of spotless purity in comparison to the jewish nastiness.")[16] In later years, when Florida had the audacity to send a converted Jew to Congress (David Yulee, a pro-slavery firebrand), Adams referred to him as "the Jew delegate."[17]

This political shift had little to do with Jews, at least at first. The French Revolution exploded in 1789, and initially won warm applause from Americans, who welcomed a sister republic. The French, however, pursued a more profound revolution than the Americans. Within a few years, Louis XVI was dead and the guillotines began their work. American politics in the 1790s became wrapped in the language and imagery of the convulsions in France—as well as the 1791 revolution in Haiti that made free people of the colony's enslaved.

The alarm over the French and Haitian revolutions spread with the emergence of the Democratic-Republican societies—a new kind of political organization. These societies (sometimes called "clubs") were made up of like-minded Americans who opposed Washington's political program. They did not want a national bank, or the assumption of state debts, or a closer relationship with England—all of which were Federalist priorities. Over time, these clubs became a coherent political opposition, and Thomas Jefferson became their standard-bearer. By 1800, such clubs were known as "Democratic-Republicans," "Republicans," or "Jeffersonians." Democratic-Republican societies saw themselves as loyal to the nation and the American Revolution, but opposed to the Washington administration. At heart, these societies exemplified the idea of a loyal opposition, a way of developing an alternative to those in office without having to win an election first. Federalists, however, did not see the societies that way. Democratic-Republican societies reminded the Federalists too much of the radical Jacobin clubs of revolutionary France. One Federalist paper said that the Democratic-Republican societies intended to "unhinge all law, all subordination to the civil magistrate," and "pave the way for the reign of anarchy."[18] Democratic-Republican societies appealed to a strong anti-British strain in American life, painting the Federalists as tools of America's former king.

In New York and Philadelphia, many of the newly arrived Irish—fellow enemies of Britain's George III—flocked to the societies. Federalists saw a conspiracy to replace Anglo-Americans with foreigners and dupes. For the Federalists, the nation *was* the Washington administration, and voices in opposition corroded trust and confidence in the new republic, harming the people and nation. Federalists happily condoned meetings of those supportive of the government, however.[19]

Philadelphia Federalists who feared the Democratic-Republicans clubs often stopped and stared at Benjamin Nones, the parnas of Mikveh Israel and a leading Jeffersonian in the city. Nones had escaped Bourbon France, joined the Continental Army, and received a commendation for bravery.[20] By 1782, he was in Philadelphia, helping to re-found Mikveh Israel. By 1793, Nones had become an ardent defender of natural rights. He joined Philadelphia's Democratic-Republican club and personally welcomed the French ambassador to the city. That same year, he also joined Philadelphia's abolitionist club, and attempted to convince arriving French refugees from Haiti to manumit their enslaved persons. A foreign-born Jew interacting with Haitian refugees and French officials, and an avid Democratic-Republican as well: Nones was an object of Federalist derision. They called him "Citizen N."[21]

It did not help Nones's reputation that the first Democratic-Republican club, founded in Philadelphia, took advice from Edmond Genet, the same French ambassador that "Citizen N" had welcomed to town. Genet was the French Revolution's envoy in America and believed that the two sister republics would naturally have the same goals, and the Americans would side with the French against the British. The Washington administration felt otherwise. But Genet did not take no for an answer. Rebuffed by Washington, he began addressing the American people directly. Genet thought he could simply go over the head of the president to his constituents, whom he saw as the real power in America. Federalists howled. Democratic-Republican societies evolved well beyond Genet, but in Federalist eyes they were tainted by association.

Then a crisis on the Pennsylvania frontier brought matters to a head. Opposition to Hamilton's whiskey tax grew into armed revolt in 1794 and the so-called Whiskey Rebellion. Washington rode at the head of the federal army to quash the rebellion. Armed protests did not emerge from the Democratic-Republican societies, but Federalists saw their political opposition as the brainchild of such insurrection. Washington addressed

Congress and blamed "self-created societies" for the revolt. It was an odd tack for Washington, since he himself led the most famous "self-created" society of all—the United States. But the Federalists were keen to stifle the revolutionary impulse in the wake of the Constitution. For a while, the societies fell silent, ashamed or intimidated by Washington's rhetoric. But when John Jay signed a treaty with Britain—one particularly favorable to their old colonial oppressor—the Democratic-Republicans forged themselves anew. These civic groups arrayed against Washington soon evolved into an organized political party.[22]

Many Federalists were revolutionary leaders of a traditional cast, bred in staid Protestant traditions, career men in law or plantation agriculture. Their shock at seeing opposition to Washington was less a passion to prevent people from obtaining rights as it was a horror at who already had obtained rights in the United States. Federalists feared the politics of the Democratic-Republican societies as much as they feared the people in them. The "character" of the new country had embraced French radicals, the working class, merchants, free Blacks—and Jews.

In the summer of 1793, a political cartoon appeared in the pages of the Philadelphia *Gazette*. Entitled "A Peep at the Anti-Federalist Club," it depicted a motley crew of radicals, political outsiders, and the devil, all making the case for an overthrow of the government. At the center, a tall man asks "To be or not to be, a Broker is the question," whether 'tis nobler to "Contrive some means of knocking down a Government and on its ruins raise myself to Eminence and Fortune." An African American dubbed "Citizen Mungo" replies, "Our turn nex." Edmond Genet holds a plan marked, "The entire subversion of government." The astronomer David Rittenhouse (a Jefferson ally) gazes through his telescope and cries, "Oh! For such a government as they have on Saturn!" The devil nods approvingly. The "Creed of the Democratic Club" flanks the scene, declaring, among other things, "All power in one body and that Body Ourselves" and "Liberty is the Power of doing anything we like."[23]

The tall man is sometimes identified as Jefferson or Aaron Burr, but neither of those men were brokers or merchants, and the figure's further claim that he can turn "dirt into Gold" seems unsuited to the well-born Burr and Jefferson. One historian thought the tall man was Israel Israel, a leader of the Philadelphia Democratic-Republican Society. His thoroughly Jewish name and descent from a Jewish father made Israel the frequent target of anti-Semitic animus, though he was in fact a Universalist. His apparent election victory in 1797 was branded as "the triumph of the Jews over the Gentiles."[24]

If the tall man was Israel Israel, then the "Peep" parody earned a dubious distinction: the first time in American history in which Jews, Blacks, and immigrants were portrayed as co-conspirators.[25] The "Peep" was a response to the liberties created by the American experiment. Jewish rights had already arrived, a fact that traveled the world. In 1796, as the Dutch debated emancipation for Jews in Holland, one delegate spoke for the policy based, he said, on "how the emancipation of the Jews in France and North America has contributed to the progress and prosperity of these countries." When the French Revolution began, the Jews of France pointed to American precedent in their petition to the National Assembly for full political rights.[26]

The anger and anti-Semitism of the Federalists was less of a warning that Jews might become citizens than it was disbelief that Jews already were citizens. Faced with the fact that Jews were Americans, Federalists attacked Jews for ruining American character. Jews were a cautionary tale, according to the "Peep"; Blacks and foreigners were next. In that sense, the Federalist case against Jews was minor compared to the fury vented at free Blacks, the Irish, and immigrants.

The 1795 Jay Treaty took party politics to flood stage. The treaty solidified the Washington administration's alignment toward London over Paris. British ships on the high seas were now allowed to search American ships for cargo bound for revolutionary France. The treaty was Hamilton's brainchild, and it sparked a furious backlash among Americans who felt President Washington had bargained away American sovereignty and independence. When Britain's Isaac Weld visited Pennsylvania, he noted, "It is scarce possible for a dozen Americans to sit together without quarrelling about politics, and the British treaty." Weld spent a night at the inn where the arguments lasted through dinner and into bed, until "at last sleep closed their eyes, and happily their mouths."[27] Elections in 1795 were often fought between "Treaty" and "No Treaty" parties. In Philadelphia, Israel Israel ran on the "No Treaty" ticket.[28]

In this atmosphere, the Federalists took a second look at anti-Semitism. On October 7, 1795, "A Federalist" published a newspaper essay asking whether the Democratic Societies and the No Treaty ticket could "represent the People of this district generally," or simply members of their own society. The "Federalist" then suggested that all the Democratic-Republicans move to the Northwest Territory, which would be "a second going out of the Children of Israel, or rather of *Israel Israel*." The point was clear: Democratic-Republicans were Jews, and they did not belong. In case anyone missed the point, a few days later another Federalist paper referred to Israel Israel as "once a Jew and . . . now an ugly Christian."[29]

Israel lost the election. He did not take it well: He tried to beat up the Federalist publisher John Fenno. Nothing came of the altercation, but when Israel apparently won an election in 1797, Fenno printed the notice that "A Jewish Tavern Keeper, with a very Jewish name (viz. Israel Israel) is chosen one of the Senators of this commonwealth for the city of Philadelphia solely on account of his violent attachment to French interests."[30]

In New York, Federalists reminded readers that Democratic-Republican Societies admitted Jews. Solomon Simson (former Shearith Israel parnas) actually became vice-president of the club. Federalist printer James Rivington published a British novel called *The Democrat*. Rivington also wrote an introduction to the book, connecting the novel's anti-French themes to the American situation. Rivington told readers that Democratic-Republicans could be spotted by "their physiognomy; they all seem to be, like their Vice-President [Simson] of the tribe of Shylock . . . that leering underlook, and malicious grin." These Jewish Jeffersonians, Rivington warned, had "unlimited powers for rousing the mob to 'holy insurrection.'" Rivington also implicated Jews and Democratic-Republicans in the Haitian refugee crisis and revolutionary calls for racial equality. Simson had the last laugh, however. He became president of the Democratic-Republican club and was elected to public office (assessor of New York City's Second Ward) in 1794.[31]

A handful of Jews joined Simson on the ballot in the 1790s. These early Jewish politicians mostly ran for local offices, and they did not make their religion a point in the contest. Few of them recorded notes on their campaigns, perhaps because some of those campaigns went poorly. Moses Michael Hays put his name forward for the state senate in Massachusetts; he received one vote. Abraham Seixas said little about his 1790 electoral bid, where he finished dead last.[32]

But Jews did win office. Even before Virginia's Act for Establishing Religious Freedom had passed, Isaiah Isaacs ran for Richmond's Common Hall (city council). In 1795, Jacob Cohen won election to the Common Hall; Moses Myers won election to the Norfolk Common Council in 1794.[33] Mordecai Sheftall, as we've seen, served in numerous civic roles in

Savannah after the war; he became justice of the peace, and in 1796, a state representative. In South Carolina, Levi Myers went to the statehouse that same year.[34]

These local elections are quiet testaments to the work and tenacity of Mikveh Israel and the patriot Jews as well as the general tenor of the early American electorate. Jews ran for office; when they won, they served. Federalists attacked the Jews not because they feared a coming republic of religious equality but because that equality appeared to have already arrived.

And then came the Alien and Sedition Acts. By 1797, France and Britain had gone to war and of course the Jay Treaty allowed British ships to search American vessels for cargo bound for France. In response, the French stopped and searched American vessels for cargo bound for Britain. President Adams sent envoys to discuss the diplomatic crisis with Paris. The French envoys (codenamed X, Y, and Z) demanded a bribe. This "XYZ" affair turned public opinion decisively against France and the Democratic-Republicans. With a rallying cry of "Millions for defense but not one cent for tribute," the Adams administration doubled down on opposition to France, launched an undeclared naval war with France—and won the 1798 elections, securing a few more Federalist seats in Congress. Jefferson described the situation as "almost insane." John Adams—dressed in full military regalia—rallied his Federalists in Philadelphia. The Federalists then rioted, destroying Jeffersonian print shops.[35]

The Federalists intended to destroy the Jeffersonians. In Congress, their preferred weapons were the Alien and Sedition Acts, laws that narrowly passed through Congress in 1798. (The vote in the House was 44–41.) Among other things, the acts increased the residency period required to apply for American citizenship from five to fourteen years and gave the president the power to deport at will anyone not naturalized. The Federalists were not shy about revealing their intentions. A Federalist printer named William Cobbett declared, "Every United Irishmen ought to be hunted from the country, like a wolf or a Tiger. . . . As well might we attempt to tame the Hyena, as to Americanize the Irishman." Congressman Harrison Gray Otis of Boston feared "hordes of wild Irishmen . . . who come here to disturb our tranquility."[36]

Meanwhile, the sedition law made it a federal crime to publish anything insulting to the American government or the president. Newspaper publishers could now be arrested and imprisoned, as indeed they were under Secretary of State Timothy Pickering. The sedition laws equated critique of the government with opposition to the government. It was no longer legally possible to be an American and complain about the president. Sixteen men and one woman were arrested under the new sedition laws; twelve of them were printers. Almost all of them faced charges in the election year of 1800. All of the accused were Democratic-Republicans. Federalist publishers freely called for more arrests. As John Fenno wrote, "It is *Patriotism* to write in favour of our government—it is Sedition to write against it." Very few deportation orders were signed under the Alien Acts—although Pickering helpfully sent John Adams a stack of blank orders for the president to fill in at his leisure. Nevertheless, Attorney General Charles Lee declared in 1798 that the Alien Act "has produced the most desirable and salutary effect. . . . It has suggested to Alien French men the necessity of departing out of our territory." This would, Lee declared, "prevent an invasion of our country by the French republic."[37]

American Jews did not figure prominently in the enforcement of the Alien and Sedition Acts. They were vastly outnumbered by Irish and French immigrants, and no Jew published a newspaper in 1798. Pickering seemed particularly incensed by Irish Catholics, his previous work for religious equality forgotten. Yet Federalists still intended to let Protestants know that Jews were not real Americans and should be classed with French radicals, the Irish poor, and Jeffersonian politicians as people who did not truly deserve or understand freedom. On June 30, 1798, authorities arrested Benjamin Franklin Bache— grandson of his namesake and publisher of the *Aurora*, a leading Jeffersonian paper. After Bache was arrested, William Cobbett pulled together a mob to attack Bache's printing press, crying out that Bache deserved no better than "a Jew, a Turk, a Jacobin, or a dog."[38] Bache died before his trial, and the *Aurora* passed into the hands of William Duane—whom Cobbett also called "once a Jew," which he was not, and a "Jew clothesman in London," which he also was not.[39] Cobbett had a predilection for creating Jews when he needed them: his paper published a letter by "Moses S. Solomon," which purported to be a Jewish voice against the candidacy of Jefferson for president. Duane's *Aurora* pointed out that no such person lived in Philadelphia.[40]

These kinds of attacks on Jews persisted throughout the Adams administration, particularly in the run-up to the election of 1800. When John Israel (son of Israel Israel) started a Jeffersonian paper in Pittsburgh, Federalists tarred it as "the Jew press," "published by a Jew," and "the mother of sedition."[41] Another essay against Israel and his Christian associates accused them of having "placed Strumpets on Altars," but the author expected as much: "I do not wonder that a Jew . . . denies the New Testament."[42] In Maryland, Solomon Etting requested the state legislature to amend its test act, so that he could run for office and "be put on the same footing with other good citizens."[43] The Federalist legislature refused to consider the question "at this advanced stage of the session." (The House continued to meet for the next four weeks.)[44] Cobbett accused Benjamin Rush of deliberately providing false medical diagnoses in a yellow fever epidemic. Rush sued Cobbett for libel and hired Moses Levy as his lawyer. Levy was a Jewish convert to the Episcopal church. In an apoplectic essay, Cobbett declared that whatever Levy said, it "never could have been engendered but in the mind of a Jew!" You could not expect that Jew lawyers would ever believe the things they said in court: "He vash working for all monish dat vash all."[45]

Then and now, inserting dialect into the mouths of ethnic minorities has often been a way to mock and stereotype them. (See the language applied to "Citizen Mungo" above.) In the politics of the 1790s, American Jews were given East European and German accents by Federalist presses in order to emphasize their supposed "foreign" origin. Even Benjamin Nones—who would have had a French accent, if any—was parodied by the Federalist press as asking for clemency because "de monish ish very scarch."[46] Indeed, "de monish" became a kind of anti-Semitic shorthand in the decade, as when the New York *Journal* published "A Favorite Song" of "A Jew Broker" with three references to "monish."[47] A 1792 novel gave a Jew a monologue on "de love of de monish."[48]

In 1800, Jefferson and Adams faced off in a presidential campaign envenomed by dirty tricks and outright lies. Each camp believed that if the other man won, the republic would fall. Christians in Massachusetts were advised to hide their Bibles in wells lest Jefferson confiscate them. The printer Matthew Lyon told voters that Adams was driven by "an unbounded thirst for ridiculous pomp, foolish adulation, or selfish avarice." Tunis Wortman called Adams "a political divine" and therefore "a dangerous character."[49] Timothy Dwight preached that if Jefferson won, "we may behold a strumpet impersonating a goddess on the altars of JEHOVAH." The Bible would be "cast into a bonfire, the vessels of the sacramental supper borne by an ass in public procession, and our children, whether wheedled or terrified, uniting in chanting mockeries against God." For good measure, "we may see our wives and daughters the victims of legal prostitution."[50]

For the Federalists, the political response to the election of 1800 had to be religious, for only religion could hold off French atheism. By extension, the Jews and the deists had to go. But Federalists also knew that Jews and deists had rights in America, so the obvious response would be to eliminate those rights, cut all contacts with France, and thereby promote "true religion." The Federalist theologian Dwight—who had no part in framing the Constitution—insisted that American government "stands on the single basis of Christianity." Federalists thought America must Christianize before it could unify.[51]

Jews fought back and found some unexpected allies. On August 5, the *Gazette of the United States* again lampooned the Democratic-Republicans of New York, describing them as "the very *refuse* and *filth* of society," with "sacreligious hands," a cabal of Blacks, immigrants, and Jews. Jews were represented by "Citizen N-----" (Benjamin Nones), who refuses to pay his fines because he had just been released from prison because of "de Insholvent Law." He was, of course, short of "de monish" as well.[52] Nones shot back with a full-throated defense of democracy and the Jew's place in it, published in Duane's *Aurora*. "I am accused of being a *Jew;* of being a *Republican;* and of being poor," Nones wrote, and he proudly admitted to all three. "How can a Jew but be a Republican? especially in America."[53]

Nones went through the full defense of Jewish citizenship as he had learned it in the reestablishment of Mikveh Israel in Philadelphia. He recounted his service under fire in Georgia and the Carolinas, "an American throughout the whole of the revolutionary war." Both the synagogue and the Democratic-Republican club, Nones suggested, were full of veterans, but those who sought to silence them "cannot have known what it is to serve his country from principle in time of danger," for if they had, such Federalists would not now have become "reviler[s] of those who have done so." The test of citizenship, Nones implied, was not a party platform or a religion, it was service—a direct charge against the Anglophilia of the High Federalists.

Jews had a greater reason to be republicans. "In republics, we have *rights*, in monarchies we live but to experience *wrongs*," wrote Nones. In republics, "we are treated as men and brethren" and a Jew understood "the glorious and benevolent cause of the difference between his situation in this land of freedom, and among the proud and privileged law givers of Europe." Jewish freedom shared its origins in the broader American opposition to monarchy; both were set against the "Kingly governments" and "the pious priesthood of church establishments." Such aristocratic institutions had held down the people and the Jews as well. That persecution had not swayed the Jews from the performance of their ancient religion, however: "We and our forefathers have *not* sacrificed our principles to our interest" and so; "no wonder we are objects of derision to those, who have no principles, moral or religious, to guide their conduct."

Nones delivered both a defense of Jewish citizenship and a political argument on behalf of the Jeffersonians: Jews could be trusted to protect religious freedom, while Federalists planned to put churchmen in charge of everything. Jews had virtue; conniving Federalists did not. Or as another Jeffersonian paper put it, the Federalists would first strike at the Jews, and "amend that part of the Constitution that admits a Jew as President" and then create "an established religion of some sort."[54]

Even Gershom Seixas spoke out against the Federalist rollback. The "rabbi" of New York published a sermon in 1798 condemning political partisanship and war without mentioning any specific politicians. (He urged Americans to "guard ourselves against evil bickerings, discords, and schisms" so as to achieve a "well-regulated society.")[55] It was not openly Anti-Federalist, but it was published by an Anti-Federalist printer and advertised in Anti-Federalist newspapers.

The most serious effort to restrict Jewish rights and upend religious equality came in a court of law. Despite the predilection of Jews for the Jeffersonians, it was a Federalist who bucked his party and backed religious rights: Alexander Hamilton. The former cabinet secretary argued the case in front of New York's highest appeals court, then known as the Court of Errors.

At issue was the question of whether any Jew could be believed under oath. The case has mostly been forgotten, but at the time it was big news; "You can scarcely conceive the public attention," wrote one contemporary.[56] The case began as a commercial issue: Louis Le Guen—a French Gentile—arrived in the United States in 1794 with a cargo of indigo and cotton. Le Guen entered into partnership with two Christian New York merchants, Isaac Gouverneur and Peter Kemble, to sell the cargo. Demand was weak in New York, so they shipped the goods to Europe under the care of Isaac Gomez, a Jewish merchant. Gomez found no buyers in Holland or Germany, and eventually returned the goods at a loss to the London agents of Gouverneur and Kimble. At that point, Le Guen sued, arguing that he had not agreed to the sale and that his partners owed him. Gouverneur and Kemble countered that it was the low quality of goods that had forced them to sell at a loss, and that Le Guen was guilty of fraud. It was a "morass of conflicting allegations."[57]

The religious issue entered the proceedings over the question of evidence and witnesses. Gomez testified that the *demand* in Holland and Germany had been weak, and that was why he returned the goods unsold. Gouverneur and Kemble insisted that the *goods* were inferior. Gouverneur Morris, the peglegged Founding Father, took up the case of his cousin Gouverneur. Morris's legal argument was simple. He informed the court that Gomez was a Jew and "Jews are not to be believed upon oath."[58]

No official court transcript survives, and Morris left little in his own writing on the case except for a few lines praising his own acumen.[59] The arguments must be reconstructed from Hamilton's own notes. From those, one recent historian suggested that Morris might have been reaching back to some of the medieval era's greatest hits of anti-Semitism: the myth that Jews had a religious obligation to ignore their oaths. This old chestnut was knocked about Europe, and in theory draws from a misunderstanding of the sacred *Kol Nidre* prayer on Yom Kippur. In that prayer, the head of the congregation asks God to forgive all religious vows made in the coming year. It is an act of repentance for the failures everyone will make before God and themselves. *Kol Nidre* is an act of humility; humans so often fail. Rabbis have always been clear that the prayer refers only to religious promises, not legal oaths. Anti-Semites twisted the words to convince Christian courts that Jews believed in lying and had no respect for oaths. It is possible Morris had this on his mind.

It is also possible that Morris had in mind a much simpler notion: All Jews were cheats and liars, and since that was what "everyone" really thought, it was therefore a valid if unwritten legal truth. Morris indeed admitted that there was nothing in law books to back him up, and that he instead decided to "appeal to the principles written on the heart of man." As witnesses, Jews were "unworthy of Credit." Hamilton jotted down an inscrutable note: "*Jews are in* capacity to be every thing?" Perhaps Hamilton and Morris were debating the question of whether Jews occupied the same civic position as Christians, or whether Christians were to have pride of place in the republic.

Hamilton rose to the occasion. One of the opposing lawyers wrote that Hamilton "has pushed this cause to the utmost extremity. . . . I never knew him on any occasion so heated."[60]

Hamilton attacked Morris's anti-Semitic claims. Christians had to accept Jewish evidence, after all, since Jews were the original witnesses of Christianity (a point Morris had apparently scoffed at). More important, Hamilton argued that the demand of justice cannot be subject to any racial or religious claims. Justice "knew no birthplace" and clothed "Jew, or Gentile, or Christian, or Pagan . . . with her mantle, in whose presence all differences of faith or births, of passions or of prejudices—all are called to acknowledge and revere her supremacy." The case involved a Jew, but Hamilton framed the legal question to address citizenship and religious diversity.[61]

Morris thought Hamilton went "beyond the Bounds," but chose not to respond.[62] The vote was not close. The court ruled in favor of Hamilton and Le Guen, 28–6.[63] The case had other aspects, yet if the Court of Errors had truly felt that certain religious beliefs prevented full citizenship, the decision would have gone the other way, with untold consequences for religious freedom, legal precedent, and Jewish life.

The Le Guen case, now forgotten, came in the middle of the efforts by the Adams administration to regulate the kinds of persons who could be Americans. Morris's argument was a test of the recurring supposition in American life that the broad protections and definitions in American law and government did not really mean what they said. Morris simply told the court that "principles written on the heart" were more important. You know how the Jews are. A Christian lawyer asked Christian judges to affirm that legal equality before the law only applied to Christians, even though that was not what the Founders, the federal Constitution, or the laws of New York state required. Christian judges disagreed.

In years to come, multiple commentators and historians would insist that because the Founders were Christian and believed in God, American law itself gave Christians special protections to which others were not entitled. In the Le Guen case—as happened repeatedly throughout the revolutionary era and the early days of the Constitution—a court was specifically asked to apply a different standard of proof to a non-Christian, solely because of religious belief. In an age of religious discrimination, when Jews could not vote in Britain and pogroms exploded across Russia, the American court flat-out rejected the idea that Jews were legally different from Christians.[64]

Religious equality was not a grant given by a Christian government, one which then expanded, at its leisure, to the Jews; it was created by the

Americans in the separation from Britain when Jews were accepted into the revolutionary ranks as soldiers and patriots. Religious equality did not gradually appear over time. It emerged with the revolution. None of this should obviate the enormous inequalities that remained after the revolution; the perpetuation of slavery, discrimination, and manifold other sins are all too obvious. Yet the revolutionary settlement did not merely recast existing legal structures with new power brokers. At least in the case of religious equality, huge changes had occurred—and Hamilton and Jefferson, disagree as they did on almost everything else, both accepted that.

Jefferson won a narrow victory in the election of 1800. Mordecai Myers was elated, having worked with the Jeffersonians in New York, drawing up election lists and giving speeches. Myers was part of Aaron Burr's team canvassing New York neighborhoods, going to "each voter . . . house to house, seeing and conversing with as many as possible." He rejoiced that "the result of the election destroyed the hydra monster, Federalism."[65] The new president made similar remarks; Jefferson called the age of Federalism a "reign of Witches," and the election validated his prediction that "We shall see . . . their spells dissolve, and the people recovering their true sight, restore their government to it's [sic] true principles."[66]

Once in office, Jefferson appointed numerous American Jews to federal positions, more than either of his predecessors. He named war veteran Reuben Etting as federal marshal for Maryland in 1801. The state constitution there required a Christian oath, but federal offices did not, so Etting took the job. Jacob I. Cohen became a prison inspector in 1807.[67] Jefferson appointed Moses Myers of Norfolk as a federal Commissioner of Bankruptcy in 1802, although Myers declined the appointment.[68] James Monroe recommended Jacob I. Cohen as a commissioner, too, though Monroe also felt it necessary to add that Cohen was "a jew & foreig[ne]r, but very worthy character."[69]

Offices like prison inspector or commissioner of bankruptcy were not plum jobs, nor did Jefferson ever suggest that he appointed these men because he had to appoint a Jew or because he wanted to "reward" the Jewish community. He was simply filling positions, and Jewish Americans had become some of his strongest supporters. Jefferson—more so than even Washington—acknowledged the "possibility of Jews" as members of the body politic and as officers of the law. When Nones applied for a position in the Jefferson administration, he recounted his political qualifications like everyone else—"principles and opposition to the measure of Mr.

Gershom Seixas (1745–1816): The revolution's rabbi, Seixas moved his congregation into Connecticut in 1776 rather than live under British rule. He then created the first national Jewish congregation in Philadelphia. American Jews, Seixas wrote, should view themselves "as possessing equal rights & privileges"—and Seixas himself petitioned and sermonized to make that true. Image courtesy of the Museum of the City of New York

Prayer of the Richmond Synagogue for President Washington, 1789. This benediction is a variation of the traditional prayer of the Jewish community for the country in which they live. In this case, the Jews of Richmond turned the prayer into a Hebrew acrostic, spelling out the name "VASHINGTON" on the right side. It suggests the affection and loyalty American Jews felt for their new country and its first president. Image courtesy of the Weitzman National Museum of American Jewish History

Jonas Phillips (1736–1803). The *alter kaker* of the Revolution, Jonas Phillips dubbed the American army *rookim.* He served in the militia, wrote to Washington and the Constitutional Convention, and led Mikveh Israel in its petition drive for full civil rights in Pennsylvania. He was also the brash and uncompromising parnas of KKMI who refused to surrender the synagogue's deed to his successor. Image courtesy of the American Jewish Historical Society

Jacob Cohen (1744–1823). A militiaman in the Revolution, Cohen joined Mikveh Israel in Philadelphia, then defied its authority to marry Esther Mordecai despite her Gentile origins. Instead, the couple headed to Richmond, where Cohen founded Richmond's Beth Elohim. In the new United States, Jews themselves and not yeshivas would make the rules. Courtesy of the Maryland Center for History and Culture

fhip under full fail, and the motto, *Deus nobis hæc Otia*
  t.

58. No perfon fhall be allowed to plead in the courts
of law, in this ftate, except thofe who are authorifed fo
to do, by the houfe of affembly; and if any perfon fo
authorized fhall be found guilty of mal-practice before the
houfe of affembly, they fhall have power to fufpend them.
This is not intended to exclude any perfon from that inherent privilege of every freeman, the liberty to plead his
own caufe.

59. Exceffive fines fhall not be levied, nor exceffive bail
demanded.

60. The principles of the habeas corpus act, fhall be
part of this conftitution.

61. Freedom of the prefs, and trial by jury, to remain
inviolate for ever.

62. No clergyman, of any denomination, fhall be allowed a feat in the legiflature.

63. No alteration fhall be made in this conftitution
without petitions from a majority of the counties, and the
petitions from each county to be figned by a majority of
voters in each county within this ftate. At which time
the affembly fhall order a convention to be called for that
purpofe, fpecifying the alterations to be made, according
to the petitions preferred to the affembly by the majority
of the counties, as aforefaid.

By the above Constitution of Georgia there is no impediment of a Jew being either Govr. Councellor or Representative in Assembly or any other Office of Trust or proffit either Civil or Milita. and altho in Article 6. the Representatives must be protestant, a Jew being a protestant, is not incapacitated. — Philada. 13. Jany. 1783.

Notes from Congregation Mikveh Israel, 1783. When the revolution
ended, Gershom Seixas and a committee from Mikveh Israel bought
copies of all the constitutions of the new American states and set
out to determine the nature of religious freedom in the new nation.
Their work led to the petition to the government of Pennsylvania for
an end to its test oath. Here, in Seixas's handwriting, the committee
has written, "By the above Constitution of Georgia, there is no impediment of a Jew being Govr. Or Councellor or Representative in
Assembly," though in order to reach this conclusion, the committee
chose to also classify Jews as Protestants. Image courtesy of the
Rosenbach Museum and Library

Grace Seixas Nathan (1752-1831). Grace Seixas's marriage to Simon Nathan was one of several matches made among the patriot Jews of different regions when they gathered in Philadelphia to found Mikveh Israel, cementing the national character of American Judaism. In later life, she left records of her patriotism in the War of 1812, daring the British army to invade America. Image courtesy of the American Jewish Historical Society

St. Eustatius. The Dutch-controlled island of St. Eustatius was a center for the black-market supply of American forces in the Revolutionary War. It also hosted a sizable Jewish community. When Sir George Rodney attacked the island in 1781, ostensibly to cut off American materiel, he blamed and exiled the Jewish community there. The Jews, Rodney wrote, "are notorious in the cause of America and France." Image from *Gezigten uit Neerland's West-Indian,* courtesy of Rijksmuseum, Amsterdam

Jodensavanne. This Jewish settlement in Suriname had a synagogue and a rabbi long before any city in the British colonies. Jodensavanne depended on enslaved labor, and its synagogue exercised significant central control over the religious lives of Jews. This approach to the Jewish New World would be overtaken by the democratization of United States Jewry. Image from *Gezigten uit Neerland's West-Indian*, courtesy of Rijksmuseum, Amsterdam

Sarah Brandon Moses (1798–1828). Born in Barbados, Sarah Brandon Moses underwent a mikveh in Suriname to become a Jew. Her mother, Sarah Esther Gill, was an enslaved woman of African descent. The synagogue at Barbados refused to perform the mikveh. Sarah's father sent her to Suriname for the ceremony, and from there, Sarah went to London and then the United States. In New York, she assimilated into white Jewish society. This portrait in ivory is the first known likeness of a biracial American Jew. Image courtesy of the American Jewish Historical Society

Traveling Menorah. Just as itinerating Christian ministers took portable communion kits with them in the early republic, so too early American Jews crafted and carried this tiny, portable menorah, for use while traveling in Hannukah in the mobile world of the early United States. Image courtesy of the Weitzman National Museum of American Jewish History

Rebecca Gratz (1781–1869). Gratz pioneered a series of new democratized institutions in American Jewish life, including poor-relief societies and Hebrew Sunday school. She probably did more to shape American Judaism as a lived religion than anyone else in the early republic. Image courtesy of the Rosenbach Museum and Library

Aaron Lopez (1731–1782). New England's most prominent Jewish merchant struggled to become a British subject in the colonies, then sent aid to Connecticut communities trying to break away from Britain. His patriotic ambivalence and his engagement with the Atlantic slave trade have left a long shadow across colonial Jewish history. Image courtesy of the American Jewish Historical Society

SPEECHES

ON THE

JEW BILL,

IN THE

HOUSE OF DELEGATES OF MARYLAND,

BY H. M. BRACKENRIDGE, COL. W. G. D. WORTHINGTON,
AND JOHN S. TYSON, ESQUIRE.

TOGETHER WITH

AN ARGUMENT ON THE CHANCERY POWERS,

AND

AN EULOGY

ON

THOMAS JEFFERSON AND JOHN ADAMS, &c.

BY H. M. BRACKENRIDGE.

PHILADELPHIA:
J. DOBSON, (AGENT,) No. 108, CHESNUT STREET
JESPER HARDING, PRINTER.

1829

Debates on the Jew Bill. In 1823, the state of Maryland attempted to remove language in its constitution barring Jews from public office. The debate provoked tremendous political furor and reshaped an election cycle. Publications like this one boldly made the case for full religious freedom, and after years of work, Jews were allowed to hold office in the state. It was in the 1820s, and not the 1770s, that claims that America had been legally founded as a Christian nation emerged. Image courtesy of the Maryland Center for History and Culture

Solomon Etting (1764–1847) Etting pushed for an end to the test oath in Maryland, then got elected to public office himself. He also served as shohet, purchased land for Maryland's first Jewish cemetery, and served in the defense of Baltimore against British invasion in 1814. Courtesy of the Maryland Center for History and Culture

Newport's Touro synagogue today. The colonial Jews of Newport raised a house of worship despite an uncertain legal status in the years before the revolution. Perhaps because of this. the synagogue has no outward indication that it is a religious building. Image courtesy of Lew Keen.

Interior of the Touro synagogue. The worship space is modeled on synagogues in London and Amsterdam. Outside the sanctuary, things were much different. When hazan Moses Seixas petitioned George Washington about Jewish rights, Washington responded with a clear vision of a broadly inclusive religious freedom in the United States. Image courtesy of Josh Edenbaum

Adams' Administration."[70] Jefferson even considered Moses Levy for attorney general in 1804. The president wanted a Pennsylvanian for the
job, and Levy's name came up. Treasury Secretary Albert Gallatin advised
against it, doubting that Levy would "exchange Philada. for Washington,"
and assessing Levy as "second-rate." Jefferson went with John Breckinridge
instead.[71]

Levy's candidacy generates a certain "wow" factor in a modern
reading—a Jew was up for the cabinet in 1804? Jefferson and Levy both deserve credit, though it's not clear how seriously Jefferson considered Levy
for the job. (Also, Levy was a practicing Episcopalian by then.) Moreover,
cabinet appointments in 1804 were much less sensational and fraught than
they are today. Gallatin even rejected another (Gentile) applicant for attorney general because he didn't think he'd accept the salary. Nonetheless,
there was no doubt that Jefferson brought Jews into the government as full
members. Appointment (and election) to high office allowed them to hold
authority over fellow citizens—and in America, that meant authority over
Christians. Indeed, in the case of Reuben Etting, a Jew exercised a legitimate authority with federal jurisdiction in the state that denied Jews state
jurisdiction. It took place almost silently, with no fanfare or hullaballoo.

Jefferson has received far more attention for his declaration of a "high
wall of separation between church and state" than for this quiet religious
revolution in appointments. Jefferson was actually implementing the republicanism that he had been promoting since the Virginia Declaration of
Religious Freedom. "Difference of opinion is advantageous in religion," he
had written in 1785. Therefore, Jefferson believed the United States needed
and had already created a political system where character did not relate to
confession. So Jefferson appointed officials and built a political coalition
without regard to religious differences.

Jefferson didn't particularly like Judaism. The "Reign of Witches" letter
itself mentions Jews, and not in a good way. Jefferson called New England
Federalists "marked, like the Jews, with such a peculiarity of character, as
to constitute from that circumstance the natural division of our parties."
To Jefferson, Judaism was not equivalent to Christianity. His private
writings about Judaism are mostly filled with criticisms of Old Testament
priesthood and the futility of its modern successors. "Moses had bound
the Jews to many idle ceremonies, mummeries & observances of no effect towards producing the social utilities which constitute the essence of
virtue," wrote Jefferson to William Short. "Jesus exposed their futility &

insignificance." Judaism originated in "the fumes of the most disordered imaginations . . . recorded in their religious code, as special communications of the deity." Such things, Jefferson continued, have "preserved their credit with the Jews of all subsequent times," as well as with Christians.[72] Jefferson consumed numerous religious books in his lifetime, but his lone reference to the Talmud was to repeat someone else's assessment that it contained insufficient ethics, and that it was "impossible to collect from these writings a consistent series of moral Doctrines."[73] For Jefferson, ancient Judaism provided the template for "priestcraft"—control of the public good by clergy, whether Protestant or Catholic.

Another time, Reverend Ezra Stiles Ely asked whether Jefferson was a Christian. Jefferson replied, "I am not a Jew." (Not a surprise there.) Jefferson then explained that Jews presupposed a god of infinite justice who nevertheless "punish[ed] the sins of the fathers upon their children, unto the 3rd and 4th generation." By contrast, Jefferson praised Jesus, whom he said "teaches us to love our neighbors as ourselves" and "has told us only that god is good and perfect, but has not defined him." That led only to "doers of good & eschewers of evil." Religious animosities came from "those who call themselves his ministers. . . . I am sometimes more angry with them than is authorised by the blessed charities which he preached."[74]

Jefferson maintained he was a Christian—on very specific terms: "in the only sense in which he [Jesus] wished any one to be; sincerely attached to his doctrines, in preference to all others, ascribing to himself every human excellence, and believing he never claimed any other." He wrote to Joseph Priestly that Jesus had been trying to bring the Jews to the "principles of pure deism."[75]

The president was likely a closet Unitarian, believing in Jesus's teachings and the existence of God, but not in the miracles described in the Bible, and certainly not trusting to church authorities to interpret God's word. Indeed, Jefferson spent several weeks while president rearranging the New Testament. It was a simple matter, he later explained: "I find many passages of fine imagination, correct morality, and of the most lovely benevolence: and others again of so much ignorance." It could not all have come from the same source, so Jefferson decided to "separate . . . the gold from the dross." He removed all the supernaturalism in which he could not believe. Jefferson's Bible has no healings, no exorcisms, no feeding of the 5,000, no resurrection. The Jefferson Bible ends when Joseph and Nicodemus take Christ's body down from the cross, wind it in a cloth, and lay it in the cave, "And they rolled a great stone to the door of the sepulchre, and departed."[76] The End.

Jefferson's redacted bible also removed almost all the associations of the Jewish people with bloodguilt for the crucifixion of Christ. Jefferson relied on Matthew 27 for his account of Jesus's trial before Pilate, but he excised Matthew 27:24–25—the infamous verse wherein the Jews take responsibility for the execution of Christ. ("His blood be on us, and on our children!") That line had long found use in Christian anti-Semitism as a curse and a justification for discrimination against Jews. There is no doubt that Jefferson cut it deliberately, as he included the story from verse 13 to 23, and then picked back up with verse 26. Jefferson's Bible quietly removed the verse most associated with anti-Semitism. (The general public knew nothing of this; Jefferson kept the project private and the volume wasn't published until 1902.)

Jews stayed with the Jeffersonians even after Jefferson left office. Jefferson's successor, James Madison, received substantial (though not universal) support from American Jews. Isaac Harby purchased a newspaper in Charleston, changed its name to *Southern Patriot*, and "supported with great ability the administration of MR. MADISON" as the "eloquent champion of the republican cause."[77] Moses Sheftall ran for the Georgia statehouse as a Jeffersonian three times in Savannah between 1807 and 1809; he never won.[78] Myer Moses won on a Democratic-Republican slate in 1810 in South Carolina, thumping the Federalists.[79] Grace Seixas Nathan and other Jews backed the Madison administration's 1812 war against Britain: "I cannot for the life of me feel terrified," of a British invasion, she wrote. "Besides I am so true an American, so warm a patriot, that I hold these mighty armies and their proud, arrogant, presumtious [*sic*], and over-powering nation [Great Britain] as beings that *we* have conquered and *shall* conquer again." Nathan probably should have worried, given how badly Madison mishandled the war. (The British burned down the White House, after all.)[80]

Despite strong Jewish support, President Madison managed to flub the appointment of the first Jew as a US consul. He appointed playwright and editor Mordecai Manuel Noah (grandson of Gershom Seixas) as consul to Tunis. The embassy in Tunis served as the American diplomatic mission to the Barbary states, a loose confederation of North African principalities whose toleration of piracy strained their relations with the United States. Noah got the job thanks to his full-throated editorial support of Madison in the 1812 election. Madison returned the favor in March 1813 by sending the twenty-seven-year-old redhead off to Tunis. Noah had shown interest in the post as early as 1811 and stressed his Jewish heritage as an advantage. The Dutch and the British had also sent Jewish envoys to the Barbary states, following an old tradition of using Jews as go-betweens in Christian-Islamic affairs.[81] In April, Secretary of State James Monroe added a secret mission to Noah's portfolio: Arrange for the release of a host of American sailors captured by the Algerian navy. Noah was forbidden, however, to let anyone know he was acting under official government orders; he must act as a private agent, with a circumscribed budget.[82]

Noah's efforts at freeing the captives went over budget and involved little subterfuge. Asked to assess Noah's performance, cabinet member Richard Rush replied, "Secrets are prone to escape through much smaller openings."[83] The State Department, meanwhile, lent its ear to Johan Norderling, Swedish consul at Tunis and noted anti-Semite, who explained that "a Jew was not a fit subject to send to Barbary." President Madison himself agreed that Noah needed to be fired, but also that "it might be well to rest the reason pretty much on the ascertained prejudice of the Turks [Muslims] against his Religion, and it having become public that he was a Jew." Monroe followed suit, and fired Noah for being Jewish. He wrote to Noah with the explanation that the "religion you profess . . . would produce an unfavorable effect" in the Berber states.[84]

Noah got the letter while in Tunis. After reading it, he walked to a rocky promontory overlooking Cape Carthage to consider his response. The method of termination "violated one of the most sacred and delicate rights of a citizen," he wrote.[85] He blamed Madison personally: "He should have remembered that the religion of a citizen is not a legitimate object of official notice from the government." If Muslims were not prepared to deal with a Jew—and Noah refused to concede that point—did that mean Americans had to play along? "Are we prepared to yield up the admirable and just institutions . . . to gratify the intolerant views of the Bey of Tunis?" he wrote in his memoir. "Have we fallen so low?"[86]

Noah did not think so. He hid Monroe's order and stayed at his post long enough to complete some perilous negotiations, then returned to America "more attached to the soil, to the character of the people, and national institutions" than ever before.[87] He sought personal apologies from Monroe and Madison, and when those were not forthcoming, wrote extensively about his experiences in public print, winning over skeptics and ultimately forcing the state department to acknowledge that his termination had been wrong.[88]

Moreover, Noah published two books on the experience—a travelogue of North Africa, and a collection of documents exonerating his conduct as consul. He did not frame the problem as one of Jewish rights, but of American rights. Noah had been wronged as an American. "I was a citizen of the United States, protected by the constitution in my religious as well as in civil rights." Nor was it necessary "for a citizen of the United States to have his faith stamped on his forehead; the name of freeman is a sufficient passport."[89] Whatever the customs of the country, Americans did not need to validate their faith as long as they followed the law. Judaism was not an addition to Americanism that needed a special dispensation. Americans got to choose their faith. The threat was to the republic itself: "This is the first attempt since the adoption of the Constitution of the United States, to make the religion of a citizen an objection to the possession of office," a move "so dangerous to the liberties of the country, that citizens cannot be insensible to the new and dreadful features which it exposes."[90]

Noah went on to explain that freedom of religion did not mean that he could pick and choose which laws he followed, but rather that the law must treat him equally. He cited his raising and lowering of the flag on Christian holidays, and his reception of the various Christian clergy of Africa, as proof of his indebtedness to the majority faith of the United States. He referred to the United States as a "Christian nation," yet also cited the Barlow treaty of 1798, quoting the lines that "the government of the United States [of] America is not in any sense, founded on the Christian religion." In other words, the agents of government should respect Christianity—but they could not be held to a religious standard of office.[91]

Isaac Harby of Charleston echoed Noah and George Washington in his pro-Madison newspaper. Harby objected on "the principle, not of *toleration* (for man has no *power* to tolerate Religion, that is a concern between man and his maker) but upon the principle of equal inalienable, *constitutional Rights.*" And if so, how was it "that *Religion* disqualifies a man from the exercise of his political functions?"[92]

As it became more generally known that Noah had been fired for his religion, Madison hurried to appoint another Jew, Moses M. Russell, as consul to Latvia. Madison encouraged Russell to write a few public letters about how religion was never a topic in White House appointments.

When Monroe succeeded Madison, he made Nathan Levy consul at St. Thomas.[93]

By 1817, the attorney general reviewed the case, determined Noah was in the right, and offered the diplomat-turned-playwright the remainder of the money due to him from his expenses at Tunis. Madison—then out of office—finally responded to Noah. The ex-president praised a sermon Noah had sent to him, and found it "agreeable" that "your accounts have been closed in a manner so favorable." Madison added that Noah's Judaism "could not be a motive in your recall," in either deliberate or apparent ignorance of Monroe's letter.[94] Noah also apparently felt the issue was settled. By 1820, he sought a position in the Monroe administration without any reference to former events.[95] As in the Le Guen case, the revolutionary model of religious citizenship prevailed over older notions about who had rights in the state.

The extent of this change from traditional law to constitutional citizenship is revealed by one of the stranger coincidences in Jewish history—the case of the two Jews elected in 1808. That year, Ezekiel Hart in Canada and Jacob Henry in North Carolina both won elections to their local legislatures. In both places, fellow legislators attempted to have them removed from office, based on their inability to take a Christian oath of office. In Canada, the prominent French Canadian leader Pierre-Stanislaw Bédard argued against seating Hart because Jews were not and had never been citizens of England or any "Christian lands: that none accorded them the rights of a citizen." Canada was English. England had never given Jews citizenship rights, and therefore no Jew could be a lawmaker in Canada. Hart's fellow legislators voted to exclude Hart from the House by a vote of 21 to 5. England's principalities had to set different standards for believers and non-believers.[96]

The outcome was different in North Carolina. Carteret County sent Jacob Henry to the state legislature in 1808 and he was reelected in 1809. Henry remains a cipher in Jewish history. Little is known about him. He was the son of Amelia Henry, a Jew from Bermuda who found her way to the mainland colonies. Neither Jacob nor Amelia joined an American synagogue. The family is notably absent among Mikveh Israel patriots. Even Henry's birth year is unknown, although he was listed as "forty-five and upward" in 1820. His social standing in the predominantly Gentile town of Beaufort, North Carolina, must have been substantial—Jacob and his father both held enslaved people in their households.[97]

Henry was, however, unquestionably Jewish, and North Carolina's state constitution forbade office to any person "who shall deny the being of God or the truth of the Protestant religion, or the divine authority either of the Old or New Testaments" from taking the oath of office. Henry had simply not bothered to take the oath in 1808; no one noticed. After reelection in 1809—and nearly two weeks into the legislative session—Hugh Mills of Rockingham County objected to Henry's presence. It was "contrary to the freedom and independence" of the United States, "that any person should be allowed to have a seat in this Assembly, or watch over the rights of a free people, who is not constitutionally qualified for that purpose." Mills then announced that "a certain Jacob Henry, a member of this house, denies the divine authority of the New Testament." Mills asked that Henry's seat be vacated.[98] In so doing, Mills did not claim that Jews could not serve because they had killed Christ or because they were untrustworthy; he merely pointed to the legal ban. "Freedom and independence" could not stomach a Jewish legislator, Mills claimed, because it would violate the law. In essence, this was the case of the British against the patriots of 1776: Law matters more than rights. The statehouse duly considered Mills's measure, and dedicated a day of debate to the measure. Eventually they referred it to committee, who "after some time" reported that "no proof had been adduced in support of the charges," and Mills's motion was rejected.[99]

Fortunately, someone wrote down at least one of the speeches: Henry's own. He defended himself in the statehouse, referring to his fellow legislators as "colleagues." His right to free religion in North Carolina's bill of rights preceded the constitution, he argued, and the declaration of rights "is to the Constitution as the Constitution is to a Law; it controls it and directs it absolutely." That bill of rights declared that "all men have a natural and unalienable right to worship Almighty God according to the dictates of their own consciences." Henry argued that religious freedom was "undoubtedly a natural right, and when it is declared to be an unalienable one, by the people in their sovereign and original capacity, any attempt to alienate it either by the Constitution or by Law, must be vain and fruitless."[100]

"The people in their sovereign and original capacity": The people made the government, not the other way round. The law could not violate the compact created at the moment of independence, and that moment had not been exclusive to Christians or any sect thereof. This was the same position as held by the Mikveh Israel patriots, as Benjamin Nones, as Madison and Jefferson and a host of others. Governments sprang from the people as a whole, and therefore, no particular church could exercise control over government or validate its members. More important, "the people" already included Jews, Catholics, Baptists, Calvinists, Presbyterians, and Unitarians, as Henry explained. He offered a long list of religions of North Carolina and pointed to their representation already in the state house of 1809. The government of North Carolina was not divine, and therefore could not bind its members on religious beliefs: A citizen "ought to suffer civil disqualification for what he does and not for what he thinks."[101]

Henry never mentioned the word "Judaism" in his speech, although he defended his belief in a religion that "inculcates the practice of every virtue, and the detestation of every vice." He briefly considered asking how such a religion could be founded upon "the denial of the divine authority of the old and new Testament?" but wisely took that out. The issue of the origin of his religion was immaterial—only that it produced virtue and loved republican government.[102] Henry's speech was reprinted across the United States, and by 1824 had been included in a collection of American oratory.[103] Schoolchildren in the early republic would have learned about the relationship of religion, state, and virtue by reading the speech of a Jewish man defending his right to hold the seat to which his Christian neighbors elected him.

Judaism and Jewish freedom were not abstract issues in the early United States. The world where all Americans were church-going Protestants never existed—nor did many of those Protestants want such a world. Christians advocated non-Christian citizenship because they saw political power emanating from the people. Freedom was the ability to worship according to one's conscience, and to suffer no civil disabilities because of it. The nation was not the finger of God, meant to keep the people pure. The nation was the creation of the people, whose worship had to proceed from their own ideas, experiences, and conscience.

This was the Jewish contribution to American statecraft and it did not merely affect Jews. As disestablishment took hold, some Christians changed how they worshipped—and how they preached to Jews. As political protections for Jews became confirmed in the early nineteenth century, these Christians found new religious ways to think about their fellow Jewish citizens—and new ways to preach to them. Jews found ways to respond.

9

Democratization

REBECCA SAMUEL OF VIRGINIA WAS frustrated. She lived among Jews she considered "not worthy of being called Jews," who worshipped on Yom Kippur without a Torah and without a *talis*. "Anyone can do what he wants," she wrote in 1791. "There is no rabbi in all of America to excommunicate anyone."

Samuel found a silver lining, however. The post-revolutionary Jewish situation was also "a blessing," because "Jew and Gentile are as one." In Virginia, she wrote, "There is no *galut*"—segregation between Jews and Gentiles. Samuel longed for stricter obedience to Jewish traditions. At the same time, she knew transformations in Jewish life shared an origin with the new religious rights. A state that could not compel religious obedience would also be a state where religious traditions were going to change.[1]

That change could become violent. In 1812 something like a riot broke out at Congregation Beth Elohim in Charleston, "a state of warfare sanction & approved" by the hazan and "unheard of in the annals of religion," according to Mordecai Noah. The trouble began when the adjunta ordered the hazan, E. N. Carvalho, to avoid "the discordance which attends every synagogue." Carvalho apparently taught the synagogue's children to sing in a regular manner, but then for some reason "discontinued the ceremony & forbid [*sic*] the children to sing." The adjunta wanted the song, and Carvalho "treated the adjunta with disrespect." The adjunta therefore suspended Carvalho for five days. Undaunted, the hazan marched into an adjunta meeting on Saturday night, surrounded by supporters (or "a rabble comprised of all the vagrant Jews," as Noah put it). Soon enough, "the whole meeting parnas & all were battling with clubs & bruising boxing &c.," and Carvalho in turn "aided and abetted the confusion and riot."[2]

Fistfights broke out in houses of worship regularly in early America. A French Catholic priest in Charleston needed a militia escort to chant a *Te Deum* on the downfall of Napoleon. A congregant attacked him with a dagger anyway.[3] Methodist preacher Peter Cartwright found a disruptive young man at his revival and sent two heavies out to threaten him and cut his hair off. Cartwright himself ran a miscreant off with a cudgel, and then "the power of God fell on the people gloriously."[4] Mormon preachers frequently had threats made against them; visitors bombarded them with books, ink, and in one case a stink bomb, "an odious smelling thing . . . that raised confusion in all the house."[5] American religion became passionate, profound, and rowdy in the wake of the revolution. Respect for tradition ebbed and institutions crumbled in a world where religions had to compete for people's attention.

Historians of Protestantism have called these changes "the democratization of American Christianity." "Democratization" refers to a widespread process of leveling in American Christianity. Between 1790 and 1830, churches with hierarchies and formal worship shrank, and egalitarian and informal churches prospered. In the colonial era, state churches that relied on a college-educated clergy (such as Congregationalism and Anglicanism) easily held on to the majority of Christian supplicants. Congregationalists had twice the clergy of any other denomination in 1775. By the early 1820s, Methodist preachers outnumbered Congregationalists tenfold.[6] Baptists and Methodists relied on self-governing churches and itinerating ministers (respectively), encouraging self-trained preachers and enthusiastic layfolk to forge ahead in new, independent ways. Tradition and education no longer held the authority they once did in American churches. When one itinerating preacher (Nancy Towle) criticized the Mormon prophet Joseph Smith for being "no more than any ignorant plough-boy," Smith replied, "The gift has returned back again as in former times, to illiterate fishermen."[7]

Indeed, the push for church reform sometimes went farther than the revolution. People who remained outside the bounds of political citizenship made claims to spiritual equality. Women, Native Americans, and African Americans all founded successful churches in this era. Black preachers organized the first independent Black Baptist churches, the African

Methodist Episcopal Church, and the African Methodist Episcopal Zion church before 1822. Handsome Lake and Tenskwatawa built new indigenous religions; each man claimed sacred authority from the "Master of Life," a previously quiet deity. Tenskwatawa's religion became a rallying point for opposition to fraudulent US treaties with Native American nations—so much so that the federal government actually sent the army after Tenskwatawa's followers at the Battle of Tippecanoe in 1811.

Women became "exhorters"—ignoring Pauline injunctions about keeping silent in church and giving what were sermons in all but name. Upstart denominations frequently called on women to give public testimony of their faith and religious journeys. New sects like the Freewill Baptists, African Methodists, and the "Christian Connexion" movement went further and allowed women into the pulpit. Abigail Roberts found no preacher of the Christian Connexion in her New Jersey town, so she appointed herself preacher and established several congregations. The well-born Harriet Livermore believed God had chosen her to be a preacher and religious writer; she itinerated around the country, outside the bounds of formal congregations as a self-appointed preacher.[8]

Thus when American Jews found themselves training their own hazans instead of hiring formally trained rabbis, they followed the general path of postwar American religion. Jacob Mordecai complained, "In this country . . . everyone does as he pleases." American Jews "consult so-called 'scholars,' thoroughly corrupt individuals" who "contrive egregious legalistic loopholes." Mordecai echoed Anglican minister Devereux Jarratt, who worried that American religion had fallen "under the supreme direction and control of tinkers and tailors, weavers, shoemakers, and country mechanicks of all kinds, men illiterate and wholly unacquainted with colleges."[9] Jarratt wanted baptisms and Mordecai wanted mitzvahs, but they were talking about the same process. Americans needed no permission from ecclesiastical superiors to read the Bible as they liked. Churches ceased to be state-supported institutions charged with public order, and became instead voluntary associations—groups of like-minded Christians who agreed to worship together. The same forces and laws applied equally to Jews. The Judaism of European cities and church-state alliances could not survive in Washington's America.

The challenges for American Judaism in the early American republic were not the challenges of "Americanization" faced by Jewish immigrants in the late-nineteenth and twentieth centuries. Those communities by and large brought religious authority with them from Europe. Nineteenth-century Jews arrived with rabbis and communities in tow, reinforcing a transported religious structure. Anzia Yezierska captured the alienation of this generation in her 1925 novel, *Bread Givers,* the story of Sara Smolinksy. Smolinsky lives crammed into a New York tenement with her immigrant family, proscribed by father and community from doing things the American way. "I got to do something!" she cries. "I want to go into business *like a person.*"[10] Yezierska's protagonist longs to go into American culture; her Jewishness holds her back.

A hundred years earlier, in 1833, Penina Moïse emphasized just the opposite: Judaism belongs in America. Moïse's *Fancy's Sketch Book*, the first book of poetry published by an American Jewish woman, invites Jews to the United States: "Not as Strangers shall your welcome be,/ Come to the homes and the bosoms of the free!" *Fancy's Sketch Book* lacks the literary depth of *Bread Givers*, but then, *Fancy's Sketch Book* was not born out of a need to square religious tradition with economic and political dislocation. (It also emerged from a world of plenitude, in contrast to Yezierska's impoverishment.) Moïse's work emerged instead from a world where Jews and Christians were remaking religious authority. The problem was therefore not quite an issue of "Americanization," for Americans were figuring out who they were with the Jews already attached. For American Jews, the issue of democratization of the synagogue was a question of assessing how, as religious institutions, they could gauge the feelings and choices of their own members. The result was that in most synagogues, "everyone does as he pleases." A huge number of institutional and liturgical changes transformed the American synagogue from 1783 to 1820. Rules became looser, synagogue authorities weaker. Historians have not always seen this shift as an indication of the religious preferences of Jews. They have seen these issues as a problem of "little Jewishness" (*vinig yidishkayt*), as Haym Salomon famously described his life in republican Philadelphia.[11]

Before we accept this kind of wan regret for Jews "not worthy of being called Jews," however, we should consider that most of the changes in American Jewish life came from Jews themselves. For the first time in centuries, Jews in the pews and not the yeshiva had a choice about what counted as Jewish law and practice. They built their own institutions, and they deliberately made them weak, forgiving, and flexible. And they seemed to like it. *Vinig yidishkayt* was by design.[12]

New York, Charleston, Savannah, and Richmond all founded or re-founded their synagogues in the 1780s and '90s. All of them were led by patriot Jews from Mikveh Israel; all of them modeled their organizations on Mikveh Israel's 1782 constitution. Mikveh Israel had declared the synagogue a contract among those who chose to join. The KKMI constitution was binding only on those who signed it in 1782 or subsequently agreed to join. Jews did not have to join the synagogue; religion was not simply a matter of birth. For good measure, KKMI also restricted the powers of the parnas and increased the ability of rank-and-file membership to appeal the decisions of the leadership. Even the word "constitution" was a nod to the new idea of a synagogue as a voluntary society. The more traditional term "hascamoth," hearkening back to Talmudic justifications, fell out of favor.[13]

Other synagogues pushed these ideas further. New York's Shearith Israel opened its 1790 constitution with a preamble that hearkened back to the US Constitution: "We, the members of KK Shearith Israel." The preamble celebrated living "in a state happily constituted upon the principles of equal liberty, civil and religious," and the document concluded with a bill of rights for the members. KKSI's constitution offered membership to all free Jewish males aged twenty-one and up. New members who joined were "in every respect on an equality with those now convened"; there was no rule by seniority in this revolutionary house.[14] By 1794, the synagogue adopted the secret ballot for adjunta elections.[15]

Savannah's congregation named itself after Philadelphia's 1782 synagogue, though they spelled it Mickve or Mickva Israel. Their 1791 constitution provided for annual elections for adjunta and parnas, but any decision by the adjunta could be reviewed by the full membership if three unrelated members requested it. All congregants were expected to observe Shabbat, but joining the synagogue was voluntary.[16] In Philadelphia, the breakaway synagogue Rodeph Shalom required those who joined to share the burdens of Jewish life equally. If a member became ill, every other member was required to sit up with them in groups of two until "each member in the Society shall have served a tour, and to commence again with the first members if necessary."[17]

Richmond's Beth Shalome became the most democratic synagogue of all. Any "free person professing the Jewish religion, and who lives according to its precepts" could become a member. It was intent and choice that made a Jew, according to this document. For good measure, Beth Shalome reduced the application time to three months when other synagogues might make an applicant wait a year.[18]

The new synagogue constitutions largely placed institutional power in the hands of the congregation. In Richmond, a member could object to any rule or regulation and it would trigger an automatic review by "a meeting of all the members in toto," or at least two-thirds of them. By 1805, Shearith Israel abandoned assigned seating. Members purchased seats (as in churches) on a first-come, first-served basis.[19] Richmond's synagogue allowed no fines or excommunication. By 1821, Philadelphia and New York followed suit.[20] Where rules remained, enforcement was sometimes lax. Isaac Polack was called before Savannah's adjunta for keeping his store open on Shabbat. Polack simply explained that Saturday was the only day he could get goods delivered from Charleston, and the adjunta ruled he had not violated the constitution. Individual circumstance and personal choice determined American *halakha*, not rabbinic decree. American Jews seemed fine with that.[21]

By contrast, in the Caribbean colonies, the state continued to empower synagogues to rule over the Jewish population and used force and law to back the synagogue against recalcitrant Jews. When biracial Jews of Suriname formed their own prayer group and threatened to leave the synagogue if they were not recognized as full members, the synagogue dissolved the prayer group and appealed to the state—who vested the synagogue with the power to enforce the ban. Jews violating the decisions of the synagogue would be arrested for disturbing the peace, a harsh fate for biracial people in nineteenth-century Suriname. Jewish religious authority in Suriname ultimately belonged to the state.[22]

The American Revolution gave rise to a different Jewish world. Average Jews challenged and changed synagogue rules, and they did so in the language of the American Revolution. Benjamin Judah refused to sign the 1790 constitution of Shearith Israel, as he found it "of a most arbitrary and tyrannical nature . . . not consonant with the liberality of the Constitution of the Land in which we reside." Specifically, Judah wanted all infractions of synagogue rules heard by a jury, not the adjunta. He finally signed the constitution in 1812, "notwithstanding the objections." Isaac Gomez also signed in 1812 "to establish peace and harmony." However, he insisted on placing an addendum to his signature that he still believed the synagogue laws "are Tyrannical . . . being in opposition both to the sacred Rights of our Religion as well as to the Laws of the Land in which we dwell."[23]

When members refused to abide by synagogue decisions, synagogues found themselves powerless to enforce their decisions. In Charleston, Emanuel de la Motta and the adjunta disagreed over how to bury his recently deceased father. The adjunta insisted that Isaac had wanted to be buried in the congregation's large burial ground; Emanuel believed his father wanted to be interred in the congregation's other burial ground, near his children. The adjunta refused to grant Emanuel's request. A grieving Emanuel wrote that he "would not be subject to the despotic humours of any man or set of men," and the parnas and adjunta were "rascally, infamous, unjust, arbitrary and despotic, that I would not abide their unlawful & Tyranick mandate." If the congregation did not grant his request, Emanuel promised "that I myself would wash his Corpse, Digg his grave, bury him."

Emanuel kept his word. He hired a carpenter at eleven in the evening, washed his father's corpse, dug the grave, and had his father buried before morning. The adjunta summoned him for having "ill treated" them. Emanuel demanded to know what law he had been accused of breaking, and when the adjunta could not name a specific provision, declared that as a free man he could not be indicted without charge. He called their proceedings "ex post facto" (referring to a set of laws forbidden by the US Constitution). It was in Emanuel's words "despotic & unprecedented," and "I would not be dragooned into any arbitrary measures they would adopt, particularly as I had not infringed any Law of the Congregation." Then he left.[24]

Changes in Jewish life went beyond ritual and synagogue worship. Freedom of movement and freedom of the press—both largely missing from Jewish life in Europe—meant that American Jews would encounter multiple sects of Christianity, read all kinds of theological and moral writings, and get into all sorts of religious arguments. Jews encountered new ideas and incorporated them into their religious life.

Consider Edward Rosewater, a footloose Jew on the nineteenth-century frontier who bounced from Ohio to Tennessee to Kentucky. His letters and writings mentioned Valentine's Day and Washington's birthday, but rarely Jewish holidays. He attended some of the emerging synagogues in the trans-Appalachian West, but also attended a Tennessee tent revival and Methodist, Baptist, and Catholic services. He read the Book of Mormon, which he dubbed "a big lot [of] trash," and happily ate pork barbecue in

Alabama. By the 1860s, however, Rosewater still identified as Jewish and helped found the Hebrew Benevolent Society of Omaha, Nebraska.

Historian Shari Rabin, who uncovered Rosewater's hodgepodge religious history, warns against seeing him as a case of "religious deterioration through secularization, Protestantization, assimilation, or apathy." Rosewater was, rather "an exemplar of American religion," moving through congregations, denominations, theologies, religious texts, and even identities as he needed them. In the outburst of organizations, ideas, and enthusiasms that was post-revolutionary American religion, Rosewater took each as it came and built himself through it, even though he began and ended his life as a Jew. The notion that American religion involves picking a tradition and sticking with it, Rabin argues, is nonsense. Rabin finds in Rosewater a precursor of the modern-day American religious "nones"—the quarter or so of Americans who define their religion as "nothing in particular" or simply a non-specific "spirituality." Rosewater's religious yearnings took him out of the synagogue and across the country. At the end of his life, he called himself a Jew. His friends reported his "tender feeling towards his co-religionists, notwithstanding that he manifests no interest in congregational affairs."[25]

Jacob Mordecai followed a similarly peripatetic intellectual and geographical journey to end up in a very different place. Born in Philadelphia in 1762, he served in the Pennsylvania militia and married Judith Myers, of the patriot Myers clan, when she relocated to Philadelphia during the war. He contributed to the new Mikveh Israel building. But as the son of Esther Mordecai—whose marriage to Jacob Cohen showed the limits of synagogal authority—he eventually followed his mother and stepfather to the new Richmond synagogue. Soon after that, he founded an academy in Warrenton, North Carolina, where he became one of the few Jews in the state.

Like Rosewater, Mordecai attended Christian services, accompanying his Gentile students to church on Sundays. When Judith died, Mordecai declared himself a deist, encouraging his children to follow Judith's example of loving "virtue in whatever garb it appeared."[26] Mordecai's son Solomon wrote that his father's liberality on points of religion made his children "Jews but by name."[27] In 1810, Jacob attended a series of Christian revivals in Warrenton, and word began to circulate that he had converted. Instead, he returned to the faith of his childhood, "strengthened [in] my faith & hope in the only true God—the Lord of Hosts, the God of Israel."[28]

Mordecai began a new career as a theologian, bringing "my attention to religious researches in a degree much greater than formerly." He began a long series of informal defenses of the faith. His handwritten letters on Judaism circulated at Richmond's Beth Shalome. "Jews who took their religion seriously admired his scholarship," writes Mordecai's modern biographer, and he spent considerable time working out the arguments for "the reasonableness of our laws." Jacob's subsequent letters and public defenses became an informal, handwritten guide for the next generation of Jewish leaders. Mordecai coaxed a young Isaac Leeser to become hazan at Richmond, Leeser's first stop on an institutional career that spanned the nineteenth century. When he died in 1837, Mordecai was a pillar of Virginia Jewry both socially and theologically.[29]

Mordecai's theology nevertheless did not advocate acceptance of rabbinic authority. He interpreted Jewish law and custom for himself: "You know me *too well*," he wrote his son, "to believe that I think a strict adherence to *all* the numerous days observed by the most superstitious of our sect, *necessary* to its *salvation*."[30] The main thing was that "we ever have & must ever be free." When Christians pointed to the miracles of Christ as evidence, Mordecai countered that it was law, not supernatural events, that provided legitimacy: "The public giving of the Law, *only*, could . . . impart satisfactory authority." Moses, he argued, had "no need of credentials, this divine commission being given *in the hearing of the whole nation*." Belief in a revealed religion was therefore "not founded in *miracles*, but on a public legislation."[31] Mordecai extended his democratized faith back to the revelation at Sinai.

His daughter Ellen went even further: she dismissed both Old and New Testament miracles and had more faith in the deist philosophers, such as Viscount Bolingbroke and the Comte de Volney, than the Bible. Yet Ellen too went on a spiritual journey and converted to Christianity in the 1830s.[32] Other Mordecai siblings followed, and Jacob dealt with crises as he usually did, by making a pastiche of Jewish tradition, experience, and Enlightenment philosophies. He refused to bless his daughter Caroline's marriage to the Catholic instructor of French at Warrenton Academy, but years later wrote asking forgiveness and promising to "for ever drop the subject."[33] Though Mordecai's dalliance with Christianity was shorter and his defense of Judaism more prominent, Rosewater and Mordecai shared the same independent, informal, self-creating Judaism in early America.

Sometimes the synagogues seemed vague on the details, too. As late as 1814, letters exchanged at Philadelphia's Mikveh Israel seemed confused over the difference between a *hacham* and a *hazan*, and other points of basic synagogue organization.[34] In 1790, the merchant Manuel Josephson described American Jews as a people with "no regular system." He traced the lack of clear rules to the polyglot nature of American religion—"every new comer introduced something new, either from his own conceit and fancy, or . . . from the Custom of the Congregation where he was bred."[35] There were not even words in Hebrew for the new nation; an 1807 Hebrew contract had to write *"medinot America"* for "the United States."[36]

All sorts of behaviors and practices bubbled up among these first disestablished synagogues. New York found an increasing number of men who chose not to wear a *talis* during worship. A committee on the subject "cannot find any law relating to this particular subject." All they could claim for it was "tradition," and only in 1825 did they try to enforce it.[37] Gershom Cohen in Charleston wrote to ask about whether synagogues should be "imitating the Christians by having services on Sunday."[38] In 1815, Mikveh Israel hired Carvalho as hazan, even though Carvalho had a reputation for eating non-kosher food.[39] Moses Hays broke Jewish tradition and requested his body be cremated. Judith Mordecai asked on her deathbed that her funeral might "omit such parts" as would "appear ridiculous . . . among people unaccustomed to our religious rites."[40]

Jews often had approximated rules regarding Jewish life and holidays, and they did not seem to mind. In the early republic, Shabbat became less important. By 1825, one New York Jew complained of only "three heads of household" showing up for Saturday services.[41] Other Jews might mark the day even away from synagogues. On an overland trip in 1826, Shabbat sundown overtook Henry Etting while still on the road. He did something, he told his brother—someone produced a candle, "pronounced the *Barocha* and lighted the lamps." But, Etting added, "I ain't going to give you the particulars."[42] When Solomon Cohen went to England, he was "much confused" by Jewish wedding ceremonies, having no knowledge of them from his American childhood.[43] Benjamin Rush attended a Jewish wedding in 1787, but speaking no Hebrew he was mostly impressed by "the freedom with which some of them [the guests] conversed with each other" during the prayers. (Rush noted the breaking of the wine glass as a sign of "the brittleness and uncertainty of human life.") The handful of Jews in 1807 North Carolina carefully observed Passover. When their Passover supplies did not arrive in time, they did without bread of any kind—though their remaining loaf of wheat bread remained in the house, providing a sore temptation.[44]

Samuel Nunes Carvalho headed west with John C. Frémont to mark out a path for a transcontinental railroad. The Jewish explorer had to guess and compromise on kosher rules when food ran low. He agreed to eat horse, "the strange and forbidden food, with much hesitation, and only in small quantities." But he refused to eat the equally *traifa* porcupine because it "looked very much like pork."[45] In New York, Naphtali Phillips scribbled out dozens of pages about the differences between "tripha" and "Cosher," a handwritten guide for Jews who had no easy access to a kosher butcher.[46]

The gift-giving of Hannukah received scant notice until the mid-nineteenth century. That was when Clement Clark Moore ("'Twas the Night Before Christmas") and other American Christians domesticated Christmas from a time of pranks and street fights into a family-centered, pious affair.[47] Meanwhile, Purim in the colonial British empire adopted a carnivalesque air, a kind of Jewish Mardi Gras. In Suriname, Christians as well as Jews purchased masks and joined in raucous marches and celebrations—as did the men and women enslaved to Jewish landowners.[48] In 1789 Richmond, Joseph Darmstadt wrote a Purim poem mostly focused on alcohol; it recounted the joys of porter, brandy, sherry, and gin, but only once mentioned Esther.[49] For a New York Purim, Gershom Seixas led children "full of the frolic" up well past bedtime telling stories. Seixas enjoyed remembering such times when he got bored at trustee meetings.[50]

Some Jews began to push for choirs in synagogue "to give to the service that solemnity that our prayers and psalms should have," according to a Shearith Israel committee. The New York committee sidestepped the question of whether choirs were really Jewish by recommending that the congregation should not become dependent on a small number of singers who might take ill or move.[51] Clearly, however, some Jews agreed with Charleston's Gershom Cohen, who preferred choirs. Their "Singing was regular (they having Practiced for a whole week)." Cohen found such singing "more decorous & decent." It occurred at the dedication of the Charleston synagogue in 1791, with the city's Board of Commissioners and City Council in attendance.[52] In 1825, Rebecca Gratz attended the rededication of Mikveh Israel, where Jacob Seixas led a choir, and heard Gentiles declare "there has never been such church music performed in Phila[delphia]."[53] When Charleston dedicated its new synagogue in 1820, an organ accompanied the service, played by the music director of one of the city's Presbyterian churches.[54]

American synagogues also embraced the patchwork nature of their clergy. Rebecca Samuels meant it literally when she said there was "no rabbi in all of America." Caribbean communities sometimes hired yeshiva graduates, but US synagogues did not. For decades, synagogues in New York, Charleston, and Philadelphia preferred educated layfolk to ordained rabbis. An informal clergy was not just practical—it was part of the broad shift in American religion. The American *bimah* that had been spackled together in the 1700s suddenly appeared to be on the vanguard in the 1800s.

Jews appointed leaders based not on their knowledge of tradition but on their ability to engage their audience. The American hazan had to speak to the people, not necessarily to the law. Rebecca Gratz described Moses Peixotto—Seixas's successor in New York—as "not a learned man, nor indeed a very sensible one," but "a good man" and "very popular with the congregation and reads the prayers in a manner as to make his hearers feel that he understands and is inspired by their solemnity."[55] Peixotto was a merchant before becoming hazan. Richmond's new synagogue made Jacob Cohen their hazan, despite (or perhaps because of) his insistence on interpreting marriage law for himself. Cohen had no formal religious training, but in 1791 he signed a ketubah as "Jacob Cohen, Rev."[56] Later, Richmond did away with the hazan altogether, instead allowing laypeople to lead the services. The congregations of Savannah and Newport followed suit.[57] Jacob Mordecai's daughter Rachel performed most of the Yom Kippur service in Warrenton, North Carolina, although when she finished, she confessed she was "glad . . . it is over."[58] American synagogues did not have an established rabbinate. It also appears that they did not want one.

With all this upheaval, worship could become rowdy. Abraham Pinto was censured by Shearith Israel for insulting the parnas during service.[59] In Philadelphia, Benjamin Nones was the parnas and was censured by the adjunta for insulting them in an argument over the proper law regarding the shofar.[60] On the last night of Passover 1825, Philadelphia's *shammash* (synagogue functionary) had to request that several women in the women's gallery take the seats they had paid for. The women sent their brother into the men's gallery to challenge the *shammash* and "dare the Parnas or any one to order his Sisters out of the front seat."[61] The *shammash* meekly declared he "found my Selve obliged to inforse the Rules of the Congregation." These rules specifically forbade members having conversations "either in the synagogue or places adjacent" while prayer was going on. Congregation Rodeph Shalom in Philadelphia had to ask members to keep their seats during service and "hold no discussions foreign to the duties before them during Publick worship."[62] Such troubles may explain the reticence of many members to serve as officers; in 1807, fifteen different members declined the "honor" of serving on the adjunta for Charleston.[63]

Democratization was not the same as the modern Reform movement of Europe and the Americas. Shifting liturgies, untrained clergy, lax enforcement of kosher laws, and lay-led synagogues all preceded the formal splits that Isaac Harby and other Reform Jews proposed in the later nineteenth century. When in 1811 the congregants of Shearith Israel demanded the right to recognize more than one kosher butcher in the city of New York, they were exercising freedom of religion rather than trying to assimilate. Seixas asked the city to enforce his edict recognizing only one kosher butcher, but the city balked. New York Jews insisted on the right to recognize kosher butchers beyond those identified by their leadership.[64] The question of who made Jewish law, and not Jewish law itself, seems to have been the driving issue.

Even some Gentiles wanted to interpret Jewish law. American synagogues fielded requests from Christians who wanted to become Jews. James Foster traveled to Mikveh Israel in 1788 with "a desire to take hold of God's holy Covenant" and made his request "in the Name of the God of Israel."[65] Anna Barnett wrote to Mikveh Israel, "Permit one who has not the Happiness to be Born a Jewess & Favored Immediately from the God of Israel as you are to request your Attention to my Particular Case." Barnett wanted to be "admitted an Associate of your Congregation & to become a Jewess." She asked for the honor "not as a Favour" but as a way to live up "to the Divine precepts of the Bible."[66] The tone of the requests suggests an earnest desire among Christians to connect to the original text of the Bible—a frequent urge in those days of revivalism. Most of these potential converts went away disappointed. Foster was told he needed to undergo ceremonies in Amsterdam. Another initiate (known only as "Miss Mervin") received the ritual bath for converts, but questions over its validity delayed her entry into the synagogue.[67]

Efforts by Gentiles to convert to Judaism outside intermarriage suggests that while Judaism was not prominent in the American spiritual marketplace, it was still a part of the American religious firmament. In 1848

Abraham Kirkas arrived in New York from Syria. He had sought conversion in his own land, "but the Jews did not wish to make a proselyte of me for fear of the laws of the country." Kirkas then told the synagogue that "we came hither to this free country America. . . . [W]e shall not go away from here until my desire shall have been carried out." Shearith Israel accepted him as a convert.[68] Judaism was not strange or hidden to revolutionary America, and the freedom of American Jews was not hidden to the world.

With so much religious choice and unclear authority, divisions became inevitable. By 1830, there were multiple synagogues in Philadelphia, New York, and Charleston, plus a host of new Jewish organizations. These splits were also part of a more general flood of sectarian splits in American religion. If conscience alone could dictate religious choice, then the power of "tradition" would atrophy. Democratization did not create the Baptists or the Methodists, but it accelerated their rise to prominence—to say nothing of the host of smaller Protestant sects that were born or flourished in this period, including Churches of Christ, Disciples of Christ, Mormons, Shakers, Hicksite Quakers, Universalists, Swedenborgians, Unitarians, Adventists, and a short-lived Ohio church known as the "Screaming Children."

Even Mikveh Israel divided. Congregation Rodeph Shalom began as a separate prayer group within Mikveh Israel in 1795—another nod to the informality of worship. Within twenty years it was an independent congregation. Historians have sometimes defined this split as a division of Sephardic-Ashkenazic Jews, and it is true that Rodeph Shalom eventually adopted the Ashkenazic service. But Mikveh Israel had long had internal divisions. In 1782, Benjamin Nones threatened to shave Abraham Levy's beard, since the beard led "many people falsely to imagine him a distinguished member of our congregation." Jonas Phillips called the scuffle "a Riot in the Synagogue y[ar]d."[69] So the Rodeph Shalom split was not merely an ethnic division. In 1829, Rodeph Shalom decided that Jews who married non-Jews would not be expelled—as long as they raised their children as Jews. Unlike Mikveh Israel, Rodeph Shalom did not avoid would-be converts; they accepted Jacob Bar Abraham Abinu as a member in 1819 and performed the rituals of immersion and circumcision.[70] Rodeph Shalom went farther on the road to democratization than its parent congregation: They had no hazan at all. Members took turns as readers. Mikveh Israel could not keep all the Jews together. But neither could Rodeph Shalom—by 1810, they had to pass congregational rules concerning members attending *minyan* at both synagogues.[71] American Jews were choosing to follow religion in their own way.

In New York, tensions led to a planned act of religious disobedience that split the synagogue. At Shearith Israel, in the last day of Passover 1825, Barrow Cohen was called to the Torah, where he failed to make the usual *tzedaka* offering required of all those who received *aliyah*. The hazan mentioned the oversight, whereupon (in front of the Torah), Cohen pulled out a copy of "the Book of the Laws" with "an apparent view of shewing the reason or cause" for his refusal. Cohen's defense was that the requirement for *tzedaka* had been created by the trustees in 1820; it was not in the synagogue constitution, and Cohen would only take actions "according to the Constitution of this Congregation." This tactic failed to sway the hazan, and Cohen returned to his seat.

Cohen's act was not a spontaneous outburst. The "Book of the Laws" was likely KKMI's constitution, not a Talmudic or Levitical book since it was referred to as "a Book or paper" that fit in a pocket. Cohen did not simply happen to be carrying the institutional laws around with him when called to the Torah; he acted as part of a collaborative effort against the power of the trustees.

Shearith Israel had managed combative personalities prior to Cohen's Pesach performance. In 1816, Gershom Seixas died, and the congregation bickered over choosing a new hazan. The trustees picked Moses Levi Madura Peixotto, but Mordecai Manuel Noah publicly condemned the choice and considered the post "vacant."[72] David Seixas—son of the revolutionary rabbi—insulted Peixotto with "passion and temper" inside the synagogue; the board suspended him from synagogue honors for a year. That in turn provoked a crisis—seventeen members petitioned the board claiming that Seixas had a right, according the KKSI's constitution, to a hearing for his actions, and defended themselves in good republican language: "Laws . . . enacted for the rights and Liberties of individuals ought not to be precipitously disregarded."[73]

The Cohen case pushed the synagogue to its sectarian limit. Cohen and others tried to set up a separate prayer group to express "our zeal and attention to the worship of our holy religion." The trustees rejected it, and the synagogue split. The new synagogue, B'nai Jeshurun, purchased a house of worship from the First Colored Presbyterian Church and established a highly egalitarian synagogue. Membership fees were reduced from those at Shearith Israel; trustees were elected to short, three-month terms. The hazan was not to dress differently from any other member of the society, and synagogue honors were to be given out "in such a manner that each person should have an equal portion."[74]

Much the same process split Charleston's synagogue, twice. An independent group of Jews called Unve Shalom established their own cemetery in Charleston in 1785.[75] This was hardly surprising, given that in 1775 Isaac DaCosta (who joined Unve Shalom) and others had complained the existing synagogue (Beth Elohim) ruled with "an arbitrary nature . . . inconsistent for the ruling of a congregation, justly & equitably."[76] The split ended in 1791, but Charleston's Jews argued for years over which cemetery should receive the remains of departed Beth Elohim elders.[77]

A more substantial split occurred with Isaac Harby's Reformed Society in 1825, also in Charleston. Harby, a playwright and politician who did not speak Hebrew, became the leader of the dissidents at Beth Elohim. He combined revivalist feeling and deist reason with Jewish flourish: "PRAYER, to proceed from the heart, must proceed from the understanding. True piety consists not in sound, but in emotion. True religion needs no mystery, no veil, no cloud to hide it."[78] When the reformers wrote their articles of faith, they declared, "Let each one believe or reject what his heart . . . may rationally dictate to be believed or rejected." Doing so, Harby and his followers believed, would allow Jews to "break in pieces the sceptre of Rabbinical power."[79]

The changes requested by Harby included a shorter, more decorous service. As subsequent generations of bar and bat mitzvah candidates have complained, "The service continued until *twelve* o'clock, although usually commencing at *nine*."[80] They shortened the liturgy by removing repetitions and throwing out what Harby called "Rabbinical interpolations." Reformers also wanted more of the service in English so that the word of God could be understood. After all, ancient Jews worshipped in Hebrew because that was "the language of the people." The service needed to be understood, so it needed to be in English. If these changes could be implemented, Harby argued, then Jews would understand what Jewish worship was and why it mattered.[81]

The reformers promoted their changes as a "more rational means of worshipping the true God" that would promote the beauty of Judaism as well as the "practice of virtue and morality."[82] The proposals drew in part from the broader stirrings of the Reform movement, then just beginning in Europe. Still, the Beth Elohim petitioners saw themselves as American reformers. It was "in the United States, that we are to look for the experimental development of our system."[83]

In January 1825, Beth Elohim's adjunta issued a formal response rejecting the proposed changes. According to the synagogue's 1820 constitution, petitioners needed two-thirds of the membership to call for such a change, and the forty-seven Jews who signed the petition were insufficient. Harby and the reformers broke away and built the Reformed Society of Israelites in 1825, with the avowed goal of fighting apathy among Jews of Charleston.[84]

Harby compared himself to Martin Luther. (If Harby knew about Luther's anti-Semitic writings, he never admitted it.)[85] He sought a Protestant-style revision of Judaism, and for good measure, he doused the new synagogue in revolutionary language. The Society had a Committee of Correspondence, just like the patriots, and Harby declared "the birthright of ourselves . . . is equal liberty."[86] The Society persevered through 1838, then fizzled out.

Even if Harby was no Luther, Jewish communities nevertheless followed the model of the upstart Protestant sects of the Republic. The fissiparous nature of American Christianity became the institutional model for American Judaism for the next fifty years.[87] Synagogues split over divisions rather than amalgamate all Jewish voices into one. By 1850, there were ten synagogues in New York.[88] And if Jewish institutions worked like Protestant institutions, it confirmed the revolutionary notion that moral capacity was not dependent on religious confession.

As barriers eroded, Jewish men even reached acceptance in the ultimate expression of genteel culture: dueling. Once the purview of upper-class fops, dueling actually became a kind of egalitarian political exercise in postwar America. Only equals could duel—part of the complex ritual code that had endeared it to the upper classes in the first place. In the early United States, however, to demand or accept a duel became (among white men) a way to seek redress of wrongs and prove one's equality. In a rather perverse way, dueling created a brotherhood of honor and therefore, a kind of trust.[89] American duels did not always end in bloodshed; merely accepting the challenge might be enough to prove to each participant that their opponent was an honorable man. Duelists might fire into the air or aim for a leg. Taking on such a risk, and publicizing that risk in newspapers, became a way of proving honor and manliness, especially in the political realm. In 1809, Henry Clay began his political career by taking a bullet in the thigh during one of his duels.[90]

Still, a lot of people got shot. A congressman shot a former governor in an 1802 North Carolina duel. Patriot Lachlan MacIntosh shot the patriot governor of Georgia in a 1777 duel. Republican Brockholst Livingston killed Federalist James Jones in 1798. Andrew Jackson shot several men in duels in the early 1800s, and of course, Vice-President Aaron Burr killed Alexander Hamilton in 1804. (Hamilton knew the risks. His son Phillip had died in a duel in 1801.)[91]

Jewish men were accepted as duelists in the early United States, and however *meshuggis* the system, it was a clear sign of social and political equality. Duels occurred between equals; if a Jew dueled a Gentile, his presence on the "field of blood" tokened both personal honor and an equal status. (The code of dueling required that social inferiors be beaten or have their noses pulled instead.) For example, in 1812, Mordecai Noah endured a raft of duels when his essays earned the ire of the Federalist Joshua Toomer. James Hamilton, the future governor of South Carolina, delivered Toomer's challenge to Noah. Noah accepted and spent most of the rest of the day in target practice. Noah and Toomer sent their representatives into four hours of negotiations, and a gentleman's agreement was reached to call off the duel. Noah engaged with the highest levels of political authority as an equal—although lest he be called a coward, he soon fought a related duel with (in his words) "a puppy by the name of John Cantor" who "had the insolence to send me a Challenge to fight him. I accordingly met him on Sunday last and plum'd him the first Shot in the leg to the joy of all Charleston."[92]

Duels also offered a way to answer anti-Semitism. In 1832, James Stark called Phillip Minis a "damned Israelite" who "ought to be pissed upon." Minis demanded an apology. Stark gave one but then retracted it. Minis demanded a duel; Stark accepted. When Stark tried to shirk the duel, Minis met him at a hotel, called him a coward, and shot the man dead. Minis immediately submitted himself to the local authorities. A jury acquitted him of murder.[93]

In May 1811, the Christian Richard Bowden argued with the Jewish Moses Myers, and the next morning, in broad daylight, "without notice or provocation" Bowden approached Myers "& struck him with a butcher's cleaver." Myers and Bowden were separated; on hearing the news, Moses's son Samuel raced to his father's side. Moses fainted from blood loss, and Sam, "supposing his father to have been killed, rushed to the counting house of Mr. B" and shot the Christian dead.[94]

These acts of violence, in a different time and place, might have launched an anti-Semitic response. But in 1811 Virginia, public opinion fell squarely behind Samuel Myers. "So far from attaching dishonor," the shooting apparently ensured that "men will ever have a more favorable opinion of your Son," wrote Asher Marx to Moses. The reputation of the Myers clan had increased when Samuel shot Bowden, because he had revenged an insult rather than remaining "altogether inactive, when his father was abused."[95] Bowden had struck first and had not treated Myers as an equal; so Samuel had struck back, not treating Bowden as an equal. It left people, according to Marx, "relieved." Moses himself wrote a week later that Samuel had become "an astonishing favorite of all classes save a few Petifull beings." Samuel Myers was charged with manslaughter, not murder, and got off with a slap on the wrist.

The morality of all this is, of course, awful. But the question is not whether the Jews were moral but whether they were equal. (And morality was pretty terrible in many ways in the early United States.) Not only were Jews included as equals in duels of honor, but they might be perceived by Gentile neighbors as more honorable than Christians. Men's personal honor was not necessarily determined by their religious choice.

Dueling was for men; so too was synagogue membership. The synagogue was run by and for men. In 1815, Shearith Israel had 132 seats for men but only seventy-two in the women's gallery.[96] The Hebrew Orphan Society, a South Carolina organization caring for Jewish widows, was headed by a man. Despite that, Jewish women fought for the right to live their religion in their own way. As we've seen, the Judah sisters in 1785 defied the decision of the adjunta who sought to assign them seats. Gershom Seixas tried to mediate the conflict between the Judah sisters and the board of trustees. He and the Judahs' mother offered to have her pay for the new seats at the going rate, and thereby avoid "scandalous consequences."[97]

The trustees instead rebuked Seixas and took the Judah sisters to court, where the women were found guilty of trespass. The sisters and their mother all quit the synagogue. Seixas vented his rage as he rarely did: "I . . . conceived it as my duty as a JEW to use my endeavors to prevent its being carried before any Tribunal of Justice" beyond the synagogue. He defended the proposed compromise with Mrs. Judah as "founded on principles of equal and common Liberty—am sorry the Trustees differ with me." When his female congregants demanded to make their own rules, Seixas stood with them.[98]

The Judah sisters eventually returned to KKSI, on their own terms. Becky and Sally were readmitted "for the sake of peace," according to a peremptory note in the minutes of the trustees. When Abigail Judah returned, she requested an appointment as a *shammash*, figuring she could do the work as well as any Jewish man. She did not get the job, but in 1815, Jennett Isaacs *did* become a "shammashess"—doing the clerical and routine work expected of the synagogue beadle. Isaacs was the widow of the previous *shammash*. She served for six years.[99] Even as synagogues became more masculine places, Jewish women shaped their faith in republican terms, and confronted those institutions in search of the Judaism they envisioned.[100]

To do so, Jewish women made their own institutions. Locked out of leadership in Philadelphia's Jewish organizations, Rebecca Gratz invented an ecumenical one. Along with eight Jewish and fifteen Christian women, Gratz co-founded the Female Association for the Relief of Women and Children in Reduced Circumstances in 1800 and served as its secretary for twenty-two years. Gratz's group raised and distributed money to the "deserving" poor (that is, the poor they did not condemn as lazy). Gratz insisted that the treasurer of the association must be unmarried, because Pennsylvania law in 1800 declared that a wife's property became her husband's on marriage, and Gratz wanted no men taking charge of the money.[101] Gratz insisted on female control of a religious society for women.

In 1819 Gratz created the Female Hebrew Benevolent Society. The new organization provided aid for Jewish women in indigent circumstances, independent of Philadelphia synagogues and with a slate of all-female officers. Protestant poor-relief institutions assisted all comers. But Protestant relief organizations included Christian proselytizing with their assistance. Gratz sought to save Jewish women that experience.[102] In 1822, a second Jewish aid organization opened in Philadelphia; similar groups spread across Jewish America. When New York's Jewish men called a meeting to organize women into a society for care of the dead, they found the meeting lightly attended "and nothing was done." The men were baffled, because of the "Zeal displayed" previously by "the Ladies of our Holy Religion." Perhaps the women were not interested in another male-led Jewish organization.[103] These independent Jewish organizations offered ways for Jewish women, especially single women, to shape Jewish culture, practice, and morality outside the synagogue. As Gratz wrote to her Christian sister-in-law, "the offices of charity are not all engrossed by the Church"—or the institutional synagogue.[104]

In 1838, Gratz adapted another Protestant standby to Jewish ends with the creation of the first Hebrew Sunday school. Sunday schools had become routine in Christian congregations in England and the United States. Gratz wanted Jewish children to be able to live among Christians while still "respecting their own laws and practicing the virtues required of the chosen people of God." Therefore, Jews needed Sunday schools. (She also mentioned that the "want of education shuts the door of advancement in private or public station—which the Israelite might obtain in this country.")[105] Gratz somehow convinced the American Sunday School Union to provide Bibles for classes; she cut out or pasted over passages referencing Christ. As the Hebrew Sunday school model spread, Gratz recruited a company of female teachers to instruct Jewish children. Nineteenth-century democratization did not give rights to women, but Gratz and her contemporaries created new religious spaces for themselves anyway.[106]

Women also constructed Jewish thought and liturgy in the early republic. If European yeshivas were male-only, the lay-led synagogues of America were not. Like her father Jacob, Rachel Mordecai circulated some of her handwritten defenses of Judaism. Her most famous were a series of letters with Irish novelist Maria Edgeworth. Rachel Mordecai objected to Edgeworth's novel *The Absentee* in 1812, a book about English landlords in Ireland in which the bloodsucking moneylender manipulating the English is a Jewish nogoodnik named "Mordecai." Rachel Mordecai objected in a letter to Edgeworth. She had grown tired of reading novels where "whenever a *Jew* is introduced" the character was "mean, avaricious, and unprincipled." If Edgeworth knew no Jews of good character, it was because she had never been to the United States: "In this happy country, where religious distinctions are scarcely known, character and talents are sufficient to attain advancement, we find the Jews to form a respectable part of the community." Judaism did not corrupt, Mordecai argued; religious discrimination did.[107]

What began as a stern critique turned into a lifelong friendship. Edgeworth and Mordecai exchanged epistles, books, and scientific specimens for over twenty years. Edgeworth made an apology for her fictional Mordecai in the novel *Harrington*. Edgeworth's eponymous hero fears Jews until a fictional American Jew, Berenice Montenero, wins his heart. Edgeworth put Mordecai's own words about American Judaism into the novel. Berenice's father describes her as coming from "a happy part of that country, where religious distinctions are scarcely known—where characters and talents are all sufficient to attain advancement—where the Jews form a respectable part of the community."[108]

The correspondence between Rachel Mordecai and Edgeworth was not published, but news of her defense of Judaism circulated among Philadelphia and Richmond Jewry.[109] Mordecai's defense was probably more popular than *Harrington* among Jews, since Edgeworth's Berenice reveals herself as a Christian after weaning her beau off anti-Semitism. It was Mordecai's only disappointment in *Harrington*, and she duly noted it to Edgeworth, but also admitted she believed both religions were "equally capable of conducting them to the Throne of Grace."[110]

If Rachel Mordecai believed Christians and Jews were equally likely to get to heaven, it perhaps followed that she thought their services ought to resemble one another. Mordecai threw herself behind Isaac Harby and his reforms. In 1824, she advocated a "thorough revision of our English prayer book by some person of ability and judgment." Worship needed to be comprehensible and virtuous. Jews ought to place "good sense and true piety" as "the basis of our public worship, instead of . . . Rabbinical jargon." Her father, Jacob Mordecai, opposed Harby and called him an atheist. Rachel probably shaped the debate over Harby at least a little when her father, unaware of her feelings, asked her to review his jeremiad against Charleston's Reformed Society. Rachel advised non-publication or limited circulation of his response, because she believed that it might harm Jewish-Christian relations. So Jacob contented himself with an oral denunciation of Harby in the Richmond synagogue. Harby's group fizzled, and Rachel increasingly felt herself "repeating prayers of which I cannot admit the efficacy, and keeping festivals which . . . have lost their solemnity." She converted to Christianity on her deathbed. It did not please her fellow Jews. But she chose her own faith.[111]

Many Jewish women who did not convert, however, echoed Mordecai's call for "good sense" over "rabbinical jargon" in Judaism. Louisa Hart informed her Hebrew Sunday school students that "the simplicity of our holy religion" could be confounded by "arguments of falsehood." Better to keep things simple. There was one central tenet, she told them: "Judaism based on the proclamation of God's unity is the very life of life." From this principle flowed all the ceremonies and prohibitions. Students needed to know why they believed, "and action must be proof of conviction. . . . [Y]ou must teach yourself to instruct others."[112] New York's Judith Cohen could not accompany her younger brother to England in 1815, but she did write out a series of instructions for him. The first was "Fear God and keep his commandments." The rest were generic instructions of genteel virtue that presumably flowed from the first, such as "Let your actions be such that you will always deserve praise without pride" and "Keep no vicious company." Cohen admonished her brother to keep the Jewish law, but her specifics referred to clear moral actions unconnected to broader Jewish themes.[113]

This concern for virtue and morality was not an attempt to make Judaism something else. These women saw Judaism as beginning with the love of God and moral action. Grace Seixas Nathan's final written words to her son were an exhortation to him to teach his children "a just idea of their religious and moral principles, these being the corner stones of all *good*, and on which the basis of life here and hereafter may be supported." Although there was nothing specifically Jewish about her instructions, she nevertheless wrote "I *die* in the *full faith* of my *religion*."[114] Rachel's sister Emma Mordecai created a Hebrew Sunday school in Richmond, and then published a short primer under the pseudonym "A Jewess," intended for Jewish students and educators across the country. Twelve of its thirteen lessons dealt with the oneness of God as Creator of the universe. (There were also bits of Newtonian physics and botany thrown in.) Only in the final lesson did Emma reveal the notion of God's commandments, and that with a vague aphorism: "All that God has made known to men about Himself, is written in the Holy Bible." It is the only explicitly Jewish reference in the lessons. A Christian reader—who would assume the Bible included the New Testament—would find little to object to. That was partially Emma's intention. The book was "written expressly for the benefit of the rising generation of Israel" but she wrote it "to inculcate those first grand truths, in the contemplation of which *all* sects and denominations melt down into one great mass of God-adoring believers." It was a perfectly republican document. Religion was love of God and good sense, and from that arose Judaism—and others, according to Emma Mordecai. If Christians found it useful, so be it.[115]

In at least one case, Jewish women refashioned an old Jewish religious tradition to protect their own rights: the *shtar hallitzah*. Under American law, wives lost most of their legal rights upon marriage. Jewish *ketubot* (marriage contracts) protected some of those rights. Though it had fallen out of use in the eighteenth century, the *shtar hallitzah* was a medieval legal document intended as a workaround for the restrictions found in

Deuteronomy 25 (which required a wife's brother-in-law to impregnate her if her husband died without children). It required the brother-in-law to formally refuse to fulfill this obligation, at which point the woman in question removed his sandal. (They usually put something in writing, too.) Rebecca Phillips Moses received a *shtar hallitzah* the day after her wedding in November 1807. She may herself have requested it, since at the time, she was fifteen and her husband thirty-five. In 1793, Hannah Levy Hart sought a *shtar hallitzah* from her future brother-in-law. When he refused, a mild crisis ensued. The adjunta of Savannah's Mikve Israel insisted that "it was required of him," and the wedding only went forward when a legal loophole was discovered, rendering the *hallitzah* moot.[116] At other times, the language of the *ketubah* itself promised women financial rights and independence that American laws did not. Judith Hays and Samuel Myers's *ketubah* of 1796, for example, stated explicitly that she would inherit more than the one-third of her husband's estate required by law when he died.[117]

The return of the *shtar hallitzah* represented an assertion of the rights and personhood of married women. When Moses Sheftall married Nelly Bush in 1792, Bush actually went through the ceremony with Sheftall Sheftall, her new brother-in-law; she removed his sandal and that was that. Perhaps Bush wished to establish her credentials as a Jewish woman to a skeptical father-in-law, Mordecai Sheftall, who had complained about the apostacy of many members of the Bush clan.[118]

The return of the *shtar hallitzah* demonstrates that the changes in American Judaism did not always involve abandoning traditions or loosening rules. Fundamentally, American Jews democratized their religion by searching through it for the aspects that best met their new concerns and outlook. The lasting religious effect of the revolution was the same for Jews and Christians: the rise of a belief in a God of egalitarianism, a God who cared for each believer more than for hierarchies or formalities. The democratized synagogue created conflicts and splits. Some synagogues survived and some fell. But it also pushed American Judaism further in the quest to make religion vital to daily life. Judaism was a series of practical principles as well as a way of life. Perhaps American Jews felt like Rebecca Gratz, who summarized her own Jewish faith this way: "A life of usefulness is a life of enjoyment."[119]

10

The Black Synagogue

IN 1811, IN HIS LATE teens, Isaac Brandon went to Suriname to become a Jew. Born in Barbados to a Jewish father, he left home to look for a *mohel* to perform the rite of circumcision. Suriname had seven *mohels*, so when Brandon arrived, he provided the required declaration that he wished to "be considered a Jew of the Portuguese Jewish nation" and underwent the procedure. His sister Sarah, baptized an Anglican, similarly went to Suriname, underwent a *mikveh* (ritual bath), and became a Jew.

By 1820, Isaac and Sarah lived in New York. They both worshipped at Shearith Israel and both married into the prominent Moses clan. They became pillars of the New York Jewish community. Each had portraits stippled onto ivory, as befitted people of their high station. The siblings (and the broader New York community) almost never spoke about the reason Isaac had needed to go to Suriname: He had not been born Jewish because their mother was an enslaved woman of African descent. The ivory miniatures of Isaac Brandon and Sarah Brandon Moses are the oldest existing portraits of multiracial American Jews.[1]

Their mother, "Sarah Esther," went by either first name and sometimes both, and carried at different times the last name of her mother (Gill), her enslavers (Lopez), and the father of her children (Brandon). Her own preferences and intentions remain unknown to us since those who recorded the written evidence of her existence "transcribed nothing that she said and didn't wonder about what she thought," according to the Brandons' biographer, Laura Leibman. At some point in the late eighteenth century, Sarah

Esther and Abraham, a white Jewish merchant of Bridgetown, Barbados, lived as husband and wife, although they remained unmarried. These kinds of relationships were common in the slaveholding Atlantic, and it is impossible to know whether Sarah Esther gave her "consent" to the matter (if such a word even applies under the conditions of slavery). She did, however, bear Abraham two children, and those children remained his favorites and chosen heirs. It was Abraham who arranged for Sarah's manumission; Isaac's legal status at birth is unclear, but he, too, was free by 1811.

Abraham attempted to make his son a full member of the Bridgetown Jewish community. It did not go well. Several synagogue members refused to accept Isaac as a Jew, inflicting "a wound that stings Mr. Brandon to the quick," as the synagogue parnas reported. So once his children became teenagers, Brandon sent Isaac and Sarah to Suriname for conversion and then on to London for education. In London, the Brandons' effort to reclassify themselves as white began in earnest. Sarah received a finishing education at a school for Jewish girls and eventually had her ivory portrait made. She was married at London's Bevis Marks synagogue to Joshua Moses, and the couple then settled in New York near her husband's American relatives. In 1820 the US census classified both Isaac and Sarah as white, although their African ancestry remained something of an open secret. Isaac became an American citizen in 1829.[2]

Revolutionary-era American Jews lived in a multiracial society, and early American Judaism was multiracial. Sarah Brandon's journey from enslaved Anglican of Barbados to a white Jew of Manhattan was part of the shifting grounds of freedom, slavery, and race implicit in the Age of Revolutions. Classifications changed rapidly. New York passed a gradual emancipation law in 1799; shortly afterward, the Indiana Territory forbade anyone of African or Native American descent from testifying in court. Indiana also introduced one of the nation's first "blood quanta" rules—laws that required any person with African ancestry to be classified as Black. When Ephraim Waterford discovered that as a Black man in Indiana, he could not bequeath his estate to his wife, he told a court, "If that was a republican government, I would try a monarchical one." Waterford headed to Canada.[3]

Isaac Brandon's citizenship depended on his being classified as white. His Judaism did not seem to matter. "Jew" was not a racial category in the wake of the American Revolution. It remained a legal class in most of Europe, where laws dictated what Jews could wear, where they could live, and how they could earn a wage. In the Caribbean as well, census takers and militia rolls maintained the category of "Jew" in addition to "black" and "white."[4] Jewishness as a racial classification returned to America in the later nineteenth century, with the rise of European nationalism and the assertion of "scientific" racial categories. But the post-revolutionary United States largely accepted the American Jewish argument that Judaism was a religious choice, founded in moral principles and hence fit for a republic. At the same time, defenders of the slave system emphasized (Black) race as something that made people unfit for life in a republic. Thus as Jews defined themselves as republican, they also defined themselves as white. Historian Shari Rabin writes, "In the eyes of American law . . . Jews have been white from the beginning."[5]

But of course, not all Jews were white. Though biracial Jews found almost no institutional support and freedom in the United States, they continued to retain their Jewish knowledge and sometimes Jewish practice secretly. Moreover, as the new republic passed over its short-lived abolitionist urges in the 1790s, the legal right to own human property became a "freedom" that citizens could exercise. If Judaism made good republicans, and the American republic enslaved Blacks, would Jews choose to follow the American norms, or would they remember that their ancestors were slaves in the land of Egypt?

These questions have unpleasant answers. Historians of American Judaism have been reticent to broadcast details of American Jews and slaveholding when such comments can be ripped out of context and added to conspiracy-driven social media accounts advocating the total elimination of world Jewry. In 1991, the Nation of Islam published *The Secret Relationship Between Blacks and Jews*, a book that accused Jews of being the central players in the Atlantic slave trade. Henry Louis Gates Jr. called the volume a "Bible of the new anti-Semitism." Eli Faber and numerous other historians wrote well-cited refutations. The book nonetheless remains in print and can be found among citations on alt-right and neo-Nazi websites.[6]

As always with anti-Semitism, the argument seems impervious to facts. The notion that Jews funded or created the slave trade, or even that the handful of Jewish merchants involved in the trade had a disproportionate influence in its operation, have been disproved time and again by some of the world's best scholars. This kind of refutation can be helpful in correcting misinformation among colleagues, friends, and family members. It cannot stop the perpetual motion engine of hate and conspiricism.

An older generation of Jewish historians, writing in the wake of *The Secret Relationship*, wrote primarily in an exculpatory vein. One history of Charleston Jewry notes that while "Blacks and whites did intermingle . . . Jews of the city, *being white-skinned*, joined with the dominant race" and "quickly adopted the attitudes of the slaveholding society."[7] Under this mode of thinking, those Jews who enslaved people did not make a choice to do so; they were merely peer-pressured. It also assumes that the only Jews of Carolina were white.

There are also sins of omission. Steven Weisman's *Chosen Wars* describes the air of the Charleston docks of 1825 suffused with the smell of goods in that "major trading center": fish, tobacco, coffee, and citrus. It does not mention the odor of human sweat, blood, and feces that would also have suffused the docks, since the human trafficking centers—slave trading centers called "vendue markets"—sat amid the docks as well. *Chosen Wars* imagines a pre–Civil War America where free white Jews did not live alongside people in chains.[8] An outstanding 2005 history of American Jews devotes a section to Rhode Island merchant Aaron Lopez and his participation in the slave trade with the intention to show that Lopez's slave trading killed fewer people than most Christian slave trading.[9] The comprehensive *American Judaism* of 2004 does not mention slavery in any capacity until the Civil War period.[10]

Slaveholding is at its core an expression of legal and political power.[11] Some Jews in America chose to exercise that power as part of their world of "freedom." The question is not whether Jews were as a group pro- or antislavery; Jews were not a monolith. It is not what "the Jews" did or failed to do, but how Jewish people, families, and institutions adopted, adapted, and interpreted their freedom. That condition of freedom existed alongside and within a racial slaveholding system of unfreedom. That system also shaped the Jewish response to religious liberty—and gave rise to generations of interracial and enslaved Jews across the Americas who chose to live as Jews, even under conditions of Egyptian darkness. Enslaved and biracial Jews deserve to be known and included as Jews whose skin color did not afford them the same degree of choice enjoyed by Gershom Seixas—or even Sarah Moses Brandon.[12]

In Egypt and the New World, slavery was predicated on force. Legal, financial, cultural—all sorts of power were denied enslaved people, down to the level of nutrition. An 1838 narrative by "A Runaway Slave" took readers into the daily life of the enslaved in South Carolina, where "slaves had a regular allowance of food given to them the first of the week, and that was all they got.... We were not able to make the allowance last more than four or five days." The allowance was often only one kind of food—corn or peas or sweet potatoes, "they never gave us anything else." Subsisting on two meals a day, the Runaway would sometimes fall asleep in the fields, and the driver "would whip me.... I used to get my full share of whipping. All the scars on my back were made that way."[13]

The anonymous "Runaway" experienced this brutality under multiple regimes. As a child, he was enslaved to a Christian master, and "if we did not do every thing exactly to please her we were sure to get a whipping. An old man whipped us on our bare flesh with hickory switches." He went naked until he was old enough to plow. "When they whipped us they often cut through our skin. They did not call it skin, but 'hide.'" The Runaway heard another Christian master, Alfred Smith, recommend to a fellow white Christian that he ought to shoot a slave suspected of stealing pears. His friend then killed the enslaved suspect by gunshot. The Runaway likewise met a minister named Jenkins on a nearby plantation, and "We could hear his people halloo when they whipped them."

There was little difference when the Runaway was sent to live under Davy Cohen, "a Jew who lived on Ashley River." Cohen found the Runaway had stolen a musk melon, and in reprisal, tied him to a log, whipped his back raw, then poured salt into the wounds. Cohen was also known for tying enslaved people spread-eagled on the ground before whipping them. The physical and psychological torture the Runaway saw and suffered through was endemic to South Carolina's slave system. Jews and Christians both participated in it.

The evidence of the Runaway should put to rest the notion that the history of Jews in the American South was somehow different because of religion. It was not. Philip Cohen of Savannah wrote the *sh'ma*—the sacred prayer at the heart of Judaism affirming the oneness of God—in his last will and testament. In the same document, he transferred ownership of enslaved people to his friends. Clearly, his religious conscience did not touch his slaveholding practice. In the midst of war and occupation in Georgia, the Jewish patriot Philip Minis still found time to sell his enslaved property to others.[14] Joseph Cohen of Lynchburg, Virginia, murdered his enslaved man in 1819.[15] Emma Mordecai held people in bondage both as a Jew and later as a Christian convert. The difference was that as a Christian she insisted her slaves learn Bible verses and whipped them when they did not.[16]

In medieval Europe, Christian law forbade any Jew from owning a Christian slave. As European slave trading in West Africa opened up in the sixteenth century, the possibility of African "pagans" bound to Jewish enslavers appeared, both in Europe and the New World.[17] Occasionally, European states or their colonial outposts attempted to limit slaveholding to Christians only. In 1705 Virginia passed a law limiting the rights of Jews as slaveholders. Louisiana's 1724 *Code Noir* banned Jews from entry and mandated the teaching of Christianity to all enslaved persons. In 1733, Curaçao mandated that persons manumitted must receive instruction in the Christian religion.[18]

This may not explain why prominent Jewish thinkers went out of their way to defend slavery in print. Isaac Harby and Jacob Cardozo edited two of Charleston's leading papers; both papers were strongly pro-slavery. From a young age, Harby argued for moral and historical justifications of slavery. In an 1804 speech about the "moral cause" of wars, Harby claimed that Africans were "the slaves of all mankind."[19] As the editor of the *Southern Patriot*, he spent less time justifying slavery itself and more time criticizing white abolitionists for daring to attack the practice: "Let us, in America, take especial care that our best interests be not *canted away* by the false and hollow philanthropy of the . . . abolition societies." For Harby, American slaves were "those whom our British ancestors have left to our protection, and for *our* service."[20] As a young man, Mordecai Manuel Noah had written hopefully about American Blacks attaining a "greater equality of rights." As he aged, Noah's language became increasingly hostile to Blacks and abolitionists alike. He wrote essays describing enslaved people as "happy and contented," enjoying "luxurious meals" and "handsome clothing." He urged the state of New York to ban abolitionist writing and to limit the franchise to white males.[21] In a 1794 ad, Abraham Seixas wrote a repulsive poem advertising a sale of his human cargo: "To sell, all for the cash, Of various price/ To work the rice/ Or bring them to the lash." (These are not even the most offensive lines in this awful poem.) He signed his doggerel, "ABRAHAM SEIXAS, All so gracious."[22]

Synagogues often limited membership to "free men." Richmond made the restriction explicit in its 1789 constitution.[23] In 1820, Beth Elohim in Charleston announced it would not accept any white converts unless a rabbi from another synagogue vouched for them. It would not accept any "people of color" at all.[24] Shearith Israel of New York permitted membership to "every man, except a bound or hired servant, professing to be and living as a Jew."[25] "Free" seemed to outweigh "Jewish"; two indentured Jewish servants (L. E. and Polly Miller) asked Shearith Israel in 1807 to find a way to shift their indenture from "a very deplorable situation" with a Gentile to service with a Jew. Shearith Israel declined to act.[26]

Much of institutional white Christianity also showed indifference to the enslaved. The Runaway had "many masters, but never found any who cared to let their slaves go to meeting, or who talked with us about religion. Until I came into the free States a few months ago [in 1838], I did not know any thing about God or the Bible." While enslaved in the Carolinas, the Runaway illegally attended Christian worship, but had nothing to guide him: "I never could understand what the minister was preaching about. I heard a mighty hollowing and that was all." African Americans began to adopt Christianity more widely by the later 1700s. The "Black church" became a fundamentally distinct institution, reading the Bible primarily through the lens of the Old Testament redemption of Israel in preference to the New Testament's Pauline epistles. The Runaway thought whites feared teaching the Bible to the enslaved, for "they do not like to have any kind of seriousness in the slaves. *They do not want them to think.*" The Black church became a center of Black religious, intellectual, and political life—a center visible in free states, hidden in the slave states.[27]

In the Runaway's experience, many whites made a show of religion. The exception was Davy Cohen. Cohen made no effort to teach the Runaway or anyone enslaved to him the basics of religion. Most Jewish enslavers followed the same course. As a religion of practice and ritual, Judaism required more formal instruction than a religion of belief like Christianity, and for the most part, enslaved Christians were self-taught or evangelized and catechized by members of the Black church. There was no equivalent "Black synagogue" in the United States, and white Jewish slaveowners generally did not circumcise their male slaves nor induct enslaved persons into their religion.

A Black synagogue did appear, however, in Suriname—a semi-independent organization of Jews of color that confronted Suriname's coordination of church and state. Only a small minority of the enslaved men and women in Suriname chose to live as Jews, but given the enormous population of Suriname's enslaved, there were enough biracial Jews to form a prayer group.[28] Some of these biracial Jews may have been converts, but most were described (in a letter to the governor) as the offspring of enslaved mothers and Jewish European fathers, who "out of particular love for the Jewish Religion" saw that "the boys were properly circumcised and the girls instructed by a teacher, as were their descendants." Some of the biracial Jews were manumitted; some remained enslaved.[29]

The leader of this group was Joseph de David Cohen Nassy—biracial son of David Cohen Nassy, a Caribbean doctor who assisted in Philadelphia's 1793 yellow fever outbreak. Nassy Jr. helped establish Darhe Jesarim, "The Path of the Upright"—a separate religious group for Jews of color in 1759. At first, the group had the support of Suriname's synagogue, and white Jews and Christians helped raise money for a separate building for Darhe Jesarim. This was not the first effort at segregation in the Suriname synagogue; all Jews of mixed race, or European Jews who had married someone of mixed race, were classed by Suriname's synagogue as *Congregantan* (congregants) and not as *Yehidim* (meaning Jews, or full members) in the synagogue.[30]

Joseph Nassy's death and burial in 1790 led to the unmaking of Darhe Jesarim. Nassy's friend Reuben Mendez Meza equated Nassy's leadership at Darhe Jesarim with leadership in the institutional synagogue and chose to bury him with official honors. When the procession arrived at the cemetery, however, they found the grave "in a swamp and only one foot deep." When they complained, they were told "if folks do not shut up we will shut you up." *Congregaten* were not authorized to make decisions about funeral honors. The Jews of Darhe Jesarim wrote a letter of objection. The synagogue's *mahamad* again rejected the claims and insisted they continued to pay to remain *Congregantan* at the synagogue. A year later, Meza wrote on behalf of Darhe Jesarim that they paid the fees "without the least opposition" but "under protest." A year after that, still barred from full membership, the congregants of Darhe Jesarim wrote to the *mahamad* and threatened to secede from the synagogue.

Rather than make any changes for their brethren, the *mahamad* instead called in the state. The synagogue dissolved Darhe Jesarim completely and wrote a letter to Suriname's government, warning that if the synagogue's ban on biracial Jewish organizations were not upheld, manumitted people of color might think themselves equal to whites. Darhe Jesarim had been "ungrateful." Their actions would lead to "anarchy"—code for armed rebellion. Suriname's leaders, who had empowered the synagogue to rule over the Jews, backed the white *mahamad*, giving them the power to force all

Blacks and *congregaten* "to behave themselves in all respects with the subordination and the due respect towards . . . [the] Regents and Deputies of the Portuguese Jewish Nation." If biracial Jews defied the synagogue, they could now be arrested and imprisoned. By the 1820s, biracial Jews of Suriname were choosing to raise their children in Christian households.[31]

At almost the same moment, Black Christians in the United States established the first independent African American denominations. Richard Allen was dragged from prayer at St. George's Methodist Church in Philadelphia so that white congregants could get communion first. Allen and his allies founded the Bethel African Methodist Episcopal church six years later. Black Baptists set up independent denominations in Boston, New York, and Ohio. The Black church became a pillar of the Black community and the seedbed of a distinct theological tradition. American Methodists attempted to regain control over Allen in the courts by suing him. The courts sided with Allen.[32]

Meza and Allen were both born into slavery and confronted racism in the house of the Lord. Allen succeeded in constructing a new institutional church in the United States; Meza failed to build a new synagogue in the Dutch colonial world. The difference is not solely attributable to the presence or absence of a legal religious establishment, but American freedom of religion played at least some role in a free Black man defending his right to believe as he wished. No biracial American Jews built similar institutions. Indeed, institutional American Judaism closed itself to biracial Jews. And yet that does not mean that American Jews were exclusively white. Indeed, the very presence of regulations such as those in Richmond and Charleston suggests that some non-white Jews in the United States wanted to live Jewish lives.

Numerous biracial Jews lived in the shadow of Virginia slavery. Isaac Judah, the first minister at Beth Shalome, had a relationship with an enslaved woman and fathered biracial children. He provided for the freedom of two women named Maria and Betsey in his will "on consideration of their fidelity and attachment to him," and left money and land to Philip Norborne Wythe and Benjamin Wythe, identified as "free mulatto boys." The will included stipulations designed to discourage any family members from challenging the will.

Clearly, Judah was attempting to manumit and provide for Maria, Betsey, Philip, and Benjamin—a biracial family in slaveholding Virginia. Yet Judah never attempted to bring any of them into the synagogue. The same was true of David Isaacs, a Jewish immigrant living with Nancy West, a free woman of color, in Charlottesville. Isaacs and West had seven children together. They never married. That brought them into legal trouble with the state, which attempted unsuccessfully to prosecute them for illegal fornication in 1822. It caused no problem with Beth Shalome synagogue, where Isaacs remained a member until his death in 1837. Isaacs's biracial son Tucker and his son-in-law Eston Hemings had Isaac's corpse brought to the Jewish cemetery for burial. Eston Hemings was the son of Thomas Jefferson and Sally Hemings.[33]

An understanding of Judaism, however, shaped the lives and routines of enslaved men and women bound to white Jews. Jewish merchants sent enslaved people to operate shops on the Sabbath.[34] Levi Sheftall hired out one of his slaves as *shammash* for Savannah's Mickva Israel. The *shammash* did ritual work for the Jewish community, caring for the synagogue and its sacred objects. Levi never recorded which of the people he owned knew enough about Jewish law and life to undertake such a responsibility, but that unnamed Georgian slave was as close to Judaism as anyone in Savannah.[35]

The records of Suriname Jewry contain the story of "Purim"—an enslaved man who bore the name of a Jewish festival. Naming a child after a holiday was more common in African than European societies, so Purim's name suggests some combination of Jewish culture and African onomastics. It may have been a name he gave himself. Twice in 1772, Purim disrupted synagogue services—once for his namesake holiday in March, and again in October for Yom Kippur. Purim calibrated his rebellions with an intimate knowledge of the Jewish calendar. Rabbinical thought had long placed Purim and Yom Kippur as antipodes—on opposite sides of the year, with reversed stakes and styles of worship (redemption instead of judgment, revelry rather than atonement). Purim marked the ritual year of his enslavers with his own acts of religion.

Purim may have considered himself Jewish. He was once discovered in the act of sacrificing a goat. This may have been an attempt to recreate ancestral worship practices from Africa, but he may also have been attempting the Levitical sacrifice of a sin offering. Alternately, he may have been trying to enact the selection of the scapegoat in Leviticus 16.[36] These are speculations—but there is no doubt that if Purim did not consider himself Jewish, he was deeply versed in Jewish thought and practice.

A similar combination of Black Atlantic culture and Jewish holidays appeared in Savannah. In 1795, Samuel Benedix and Moses Simon blew the shofar call for Rosh Hashanah on a conch shell rather than a ram's horn.[37] The conch was an odd choice for a Jewish ritual—it's just as unkosher as clams and mussels. However, the conch had long been used among Afro-Caribbean communities as a marker of time and occasionally as a call to arms. Some participants in the 1791 slave revolts in Haiti had initiated their rebellion with blasts of the conch shell. Benedix and Simon were both temporarily suspended from the synagogue. Both men were classified as white, but they had blown their unkosher shofar at home. Were they mimicking an enslaved religious practice? Did they mean to extend the new year to enslaved Jews?

Other enslaved people showed the same understanding of Jewish life. Some of these actions may have been deliberate acts of disobedience or repudiation. E. N. Carvalho in 1809 instructed an enslaved person to superintend his meals to ensure they were "Casher." That same year, Carvalho was accused of failing to keep kosher. Did Carvalho's slave deliberately feed him unkosher food in an act of rebellion?[38] An enslaved Jew who identified himself as "Paul the Jew" lived to see the Civil War. In Virginia, he converted to Christianity as a way to celebrate his "Christian freedom" from enslavement—but he continued to worship on Saturday.[39] Francis Lewis Cardozo certainly knew Judaism. His father Isaac Cardozo was Jewish and lived openly in a common-law marriage with Lydia Williams, a free woman of color. Though born to a practicing Jewish father, Cardozo chose to become a Presbyterian minister. During Reconstruction, he became South Carolina's secretary of state.[40]

Other biracial Jews practiced the religion more formally, even when they were denied official sanction in the early republic. Sarah Esther Brandon-Gill (mother of Isaac and Sarah) was not classified as white and yet received burial at Shearith Israel in New York in 1823.[41] A man identified as "Brother George" in North Carolina was identified in an African American baptismal record as "long a practitioner of the Israelite faith."[42] Billy Simons worshipped at Beth Elohim in Charleston in the 1840s; he claimed to be an African Jew from Madagascar. Documents at the time describe him as one of the regular attendees at services, where he worshipped in spite of the ban on "people of color."[43] Simon was not the only Black Jew worshipping there. A German visitor in 1857 found several women of African descent in the synagogue pews—biracial Jews born enslaved in Suriname and later brought to America.[44]

Some white American Jews chose to demonstrate their freedom by freeing others rather than by perpetuating enslavement. Moses Judah joined the New York Society for Promoting the Manumission of Slaves, eventually serving as an officer. The society did not simply advocate abolition: it became actively involved in freedom suits, a long-term legal process that eventually brought fifty enslaved persons (or those signed to spurious long-term "indentures") to freedom.[45] Joseph Tobias III purchased the woman Jenny and manumitted her on the same day.[46] The immigrant Jewish brothers Joseph and Isaac Friedman purchased their enslaved friend Peter in Tuscumbia, Alabama, in 1849. Local Christians lamented the sale to Jews, "who had no higher wish than to make money," as a published account went. The Friedmans arranged for Peter to buy himself, then took him to Ohio, where he was free.[47] Isaiah Isaacs of Charlottesville, inspired by revolutionary rhetoric, manumitted his enslaved people in his 1803 will, because he was "of the opinion that all men are by nature equally free."[48] Some may be inclined to praise Isaacs for following through on his belief in equality in the end. The tragedy is that he did not do so in the beginning— and that, in this case, the nature of his historical record means that we know more about the moral arc of the enslaver than we do about the lives of the enslaved.

When the First African Baptist Church was founded in Savannah in 1790, Mordecai Sheftall defended the right of people of color (enslaved and free) to worship there, at least from sunrise to sunset: "All men have the right to worship God their own way." Sheftall was quite ready to defend religious liberty—without granting the idea of full liberty. The enslaved populations of the Americas lived under a regime of depersonalization— treated as objects to be traded, tortured, and sold—and had no legal right to choose their religion. But they did choose their religion, of course. One does not need to be legally free to believe in God. Some few chose to live like Jews; others made different choices despite their close contact with Jews. Indeed, one of the deacons of the First African Baptist Church was a free butcher named Adam Sheftall. Whether Mordecai defended Adam's right to worship because the men were related remains a mystery.[49]

II

The Converts

JAMES MORRISON ARNELL LOVED JEWS, especially when they converted. As a member of the American Society for Meliorating the Condition of the Jews (ASMCJ), Arnell subscribed to the belief that America had the perfect conditions for a mass conversion. In America, "bigotry had no power, and even *toleration* is not an appropriate term" to describe "this land of civil and religious liberty." Americans, as one ASMCJ supporter wrote in 1823, would convert Jews to Christianity because "we have not disfranchised them. . . . [I]n the intercourse of society, no difference is made between them and Christians." The conditions of liberty would break down barriers between Jew and Gentile. Conversion would follow.[1]

Arnell tested that theory on an 1822 missionary journey with Joseph Samuel Christian Frederick Frey, a converted European Jew who spearheaded missionary efforts in Britain and the United States. Arnell and Frey traveled from Philadelphia to Georgia to proclaim Jesus Christ to American Jews. Frey drew crowds wherever they went. Jews and Christians both attended, although more Christians than Jews. They had advance notice from *Israel's Advocate*, the society's newspaper, which touted the trip and noted that the United States "has the glory of being the only nation in the world, which acknowledges Jews as citizens." Indeed, Arnell spent part of his missionary journey campaigning to remove Maryland's remaining test oath. He defended the rights of Jews to hold office to anyone who would listen and celebrated when the test oaths were removed.[2]

Still, while Christian audiences came to listen, Arnell found Jews "not very well satisfied with his discourse," and "much dissatisfied" with Frey's sermons. In South Carolina, Arnell got into a public argument with a "Rabbi" over the meaning of Isaiah 9 ("Unto us a child is born, unto us a son is given, and the government shall be upon his shoulder.") Arnell claimed it was prophecy about Christ, and the "rabbi" (identified only as the Jew "most learned among them") said it referred to the Old Testament king Hezekiah. By April 1823 Arnell seemed to lose hope: "I observed that the Jews today did not like Mr. Frey's object and they spoke very harsh things about him." At journey's end, he concluded that some Jews simply "put more faith in what the Rabbis said than in what God hath declared." Frey and Arnell had interested many Christians in the Jews, but they had not converted any Jews.[3]

Around the same time, another minister traveled to Richmond intending to argue Jacob Mordecai out of Judaism. Mordecai was prepared. The Jewish schoolteacher had studied the Christian scripture with "a sincere and honest determination to follow the doctrine of Christ," if he could be "satisfied of its superior claim to the truth." But he had not found it so. Indeed, "if the Old Testament contains a revelation from God, then the New Testament is not from God," he wrote, because "the New Testament is contradictory" and "God cannot contradict himself." Mordecai wrote his own account of the New Testament, book by book, listing what he saw as its flaws and mischaracterizations of God. He defended Judaism based on its theology, not its tradition, and had no problem condemning the Christian system as he did so, likely stunning the "Zealous Episcopal minister" who had been his primary teacher.[4]

Arnell, Frey, and Mordecai's unnamed missionaries were not the first Christians to believe they had found the key to Jewish conversion. They were, however, among the first in many centuries to hear Jews give as good as they got. The very civic equality that the ASMCJ members praised as a bridge to conversion allowed Jews to formulate and publish responses to Christian evangelization. American Jews could say that Jesus was not the Messiah without fear of having their tongues bored through or their property seized. So Jewish apologetics shifted in early America to meet the missionaries. The missionaries, in turn, adapted their rhetoric. American freedom of religion created a new thread in Christian missions, which in turn created a new kind of Jewish apologetics. Neither group left the encounter unchanged. The revolution made religious freedom, and religious freedom changed how Jews and Christians talked to each other about God.

Bitterness between the two faiths goes back to the first centuries of Christianity. The second-century bishop Melito of Sardis first accused the Jews of deicide; rabbinic literature occasionally offered a rejoinder warning Jews against Christian theology. With the Christianization of Rome, Jewish freedoms to write and preach came under severe limitations. In the Eastern (Byzantine) empire, the Justinian Code (535 CE) restricted Jewish practice and shuttered synagogues. In Western Europe, Pope Gregory the Great (served 590–604) proclaimed protection for the Jews, but by the late medieval period that tolerance had evaporated. There was no such thing as Jewish freedom of thought. Jewish books were burned by the thousands. Jews were forced to attend conversionist sermons. Numerous countries expelled their Jews or required them to live in certain places and wear distinctive clothing—making them easy targets for pogroms. It was not an atmosphere where a meaningful exchange of ideas took place. Where Jewish communities hung on, rabbinical authorities discouraged Jews from discussing religion with Christians. In the eighteenth century, London's major synagogue declared, "No Jew may hold dispute or argument on matters of religion" with Christians.[5]

But conditions were different in America. A state without a church meant that conversion provided no new political or legal freedoms. Any conversion therefore had to come from personal faith, not a desire for security. John Livingston, vice-president of the ASMCJ, declared, "Every foot of ground within our boundaries is consecrated to liberty. Every part is equally sacred to the honest emigrant, whoever he may be, Jew or Gentile. The moment he lands on our blessed shores he is safe."[6] The ASMCJ thought that meant a field ripe for harvest.

Frey arrived in the United States in 1816 to begin gathering. Many old standbys of the revolution signed on to his efforts. John Jay and John Quincy Adams were all early figureheads of the ASMCJ. Jay and Adams harbored anti-Jewish resentment as well, and anti-Semitic caricatures sometimes filtered into the ASMCJ. *Israel's Advocate* often printed letters of society members who referred to Jews as "monuments to [God's] displeasure" or a "desolate nation." The *Advocate* once referred to a foreign Jew having "rabbinical horns"—an allusion to the medieval myth that Jews had horns.[7] Frey, however, was adamant about "barbarity and cruelty with which the Jews are oppressed in most parts of the world," and the consequent need for civic equality.[8]

Others had preceded Frey. In 1816 Hannah Adams, one of America's first historians, founded the Female Society for Boston and the Vicinity for Promoting Christianity Among the Jews. (Nineteenth-century religious organizations favored long names.) Adams's organization, like Frey's, encouraged donations from around the country. Frey followed a similar pattern, establishing multiple local groups to convert the Jews. Those independent local groups could then feed funds and missionaries to the national organization. In 1836, Isaac Leeser discovered one such local missionary in the doorway of the Charleston synagogue after Shabbat services, handing out "copies of a tract . . . contravening the tenets which we profess."[9]

Adams gathered information on American Jews by writing to Gershom Seixas. She wanted statistics on American synagogues for her 1812 book *History of the Jews*.[10] Seixas felt "much gratified" to contribute to the work of "a woman so eminently distinguished as a literary character." He added one request, though: Seixas knew that the persecution of the Jews of Europe and the Middle East had often been used as evidence for Christianity. Seixas had read, for example, George Stanley Faber's 1809 account of Christian prophecies, which begins by referring to the prophecy of Luke 21:24 that "*the Jews* shall be led away captive into all nations"—and therefore, that Jewish suffering was divine proof of Christian scripture.[11] Seixas cited Faber in his response to Adams. Rather than have Jewish history serve as evidence for Christianity, he asked Adams to use Jewish history as evidence for God, to take note that the "Justice (or righteousness) of Providence is manifested in the dispersion of His People—for they have never been driven from any one country without finding an Asylum in another."

Adams didn't listen. She opened her book by telling readers that Jews were best understood as "a standing monument of the truth of the christian religion."[12] She acknowledged that Christian anti-Semitism showed the "professed disciples of the benevolent Redeemer violating the fundamental precepts of the gospel." Still, Adams also blamed the Jews, who, she wrote, chose "to oppose oppression by fraud" and to direct "all the energy of their minds . . . to the pursuit of gain." In the end, Jews had been "by turns persecuted by Pagans, Christians, and Mahometans; continually duped by impostors, yet still persisting in rejecting the true Messiah."[13] It was not their fault, except when it was.

If Seixas noticed what Adams was up to, he left no mention of it. New York's leading Jew rarely engaged in public polemics. He was far more interested in finding ways for Judaism to coexist with Christian neighbors. Seixas never preached against missionaries, but he did seek to end "the spirit of profaneness" and openly called for religious cooperation: "Let those who are on "the Lord's Side' unite & cheerfully associate to suppress this hideous monster." Rather than compare Jewish to Christian theology, Seixas counseled Jews to "promote peace & concord among our brethren; that we may dwell quietly in our habitations."[14]

Privately, Seixas was less circumspect. In his letters to his daughter Sarah Kursheedt, he delved into grittier details of Christian claims. He was open about "the pretended Messiahship" of Jesus Christ. But he also accepted "the real principle of free agency" that governed "religious, moral, or perceptive obligations." If all people were free to decide, then theological disputations had to take place. Nonetheless Seixas avoided direct confrontation.

The iconoclastic theologian George Bethune English also tried to draw Seixas out. In 1813, the American-born English published *The Grounds of Christianity Examined*, a deist work that denied the Christian Trinity. Like Adams, English wrote to Seixas asking for help. English thought Seixas could provide some books on the subject of Christian error. Seixas had none to give, but English sent Seixas a copy of the completed work anyway. Seixas agreed with English's denial of Christ's divinity but found English too indebted to "Spinosa (the apostate Jew) who was the first that broached the doctrine of free-thinking."[15] Seixas shared his views with Sarah, not with English. He defended Judaism; he had no interest in condemning Christianity.

When Seixas discussed religion, he discussed it in the moral terms upon which he had relied during the revolution. Virtue made someone a citizen, and Judaism's most salient component was the production of virtue. The "practical duties of our religion" Seixas preached, "universally lead us to virtue." And again, near the end of his life: "By the sacred history we are informed of all the preceptive & practical duties, necessary to establish the *religious & moral law*; to conduct us to virtue—to happiness."[16] It was not that Judaism was right and Christianity was wrong; both were virtuous. Gertrude Meredith, a Philadelphia Gentile, agreed. She publicly defended "a virtuous Jew" by arguing that "virtue is the same" no matter in whom it is found. Unlike Jefferson, Meredith had many Jewish acquaintances, and even cooked kosher food when they came to dinner.[17]

A series of pamphlets from Britain republished in America in the 1810s adopted the same approach: Judaism was moral, and therefore conversion was unnecessary. Jacob Nickelsburger wrote *Koul Jacob* in 1814 (US edition 1816) in response to Frey's autobiography, but Nickelsburger emphasized that his work was "not against any religion whatsoever." Good people existed in every religion, he wrote, and so "much less do I, or any one of my nation wish or attempt to make proselytes to our opinions." The pamphlet defended Judaism, but it adhered to the old taboo against speaking ill of Christianity.[18] In *Elements of the Jewish Faith* (1817), Solomon Jacob Cohen pointed out that God intended the law for Jews only, so "we are not commanded to spread them forth among other nations, or to send missionaries to distant places." In fact, if any person applied to join the Jewish nation, Jews should "use every endeavour to dissuade him, and advise him to decline it."[19]

If Judaism was a system of virtue, then by extension "all religions, the foundations of which are constituted on moral principles . . . render [people] happy both here and hereafter," as *Elements* put it. As a practical guide for Jews, however, this apologetic approach had a major flaw. If Judaism created virtue just like other religions, there ought to be no reason to leave. But there was also no reason to stay. In an 1824 letter, Shinah Schuyler explained to her niece how to find a good husband: "Let esteem for virtuous principles be the first basis for love." Schuyler herself married a Gentile and left the faith.[20] Sol Mordecai thought similarly: "If . . . all religions are equally good," then why *not* marry a Christian and allow the children to be brought up as Christians? And if that were so, maybe he should convert as well: "Why should I not observe those tenets which it would be my duty to inculcate in the minds of my children?"[21]

This question upended the religious lives of several generations of the Mordecai family. Jacob Mordecai instructed his children in 1796 to follow the example of their late mother: "Impressed with the ideas of Religion and with piety unaffected she offered her adorations to the Throne of Mercy and Grace. Her sentiments on this subject were most liberal. . . . [S]he loved virtue in whatever garb it appeared."[22] That left Sol Mordecai wondering if he was "an Israelite by name rather than in principle." If Christianity was virtuous and Judaism virtuous, were they not "equally good"? And should he then convert? His sister Ellen asked him to ignore the practices and liturgy of Judaism (which she thought were "superstition") and focus on the tenets. But in the end, she wrote, "Let your *conscience* answer every question." Whatever choice he arrived at, she promised that she would support him.[23] In the end, both Sol and Ellen left the faith. Their sister Caroline also joined a church and credited a similar intellectual decision. She wrote to Ellen, "If I ever become convinced I am in error I will tell our dear parent immediately." She never did.[24]

Thinking of religion as virtue may have opened the door to intermarriage, which rose in the wake of the Revolutionary War.[25] Probably the most unusual match occurred in 1806, when Abraham Hyam Cohen, the hazan of Mikveh Israel in Philadelphia, married Jane Picken, the daughter of a Presbyterian minister. In this case, Picken converted to Judaism, but this did not sever her ties to Christians. Instead, she found her "connection with the Jewish people" made her an object of interest and inquiry among philo-Semites.[26]

Middle-class Jewish men were more likely to travel from home and thus had more exposure to potential Gentile spouses. By extension, Jewish women faced a shortage of potential husbands. It was not, of course, impossible to make a Jewish match. Jews often found each other in unusual places. Sarah Ann Hays met her future husband at a White House soiree in 1830. Both were Jewish.[27]

For Jewish women, however, the problem was compounded by questions of Jewish practice. As Judaism became increasingly defined as a system of virtue, some women found little to praise among Jewish men. "I should like much to know from what arose the command," wrote Slowey Hays of Virginia, "to unite ourselves alone to those who possess the same tenets." Few men bothered to keep "the exactitudes a woman subscribes to." Too many Jewish men complied only with "superficial Duties of life," she wrote in a letter to her friend Rebecca Gratz. "I would rather unite my fate with that of a Mahometan who gave dignity to the religion he professed by an adherence to its morals and forms than to one of my owne who neglected any part of his Duties." She understood that she was bound to marry a Jew, but she also found American Jews too lax in their practice. She was not really going to marry a Muslim, but she wanted Judaism to be something other than what she found. Hays wanted virtue, consistency, and Judaism. To have all three, she decided not to marry at all. Hays made her own decisions about what constituted a virtuous Jewish life.[28] Numerous other Jewish women followed suit, preferring to live an unmarried life dedicated to their family of origin or to the Jewish community in general. Louisa Hart of Philadelphia found being single in older life "very happy," though the road had been "a very sad one to travel before one reaches the climacteric [menopause]." The Jewish world of early America had many Louisa Harts. As many Jewish women did not marry as did.[29]

Synagogues remained officially opposed to intermarriage. A 1798 revision of the Shearith Israel constitution held that any male or female Jew marrying outside the faith would forfeit membership and their "name shall be erased from the books (of the congregation)."[30] Such measures were, however, less strict than elsewhere in the Americas. In Suriname, the governor enforced a law banning marriages between Ashkenazic and Sephardic Jews.[31] Moreover, American synagogues sometimes ignored their own rules, particularly when the men remained Jewish. Moses Nathans "lived with in a public way with a *goyah*" and had two children by her at the same time he was a member of the board of Philadelphia's synagogue. In 1793, she became a Jew and the couple married the next year.

Synagogues could also set such high standards for returning converts that it discouraged leaving in the first place. Mary Ann Suares left Judaism to marry a Christian in 1829. By 1841 she wished to return. Charleston's Beth Elohim took her back, but required her to publish a card to friends and the general public declaring that she "with a sincere and repentant heart expressed her deep regret at having abandoned the Jewish faith, and also her earnest desire to return to the religion." Suares agreed "to undergo any penalty" to worship "at the same altar, at which You and my ancestors worshipped."[32]

The question of conversion in a free republic, however, went beyond the issue of intermarriage. The United States had made religion a personal choice, so American Jews were now figuring out which traditions mattered to them. Those decisions drew upon the idea of Judaism as virtue that had blossomed among the patriot Jews. The traditions were multiform, the freedoms unprecedented, the possibilities unknown. The Mordecai family left extensive records of its struggles and heartbreaks over conversion. Ellen described her dread at revealing her Christianity to her family, "the apprehension of causing pain to them, or of enduring their displeasure."[33] Gershon Lazarus—Jacob Mordecai's grandson—also began visiting churches after observing a "want of decency" in Charleston's synagogue. Gershon began asking around about the divinity of Christ, and while still a teen he read his one of his grandfather's tracts on the false messiahship of Jesus. It did not take, and Gershon wrote his father a letter in 1823 containing his "enthusiastick declaration of his conviction of the truth of the Christian faith and every article of his creed." His father replied with a terse letter forbidding Gershon from receiving baptism and requiring him to study with Jacob Mordecai. If Gershon felt the same at twenty-one, said his father, he could follow "the dictates of his conscience."[34]

So began the battle for the soul of Gershon Lazarus. The young convert headed to Richmond, where he studied with both grandfather Mordecai and Anglican bishop Richard Moore. It was his father's wish that his son "should investigate so momentous a subject as completely as possible that he may be in no future danger of vacillation."[35] Gershon came back to Judaism, becoming in his father's words, in "principle what he was first, from accident."[36] Principle, not birthright, made a Jew. Twenty years later, Emma and Ellen Mordecai would have a similar struggle over the soul of Julia Lazarus, who was all of fourteen at the time. Julia ultimately decided that birth did make her a Jew: "She was born a Jewess and a Jewess she must remain."[37]

Not so for Rachel Mordecai. Like her sisters Caroline and Ellen, Rachel ultimately left Judaism after long experience with Christianity. Her previous defense of Judaism against literary stereotypes (in those letters she wrote to Maria Edgeworth) made her a heroine among American Jews. In the 1820s, Rachel agreed to exchange religious texts with Lucy Ann Lippitt of Rhode Island. Rachel found Lippitt's conversionist texts persuasive, and by 1828 she considered herself a Christian.[38]

Shortly after Rachel converted, Joshua Seixas took a job teaching Hebrew to the Mormons. The grandson of the patriot hazan Gershom, Joshua devoted his life to the study of Hebrew, serving as chief Hebrew instructor for Shearith Israel in 1825 and later developing his own course of study—which he advertised as allowing anyone "in a short time and with little trouble, to read [Hebrew] with much pleasure and satisfaction."[39] By the 1830s, however, he had converted to Christianity. The Unitarian minister James Walker wrote to Seixas about "our views of Christianity" and "the subjects that most interest us: the power, the satisfactions, & the prospects of true Christianity." Around that time, Seixas changed his name to James (possibly after the most Jewish of the epistolary New Testament authors). He wrote and published a Hebrew grammar and relocated to Ohio.[40] There, the Church of Jesus Christ of Latter-day Saints (the Mormons) found him. The Mormon prophet Joseph Smith Jr. wanted to provide formal Hebrew instruction for his burgeoning church, and Seixas seemed both suitable and available. For several months in 1836, Seixas taught Hebrew to the Mormon elders in the LDS enclave of Kirtland, Ohio. The Mormons continually referred to Seixas as Jewish. Either Seixas kept his conversion quiet, or the Mormons wanted him to be Jewish to provide a more "authentic" knowledge of the Hebrew Bible. Smith "conversed with Mr. Seixas on religion," but Seixas never became a Mormon. When Seixas left Kirtland, numerous Mormon apostles praised and thanked him. The knowledge Smith gained under Seixas was later employed in Mormon exegesis, and in the name of the Saints' Illinois town: Nauvoo, Hebrew for "beautiful place." Seixas also taught Theodore Parker, the future Transcendentalist reformer of Unitarianism, thereby shaping two very different American religious leaders.[41]

The ASMCJ played no discernible role in any of these conversions. Almost no Jewish converts mentioned Joseph Frey. Rachel and Ellen read their way into Christianity through other authors. Jewish convert Jane Picken returned to Christianity in 1821 when she had a vision of Jesus. "This was conversion," she wrote, "deep and heartfelt conversion— such as baffles the pen of description; for language can give no idea of it." The hubbub over conversion among Jews led Jacob's grandson, Marx Lazarus, to drop all religions; the Old and New Testaments, he wrote, were "like the Kilkenny cats, and when the fur had done flying, there were no cats left."[42]

The vast majority of American Jews remained in the religion, but Jewish writers and leaders began to realize they needed an additional kind of apologetics for a new religious landscape. So for the first time in centuries, a group of Jewish writers (publicly and privately, formally and informally) began to make the case that Christianity was wrong.

Jacob Mordecai put it in the strongest terms: "All the books of the New Testament were written by infatuated, ignorant men." (Mordecai might have been venting some personal frustration, since three of his daughters had left Judaism for Christianity.) In the 1820s, Mordecai completed an extensive, handwritten review of the Christian scriptures. He did not deny that Christianity could produce virtue, but he had no compunction in declaring Christianity untrue and inconsistent with the Hebrew Bible. He even asked a question many Jews then and now have when presented with Christian interpretations of Jewish prophecy: If Isaiah says the messiah will be called *Immanuel*, why does Mary name her child *Jesus*?[43]

Mordecai borrowed much of his polemic against Christianity from other works. Like Gershom Seixas, Mordecai had read George Bethune English's *Grounds of Christianity Examined*; unlike Seixas, Mordecai liked the book. Similar to English and other deists, Mordecai took painstaking care in listing the contradictions in the gospel accounts of the life of Christ. He began his commentary by comparing the lineage of Christ presented in Matthew 1, which traces Christ's ancestry from Joseph to Adam. Yet Mordecai already had a problem, because Luke 1 insists the Holy Spirit sired Christ: If so, then "the genealogy of Joseph has nothing to do with Jesus." Almost the exact same phrase occurs in *Grounds of Christianity*.[44] Paine's *Age of Reason* made the same point: "If they lied in one genealogy, why are we to believe them in the other?"[45] Or as Mordecai wrote: "If we credit Luke, Matthew must necessarily have said a falsehood & vice versa."

Mordecai continued with the classic inconsistencies of the New Testament. Matthew says Judas hanged himself; Luke says his body swelled and burst. The apostles have power over spirits in Matthew 10 but not in Mark 9. In John 18, Jesus identifies himself to the centurions; in all the others Judas betrays him with a kiss. Galatians 1 identifies James as the brother of Jesus; John 7 claims Jesus's brethren didn't believe in him. And so on. Mordecai and English both noted that Isaiah's promise that "a virgin" shall conceive might be better read as "a young woman" shall conceive. (The Hebrew term is the word *almah*, and its translation is an old question.) If Mordecai had not read about that word in *Grounds of Christianity*, he could have found it in *Age of Reason*.[46] English and Mordecai both highlighted the words of Jesus in Mark 21, that false Christs will come and offer miracles—and therefore they conclude that Jesus's own miracles can't stand as evidence.[47] Paine and Mordecai both wondered why the massacre of infants in Matthew 2 cannot be corroborated by any other ancient source, and is not mentioned anywhere else in the New Testament.[48]

Interrogating the gospels for miracle accounts was a standard religious approach of the early nineteenth century. Much eighteenth-century Protestant discussion focused on affirming the validity of Christ's miracles while discounting the continuation of miracles claimed by Catholics and enthusiastic Protestant sects like the Quakers and Methodists. John Locke's *Discourse on Miracles* (1701) addressed the question by determining that whoever had the most impressive miracles had the true church. (Locke's vote: Christianity.) Other theologians instead emphasized the reliability of the witnesses to the miracle. Theologian Thomas Sherlock wrote a defense of Christ's miracles as a courtroom drama, with public miracles and reliable witnesses verifying the ministry of Christ. American editions of Sherlock's book appeared in 1788, 1800, 1804, 1808, and 1809. Yale's prolific minister, Timothy Dwight, declared that modern miracles were simply "pretensions to miraculous powers," but that biblical miracles were true, because God needed to prove his apostles were "inspired with a knowledge of the divine will." Miracles had actually become more important to American theology by the 1820s.[49]

As this view became more prominent among Protestants, freethinkers moved in to exploit the loophole: If miracles proved divine intention, disproving them could "disprove" Christianity. Thomas Paine took the lead: "In every point of view in which those things called miracles can be placed and considered, the reality of them is improbable, and their existence unnecessary." Moral principles did not need a miracle to be true, Paine argued, and to drive his point home, he went through numerous biblical miracles and dismissed them all. Indeed, he wondered why some biblical miracles didn't go bigger. It was fine to have the whale swallow Jonah, Paine wrote, but it would have been more convincing if Jonah swallowed the whale.[50]

Mordecai used the same logic in his discussion of Matthew 21, where Jesus curses a tree out of season when it does not bear fruit: "It would have been a greater miracle and relieved his hunger if he had caused it to bud, flourish, & bring forth fruit out of season." If Simon Magus in Acts 8 performed magic spells that did not come from God, then why (asked Mordecai) shouldn't readers also accept that Jesus's miracles arose from the same source? Mordecai was taking direct aim at the theological proof from miracles. If "miracles ascribed to Jesus are appealed to as evidence of his being the Messiah," and if Jews were invited to receive them as such, Jews should "reject the miracles as *unnecessary tests* of his mission." Moreover, "Jesus proved that *others*, as well as himself, can perform them so completely." Somewhat disingenuously, Mordecai claimed that God performed miracles in front of an entire nation in Exodus, but only a handful of people supposedly saw the resurrected Christ.

Mordecai recycled arguments; he did not create them. What was unique was that he made his critique as a Jew. Deists usually went after the Jews along with everybody else. Elihu Palmer's 1801 *Principles of Nature* described Moses as an "eminent murderer of antiquity," ruling over the Jews "with a rod of iron, and a military despotism."[51] Paine called Moses the inventor of holy war, who "committed the most unexampled atrocities that are to be found in the history of any nation."[52] But Mordecai was not in the business of the taking down all religion. He critiqued Christianity to defend Judaism. In the United States, Jews like Mordecai could openly declare that Christians had misread the Old Testament. After all, those books contained "*no* prophecy of a Messiah who was to be called Jesus Christ."

Mordecai had a strong grasp of Christian doctrine. He abbreviated "Christ" with a fish symbol in shorthand notes, and referred to Saint Jerome, Edward Gibbon, and the Roman-Jewish historian Flavius Josephus as he went along. As he noted, he had apparently once considered becoming a Christian and decided against it. Unlike Seixas, however, Mordecai did not pass over the slights he felt Jews had received, even in the new land of liberty. He noted the dark history of certain chapters in Luke and John which attached bloodguilt for the crucifixion on the Jews forever. Reflecting on Luke 6 ("love your enemies, do good to them which hate you"), he wrote simply, "We have never met with any Christian who observed these precepts."

Rachel Mordecai convinced her father not to publish his treatise. Instead it circulated in longhand among the Richmond Jewish community, and Mordecai became known as "a prophet in Israel" among his fellow Jews. When Isaac Leeser published an American compendium on the Mosaic law in 1833, he thanked Mordecai for leading the way.[53] In 1822, Mordecai gave a discourse at Beth Shalome in Richmond, and sketched out the basics of the new Jewish apologetics. Jews, he declared, had both divine and moral precepts; the religion was both virtuous and historically valid, both "consonant to his [God's] holy laws and conformable to the principles of moral rectitude." The Children of Israel had received particular commands "few indeed in number but applicable to every situation." They were a particular people of God, not "seceders from another sect."

Mordecai's public address noted that Hebrew scriptures "are referenced by the professors of that religion, which is the most prevalent" and "on *that* belief rests the foundation of their faith." He avoided saying Christianity was equal to Judaism, instead making the point again that believers in the New Testament had to accept the Old Testament a priori. He left his manifold problems with the New Testament unsaid but implied. As far as other beliefs went, however, Mordecai insisted that when God commanded Jews to "seek the peace of the city" where they live, God meant "the whole human family, however diversified by religious faith, all our fellow human beings who believe in God."[54]

Other Jews joined Mordecai in this revised defense of Judaism. In 1823, the first American Jewish periodical appeared—Solomon Jackson's *The Jew*, devoted exclusively to countering the arguments of the ASMCJ and Frey. The ASMCJ had launched its own paper, *Israel's Advocate*. Jackson thought it should be called *Israel's Accuser*—since the missionary magazine still blamed Jews for the death of Christ. Jackson sometimes resorted to snark. He wondered, for example, why the Society published conversionist tracts in foreign languages for European Jews but not English ones for Americans: "Are you afraid that you will be paid in your own coin? that you will receive as good as you send?" The tone was more assertive than Seixas, but less confrontational than Mordecai. Cohen also made much of miracle claims, asking if the missionizers could produce any of their own. Like Mordecai, he mentioned Isaiah's translation of *almah* as virgin/young woman, and discussed other Old Testament prophecies to show that they did not refer to Christ or had been mistranslated by the Christian church. He claimed to do so not just in defense of Judaism but because the "mischief" of mistranslations "give a handle to the disbeliever in revelation to turn the whole into ridicule."[55]

An anonymous 1820 book, *Israel Vindicated*, similarly argued that the absurdities of the Christian system "furnish the adversaries of the truth with weapons to attack revealed religion." Written by "An Israelite," the tract was presented as a series of letters between Jewish friends. It aimed to provide Jewish readers with direct responses to Christian missionaries. Jews would have already gotten around to this, the author explained, if "not prevented by stakes, gibbets, bolts, bars, prosecutions, persecutions, and proscriptions."[56]

Israel Vindicated was probably the work of George Houston, a Gentile deist from London who fled across the Atlantic after one of his books raised cries of blasphemy. *Israel Vindicated* also faced blasphemy charges in the United States, which was odd for a book that declared that in America, "each may discuss the dogmas of his religion in perfect security, and publish them to the world." Perhaps so, but in addition to the usual arguments about the misreadings of Hebrew prophets and the supposed unreliability of gospel accounts, *Israel Vindicated* surpassed even Mordecai in its attacks on "the Nazarene religion": "an endless jargon of contradictory systems" and "a rotten prop to morality." Houston anonymously accused Christianity of lowering moral standards by honoring men like Luther and Calvin who oppressed those who disagreed with them.[57] Few Christians likely read the text. It was clearly intended as a tool for Jews facing missionaries, and it made a point to distinguish between most Christians and the repressive regimes of Luther and Calvin.[58]

The new apologetics did not stop the ASMCJ. Bad planning did that. The society raised little money, and it launched an ill-fated scheme to colonize Christianized Jews in upstate New York. The plan alarmed many American Jews. Solomon Jackson said that Jews who converted were in it for the money, "swayed by . . . motives of bettering their situation by becoming settlers in your colony."[59] Frey conceived of an American colony as a way to convert European Jews. The conditions in Central Europe were hopeless; Jews had no rights and no means of leaving the ghetto. For Frey, that meant they would never have a reasonable chance of hearing the gospel from concerned Christians with pure motives. But if the ASMCJ could offer refuge in the United States, —say, in the form of housing and economic opportunity in a designated colony—Frey could "reasonably expect an extensive spread of christianity" among the Jews.[60]

The society loved the idea but never got around to working out the details.[61] Two years passed between incorporation and any significant effort to organize a colony. Possibilities abounded: The founder of the American Bible Society bequeathed land in Pennsylvania—but only enough for fifteen families.[62] A German noble, Adelbert Von der Reke, established what Frey called "a *nursery* to our settlement"—an asylum in Europe for Christianized Jews, who would then be sent to the United States.[63] When the committee tasked with crunching the numbers delivered its first report, they advised that "such a colony ought to be abandoned."[64] A faction within the ASMCJ wondered why European converts could not just settle anywhere in the United States and enjoy "the civil and religious privileges of our happy country."[65] "An asylum! From what?" asked John Livingston. "What danger, what insult, what opposition, what injury has a believing Jew to fear in America?"[66]

The ASMCJ embraced the idea of an American refuge for the Jews, even as they skimped on devoting time or resources for it. The Society considered land near Lake Champlain that was so forbidding Livingston worried any arriving Jews would turn around the minute they saw it. They did buy some land near New Paltz, a town in the Hudson River Valley in upstate New York, but the board of directors constantly became sidetracked by small-scale issues over questions like whether the converts should pursue manufacturing or agriculture, the settlement's size, and the exact terms of lease. An ASMCJ committee suggested a smaller refuge, where the ASMCJ could provide schools, agricultural training, and ministry—and where the board of directors could remove any Jewish emigrant at any time if they threatened to "corrupt the morals of the other members of the settlement."[67]

That kind of language insulted the handful of converts who might have been interested. Eratus Simon led other Jewish Christians in declining the honor of settling in the ASMCJ's refuge. All four men were committed Christians, but they refused to submit to the oversight of the ASMCJ. The ASMCJ insisted on the right to monitor morals, choose a minister, and forbid a common treasury. The converts wrote to the society that such rules "rather belong to the regulations of an almshouse or an asylum, than a free community." They would not compromise on the right to keep a common treasury and to select their own minister; they chafed at the notion that as Jewish converts, they somehow occupied a lower or infantile station in the church. Indeed, "Hebrew Christians are themselves fit instruments to give Christian instruction to their brethren."[68]

The colony never got off the ground, and the ASMCJ fell apart. Frey eventually left to become the first professor of Hebrew at the University of Michigan.[69] For most practical purposes, the society was defunct by 1828, although occasional efforts were made to revive it. The idea of a refuge for converted Jews drew attention, but not action.

The shifts in apologetics provoked by the proposed colony lived on. *Israel Vindicated*, for example, had a second career as an anti-Semitic prop. In 1821, the Jeffersonian stalwart Mordecai Manuel Noah was appointed sheriff in New York County (Manhattan). When he sought a full term in 1822, the New York *Evening Post* ran excerpts from *Vindicated* as proof that Jews, once offered "privileges" by Christians, would commit "open and outrageous attacks upon the religious faith." Noah despaired. The election "has become a religious one. . . . [T]he words now are, Jew and Christian." He lost. The recording secretary for the ASMCJ that year forgot about being kind to Jews, and gave a sermon blaming a yellow fever outbreak on "men of high consideration and influence . . . publicly abetting the election of an infidel in preference to a Christian." Noah tersely replied, "We are no infidels."[70]

Noah himself developed a novel response to the ASMCJ. When the society began developing plans for its colony, Noah countered with a colony of his own. In 1820, he approached the New York legislature with a proposal to found "a town or a city to be inhabited by a community of Jewish emigrants." He would bring European Jews across the Atlantic to live in America, "a country, in which persecution is unknown." Noah emphasized that he wanted to place his town on Grand Island in the Niagara River. Putting Jews there would solve an American security risk, an "exposed situation on the borders of Canada" that "will not readily find settlers." Canadian squatters had already landed and been forcibly removed. Let the Jews come, Noah argued, and "as citizens of the republic, and under the benign protection of the constitution," they would defend their homes for free. It was to be "an asylum to the Jews," a place where perhaps all the world's Jews might congregate, in America, "a country which they want, and which wants them."[71]

Some members of the New York legislature agreed. They thought that "the recent persecution of the Jews in various parts of Europe, may favor the views of the petitioner." They, too, thought "the settlement of Grand Island would be a desirable object."[72] The island was under questionable jurisdiction, and in the previous ten years had been claimed by Canada, the United States, and the Seneca Indian nation. According to the committee, there could "be no objection . . . to the grant."[73] The petition became a bill before the entire legislature. It was rejected.

Noah continued to work on the idea, on and off, writing editorials about it and contacting European Jews. For a while, he considered a more daring scheme. Perhaps land could be purchased elsewhere, "fertile land of one hundred square miles." Jews would emigrate there, "and in due time let it be admitted in the Union as an independent state . . . with their Senators and members of Congress, they will be restored to as much liberty as they can expect in the world."[74] By 1825, Noah had secured sufficient funds to purchase land on Grand Island himself. On September 15, he marched in a parade down the streets of Buffalo, from which the woods of Grand Island could be seen in the distance. He wore a costume from a local production of *Richard III* and led participants from the masonic hall to the Episcopal church. Handel's *Judas Maccabeus* welcomed visitors as Noah dedicated an enormous cornerstone. It was inscribed with the *Sh'ma* in Hebrew, and then, in English: "ARARAT, A City of Refuge for the Jews, founded by MORDECAI MANUEL NOAH, In the month of Tzri [Tishrei] Sept.

1825 & the Fiftieth Year of American Independence." The stone can be found on Grand Island today—all that remains of the Ararat project.

Then, if they had not already done so, things got weird. Noah declared himself a "Judge in Israel" and invoked himself "as a humble instrument of [God's] divine will."[75] He lauded the American situation, where Jews possessed "a constitution founded upon an equality of rights, having no test oaths, and recognizing no religious distinctions." He called for a census of world Jewry, and, in keeping with his new role as judge, formally united world Jewry and America: "I revive, renew, and *reestablish* the government of the Jewish Nation, under the auspices and protection of the constitution and laws of the United States of America."[76]

Noah had an array of bad publicity after laying the cornerstone. *Niles Weekly Register*, a Baltimore periodical, thought the whole thing was a land-jobbing scam and a "strange mixture of Christianity and Judaism." A New England paper called Noah "his rigmarole highness." Another paper asked for volunteers to found a lunatic asylum on Ararat.[77] The chief rabbi of Paris accused Noah of "an act of high treason against the Divine Majesty."[78] A Jewish newspaper in Vienna lambasted him for "assuming the dignity of governor of the new settlement" and commanding Jews "as though he were their undisputed ruler whose beck and call they must obey."[79] Some observers became confused as to whether Noah really thought himself a king of Israel. Only *Niles Weekly Register* understood the metaphor—and then joked about it. Why should Noah stop at being governor and judge, wondered the editors, when he could have dubbed himself "the forerunner of the expected Messiah!"[80]

One question is whether Noah took Ararat seriously. He was known for a humorous political streak. In 1824, he launched a faux campaign for president: "It is time there should be a Jew President," he announced; "it would be unanswerable proof of the perfect freedom of our institutions."[81] Ararat might have been similarly intended. Noah never really specified just what Ararat was supposed to be. Sometimes he referred to it in millennial or messianic terms that seem so out of place they might have been a joke; for example, he once referred to Ararat as a kind of internship for the Jewish people: "Where our people may so familiarize themselves with the science of government . . . as may qualify them for that great and final restoration" to Judea, the Holy Land. Yet Noah more frequently wrote of the United States in its entirety as a city of refuge. It was "the country which the Almighty has blessed, & in which Israel & Judah may repose in safety & happiness."[82] In Europe, Noah's calls for citizenship were seized by Austrian police; they forbade their distribution to any Jews living under Hapsburg rule.[83]

Noah's attention to Ararat seems to have waxed and waned in tandem with the ASMCJ's fickle efforts to make a Jewish Christian colony. Noah had applied to the state legislature in 1820, the same year the ASMCJ incorporated its colonization scheme. Noah wrote to Simon—the Christian Jew—soon after Simon objected to the ASMCJ's proposed colony. Noah assured Simon that soon, "the presence of many Jewish emigrants in this country shall dissipate all doubts" about a Jewish colony.[84] The ASMCJ understood Noah's intention. Indeed, at least one ASMCJ contributor was confused as to whether he was giving money to the society for "the land that Mr. Noah wanted to purchase." The ASMCJ had further concerns about Noah. They wrote in 1827 that if they could not prop up their failing efforts at forming a colony, what was to prevent Christians and Jews alike "from cooperating in building *Ararat*, with the first Judge of Israel?"[85]

Noah had intended his colony to offer an alternative to the ASMCJ. His goal, however, was not so much to bring Jews into America as to show how they were already protected in America. As he declared at Buffalo, "If the attempt shall result in *ameliorating* the condition of the Jews, and shall create a generous and liberal feeling towards them ... who shall say I have failed?"[86] Real melioration had already occurred. Perhaps Noah found that Americans had already accepted his vision of religious freedom, and thus they no longer needed his vision of a Jewish city to defend the American border.

Other American Jews also proposed new institutions to stave off conversion. Isaac Harby's Reformed Society of Israelites began in part from his reaction to Frey and Arnell's journey to Charleston in 1823. Harby's 1824 call for reform contained the warning that "other sects" were "offering the most flattering inducements to *all denominations*." Christians were trying to convert the Jews out of religion, but the Jews were not trying to keep anyone in.[87]

Like the ASMCJ, Harby's movement attracted more attention from Christians than Jews. The national *North American Review* reported that Harby's words made them hope that the "uncouth and unreasonable" worship of Jews could be reformed, and possibly the Jews might be open to religious dialogue. Harby himself even had "susceptibility to the beauty of true Christian feeling." Anglican minister Edward Rutledge wrote that "the success of the reformed Israelitish Church" would allow Jews "to listen to fair and honourable argumentation." Rutledge, an old ally of the Jewish community from the revolutionary days, clearly saw the reform effort in Charleston as logical, virtuous, and likely to bring Jews closer to the Christian faith. Even the ASMCJ gave Harby praise the reformer did not want. *Israel's Advocate* was "gratified to learn" that Harby's "service is to be performed in English, many rabbinical institutions and useless ceremonies are to be laid aside, and music is to be introduced, as in Christian churches."[88]

Jewish apologists assailed the "Reformed Society." Mordecai Noah feared Gentiles might believe the changes were "intended to lead [Jews] to a conversion from their ancient faith." Noah—trained as we've seen in the arts of politics and theater—assured readers that "the reform contemplated, originated with a few persons . . . unacquainted with the essential forms of the religion." A member of the Reformed Society wrote that whatever names Noah called them, "his title as Governor and Judge of Israel will not be acknowledged." Jacob Mordecai penned a handwritten response that circulated among the American Jewish communities. Mordecai referred to Harby's self-description as a "Jewish Luther" as perhaps not the best analogy to call on, since the Protestant Reformation gave rise to "the fire and the stakes" as well as "the variant faith of the hundreds of sects" that came out of it.[89]

Like the ASMCJ and Ararat, the Reformed Society of Israelites could not sustain itself. Harby left Charleston for New York in 1828. His subsequent death of typhoid fever—he was barely thirty—deprived the Reformed Society of its staunchest advocate and best organizer. By the 1830s the organization was defunct. Reform Judaism would have a bright future in the United States, but it did not grow out of the Reformed Society.[90]

Meanwhile in Florida, one final Jewish reformer sought to merge Harby's reforms with Noah's colonial scheme. While Ararat found no takers, a handful of European Jews did emigrate to Moses Levy's Pilgrimage, a Florida experiment Levy referred to as "fields of simple flowers & sweet herbs" that persecuted Jews "will soon flock to." Born in Morocco, Levy eventually found his way to the United States in 1820 and shared his visions of new Jewish institutions with Moses Myers and other American Jews. Like Harby, Levy sought to limit or remove Talmudic and rabbinical interpolations in Jewish life. Levy acknowledged the authority of the Hebrew Bible, and declared that "the House of Israel . . . had an office to perform in the eyes of God" but had little patience for the traditional synagogue of the nineteenth century.[91] Instead, Levy wanted communal Jewish towns, where traditional prayers and rituals would be replaced by discourses on morality and philosophy.[92] Then he actually built one in the small hamlet of Micanopy, Florida.

Unlike Ararat, Levy's Pilgrimage got off the ground. Levy purchased 1,000 acres, 120 of which were cleared for agriculture. His work in Florida actually predated Noah's 1825 Ararat speech; indeed, Noah was an investor in Pilgrimage and offered to "put my shoulders to the wheel" to share the "blessings of civil liberty & religious toleration" with European Jews.[93] By 1823, the English Jew Frederick Warburg arrived with over twenty European Jewish settlers, virtually none of whom had any agricultural experience. To compensate, Levy urged the use of alligator dung as fertilizer—and also permitted the use of enslaved labor. Between ten and thirty-one enslaved persons were forced to work at Pilgrimage, and the crop Levy chose to grow was sugar, which had given rise to some of the most brutal slave regimes in the New World. Levy had a biblical notion to emancipate all slave children by the age of twenty-one, but Pilgrimage didn't last that long.[94]

Little is known about the Jewish residents of Pilgrimage. There were likely no more than five families ever present at one time, and at least one settler left. Each family was to have its own private residence. There was also a sugar mill, stable, blacksmith shop, and the cabins reserved for the enslaved, a "range of tenements." All of it burned in the Second Seminole War, as the indigenous nations of Florida rose up to throw off American land jobbers. Given the almost total absence of Jewish documents, rituals, or buildings at Pilgrimage, it seems likely that Levy's dream of a Jewish agricultural utopia quickly became just another slave-labor plantation.[95]

Four separate efforts to create far-ranging, possibly world-changing, Jewish institutions in the United States failed in the 1820s: the ASMCJ, Noah's Ararat, Levy's Pilgrimage, and the Reformed Society of Israelites. All were attempts, at least in part, to reinvent the ways in which Jews could live among Christians. Their failure, however, suggests that American Judaism was doing just fine without them; it was growing and establishing new auxiliary societies, breakaway synagogues, and a new form of apologetics. A new context for American evangelism certainly posed problems to American Jews. Nevertheless, even when institutional responses failed, American Judaism did not drown in a sea of conversion. American Jews were learning to live with the challenge of religious freedom. And while

Frey and Arnell might have been annoying, most American Jews agreed with Noah that they were far better than the alternative. The philo-Semitism of the ASMCJ still engaged in stereotypes and discrimination, but the society's acknowledgment of Jewish suffering at the hands of Christians was a significant (if not universal) step forward. By and large, American Judaism was doing what religious institutions elsewhere in the United States were doing: democratizing and adapting to a new framework of religious freedom.

And then Maryland said no.

12

The Jew Bill

AN 1823 ELECTION FOR THE Maryland House of Delegates turned on an important political question: "Did or did not the Jews of old crucify Jesus Christ?" That at least was how one of the candidates, Benjamin Galloway, framed the election for voters in the May 18, 1823, issue of the Maryland *Herald*. Galloway's opponent was Thomas Kennedy, a genial man who had for several years been seeking to change Maryland's constitutional requirement that officeholders take an oath to support the Christian religion. Kennedy sought to expand the rights of officeholding to Jews, despite the fact that he himself claimed he didn't know any Jews. Kennedy's efforts were known as "the Jew Bill."[1]

Galloway tore into Kennedy, "Does he or does he not believe that the Jews of the present day, possess, and profess too in their synagogues, the very same principles and opinions that the Jews of old did, who crucified our Saviour?" And if so, Galloway asked, did Kennedy "wish to arm Jews with power to act in our Christian state?" All Jews "abhor the Christian religion" and if they could "obtain and maintain ascendancy in our state councils," they would "abolish all belief in the Christian religion." For the record, Galloway thought Unitarians were equally as bad.

Galloway ran on a slate known as the "Christian Ticket" or the "No Jew Bill Ticket," and on election day, he received 196 votes out of over 8,000 cast. However, the other four members of the "No Jew Bill" ticket all won. Kennedy and his allies—a group of Gentiles known as the Jew Ticket or Jew Bill Ticket—all lost. Galloway's virulent anti-Semitism did not sell in western Maryland, but neither did the Jew Bill. Few public opponents of the bill joined Galloway in asserting that Jews could not hold office because Jews had killed Christ, but many opponents agreed with Galloway that a "Christian state" could not have any Jewish officeholders.

The upheaval over the Jew Bill marked an uptick of anti-Judaism in the early republic, nearly simultaneous with Mordecai Manuel Noah's firing as consul in Tunis and the rise of the ASMCJ's (American Society for Meliorating the Condition of the Jews) missionary outreach. Having secured freedom in the 1790s, by the 1820s American Jews were being challenged as citizens. Freedom does not necessarily proceed in a linear fashion. Jews in the United States had already achieved some degree of equality when they faced an organized anti-Semitic movement to withhold their rights. As in the Age of Revolution, American Jews and other advocates of religious liberty fought back to establish their rights. Religious freedom needed to be built and rebuilt.

The First Amendment did not apply to the states in 1823, so the Maryland state constitution broke no laws by mandating one of the last remaining test oaths in the United States. Maryland law declared that "all persons, professing the Christian religion, are equally entitled to protection in their religious liberty" and that "no person ought by any law to be molested in his person or estate on account of his religious persuasion or profession." These rules notwithstanding, "the Legislature may, in their discretion, lay a general and equal tax, for the support of the Christian religion," with proceeds divvied up as taxpayers saw fit, either to a particular church, or to "the poor in general." Finally, anyone holding office needed to take an oath of fidelity to the state and "a declaration of a belief in the Christian religion."[2]

The law was not specifically directed against Jews, but functionally, it banned Jews from running for office and from practicing law (the office of solicitor then being classed as an "office of profit or trust" which required the constitutional oath).[3] Meanwhile, all Christians could take office, since the state constitution provided a specific exception for members of Christian sects who refused to take oaths, such as Quakers, Dunkers, and Mennonites.[4] Maryland probably came closer than any other state to having a broad "Christian" establishment.

These regulations did not encourage Jewish emigration. Even as Baltimore grew into a major trading hub, its Jewish population remained tiny. By 1810, Baltimore surpassed Boston to become America's third-largest city—which also made it the largest American city without a synagogue.[5] Maryland's Jewry functioned as an extension of Mikveh Israel in Philadelphia. Some of Baltimore's Jews were members at Mikveh Israel. Abraham Cohen, once the hazan at Mikveh Israel, moved to Baltimore in 1816.[6] When Baltimore's Isaac Abrahams saw a Jewish visitor from Philadelphia shaving on the Sabbath, he duly reported it to the adjunta— at Mikveh Israel.[7] A hundred miles was far to travel for worship, but religious Baltimore Jews apparently did so. Solomon Etting, the first man to challenge the test oath, paid for a pew at Mikveh Israel as late as 1824.[8] Other Jews in Baltimore found other places to worship. When Zalma Rhine arrived in Baltimore on Yom Kippur and failed to find a synagogue, he walked into an establishment marked "Levy & Solomon" and joined "them in due solemnity and devotion," breaking the fast together at sundown. Levy and Solomon were both from Pennsylvania.[9]

The Etting brothers became the leading Jeffersonian Jews of Baltimore. Their father Elijah was born in Germany but became a "natural born subject" of the British Crown in 1765. His certification noted that "being a Jew" he should not have been naturalized, since the law limited the privilege to Protestants. Officials waived the technicality, but the Etting children would have grown up knowing that, legally, their father's status had come down to a clerical error. In a world of revolution, shifting allegiances, and imperial crises, that kind of status could not have provided much comfort.[10]

Solomon Etting married Rachel Gratz in October of 1791, and by the end of that year they had settled in Baltimore. Rachel was "much taken with the place."[11] Solomon's older brother Reuben followed, and they were soon involved in the emerging merchant operations of the city. Solomon helped form the Baltimore Water Company and became one of its directors. In the War of 1812, he represented Baltimore's First Ward on the General Committee of Vigilance & Safety, and helped plan the city's defense when the British attacked in 1814. He even went so far as to write to inventor Robert Fulton about the feasibility of building a "steam Vessel of War" in the 1810s, though the communications never came to anything. In 1816, he was named to a committee to survey territory added to Baltimore; the streets were named for the committee members. Etting Street in Baltimore is a tiny, two-block street, a stone's throw from the Enoch Pratt Free Library.[12]

Solomon seemed committed to his Judaism, despite living most of his life in towns without a formal synagogue. At eighteen years old, he became

certified as a *shohet* for Lancaster, so that the small religious community might have kosher meat. His opportunities for Jewish leadership in
Baltimore were more limited. His father-in-law had to send him a Jewish
calendar; apparently none could be found in Baltimore. Etting donated
money to Shearith Israel for a new synagogue in 1817.[13]

The Etting brothers felt ready to enter the political arena by the end
of the 1790s, but the test act barred their way. In 1797, Solomon and his
father-in-law wrote to the state legislature, explaining that the test act deprived them "of the invaluable rights of citizenship" and requesting to "be
put on the same footing with other good citizens."[14] In December of 1797,
the committee of the Maryland legislature assigned to address the request
reported that "the prayer of the petition is reasonable, but as it involves a
constitutional question," the committee declined to act.[15]

So began a political odyssey. In 1801, a Baltimore legislator introduced
a bill to amend the state constitution to allow people "of the sect called
Jews" to take an oath on the Five Books of Moses. The bill was postponed
on a 35–24 vote.[16] In 1802, when unnamed Baltimore residents (probably
the Ettings) again clamored for the bill, the Maryland House referred it
to "the committee appointed on the petition of sundry Jews." The bill
reached the House floor and was defeated without debate, 36–17.[17] In
1804, a similar bill failed on a 39–24 vote.[18] After that, the Ettings apparently let the matter drop. Reuben leapfrogged from state to federal politics
when Jefferson appointed him as US marshal for Maryland. But in 1817,
Solomon and Rachel's son visited Frederick, Maryland—home of Thomas
Kennedy. Soon after, Kennedy began his advocacy for the Jew Bill.[19]

Kennedy was a Scottish immigrant and sometime poet elected from
Maryland's western panhandle. His poetry concerned (among other
things) the Mammoth Cheese—a wheel of cheese thirteen feet in di-
ameter, made for President Jefferson by the Baptist partisans of western
Connecticut. John Leland, the Baptist stalwart, brought the cheese by ship,
sleigh, and wagon to the White House as a thank-you for Jefferson's strong
support of religious liberty. In response, Jefferson penned his famous letter
to the Danbury Baptists declaring his belief in a "wall of separation" between church and state. (The cheese, however, was described as "very far
from being good.")[20]

On the day the cheese arrived in Washington, Kennedy penned his
Ode to the Mammoth Cheese: "Most Excellent—far fam'd and far fetch'd
CHEESE! Superior far in smell, taste, weight, and size, To any ever form'd

'neath foreign skies." Kennedy loved Jefferson, religious freedom, possibly the cheese, and by 1818, the Jews: "As a Christian I rejoice that there is such a nation as the Jews. . . . Christ himself, the Saviour of the world, was a Jew."[21] Kennedy proposed altering Maryland's constitution to read that "no religious test . . . shall be required from any person *of the sect called Jews*, as a qualification to hold or exercise any office."[22]

Around the same time, Jacob I. Cohen Jr. wrote to Baltimore legislator Ebenezer S. Thomas. Cohen was a young Jew, a War of 1812 veteran, and son of the iconoclastic Jacob Cohen of Richmond. The younger Cohen described the "pressure of religious intolerance" and "shackles of temporal jurisdiction." He contrasted the "indignity of our situation" in Maryland to the protections of the federal Constitution, whereby "an Israelite is placed on the same footing as any other citizen in the Union." Cohen asked for Thomas to act on the bill so that he might experience "an equal enjoyment of civil rights" without having to "*abjure* the principles instilled in him of worshipping the Almighty according to the dictates of his own con-science." It was almost exactly the revolutionary Jewish construction of the rights of citizens.[23]

The Maryland legislature's initial report—produced by Thomas, Kennedy, and Henry Marie Brackenridge—agreed with Cohen that "no law can touch the heart" and therefore, civil and political duties were un-connected with religion. Pointing to the Jewish roots of Christianity, the committee reminded their fellow legislators that Christians needed to have special concern for "that wonderful people the Jews." even if the persecu-tion fell on some other group, however, the committee felt that the New Testament still required full religious liberty for all, for God "sendeth rain on the just and on the unjust."[24]

Brackenridge addressed the Maryland legislature, however, by making the case that Jews were Christians-in-waiting. Thus when Jesus returned, "We shall, on that day, all be Christians."[25] Still, there was "no reason why we should not extend the same principle to other classes of society." Removing religious compulsion from the state, Brackenridge argued, would allow true Christianity to blossom. The Jew Bill—as it was being called by this point—would make the people of Maryland more Christian: "In no coun-tries are there more *atheists* and *deists*, than in those where but one religion is permitted."[26]

Kennedy expected the bill to pass unanimously. It failed on a 50–24 vote. Kennedy brought the bill up again in the 1819–1820 session, and again it went down to defeat. In 1822, an amendment to get rid of test oaths altogether narrowly passed Maryland's House. The Maryland Senate rejected a more limited Jew Bill, 8–7, then adopted a wholesale dissolution of the test oath, 9–5.[27] Under Maryland law, however, any amendment to the state constitution had to pass both houses of the legislature in two consecutive years. Maryland at that time had yearly elections for the statehouse. For the removal of the test oath to become law, it would have to pass through one more session.

So the Jew Bill became a critical issue in the 1823 election cycle. Oddly enough, even though this version of the amendment would allow complete religious freedom, the act was still known as "the Jew Bill." Alternatively, some called it a "*Camel Bill*, which was to swallow up all our Christian institutions." Others referred to it as a "Turk Bill."[28] Brackenridge instead called it "a true American bill." Perhaps the "Jew Bill" name stuck so that its opponents could tie the efforts of Maryland in 1823 to the English Jew Bill of 1753—whose passage was swiftly revoked amid an outpouring of anti-Semitic fervor.[29]

Opponents of the Jew Bill proceeded to give the loudest denunciation of Jewish civil rights as a threat to Christian belief yet heard in the independent United States. A writer in Annapolis thought the Jews were "only made a stalking horse. . . . [T]he real design is to open the door to infidels and atheists, and a vain attempt to mock the holy religion of the Redeemer."[30] Even if Jews "alone were to be let into office by this law, it would still be objectionable," went a letter to the editor, "as they are known to be hostile to Christians as such, & consequently must be hostile to all such parts of our government, as are founded on Christian principles."[31] Opponents claimed the Bill would encourage Jews to settle in Maryland— an argument Brackenridge sidestepped by suggesting the First Amendment was already bringing Jews to America. Nevertheless, some of the opponents simply did not like Jews. Benjamin Forrest, a Montgomery County delegate at the 1820 debate, did not want any Jews to emigrate to Maryland.

A newspaper editorial opined that all may "become members of our political family," but not all could "share in all the rights and all the powers of the government."[32] Opponents were making the case that freedom meant presence, not power. The state belonged to Christians. A letter signed by "A Christian Voter" in the Hagerstown *Torch-light* declared that it would be fine if all of the world's 12 million Jews came to Maryland: "We will give them anything but our country." To emphasize the point, the author added: "This is the Christian's Country! It is the white man's country." The state was the property of Christians, and any freedoms were gifts from Christians, not rights of citizens.[33]

Henry Brackenridge got an earful from John M. Young, a family friend who wrote that Judaism was "infinitely more disagreeable to my feelings than either Catholicism or Mahometanism." Young seemed at pains to assert that Jews had some rights—"I do not entertain the least idea of persecuting them or any other on account of their evil heart," he wrote— but at the same time, Jews "don't possess Conscience." Their historical and theological status made them unfit to hold office. Christians should "let them live," but no more. Young did not want Brackenridge to think him unkind to the Jews themselves, a "stiffnecked & rebellious people for any one of whom I would be happy to do any truly good act."[34] But the state of Maryland belonged to Christians.

Brackenridge stuck to the revolutionary line; citizenship preceded confession. The "U. States has guaranteed to every American citizen the right of worshipping God in the manner he deems most acceptable to him." This right was violated whenever a citizen's religion resulted in "*direct bodily inflictions, or by disqualifications.*"[35] Religious freedom was violated not in questions of convenience, but in questions of bodily harm and civic incapacitation. "Whatever tends to restrict the free exercise of conscience," declared Thomas Warner, a Jew Bill supporter from Baltimore, was "arbitrary and despotic."[36] A Baltimore paper condemned all efforts to "impose particular tests" as tantamount to making Christians "hypocrites or martyrs."[37] Other proponents assailed anti-Semitism by engaging in anti-Catholicism. One writer referred to anti-Jew Bill hotheads as "the monk whom superstition blinds." Mordecai Noah openly blamed Catholics for the Bill's defeat in 1819.[38] Noah received a curt correction from Cohen: "Catholics within the Circle of my acquaintance," he wrote, were all in favor of the bill.[39]

As the legal battle intensified, Maryland Jews found themselves political targets. The test oath had been inconsistently applied in earlier days. As we've seen, a local militia elected Reuben Etting its captain in the 1790s, and Jacob Jacobs became head of the city watch of Baltimore in 1808. In the midst of the Jew Bill debates, however, the law was kept to the letter. The legislative notes of those sessions began recording incoming delegates' profession of the Christian religion, and when Benjamin Cohen was elected captain of his militia unit in 1823, he was forbidden to take the office.[40]

The Jew Bill received surprising support from Joseph Frey and the American Society for Meliorating the Condition of Jews. When Frey and Arnell traveled the country in 1823, they met a Maryland legislator intending to vote "against the bill and the only objection he could bring against it was that it was undermining the Christian religion." Arnell replied "that if Christianity was not built on a basis firmer than that the few Jews in Maryland could overturn it would not be worth keeping it up." Frey took issue with the delegate, and when he told him who he was, the man was silenced. In Annapolis, Frey preached to several members of the legislature, likely making the case that only civic freedom could ensure true conversion. When Frey heard that the Bill had passed, he celebrated.[41]

Benjamin Galloway did not. He called the bill "the infidel act" and the "anti-christian act," and admitted that "I do not solicit the support of Jews, Deists, Mahometans or Unitarians. . . . Indeed I most earnestly request that they may be counted among my adversaries."[42] John Tyson, a Jew Bill supporter, described the opposition as "an opinion inculcated among the people," that the bill would make Maryland "another Judea, and Baltimore another Jerusalem."[43] Opponents defined religious freedom as an agreement among Christians, who could trust one another.

Thus, nearly fifty years after independence, American politicians began to speak of the revolution as a kind of religious compact. As one Maryland newspaper put it, "All government of right originates from the people . . . founded in compact only." If so, the essay continued, then at the moment Maryland's rights were codified, "the *people* were not Jews, nor Atheists, nor Hindoos, nor Mahometans—no, the word *people* meant no more *nor* no less, than those christian people, and nations, and languages, of Europe." Not having been in the original compact, Jews were excluded. The "Christian nation" referred to the moment of the founding, and its religious makeup was to be perpetual throughout time.[44]

The notion is demonstrably false, as this book has shown. Jews had been present, and active, at the moment of revolution. Moreover, the revolutionary generation had never made religious uniformity a precondition of citizenship; indeed, most states abandoned their state churches. Washington had made specific efforts to include non-Christian and minority religions as part of the "great governmental machine," and not as mere residents. And while most Founders credited God (or, in Washington's words, "some unaccountable something") for preservation in battle, they did not call for a Christian republic or a republic staffed by

Christians. Many Founders—and the Jewish Patriots—were clear that they sought moral virtue rather than Christian virtue.

It was the generation after the Founders that spoke of a "Christian country." The proof text for their position came out soon after the Jew Bill debates in Joseph Story's 1833 *Commentaries on the Constitution*. Story, an associate justice of the Supreme Court, offered much the same logic as the Jew Bill opponents. He wrote, "The real object of the [First] amendment was, not to countenance, much less to advance Mahometanism, or Judaism, or infidelity, by prostrating Christianity, but to exclude all rivalry among Christian sects, and to prevent any national ecclesiastical establishment." Story buttressed his case by noting that in "some of the states" Christianity continued to be established "down to the present period, without the slightest suspicion, that it was against the principles of public law, or republican liberty." Story's text became a standard of nineteenth-century jurisprudence.[45]

Story was profoundly mistaken. American Jews and Founding Fathers objected repeatedly to establishments and test oaths as inimical to republican liberty—and bad for Christianity, as well. The Jews stood up for their rights and objected to religious discrimination in the political sphere in every state where they lived. In Pennsylvania, Mikveh Israel petitioned the Censors. In Georgia, the Sheftalls confronted *Men and Measures*. In South Carolina, the Jews backed candidates committed to ending the state church. In North Carolina, Jacob Henry spoke out for his own election. In Rhode Island, Moses Seixas went to Washington himself in search of protection for Jewish rights. And that was just the Jews. Numerous Americans objected to state interference in religion. Baptists demanded full disestablishment in Virginia in 1786; they spent decades more pursuing it in Massachusetts and Connecticut. Catholics sought political relief from legal prohibitions in New York state. The tiny sect of pacifist, celibate Shakers became something of a political cause when their homes were attacked in Massachusetts, Ohio, and Kentucky. And the Jew Bill provoked an outpouring of political and religious turmoil in the same years Story falsely declared that not "the slightest suspicion" had arisen over whether non-Christians had rights in the United States.

Story may have been ignorant of the history of fights over disestablishment in the revolution, or he may have been deliberately trying to undermine the vision of church and state proclaimed by his nemesis Jefferson. (Tellingly, he published his views after Jefferson had died.) Intentionally or not, Story passed over the first fifty years of American history without inquiring as to whether religious freedom had ever come up. In so doing, he laid the foundation of a myth that the first generations of Americans were uniformly Christian with no religious conflicts. The revolutionary Americans were in fact a religiously diverse group. They had religious conflicts and culture wars, just as we do. The creation of the separation of church and state came from the arguments, disagreements, and compromises that arose as they created the American Republic. Story's argument that the First Amendment was not meant to protect non-Christian religions is a false summary, one made decades after the revolution. Washington, Franklin, Jefferson, Adams, Madison, and host of Jewish Patriots never saw disestablishment that way. Story's narrative feeds the ongoing mythology that religious diversity is a later addition to the American character. But religious diversity has been with America from the revolution.

Even today, Story's ahistorical summary is often credited over and above the actual writings and actions of Washington, Jefferson, or Franklin. Chief Justice William Rehnquist quoted Story in justifying the idea of the Constitution as a compact among Christians, where religious dissent was not an issue. (In the same opinion, Rehnquist dismissed Jefferson's "wall of separation" interpretation of the First Amendment because Jefferson did not write those words until fourteen years after the Bill of Rights. He proposed Story's interpretation as the more accurate, original intent of the Founders. Story was not even born in 1776 and was eight years old when the Constitution was written.)[46]

The Jew Bill proponents, on the other hand, went to the Founders early and often in their defense of religious freedom. Washington received most frequent mention, but advocates of the bill were not picky. "A Citizen" had a typical response, pointing to the ban on religious tests in the Constitution, "sanctioned by the immortal Washington, by Franklin, Jefferson, Adams, Madison, Hamilton and many other worthies," as a sure evidence that accepting the Jew Bill was "plain truth."[47] The authors of the Constitution, Brackenridge wrote to Young, were "the wisest assemblage of men this country ever witnessed," and "if I err, I err with them."[48] One of the Jew Bill proponents, W. G. D. Worthington, told fellow legislators, "I have in my hands proofs that the father of his country was in favor of the political equality of the Israelites"—then read the entirety of the correspondence between moses Seixas and Washington.[49] Mordecai Noah, defending the bill in the *National Advocate*, published letters from Adams,

Jefferson, and Madison.[50] And Kennedy insisted that the Jew Bill "would not injure the interests of either party" because it merely replicated "the example of the illustrious Washington."[51]

The debate also saw a resurgence of old anti-Semitic favorites. Galloway made the crucifixion and other Jewish crimes his central objection to the bill. Writing for the Maryland *Herald*, he explained that since he preferred *"Christianity* to *Judaism,"* he would oppose the Jew Bill, which was intended to undermine Christianity.[52] Others couched their prejudices in humor; Abraham Blessing, a candidate in Frederick, informed voters that "as to the JEW BILL, he would have nothing to do with it; that he had too many in his possession already, to be favorable to any such measure."[53] "The great cry in this country against the Jews," Worthington said in 1825, "is that they crucified Christ."[54]

In 1823, the No Jew Bill ticket had a resounding victory; the five members of the ticket received 5,794 votes to the Jew Bill ticket's 3,533—over 62 percent of the vote. Galloway's minuscule 196 votes represented around 2 percent of the total. The No Jew Bill ticket took every single seat from Washington County. Things did not go much better in Queen Anne's County. Three of its four delegates—James Roberts, James Wright, and Henry Pratt—voted for the Jew Bill. In 1823, Wright did not run, but Roberts and Pratt did. They were crushed, receiving less than half the votes they had received the year before. The man who voted against the Bill, William Meconekin, saw his share of the vote virtually unchanged from 1822. In Kent County, Federalist Benjamin Massey voted for the bill, and saw his vote total drop from 407 to 195—enough to lose the seat. In Baltimore County—home to the few Jews who lived in Maryland—yes-vote Edward Orrick increased his vote total but still lost.[55]

Yet while the results in Queen Anne's and Washington County were clear rebukes against the Jew Bill, the broader picture across Maryland was mixed. Several Jew Bill proponents won reelection; Henry Kemp lost 400 votes from 1822 to 1823, but eked out victory nonetheless. Tobias Stansbury and William Johnson of Baltimore increased their totals by 35 percent and 25 percent en route to decisive victories. Running on a pro-Jew Bill vote, James Hodges almost tripled the number of votes he won in his 1822 special election. And some of the "no" voters lost, too. Abraham Blessing's jokes about the Jew Bills in his pocket failed to net him enough votes for victory. It was not clear (outside Washington County) just how far the anti-Jew Bill animus had influenced the elections.

Still, the results were not good. So after several years of public silence, Baltimore Jews took action. Etting, Cohen, and Levy Solomon sent a petition to the entire General Assembly in 1824, having left the debating to the Gentiles from 1818 to 1823. Worthington (in a speech advocating the abolition of the test oath) noted that "the Jews have not made 'a great clamour,' because that would be the means of injuring both their cause and their standing." With the Jew Bill in jeopardy, Baltimore's Jewry declared publicly that they sought not "a grant of exclusive privilege" but only "equal rights." Perhaps befitting a general abolition of test oaths, the letter stressed the general nature of the rights: "To disqualify any class of your citizens, is for the people to disqualify themselves."[56] As an added bonus, the petition emphasized that "it is no part of them [Jews] to work conversion." Christian faith would not be at risk from this "sect."

The Jew Bill headed toward its crucial, confirming second vote. The galleries were "crowded to suffocation" to watch the final speeches. Not a single legislator spoke against the amendment. Nevertheless, it lost, 44–28.[57] The silence of the opposition lent some credence to Worthington's claim that members did not want to speak against the Jew Bill, merely to vote against it. Or, as *Niles Weekly Register* put it, "It would have passed if a considerable number of the members had not previously pledged themselves to vote against it, to gratify the prejudices of their constituents."[58]

Stymied at the polls, Jew Bill supporters resorted to some legislative skulduggery. They revised the amendment, so that once again it referred only to Jews. They then waited until the last day of the legislative session—when nearly a third of the House had already gone home—to introduce the bill. It passed without debate, 26–25. One vote made the difference.[59]

With the passage of the bill, both Solomon Etting and Jacob I. Cohen Jr. won seats on the Baltimore City Council. Cohen later sat on Baltimore's School Commission.[60] The legislators who fought for the Jew Bill trumpeted their success; Brackenridge published a volume of the speeches in favor of the bill in 1829, going so far as to contact his fellow legislators to assure correct copy.[61] In the wake of the bill's passage, Kennedy's Hagerstown appears to have incubated its own Jewish community. By the 1830s, the records for Maryland circumcisions listed at least ten *bris* ceremonies in Hagerstown.[62]

The passage of the bill brought mixed blessings to Maryland's Jews.[63] Jacob Cohen urged his fellow Baltimore Jews to support national Jewish institutions, to prove that Judaism still existed even "under the circumstances in which our people are situated in the State of Maryland."[64]

But even in 1827, when Cohen and Etting won their races, Baltimore still had no synagogue. When Jews attempted to incorporate a synagogue in 1830, the legislature denied their request.[65]

It is possible to view the Jew Bill episode as a last gasp of anti-Judaism following successful defenses of religious freedom for Jews across America. Yet legal and popular religious discrimination was growing, and the rise of the phrase "Christian nation" in the Jew Bill debates was a harbinger. Within a decade of the Bill's passage, American anti-Catholicism reached new degrees of ferocity, with mobs and politicians deriding Catholics as unfit for democracy. Rioters torched the Charlestown convent in 1833. Further anti-Catholic riots and arson exploded in Philadelphia, St. Louis, Louisville, and Detroit over the next twenty years. Between 1833 and 1834, Mormons were forcibly removed from Jackson County, Missouri, in an act of ethnic cleansing, because other residents deemed them unacceptable.[66]

Religious freedom does not progress in a linear fashion from theocracy to equality. It has to be built. And it has to be built upon ideas. The first generation of American Jews, fighting in the revolution, accepted the idea that government derived from the consent of the governed. Rights came from God (or at least from "Nature's God"), but the government did not earn its authority from a church or from a particular religion. It emerged through the decisions of the people. And by fighting for the Revolution and supporting the patriots against the crown, Jews made themselves citizens. Two decades of struggle followed as Jews petitioned for and secured those rights. Only then did the idea emerge that the founding had been a merely Christian movement, and that if Jews or others wanted a place in it, they needed Christian permission. This idea had a long day in the sun in the rioting and conflicts of the nineteenth century.

Yet as the Jew Bill supporters pointed out, religious freedom for all was a revolutionary ideal that became a reality as the nation achieved independence. American Jews contributed, along with Americans of all religious stripes, to the creation of religious liberty. It remains critical to note Jewish presence and rhetoric in the revolutionary era, lest we succumb to the myth that America was somehow founded only by Protestants. That does a disservice to all revolutionaries, including the Protestants. A diverse group of people fought to give America freedom. And a diverse group of Americans worked together to turn the revolution into a fight for religious freedoms. Their success is our legacy.

Conclusion

The Revolutionary Legacy

RELIGIOUS FREEDOM AND RELIGIOUS DIVERSITY were baked into the American Founding. The conditions that have made the nation today home to an endless variety of religious beliefs are not new. They were present and accounted for in the revolution. We know this because of the patriot Jews. They fought with Washington's army, prayed for military victory, walked out of cities under British rule. In Savannah and St. Eustatius, British commanders banned or exiled Jews because of Jewish enthusiasm for the American cause. And when the guns fell silent at Yorktown, Jews pushed for a straightforward answer about full rights. Was the new nation to be set up with religious institutional sanction or did the right to self-governance mean the ability to choose one's faith without political reprisal? In essence, they wished to know whether the new nation would re-establish the Christian government of the British empire. The nation did not. Almost every place where Jews lived in the early American republic got rid of its religious restrictions on citizenship directly after the revolution. Virtually any time Jews sought acknowledgment of their full citizenship, they received it. Though not numerous in the Revolutionary Era, Jews were the largest group of white Americans who practiced a non-Christian religion, and they were included in the new union from the outset.

This inclusion is not a story of Jewish "exceptionalism" or of some particular love the Founders had for the Jewish people—an idea that sometimes crosses paths with the general idea that America was founded for a

Christian millennialist purpose. Instead, it reveals just how much religious freedom expanded and changed from the outbreak of the revolution to the election of Thomas Jefferson. Jews did not do this alone; Baptists and Catholics in particular fought to create religious freedom as well. And it worked. Religious freedoms that had not existed in 1775 were established by 1800. Such freedoms were not intended merely for the majority religion and the different sects within it, but for Jews and other faiths as well. Religious freedom was meant to be wide and inclusive. Many of the revolutionary generation were already saying in 1787 that such freedoms extended outward to Muslims, Hindus, pagans, and religions of all kinds. As Jefferson wrote, religious freedom was meant "to comprehend, within the mantle of its protection, the Jew and the Gentile, the Christian and Mahometan, the Hindoo, and infidel of every denomination."[1]

In my ten years of researching and writing this book, I rarely heard the revolution referred to as the beginning of an expansion of freedom, or a moment of recognition that a people self-governed derive their fundamental rights from nature. Instead, I often hear the revolution spoken of as a kind of Eden, a space of historic purity, where all American values are realized, and where love of country surpasses everything else. At other times, I hear the revolution cast as a Fall, where promises of freedom and the language of liberty papered over the absence of change, and no real shift of power or alteration of circumstances occurred.

The story of the Jewish patriots undoes all these facile generalizations, which in the end are not only historically problematic but also insufficient for our fragile democracy. The Jews of the United States unquestionably had greater rights after the revolution than they did before. This shift did not happen because of the moral excellence or heroism of the early American Jews. And yet the rights of American Jews provide an example of how civic freedom expanded during the revolution and indeed because of the revolution. This happened even though religious equality had never been invoked as a goal, objective, or cause of the war. The revolution itself created freedoms; it did not merely name them or codify what had existed.

Many defenders of religious liberty in the twenty-first century have cast the case for religious freedom as a matter of benevolence or tolerance, stemming from concern over making others feel unwelcome. That is not fundamentally what religious freedom is about. The question for the revolutionary Jews was not whether their feelings were hurt but whether their rights had been violated. It was active rather than defensive. They wanted to know about their legal right to worship, to vote, and to run for office. Civic freedom means equality. It is not magnanimity on the part of a majority to a minority religion. As Washington wrote to the Newport synagogue in 1790, "Toleration is no longer spoken of, as if it was by the indulgence of one class of people, that another enjoyed the exercise of their inherent natural rights."

Religious freedom did not and does not require a theological acceptance of all faiths as equally valid. American patriots accepted Jews as citizens without accepting Judaism. Thomas Jefferson vocally supported Jewish rights, but he thought Judaism a fool's religion. Advocates for Jewish rights sometimes supported religious liberty because they thought it made for a superior basis on which to missionize other people. Christian missionaries began to talk about the advantages of proselytizing non-Christians under conditions of equality: "The civil and religious privileges of our happy nation," wrote one evangelist, assured that conversions could not be forced.[2] When James Madison reflected late in life on the effects of disestablishment, he wrote that "there is more religion among us now than there ever was before the change." For "every relaxation of the Alliance between Law & Religion" had turned out "as safe in practice as it is sound in Theory."[3] By removing any possible political benefit for accepting Christ, American Christians believed that they had secured their churches against false or scheming preachers. American Christians hailed the separation of church and state. The explosive growth of Baptist, Methodist, Disciples of Christ, and Catholic churches in the wake of the revolution seemed to confirm the safety and promise of a state without a church. Religious freedom was good for Christianity.

It is also good for our civic capacity—our ability to adapt, change, and value both the individual's belief and the public good. Diversity is not benevolence. It is a consequence of citizenship and equality. Jefferson and Washington did not much care what people did in church. They did care whether those people were committed to the idea of a republic. Religious freedom allows a society to judge people on their character, their civics, their ability—not on their adherence to a religious creed. In other words, religious freedom demands that citizens be judged on how they live their lives rather than what they say in prayer. The revolution changed things.

Acknowledging the revolution's creation of liberty and rights where they had not previously existed does not mean ignoring, yet again, the scorched-earth slaughter perpetuated against the Haudenosaunee, for example, or the fact that the war's rhetoric of liberty mostly failed to un-shackle the chains of the enslaved. But the creation of religious freedom might be read alongside of such events to create, as Jane Kamensky called for, an American revolution "at once faithful to the past and useful to our fragile democracy."[4] The revolution was not all heroics and noble sacrifices and untrammeled victories. But neither was it all just talk.

As I finish this manuscript, the world is facing a floodtide of anti-Semitism and other forms of hate and discrimination. This book will not change that. Nor should Jewish history be understood only in light of the patriot Jews. But we cannot understand the story of the American Revolution without the patriot Jews. Examining the American experiment at its very beginning reveals how the revolutionary generation handled the rough beast of religious nationalism and the challenge of a multireligious democracy. It was a way in which the revolution succeeded and an example of how freedom gets constructed—a case study for all people involved in the process of creating and maintaining freedom as though it was a living thing, and not a museum artifact—praised but not used, venerated but trapped behind glass.

When Jews gather at the seder table for the Passover liturgy each year, they hear the story of the exodus from Egypt. The Haggadah encourages everyone at the table to think that they themselves came forth out of Egypt—for if God had not brought the Jews forth, we might still be there to this day.

It is a useful reminder that freedom can be lost and gained. Once created it can be destroyed; rights can emerge where none were before. This is the challenge of living in a democracy. For democracy "has its evils too," as Jefferson wrote, "the principal of which is the turbulence to which it is sub-ject. But weigh this against the oppressions of monarchy, and it becomes nothing."[5]

Late in life, Gershom Seixas wrote similarly to his daughter Sarah about the turbulence of American life. "All our pursuits are . . . commixt with Blanks & prizes, more of the former, then of the latter."[6] We begin with "*hopes* of gain & not in *fear* of loss," but find "in many well-concerted plans of operation, something unforeseen occurs, & disappointment ensures. . . . Lamentations & repinings are of no avail." But perhaps thinking about his own experiences in the revolution—of making himself a patriot and a citizen, the exile from New York, the uncertainty and war in Connecticut, the unprecedented patriot synagogue he helped to build in Philadelphia—Gershom also reminded Sarah that "we are often baffled in our designs, & sometimes we find, ultimately, that all things work for good, contrary to our expectation." Democracy and freedom were not guaranteed. They required a lifetime of work and patience. And so, Seixas reminded his daughter, "wherever there is hope, there must necessarily be fear." That was Seixas's challenge, and our own.

ACKNOWLEDGMENTS

Many people helped me write *A Promised Land*. I ask forgiveness from those whom I've forgotten, and I offer the caution that everyone below helped make this book better. The flaws all belong to me.

I received enormous encouragement and wisdom from my agent Rebecca Friedman, and my editor at Oxford University Press, Tim Bent. They are both visionaries in getting at big ideas and historical changes, and also careful architects of smart sentences. Every historian should have them at their backs. I received financial and institutional support from the American Jewish Archives, who hosted me for a summer and who provided a wonderful home for cultural and intellectual history. Many thanks to Dana Herman and the entire staff. I also received financial support from the Library Company of Philadelphia and from the 2019 National Endowment for the Humanities Colloquium on the Jewish South. In 2022, Auburn University granted me leave to finish the manuscript; Christa Dierksheide and the Center for the Study of the Age of Jefferson at the University of Virginia offered me a home in their new building with access to their seemingly limitless archival resources. My research has taken me to numerous archives and libraries. I would like to thank in particular the American Jewish Historical Society, Robert D. Farber University Archives and Special Collections at Brandeis University, Georgia Historical Society, Georgia State Archives, University of Georgia Special Collections, Maryland Historical Society, Bremen Museum of Atlanta, University of Virginia Special Collections, and the College of Charleston Special Collections.

A host of scholars read and advised this project. Michael Hoberman offered ongoing commentary over the last four years and has unstintingly shared his research and insights about early American Jewish thought. Michael, Sarah Barringer Gordon, and Shari Rabin all read the entire manuscript and offered helpful critiques. I have done my best to incorporate their suggestions. Kate Carté spent a great deal of time helping me frame my argument and introduction. Other scholars read parts of the manuscript at various times, including Ben Carp, Frank Cogliano, Christa Dierksheide, Adam Domby, Joan Harrell, Meryle Cawley, Armin Mattes, Spencer McBride, Alyssa Penick, Andrew Porwancher, John Ragosta, Hannah Spahn, Heather Warren, and Nadine Zimmerli. A number of scholars also provided clarifying conversations at important points in the process; I would to thank Jonathan Sarna, Jane Kamensky, Douglas Winiarski, Susanna Lindsey, Toni Pitock, Jonathan Awtrey, Terri Halperin, and Asma Uddin. These folks may not remember talking to me, but their words helped me write the book. I learned how to do this stuff from Peter S. Onuf, and I doubt anyone else could have taught me the patience and joy of being a historian. The man who introduced me to religious history, David Holmes of William & Mary, passed away before this book saw print. I think he would have liked it.

I am grateful to my friends and colleagues at Auburn University. It is a known fact that we have the best and most collegial history department in the United States. I am honored that these folks let me work here. Our department secretaries, Alfreda Cosby and Sharon Lewis, have made my work much easier and more competent than it deserves to be. All of my colleagues have endured many comments from me about law, democracy, and obscure religious ceremonies. Special thanks to Eden McLean, Matt Malczycki, Aubrey Lauersdorf, and Kelly Kennington, who are most often the targets of my musings on *shtar halitzah* and other such things. Special thanks too to my former students who have become great friends and advisers—Dr. Rolundus Rice and Rev. Curt and Jenn Mize.

My most important thanks go to my family, who have lived with this project for some time. I do not have words to express my love and affection for Emily. Sam was not born when this project began; now he is nine. Being a father to Sam and Charlie is the greatest honor I could have, and it has shaped this book, and me, in ways I can only guess at. This book is for them.

NOTES

Abbreviations Used in the Notes

AJA   American Jewish Archives, Cincinnati, OH

AJAJ   American Jewish Archives Journal

AJD   *American Jewry: Documents, Eighteenth Century*. Jacob Rader
                Marcus, ed. Cincinnati, OH: Hebrew Union College Press, 1959

AJHQ   *American Jewish History Quarterly*

AJHS   American Jewish Historical Society, New York, NY

AJWDH   *The American Jewish Woman: A Documentary History*. Jacob
                Rader Marcus, ed. New York: Ktav, 1981

BB   *Jews of the United States, 1790–1840*. Joseph L. Blau and Salo
                W. Baron, eds. New York: Columbia University Press, 1963

CAJ   *The Colonial American Jew 1492–1776*, 3 vols. Jacob Rader
                Marcus. Detroit: Wayne State University Press, 1970

DHJUS   *Documentary History of the Jews of the United States*, Morris
                U. Schappes, ed. New York: Schocken, 1971

DHRC   *Documentary History of the Ratification of the Constitution*.
                Madison, WI: State Historical Society of Wisconsin, 1976

EAJ   *Early American Jewry*, 2 vols. Jacob Rader Marcus.
                Philadelphia: Jewish Publication Society of America, 1955

JEA   *The Jewish Experience in America*, 5 vols. Abraham Karp, ed.
                Waltham, MA: American Jewish Historical Society, 1969

JER   *Journal of the Early Republic*

JITA   *Jews in the Americas, 1776–1826*. Michael Hoberman, Laura
                Leibman, and Hilit Surowitz-Israel, eds. New York: Routledge,
                2018

MAJ	*Memoirs of American Jews, 1775–1865.* Jacob Rader Marcus, ed. Jacob R. Schiff Library of Jewish Contributions to American Democracy. New York: Ktav, 1975
PAJHS	*Publications of the American Jewish Historical Society*
PGW	Papers of George Washington. Charlottesville: University of Virginia Press, 1950–
PMHB	*Pennsylvania Magazine of History & Biography*
USJ	*United States Jewry, 1776–1985,* 3 vols. Jacob Rader Marcus. Detroit: Wayne State University, 1989–1993.
WMQ	*William and Mary Quarterly*

Introduction

1. Jonas Phillips to Gumpel Samson, 7/28/1776, *AJAJ* 27:2 (November 1975), 130–132.

2. Gratz quoted in Michael Hoberman, "How It Will End, the Blessed God Knows: A Reading of Jewish Correspondence During the Revolutionary War Era," *American Jewish History* 99:4 (October 2015), 281–313, quote at 299. The question of who counts as a "Jew" presents a quandary to historians of Judaism. As Andrew Porwancher points out, Jewish identity can be defined at least eight ways, depending on personal belief, ethnic descent, public perception, and many other factors. In general, by "Jews" I mean those people who thought of themselves as Jews. Since individual sovereignty in religion became the dominant American mode of religion by 1800, it makes sense to allow a person's own self-definition to serve as a marker of Judaism. Therefore, I will consider the crypto-Jews who practiced secret Judaism as "Jews," and I will count Jews who left the faith as Jews up until their decision to convert. (Solomon Bush, for example, became a Quaker after the war, so I consider him as Jewish during but not after the fighting.) For a quick summary, see Andrew Porwancher, *The Jewish World of Alexander Hamilton* (Princeton, NJ: Princeton University Press, 2021), 26.

3. "Some Additional Notes on the History of the Jews of South Carolina," *PAJHS* 19 (1910), 151–156.

4. On Sheftall's revolutionary career, see William Pencak, *Jews & Gentiles in Early America, 1654–1800* (Ann Arbor: University of Michigan Press, 2005), 162–167.

5. Sermon Fragments, Gershom Seixas Papers, Box 1, Folder 4, AJA. Seixas here followed the model of politicized pastors described in Spencer McBride, *Pulpit and Nation: Clergymen and the Politics of Revolutionary America* (Charlottesville: University of Virginia Press, 2016). On the relationship among religion, government, and civic virtue, see Benjamin H. Irvin, *Clothed in Robes of Sovereignty: The Continental Congress and the People Out of Doors* (New York: Oxford University Press, 2011), 30–33. Classic discussions of civic virtue and American political philosophy are in Gordon Wood, *The Creation*

of the American Republic, 1776–1787 (Chapel Hill: University of North Carolina Press, 1998 [1969]) and Bernard Bailyn, *The Ideological Origins of the American Revolution* (Cambridge, MA: Harvard University Press, 2017 [1967]).

6. "Order of Service observed in the Synagogue Shearith Israel, on a day of humiliation, fasting, & prayer, recommended by Congress," in "Items Relating to Congregation Shearith Israel, New York," *PAJHS* 27 (1920), 31.

7. For extensive examples, see John Fea, *Was America Founded as a Christian Nation? A Historical Introduction* (Louisville: Westminster-John Knox Press, 2011); Richard T. Hughes, *Christian America and the Kingdom of God* (Urbana, IL: University of Illinois Press, 2009).

8. The claim that the revolution was a Christian event often conflates the causes and justification for the war with the support of the war by Christian soldiers and pastors. James Byrd, for example, simply concludes that faith and patriotism went together in an unspecified way: "A good patriot was often assumed to be a good Christian." James P. Byrd, *Sacred Scripture, Sacred War: The Bible and the American Revolution* (New York: Oxford University Press, 2013), 17. Other historians Christianize the revolution by connecting religious "awakenings" to American political changes decades afterwards. This idea traces its pedigree to Alan Heimert, who claimed that "Calvinism, and Edwards, provided pre-Revolutionary America with a radical, even democratic, social and political ideology." Alan Heimert, *Religion and the American Mind: From the Great Awakening to the Revolution* (Cambridge, MA: Harvard University Press, 1966), viii; William G. McLoughlin, *Revivals, Awakenings, and Reform: An Essay on Religion and Social Changes in America 1607–1977* (Chicago: University of Chicago Press, 1978); Patricia U. Bonomi, *Under the Cope of Heaven: Religion, Society, and Politics in Colonial America* (New York: Oxford University Press, 1986); Thomas S. Kidd, *George Whitefield: America's Spiritual Founding Father* (New Haven, CT: Yale University Press, 2014). This position has been taken in certain political quarters as evidence that the American political tradition derives from Christian sources, and therefore that freedom is predicated on Christianity. Consider as an example the invocation of Ryan Williams at the far-right Claremont Institute: "The Founders were pretty unanimous, with Washington leading the way, that the Constitution is really only fit for a Christian people." Emma Green, "The Conservatives Dreading—And Preparing for—Civil War," *The Atlantic*, October 1, 2021.

9. Isaac Franks, "Narrative of the Revolutionary War," SC3672, AJA.

10. Lee M. Friedman, "Miscellanea," *PAJHS* 40:1 (September 1950), 77; Marcus Rezneck, *Unrecognized Patriots: The Jews in the American Revolution* (New York: Greenwood Press, 1975), 51, 65.

11. Rezneck, *Unrecognized Patriots*, 25.

12. Edwin Wolf's work on Civil War Jewry exemplified this approach, known as "name profiling." See Adrienne DeArmas, "The Methodology of the Shapell Roster," in Adam D. Mendelssohn, *Jewish Soldiers in the Civil War: The Union Army* (New York: New York University Press, 2022), 233–236.

13. *USJ*, 55.

14. *PAJHS* 10 (1902), 163–166, from Minutes of the New York Committee of Safety, January 22, 1776; *American Archives: Consisting of a Collection of Authentick Records . . .* , 4th Series, Peter Force, ed. (Washington, DC: M. St. Claire Clarke and Peter Force, 1837–1853), IV: 1066.

15. Some scholars have long claimed that American patriotism was a particularly Protestant affair—that the First Great Awakening bred revolution generations before Bunker Hill, or that a nondenominational Christian faith bound soldiers to service. See Thomas Kidd, *God of Liberty: A Religious History of the American Revolution* (New York: Basic Books, 2010); Gideon Mailer, *John Witherspoon's American Revolution* (Chapel Hill: University of North Carolina Press, 2017); Mark A. Noll, *In the Beginning Was the Word: The Bible in American Public Life, 1492–1783* (New York: Oxford University Press, 2016); Byrd, *Sacred Scripture*. The converse revolutionary antipathy to organized religion is well described in Annette Gordon-Reed, "Take Care of Me When Dead: Jefferson Legacies," *Journal of the Early Republic* 40:1 (Spring 2020), 1–17; Eric Schlereth, *An Age of Infidels: The Politics of Religious Controversy in the Early United States* (Philadelphia: University of Pennsylvania Press, 2013); Seth Cotlar, *Tom Paine's America: The Rise and Fall of Transatlantic Radicalism* (Charlottesville: University of Virginia Press, 2011). Additionally, an entire pantheon of popular books advances the proposition that various Founding Fathers were religious, often claiming Founders as evangelical Christians. Some of these books are explicitly theological, identifying America with Christian nationalist political interpretations. John Fea discusses these works in depth in *Was America Founded as a Christian Nation?*, chapter 4 and conclusion. These works form the political and cultural contexts in which twenty-first-century historians do their work. Note that I draw a bright line between the books Fea chronicles and peer-reviewed historiographies of those who emphasize the religion of the Founders, including Kidd, Byrd, and Mailer.

16. Aviva Ben-Ur, "The Exceptional and the Mundane: A Biographical Portrait of Rebecca Machado Phillips (1746–1831)," in *Women and American Judaism: Historical Perspectives*, ed. Pamela S. Nadell and Jonathan Sarna (Hanover, NH: University Press of New England for Brandeis, 2001), 63; Eli Faber, *A Time for Planting: The First Migration, 1654–1820* (Baltimore: Johns Hopkins University Press, 1992), 104.

17. Gratz and Josephson to the Jews of Suriname, 1790, in *JITA*, 215.

18. Jonathan D. Sarna, "The Democratization of American Judaism," in *New Essays in American Jewish History: Commemorating the Sixtieth Anniversary*

of the Founding of the American Jewish Archives, ed. Pamela Nadell, Jonathan Sarna, and Lance Sussman (Cincinnati: American Jewish Archives, 2010), 99.

19. Benjamin Rush, *A Memorial Containing Travels Through Life* (Lanoraie, PA: Louis Alexander Biddle, 1905), 119.

20. Ben-Ur, "Exceptional," 63. Edwin Wolf and Maxwell Whiteman, *The History of the Jews of Philadelphia: From Colonial Times to the Age of Jackson* (Philadelphia: Jewish Publication Society of America, 1975), 120; "Congregation of Jews in the City to the President and Council, read in Said council and ordered to be filed," 9/12/1782, Phillips Family Papers, Box 1, Folder 5, AJHS; Congregation Mikveh Israel, "Minutes and Correspondence of the Congregation, 1782–1790," Robert D. Farber University Archives and Special Collections, Brandeis University, 65–66.

21. Mikveh Israel, "Minutes and Correspondence," 11/20/1783.

22. Citizenship can be a tricky notion. As historian Martha Jones points out, sometimes people claimed rights simply by acting as rights-bearing citizens. This is precisely what the Jews did in the 1780s. Martha S. Jones, *Birthright Citizens: A History of Race and Rights in Antebellum America* (New York: Cambridge, 2018). My ideas of constructing citizenship are primary informed by Jones's idea that citizenship is bricolage built by law and politics but also by claims-making, and that its historiography relies on "disruptive vignettes" rather than coherent legal treatises (10). I am also influenced by Douglas Bradburn's explanation of the reorientation of citizenship along an axis of natural rights and common law, *The Citizenship Revolution: Politics and the Creation of the American Union, 1774–1804* (Charlottesville: University of Virginia Press, 2009). See also James Kettner, *The Development of American Citizenship, 1608–1870* (Chapel Hill: University of North Carolina Press, 1978); Nathan Perl-Rosenthal, *Citizen Sailors: Becoming American in the Age of Revolution* (Cambridge, MA: Belknap Press, 2015); Jonathan Gienapp, *Second Creation: Fixing the Constitution in the Founding Era* (Cambridge, MA: Belknap Press, 2018); Linda Kerber, *No Constitutional Right to Be Ladies: Women and the Obligations of Citizenship* (New York: Hill and Wang, 1998);.

23. By "religion" I mean the organized forms of institutional beliefs and practices normally understood as confessions, traditions, or denominations; I am interested in organized communities, their legal and political actions, and their recognition (or lack thereof) by others. I use the term "faith" to mean the same thing. More abstract definitions of religion, such as those dealing with interior states, are useful, but when discussing legal classification of Jews versus Christians, I believe a more general definition will suffice and that the reader will know what I mean. This approach largely leaves aside questions of Jewish practice, including *halakhah*, except as they entered public debate. On the problems of humanities and the analysis of religious terms, see Stuart Clark, *Thinking with Demons: The Idea of Witchcraft in Early Modern Europe*

(New York: Oxford University Press, 1997), 1–10; on "religion" as a term, see (among many) Jonathan Z. Smith, "Religion, Religions, Religious," in *Relating Religion: Essays in the Study of Religion* (Chicago: University of Chicago Press, 2004), 179–196.

24.   *EAJ*, 350.

25.   Some historians have argued that no such rights ever really came out the revolution, that America functionally maintained "a state-sanctioned Christianity." David Sehat, *The Myth of American Religious Freedom* (New York: Oxford University Press, 2017), 17;. These works rarely look at the Jewish experience, which is odd given that the faith presents such an obvious test case. Sehat discusses Jewish disfranchisement in Philadelphia in 1776 but not their subsequent postwar enfranchisement; see *Myth* 15–20, 27, 44. Sam Haselby, *The Origins of American Religious Nationalism* (New York: Oxford University Press, 2015), only mentions the concept of Judaism rather than any actual laws or Jewish experiences, 136, 220.

26.   Jonathan Sarna, *American Judaism: A History* (New Haven, CT: Yale University Press, 2004), 37; for similar quotes about American Judaism and rights, see Faber, *A Time for Planting*, 127–130; Rezneck, *Unrecognized Patriots*, 11, and Deborah Dash Moore, "Foreword," in Howard B. Rock, *Haven of Liberty: New York Jews in the New World, 1654–1865* (New York: New York University, 2012), xvi. David Sorkin classifies the historiographical notion that American Jews "gained equality without either emancipation or an emancipation process" into a "clean break" and a "rough edge" school. He claims that neither view can be sustained, in part because Jewish emancipation in North America needs to be seen in a Caribbean context. See David Sorkin, "Is American Jewry Exceptional? Comparing Jewish Emancipation in Europe and America," *American Jewish History* 96:3 (September 2010), 175–200. Oddly, Sorkin's comprehensive and brilliant *Jewish Emancipation: A History Across Five Centuries* (Princeton, NJ: Princeton University Press, 2019), 224–227, says little about the American Revolution; skipping directly from the colonies to the First Amendment. See also Porwancher, *Jewish World of Alexander Hamilton*, 90–105, and Stanley Chyet, "The Political Rights of the Jews in the United States: 1776–1840," *American Jewish Archives* 10:1 (1958). Historians have not, however, noticed the importance of the revolution itself in this transformation, nor how the work of Mikveh Israel contributed to the process.

27.   Robert Baird, *Religion in America* (New York: Harper and Brothers, 1844), 268. A more recent generation of scholars has challenged the notion that the Awakenings and the colonial era generally were mere rehearsals for the revolution. They see a much more profound religious disjuncture in the 1770s and 1780s, bringing in new ideas and new concepts of freedom and the church. The New Lights were not proto-revolutionaries thirsting for religious independence. Katherine Carté, *Religion and the American Revolution: An*

Imperial History (Chapel Hill: University of North Carolina Press, 2021), 6–12, 69, 114–120. See also McBride, *Pulpit and Nation*; Gregg L. Frazer, *God Against the Revolution: The Loyalist Clergy's Case Against the American Revolution* (Lawrence: University of Kansas Press, 2018). Many scholars freely use the term "evangelicalism" to describe a certain New Light pattern of belief. As Douglas Winiarski warns, modern evangelicalism has five elements of which New Light Whitefieldism shares two, so this conflation seems ahistorical. See Douglas Winiarski, *Darkness Falls on the Land of Light: Experiencing Religious Awakening in Eighteenth-Century New England* (Chapel Hill: University of North Carolina Press, 2017).

28.   Mark Twain, *Concerning the Jews* (New York: Harper, 1934 [1898]), 17. The notion that Protestants came "first" and other religions only arrived in the nineteenth century has long haunted scholarship; American religious history from Robert Baird to Sidney Ahlstrom, as Catherine Brekus notes, "judged other religions against an implicit Protestant norm" because Protestantism was "democratic and individualistic." Catherine Brekus, "Contested Words: History, America, Religion," *WMQ* 75:1 (January 2018), 3–36, quote at 9. Ahlstrom did not discuss Judaism or Catholicism upon their chronological arrival to the New World in the colonial period, but only as part of the late nineteenth-century sections of *A Religious History of the American People*.

29.   The notion of religious freedom as an immediate result of the Revolutionary War, rather than as a long process of colonial religious difference, is also at the heart of work on Protestant minorities, particularly Baptists. See John Ragosta, *Wellspring of Liberty: How Virginia's Dissenters Helped Win the Revolution and Secured Religious Liberty* (New York: Oxford University Press, 2010); Thomas Kidd and Barry Hankins, *Baptists in America* (New York: Oxford University Press, 2015), 59–75. By disestablishment, I mean the changed relationship among different sects and religions to the state and to one another; a rethinking of citizenship preceded a redefinition of faith. This is a different process from the democratization of religion explained in Nathan Hatch, *The Democratization of American Christianity* (New Haven, CT: Yale University Press, 1989). Shelby M. Balik questions Hatch's clockwork progression from revolutionary principles to legal disestablishment, "In the Interests of True Religion: Disestablishment in Vermont," in *Disestablishment and Religious Dissent: Church-State Relations in the New American States, 1776–1833*, ed. Carl H. Esbeck and Jonathan J. Den Hertog (Columbia: University of Missouri Press, 2019), 293–308. This kind of religious history is also different from the metaphorical use of ancient Israel in the American political imagination. Eran Shalev suggests that Old Testament metaphors helped shape American republicanism, but as Hoberman writes, "White Protestant hegemony lent most of these Hebraic-inflected debates a strictly abstract tenor." Eran Shalev, *American Zion: The Old Testament as a Political Text from the Revolution to the Civil War* (New

Haven, CT: Yale University Press, 2013); Michael Hoberman, "'God Loves the Hebrews': Exodus Typologies, Jewish Slaveholding, and Black Peoplehood in Antebellum America," *AJAJ* 67:2 (2015), 47–69, quote at 50.

30. Studies of Judaism in the revolution often replicate twentieth-century historiographies of American Judaism, with its emphasis on assimilation, economics, and synagogue-community relations. This reflection of twentieth-century concerns follows Jacob Rader Marcus, whose manifold volumes are the starting point for any study of early American Judaism. Other examples include Faber, *Time for Planting*; Rock, *Haven of Liberty*; Emily Bingham, *Mordecai: An Early American Family* (New York: Hill and Wang, 2003). A notable exception is Pencak's *Jews & Gentiles*, which acknowledges the presence of political anti-Semitism in the early United States but does not consider how the Jews affected American freedom. Michael Hoberman, Laura Leibman, and Hilit Surowitz Israel summarize the current state of early American Jewish historiography in their introduction to *JTIA*.

31. Isaiah Isaacs won election to the Richmond City Council in 1795. Myron Berman, *Richmond's Jewry, 1769–1976: Shabbat in Shockoe* (Charlottesville: University of Virginia Press, 1979), 33. On disestablishment, see Ragosta, *Religious Freedom: Jefferson's Legacy, America's Creed* (Charlottesville: University of Virginia Press, 2013); Steven K. Green, *The Second Disestablishment: Church and State in Nineteenth-Century America* (New York: Oxford University Press, 2010), 3–145.

32. Jane Kamensky, "Two Cheers for the Nation: An American Revolution for the Revolting United States," *Reviews in American History* 47:3 (September 2019), 308–316.

Chapter 1

1. Seixas studied the rite of circumcision through his correspondence with Abraham Abrahams, who urged him to "perform the operation with courage intermix'd with tenderness" and to "be sure to tear above the Nut and not below it." Abrahams to Moses Mendes Seixas, 6/1/1772, AJHS, Seixas Family Papers, Box 1, Folder 5.

2. Zev Eleff, *Who Rules the Synagogue: Religious Authority and the Formation of American Judaism* (New York: Oxford University Press, 2016), 10.

3. Albert Matthews, ed., "Journal of William Loughton Smith, 1790–1791," *Proceedings of the Massachusetts Historical Society*, 51 (1917–18): 20–88; Thomas Jefferson to Thomas Mann Randolph Jr., 8/14/1790, *Papers of Thomas Jefferson*, ed. Julian Boyd (Princeton, NJ: Princeton University Press, 1965), 17:390.

4. "Journal of William Loughton Smith," 21.

5. Hebrew Congregation of Newport to George Washington, PGW Presidential Series, ed. Dorothy Twohig (Charlottesville: Virginia, 1950–), 6:286n1.

6. George Washington to the Hebrew Congregation, PGW Presidential Series 6:285.

7. William Pencak, *Jews & Gentiles in Early America, 1654–1800* (Ann Arbor: University of Michigan Press, 2005), 113; Frederic Cople Jahrer, *A Scapegoat in the New Wilderness: The Origins and Rise of Anti-Semitism in America* (Cambridge, MA: Harvard University Press, 1994), 121.

8. Pencak, *Jews & Gentiles*, 84. Rhode Island had two charters, one granted by Parliament in 1644 and one given by the king in 1663. The language about the faith of Christians is in the 1663 charter. See John Barry, *Roger Williams and the Creation of the American Soul* (New York: Penguin, 2012), 308–310, 181.

9. On Judaism and emancipation in Europe, see, among many, Frederic Jahrer, *The Jews and the Nation* (Princeton, NJ: Princeton University Press, 2002); Jacob Katz, *Out of the Ghetto: The Social Background of Jewish Emancipation, 1770–1870* (Syracuse, NY: Syracuse University Press, 1998 [1973]); and Ronald Schechter, *Obstinate Hebrews: Representations of Jews in France, 1715–1815* (Berkeley: University of California Press, 2003), ch. 3.

10. Thomas Kidd and Barry Hankins, *Baptists in America* (New York: Oxford University Press, 2015), 8.

11. Quoted in Samuel Brockunier, *The Irrepressible Democrat: Roger Williams* (New York: Ronald Press, 1940), 249.

12. "Extract of a report of the King's Commissioners, 1665," John Russell Bartlett, *Records of the Colony of Rhode Island* (Providence, RI: A. C. Greene and Brothers, 1856), 2:128.

13. John L. Brooke, " 'The True Spiritual Seed': Sectarian Religion and the Persistence of the Occult in Eighteenth-Century New England," in *Wonders of the Invisible World: 1600–1900*, ed. Peter Benes (Boston: Boston University Press, 1995), 107–126.

14. Roger Williams, *Hireling Ministry None of Christs*, in *The Complete Writings of Roger Williams*, ed. Reuben Aldridge Guild (Eugene, OR: Wipf & Stock, 1963), 7:178.

15. Williams, *Hireling Ministry*, 7:178.

16. Barry, *Roger Williams*, 308.

17. Williams, *Hireling Ministry*, 1:429; Roger Williams, "Queries of Highest Consideration," in *The Complete Writings of Roger Williams*, 2:275.

18. Stiles, "Birthday Reflections, 1767," quoted in Edmund Morgan, *The Gentle Puritan: A Life of Ezra Stiles, 1727–1795* (New Haven, CT: Yale University Press, 1962), 62.

19. Brian Ogren, *Kabbalah and the Founding of America* (New York: New York University Press, 2021), 148–188.

20. Ezra Stiles, *Literary Diary* (New York: Scribner, 1901), 1:68.

21. Stiles, *Diary*, 2:510.

22. Stiles, *Diary*, 3:345. Stiles wrote of Allen, "And in Hell he lift up his Eyes being in Torment"—from Luke 16:23, the cry of the rich man denied salvation.

23. Stiles, *Diary*, 1:97, 1:32.

24.   Stiles, *Diary*, 1:7, 1:41, 1:355, 1:377. Stiles was one of the first examples of philosemitism among Protestant Americans, although the term emerged in the nineteenth century simultaneously with its unpleasant antonym, anti-Semitism. The term has remained problematic ever since, with some scholars going so far as to assume philosemitism is really just anti-Semitism disguised: merely another effort to characterize Jews as somehow different from all other people. Stiles's writings suggest both sides of the coin. See Jonathan Karp and Adam Sutcliffe, "Introduction," *Philosemitism in History* (New York: Cambridge, 2011).

25.   Lopez to Abraham Isaac Abrahams, 9/6/1767, quoted in Stanley F. Chyet, "Aaron Lopez: A Study in Buenafama," in *JEA* 1:199. See also Morris Gutstein, *Aaron Lopez and Judah Touro: A Refugee and a Son of a Refugee* (New York: Behrman, 1939). The circumcision of the Lopez men is attested by a congratulatory letter from Daniel Gomez of 10/30/1752 and is also confirmed by a reference in Stiles's diary, 3/27/1775. Stiles also heard Jewish sermons given in Dutch; see Stiles, *Diary*, 1:423.

26.   *USJ* 1:243, 251. Marcus suggests that by the early nineteenth century, the Ashkenazim were numerically dominant. *USJ* 1:221, 232. Aviva Ben-Ur dates the numerical dominance of Ashkenazim to 1720. Aviva Ben-Ur, *Sephardic Jews in America: A Diasporic History* (New York: New York University Press, 2009), 83.

27.   *JEA* 1:156–159.

28.   Robert P. Swierenga, "Dutch Jewish Immigration and Religious Life in the Nineteenth Century," in *American Jewish History*, ed. Jeffrey S. Gurock, (New York: Routledge, 2014), 1:419.

29.   "1799 Sermon," Sermons by Gershom Seixas, AJHS.

30.   *USJ* 1:278; Stiles, *Diary*, 1:299.

31.   Hayley and Hopkins to Aaron Lopez, 2/20/1775, *Commerce of Rhode Island* (Boston: Collections of the Massachusetts Historical Society, 1914), 1:9.

32.   Stiles, *Diary*, 3:24–25

33.   *JEA* 1:197.

34.   James Brewer Stewart, *Venture Smith and the Business of Slavery and Freedom* (Amherst: University of Massachusetts Press, 2010), 64.

35.   The study of New England's enslaved has grown significantly in the last decade. My summary here is drawn from Wendy Warren, *New England Bound: Slavery and Colonization in Early America* (New York: Norton, 2016); Robert K. Fitts, *Inventing New England's Slave Paradise: Master/Slave Relations in Eighteenth-Century Narragansett, Rhode Island* (New York: Garland, 1998); Allegra di Bonaventura, *For Adam's Sake: A Family Saga in Colonial New England* (New York: Norton, 2013); Margaret Ellen Newell, *Brethren by Nature: New England Indians, Colonists, and the Origins of American Slavery* (Ithaca, NY: Cornell University Press, 2015).

36.   Morgan, *The Gentle Puritan*, 125, 309; Joseph Conforti, *Saints and Strangers: New England in British North America* (Baltimore: Johns Hopkins University Press, 2006), 96. Lopez quoted in Marcus Rediker, *The Slave*

Ship: A Human History (New York: Penguin, 2007), 191. Virginia Bever Platt, "'And Don't Forget the Guinea Voyage': The Slave Trade of Aaron Lopez of Newport," in *Strangers and Neighbors: Relations Between Blacks & Jews in the United States*, ed. Maurianne Adams and John Bracey, 117–119 (Amherst: University of Massachusetts Press, 1999),, 125–126. Lopez's career furnished some of the data embedded in *The Secret Relationship Between Blacks and Jews*, a book published by the Nation of Islam in 1991 which accused Jews of being the central players in the Atlantic slave trade. Lopez was also cited by white supremacist David Duke in 2015 to prove that Jews were primarily responsible for the slave trade. Historically, this argument has little merit; the American Historical Association said as much. Academic refutation of such claims is unlikely, however, to scuttle their repetition as conspiracy theories. Yet as Ralph A. Austen writes in his review of *The Secret Relationship*, "It also does not help to accompany all discussions of Jewish slave trading with indictments of Christians and Arab Muslims as the true villains of the African slave trade." Jews who traded in human cargo must be studied "to incorporate this knowledge into the struggle to become something better." Anti-Semitic attacks on Jewish history should not prevent us from assessing and writing honestly about Jewish history. Ralph A. Austen, "The Uncomfortable Relationship: African Enslavement in the Common History of Blacks and Jews," in *Strangers and Neighbors: Relations Between Blacks & Jews in the United States*, ed. Maurianne Adams and John Bracey, 135–136. (Amherst: University of Massachusetts Press, 1999).

37. Barry, *Roger Williams*, 381; "Charter of Rhode Island and Providence Plantations, July 15, 1663," https://avalon.law.yale.edu/17th_century/ri04.asp, accessed August 31, 2023.

38. Marcus advanced this theory of the charter in *EAJ* 1:117–118.

39. *EAJ* 1:116; Pencak, *Jews & Gentiles*, 84–85.

40. *EAJ* 1:117–118; Pencak, *Jews & Gentiles*, 85–87; "Items Relating to the Jews of Newport," *PAJHS*, 27:175–176; Holly Snyder, "Rules, Rights and Redemption: The Negotiation of Jewish Status in British Atlantic Port Towns, 1740–1831," *Jewish History* 20:2 (2006), 166–167 n14. Dyre was the son of Mary Dyer, executed for Quakerism in Massachusetts in the seventeenth century.

41. Anson Phelps Stokes, *Church and State in the United States* (New York: Harper, 1950), 1:859. Emphasis added.

42. "Wicked Men's Slavery to Sin," cited in Gerald R. McDermott, *Jonathan Edwards Confronts the Gods: Christian Theology, Enlightenment Religion, and Non-Christian Faiths* (New York: Oxford, 2000), 163.

43. Increase Mather, *The Mystery of Israel's Salvation, Explained and Applied* (London, 1669), 174–176.

44. Stanley F. Chyet, *Lopez of Newport: Colonial American Merchant Prince* (Detroit: Wayne State University Press, 1970), 38–39, ascribes the denial to the struggle between the Hopkins and Ward factions in the state government.

It is possible that politics played a role, but the language of the decisions involved religion, and set precedent based on religion.

45.   Pencak, *Jews & Gentiles*, 281 n35, 36. See also David S. Lovejoy, *Rhode Island Politics and the American Revolution* (Providence, RI: Brown University Press, 1958), 76, 204.

46.   Chyet, *Lopez*, 39–40.

47.   Pencak, *Jews & Gentiles*, 103. Newport and Providence shared responsibilities as capital from 1741 until the twentieth century, but the court that handed down the decision on Lopez met in Providence.

48.   Stiles, *Diary*, 1:103; Chyet, *Lopez*, 39.

49.   Mears to Lopez, 7/30/1779, in *EAJ* 1:172; Mears to Lopez, 10/8/1779, in Marcus, "Light on Early Connecticut Jewry," *AJAJ* 1:2 (1949), 47. On Lopez's patriotism, see Marcus, *USJ* 1:50 and Michael Hoberman, "How It Will End, the Blessed God Knows: A Reading of Jewish Correspondence During the Revolutionary War Era," *American Jewish History* 99:4 (October 2015), 281–313.

50.   Stiles, *Diary*, 1:581.

51.   Sydney V. James, *Colonial Rhode Island: A History* (New York: Scribner, 1975), 342.

52.   Isaac Karigel, *A Sermon Preached at the Synagogue in Newport Rhode Island* (Newport, RI: S. Southwick, 1773), 7, 9, 12, 18.

53.   Robert Middlekauff, *The Glorious Cause* (New York: Oxford University Press, 1982), 103; *CAJ* 1130.

54.   Stiles, *Diary*, 2:27–28.

55.   Stiles, *Diary*, 2:27–29.

56.   *JEA* 1:202–206.

57.   Moses Seixas to Lopez, 6/12/1781, in *Commerce of Rhode Island* 2:137.

58.   Marcus Rezneck, *Unrecognized Patriots: The Jews in the American Revolution* (Westport, CT: Greenwood Press, 1975), 65, 122.

59.   *JEA* 1:297. According to Stiles's estimates of 1769, Touro and the Hart family represented seven of fifty-six Jews in Newport. Stiles, *Diary*, 1:11 n2.

60.   Lopez to Joseph Anthony, 2/3/1779, in *AJAJ* 27:2 (November 1975), 157.

61.   Moses Seixas to Lopez, 1/12/1781, in *Commerce of Rhode Island*, 2:118.

62.   Seixas, "Memorandum," attached to Abrahams to Seixas, 6/1/1772, Seixas Family Papers, Box 1, Folder 5, AJHS.

63.   Pencak, *Jews & Gentiles*, 90, 108–109.

64.   Stiles, *Diary*, 2:151; 1:270; 1:65. For Stiles's interaction with Lopez, see as an example 1: 226, 357, 378.

65.   Stiles, *Diary*, 1:224n.

66.   "Some Additional Notes on the History of the Jews of South Carolina," *PAJHS* 19 (1910), 151–156; Hoberman, "How It Will End," 303.

67.   Rezneck, *Unrecognized*, 47.

68.   Fritz Hirschfeld, *George Washington and the Jews* (Newark, DE: University of Delaware Press, 2005), 92; *USJ* 1:53.

69.   *USJ* 1:75.

70. G. Seixas, "Prayer for Peace During the American Revolution," undated, *PAJHS* 27:126.

71. Rezneck, *Unrecognized Patriots*, 52–53; "Items Relating to Congregation Shearith Israel, New York," *PAJHS* 27:137. Note that two Reuben Ettings served in the Revolutionary War.

72. "Reminiscences of the Seixas Family," *PAJHS* 27:346.

73. Gershom Seixas to Moses Seixas, 9/1/1790, Seixas Family Papers, Box 1, Folder 11, AJHS.

74. Manuel Josephson to Moses Seixas, 2/4/1790, "Items Relating to the Jews of Newport," *PAJHS* 27:2 (1920), 185–190.

75. "Items Relating to the Seixas Family of New York," *PAJHS* 27:348 n1.

76. David G. Hackett, *That Religion in Which All Men Agree: Freemasonry in American Culture* (Berkeley: University of California Press, 2014), 195–197; Bernard Kusinitz, "Masonry and the Colonial Jews of Newport," *Rhode Island Jewish Historical Notes* 9:2 (November 1984), 180–190; Pencak, *Jews & Gentiles*, 108.

77. Moses Seixas and Moses, Simeon, and Hiam Levy to Clinton, n.d. [177?], Henry Clinton Papers, William Clements Library, University of Michigan; Seixas to Aaron Lopez, 11/26/1781, *Commerce of Rhode Island* 2:151.

78. Holly Snyder, "Reconstructing the Lives of Newport's Hidden Jews, 1740–1790," in *The Jews of Rhode Island*, ed. George M. Goodwin and Ellen Smith (Waltham, MA: Brandeis University Press, 2004), 33.

79. Josephson to Seixas, 2/4/1790, *PAJHS* 27:2 (1920), 185–190.

80. George Washington to the Savannah, Georgia, Hebrew Congregation, May 1790, PGW Presidential Series 5:448–450; George Washington to the Hebrew Congregations of Philadelphia, New York, Charleston, and Richmond, 12/13/1790, PGW Presidential Series 7:61–64. Shearith Israel of New York had intended to create a combined address of all Jewish communities to the president, but delays in getting the project off the ground led Georgia to act alone. Seixas pointedly refused to join in the letter; the Charleston community also complained that they had been left out of the loop. See "Items Relating to Correspondence of Jews with George Washington," *PAJHS* 27:221.

81. The struggle to define Washington's religion weighs heavily in the so-called culture wars of our own day. The urge to classify Washington as either a modern-day evangelical or practicing secularist is so intense that those invested on each side have repeatedly passed over other Founders who more clearly fall into one or the other camp. For discussion of these efforts and the difficulties and politics of determining Washington's faith, see John Fea, *Was America Founded as a Christian Nation? A Historical Introduction* (Louisville: Westminster John Knox Press, 2011); Steven Waldman, *Founding Faith: Providence, Politics, and the Birth of Religious Freedom in America* (New York: Random House, 2008); and David Holmes, *The Faiths of the Founding Fathers* (New York: Oxford University Press, 2006).

82. Washington attended church fairly regularly, particularly as president, but he declined to kneel for prayer. His own diary indicates, however, that Washington sometimes visited friends, traveled, or went foxhunting rather than go to services. Fea, *Was America*, 178; Holmes, *The Faiths of the Founding Fathers*, 61–64.

83. Waldman, *Founding Faith*, 57.

84. Timothy Dwight, *A Discourse, Delivered at New Haven, on the Character of George Washington* (New Haven, CT: Thomas Green and Son, 1800), 27–28.

85. George Washington, General Orders, 8/3/76, PGW Revolutionary War Series 5:551.

86. George Washington to Joseph Reed, 12/12/1778, PGW Revolutionary War Series 18:396–398.

87. Fea, *Was America*, 178–179; Holmes, *The Faiths of the Founding Fathers*, 65.

88. George Washington to Samuel Langdon, 11/28/1789; Langdon to George Washington, 7/8/1789, PGW Presidential Series 4:104; Waldman, *Founding Faith*, 59.

89. Denise Spellberg, *Thomas Jefferson's Qur'an: Islam and the Founders* (New York: Vintage, 2013), 211.

90. Mary V. Thompson, *"In the Hands of a Good Providence": Religion in the Life of George Washington* (Charlottesville: University of Virginia Press, 2008), 33–34.

91. George Washington, General Orders, 11/5/1775, PGW Revolutionary War Series 2:300.

92. George Washington to Tench Tlighman, 3/24/1784, in George Washington, *Writings*, ed. John Rhodehamel, 555–556 (New York: Library Classics of America, 1997).

93. George Washington to the Presbyterian Ministers of Massachusetts and New Hampshire, 11/2/1789, PGW Presidential Series, 4:274–477.

94. George Washington to the Members of the New Jerusalem Church of Baltimore, 1/27/1793, PGW Presidential Series 12:52–53.

95. George Washington to the Convention of the Universal Church, 8/9/1790, PGW Presidential Series 6: 223–225.

96. George Washington to the Hebrew Congregation of Newport, 8/18/1790, PGW Presidential Series 6:285.

97. George Washington to Roman Catholics in America, c. 3/15/1790, PGW Presidential Series 5:299–301.

98. George Washington to the Baptist Churches of Virginia May 1789, PGW Presidential Series 2:423–425.

99. There are sometimes questions as to whether Washington wrote the letter; one twentieth-century editor thought the letter's distinction between "toleration" and "freedom" sounded more like Jefferson than Washington, and the secretary of state was traveling with the president at the time. (Boyd, *Papers of Thomas Jefferson*, 19:610n.) Alternately, David Humphreys has been mentioned as a possible amanuensis. (Hirschfeld, *George Washington and the Jews*, 32–33). Washington often had underlings write his letters for him,

but all indications suggest that he read what they wrote before he signed. Washington's repeated advocacy of religious liberty, especially regarding minority religions, suggests that he wrote the epistles, or at least that the letter imparted his ideas if not his words.

100. George Washington to the Hebrew Congregation of Newport, 8/18/1790, PGW Presidential Series 6:285.

101. Jonathan D. Sarna, *American Judaism* (New Haven, CT: Yale University Press, 2004), 37.

Chapter 2

1. Stanley Hordes, *To the End of the Earth: A History of the Crypto-Jews of New Mexico* (New York: Columbia University Press, 2005), 107–108. Hordes (5–6) has an excellent discussion of the terminology and etymology of the religious classification and patois in post–1391 Spain and the Spanish empire.

2. Henry Kamen, *Empire: How Spain Became a World Power, 1492–1763* (New York: HarperCollins, 2003), 21, 343; Anna Lanyon, *Fire and Song: The Story of Luis de Carvajal and the Mexican Inquisition* (Sydney, AUS: Allen and Unwin, 2011), 13–17.

3. Lanyon, *Fire and Song*, 13–17.

4. Paola Tartakoff, *Between Christian and Jew: Conversion and Inquisition in the Crown of Aragon, 1250–1391* (Philadelphia: University of Pennsylvania Press, 2012) 1, 27–29.

5. David Sorkin, *Jewish Emancipation: A History Across Five Centuries* (Princeton, NJ: Princeton University Press, 2019), 26.

6. Kamen, *Empire*, 21–22, 343; Robert Rowland, "New Christian, Marrano, Jew," 137, in *The Jews and the Expansion of Europe to the West*, ed. Paolo Bernardini and Norman Fiering (New York: Berghahn Books, 2001).

7. *CAJ*, 43; Edward Kritzler, *Jewish Pirates of the Caribbean* (New York: Anchor Books, 2008), 55.

8. Kritzler, *Jewish Pirates*, 41–42.

9. Eva Alexandria Uchmany, "The Participation of New Christians and Jews in the Conquest, Colonization, and Trade of Spanish America, 1521–1660," in *The Jews and the Expansion of Europe to the West*, ed. Paolo Bernardini and Norman Fiering, (New York: Berghahn Books, 2001), 190.

10. Shirley Cushing Flint, "La Sangre Limpiade of Marina Flores Gutiérrez de la Caballería," *Colonial Latin American Historical Review* 11:1 (December 2002), 36–54.

11. Hordes, *To the End of the Earth*, 140.

12. Kritzler, *Jewish Pirates*, 47.

13. Howard B. Rock, *Haven of Liberty: New York Jews in the New World, 1654–1865* (New York: New York University, 2012), 300, n5.

14. Fernando Cervantes, *The Devil in the New World: The Impact of Diabolism in New Spain* (New Haven, CT: Yale University Press, 1994), 38.

15. Rowland, "New Christian," 125–126.

16. Frances Hernández, "The Secret Jews of the Southwest," *AJAJ* 44:1 (1992), 414–417; Nathan Wachtel, "Marrano Religiosity in Hispanic America," in *The Jews and the Expansion of Europe to the West*, ed. Paolo Bernardini and Norman Fiering (New York: Berghahn Books, 2001), 150, 137.

17. Hernández, "The Secret Jews of the Southwest," 417; Lanyon, *Fire and Song*, 1–9 and ch. 4; Norman Finkelstein, *American Jewish History* (Philadelphia: American Jewish Publication Society, 2007), 20–23.

18. Hordes, *To the End of the Earth*, 159–161, 112.

19. Seth Kunin, *Juggling Identities: Identity and Authenticity Among the Crypto-Jews* (New York: Columbia University Press, 2009), 101.

20. Hernández, "The Secret Jews of the Southwest," 414–417.

21. Geraldo Pieroni, "Outcasts from the Kingdom: The Inquisition and the Banishment of New Christians to Brazil," in *The Jews and the Expansion of Europe to the West*, ed. Paolo Bernardini and Norman Fiering (New York: Berghahn Books, 2001), 243–245 .

22. *CAJ*, 69; Rowland, "New Christian," 132–133; Solange Alberro, "Crypto-Jews and the Mexican Holy Office in the Seventeenth Century," in *The Jews and the Expansion of Europe to the West*, ed. Paolo Bernardini and Norman Fiering (New York: Berghahn Books, 2001), 173.

23. Finkelstein, *American Jewish History*, 30–31.

24. Wim Klooster, "Communities of Port Jews and Their Contacts in the Dutch Atlantic World," *Jewish History* 20:129–145 (2006), 136.

25. Laura Arnold Leibman, *The Art of the Jewish Family: A History of Women in Early New York in Five Objects* (New York: Bard Graduate Center, 2020), 2.

26. *CAJ*, 72–74.

27. Leo Hershkowitz, "By Chance or Choice: Jews in New Amsterdam 1654," *AJAJ* 57:1 and 2 (2005), 3.

28. Leibman, *The Art of the Jewish Family*, 2–3; Hershkowits 11 notes that the details of the Jewish arrival in New Amsterdam are incomplete and the exact details of the arrival involve a certain speculation.

29. Arthur Kiron, "Mythologizing 1654," *Jewish Quarterly Review* 94:4 (Fall 2004), 583–594, quote at 584.

30. Hershkowitz, "By Chance or Choice," 1, 8–9.

31. Hershkowitz, "By Chance or Choice," 1; Megalopensis quoted in Max J. Kohler, "Civil Status of the Jews in Colonial New York," *PAJHS* 6:81–106, 84.

32. Hershkowitz, "By Chance or Choice," 1, 89.

33. Andrew Porwancher, *The Jewish World of Alexander Hamilton* (Princeton, NJ: Princeton University Press, 2021), 14.

34. Porwancher, *Hamilton*, 12.

35. Seymour B. Leibman, *New World Jewry: Requiem for the Forgotten* (New York: Ktav, 1982), 179.

36. Jessica Roitman, "'A Flock of Wolves Instead of Sheep': The Dutch West India Company, Conflict Resolution, and the Jewish Community of Curaçao in the Eighteenth Century," 91; and Jonathan Israel, "The Rise of the

Sephardi Trade System," both in *The Jews in the Caribbean*, ed. Jane S. Gerber (Portland, OR: Littman Library of Jewish Civilization, 2013), 91, 36–37.

37. Noah L. Gelfand, "To Live and to Trade," in *The Jews in the Caribbean*, ed. Jane S. Gerber, 54–57.

38. Barry Stiefel, "Counting the 'Sacred Lights of Israel,'" in *The Jews in the Caribbean*, ed. Jane S. Gerber, 147–153, 158 (Portland, OR: Littman Library of Jewish Civilization, 2013).

39. Porwancher, *Hamilton*, 27–28.

40. Porwancher, *Hamilton*, 17, 21.

41. Porwancher, *Hamilton*, 21, 24.

42. Stiefel, "Counting the 'Sacred Lights of Israel,'" 158–159.

43. Gelfand, "To Live and to Trade," 58.

44. https://encyclopediavirginia.org/entries/an-act-concerning-servants-and-sla ves-1705/, accessed August 8, 2023.

45. William Pencak, *Jews & Gentiles in Early America, 1654–1800* (Ann Arbor: University of Michigan Press, 2005), 122–123.

46. Evan Haefeli, "Delaware: Religious Borderland," in *Disestablishment and Religious Dissent: Church-State Relations in the New American States, 1776–1833*, ed. Carl Esbeck and Jonathan Den Hartog (Columbia: University of Missouri Press, 2019), 38.

47. Pencak, *Jews & Gentiles*, 146–148, 157; *EAJ*, 2:345; "To the Honorable Trustees for Establishing the Colony of Georgia in America," 12/9/1743, in *A True and Historical Narrative of the Colony of Georgia* (Charles Town, SC: P. Timothy, 1741), 37–43.

48. Mordechai Arbell, "Jewish Settlements in the French Colonies in the Caribbean (Martinique, Guadalupe, Haiti, Cayenne) and the 'Black Code,'" in *The Jews and the Expansion of Europe to the West*, ed. Paolo Bernardini and Norman Fiering, (New York: Berghahn Books, 2001), 286–313.

49. *EAJ*, 1:200; *Code Noir* available at https://digitalcollections.nyhistory.org/ islandora/object/nyhs%3A235290#page/4/mode/2up, accessed 3/13/24. Many thanks to Aubrey Lauersdorf and Emily Jortner for help with the *Code*.

50. Mordechai Arbell, *The Jewish Nation of the Caribbean: The Spanish-Portuguese Jewish Settlement in the Caribbean and the Guianas* (New York: Gefen, 2002), 174.

51. Silvia Marzagalli, "Atlantic Trade and Sephardim Merchants," in *The Jews and the Expansion of Europe to the West*, ed. Paolo Bernardini and Norman Fiering (New York: Berghahn Books, 2001), 273–275.

52. Heather Hermant, "Esther Brandeau/Jacques La Fargue: An Eighteenth-Century Multicrosser in the Canadian Cultural Archive," in *The Sephardic Atlantic*, ed. Sina Rauschenbach and Jonathan Schorsch (Cham, Switzerland: Palgrave Macmillan, 2019), 299–332; Ira Robinson, *Canada's Jews: In Time, Space, and Spirit* (Brighton, MA: Academic Studies, 2013), 17.

53. Rachel Frankel, "Antecedents and Remnants of Jodensavanne: The Synagogues and Cemeteries of the First Permanent Plantation Settlement of New World Jews," in *The Jews and the Expansion of Europe to the West*,

ed. Paolo Bernardini and Norman Fiering (New York: Berghahn Books, 2001), 397.

54. "Excerpts from the Minutes of the Society for Promoting the Manumission of Slaves . . . 1806–1809," in *DHJUS*, 118.

55. Laura Leibman, Michael Hoberman, and Hilit Surowitz-Israel, "Introduction," *JITA*, xliii, 29.

56. For a short but thorough account of these efforts, see Seymour Drescher, "Jews and New Christians in the Atlantic Slave Trade," in *The Jews and the Expansion of Europe to the West*, ed. Paolo Bernardini and Norman Fiering (New York: Berghahn Books, 2001) 442–443 and 462, n7 .

57. Laura Arnold Leibman, *Once We Were Slaves* (New York: Oxford University Press, 2021), 10–12. Aviva Ben-Ur, "Purim in the Public Eye: Leisure, Violence, and Cultural Convergence in the Dutch Atlantic," *Jewish Social Studies* 20:1 (October 2013), 32–76, provides an excellent short summary of the historiographical response to anti-Semitic scholarship in the 1980s and 1990s with the notion that Jews became a class of "benevolent masters." As Ben-Ur notes, this is not true either, and the debate itself obscures the dynamics of race, religion, and slavery in the colonial world. Ben-Ur, "Purim in the Public Eye," 36.

58. Drescher, "Jews and New Christians," 443.

59. Rock, *Haven of Liberty*, 26.

60. Pencak, *Jews & Gentiles*, 34. Evan Haefeli traces the origins of American religious pluralism to this unusual movement during England's seizure of power in New York. Evan Haefeli, *New Netherland and the Dutch Origins of American Religious Liberty* (Philadelphia: University of Pennsylvania Press, 2012).

61. Pencak, *Jews & Gentiles*, 35.

62. *USJ*, 1:26.

63. John Ragosta, *Religious Freedom: Jefferson's Legacy, America's Creed* (Charlottesville: University of Virginia Press, 2013, 42.

64. Jon Butler, *Awash in a Sea of Faith: Christianizing the American People* (Cambridge, MA: Harvard University Press, 1990), 102.

65. Faber, *A Time for Planting: The First Migration, 1654–1820* (Baltimore: Johns Hopkins University Press, 1992), 54.

66. Jessica Roitman, "Flock of Wolves," in *The Jews and the Expansion of Europe to the West*, ed. Paolo Bernardini and Norman Fiering (New York: Berghahn Books, 2001), 89; Zev Eleff, *Who Rules the Synagogue: Religious Authority and the Formation of American Judaism* (New York: Oxford University Press, 2016), 5.

67. Ben-Ur, "Purim in the Public Eye," 55.

68. Arbell, "Jewish Settlements," 306.

69. Ben-Ur, "Purim in the Public Eye," 49.

70. Rock, *Haven of Liberty*, 28.

71. Pencak, *Jews & Gentiles*, 43–44; Sorkin, *Jewish Emancipation*, 33; Leibman, *Art of the Jewish Family*, 232, n33.

72. *A Journal of the Votes and Proceedings of the General Assembly of His Majesty's Colony of New York in America (1737–1738)* (New York, 1737), 23–35.
73. Pencak, *Jews & Gentiles*, 41–45; *Journal of the Votes*, 32.
74. *Journal of the Votes*, 32–33.
75. Pencak, *Jews & Gentiles*, 43, 39.
76. *JTIA*, xxxiii; Wim Klooster, "Jews in Suriname and Curaçao," in *The Jews and the Expansion of Europe to the West*, ed. Paolo Bernardini and Norman Fiering (New York: Berghahn Books, 2001), 353.

Chapter 3

1. Jacob Rader Marcus, *The Handsome Priest in the Black Gown: The Personal World of Gershom Seixas* (Cincinnati, OH: American Jewish Archives, 1970), 16, 22; Emanuel Nunes Carvalho, *A Sermon Preached . . . on the Occasion of the Death of the Rev. Mr. Gershom Mendes Seixas* (Philadelphia: Fry, 1816).
2. Gershom Seixas to Hannah Adams, 7/23/1810, transcribed in Dan Judson, "The Mercies of a Benign Judge: A Letter from Gershom Seixas to Hannah Adams, 1810," *AJAJ*, 56: 1 and 2, 186.
3. Gershom Seixas to Sally Kursheedt, undated, Papers of the Seixas Family, Series III: Gershom Mendes Seixas and Descendants, Box 1, Folder 12, AJHS.
4. 1805 sermon, Sermons by Gershom Mendes Seixas, AJHS.
5. Marcus, *Handsome Priest*, 64; *The Letters of Abigaill Levy Franks, 1733–1748*, ed. Edith B. Gelles (New Haven, CT: Yale University Press, 2004), 75 n5.
6. Abigaill to Naphtali Franks, 7/6/1740, *The Letters of Abigaill Levy Franks*, 75.
7. Rebecca Mendes Seixas to Isaac Seixas, 5/25/1776, in "Items Relating to the Seixas Family," *PAJHS* 27: 366.
8. Abigaill Franks to Naphtali Franks, 11/9/1740, *The Letters of Abigaill Levy Franks*, 84.
9. Abigaill to Naphtali Franks, 7/6/1740; Abigaill to Naphtali Franks, 11/9/1740, *The Letters of Abigaill Levy Franks*, 76, 84.
10. Howard B. Rock, *Haven of Liberty: New York Jews in the New World, 1654–1865* (New York: New York University, 2012), 67.
11. Katherine Carté, *Religion and the American Revolution: An Imperial History* (Chapel Hill: University of North Carolina Press, 2021), 72. In contrast, Sarah Barringer Gordon argues that "shifts in doctrine and practice" actually did more than imperial or national politics to shape the legal regime of British and American religion. Sarah Berringer Gordon, *Spirit of the Laws: Religious Voices and the Constitution in Modern America* (Cambridge, MA: Harvard University Press, 2010), 1–14.
12. Carté, *Religion*, 81.
13. Dana Y. Rabin, "The Jew Bill of 1753: Masculinity, Virility, and the Nation," *Eighteenth-Century Studies* 39:2 (2006), 157–171.
14. William Pencak, *Jews & Gentiles in Early America, 1654–1800* (Ann Arbor: University of Michigan Press, 2005), 281, n. 35, 36; see also David S. Lovejoy, *Rhode Island Politics and the American Revolution* (Providence, RI: Brown University Press, 1958), 76, 204.

15. *CAJ*, 1127.

16. *EAJ*, 2:346

17. *CAJ*, 1132.

18. B. H. Levy, *Mordecai Sheftall: Jewish Revolutionary Patriot* (Savannah: Georgia Historical Society, 1999), 26–27.

19. Pencak, *Jews & Gentiles*, 179.

20. Carté, *Religion*, 53, 55, 57, 67, 69.

21. Jonathan Edwards, *Religious Affections* (*WJE Online*, vol. 2), ed. Paul Ramsey, 164–165, http://edwards.yale.edu/archive?path=aHR0cDovL2Vkd2FyZH MueWFsZS5lZHUvY2dpLWJpbi9uZXdwaGlsby9nZXRvYmplY3QucGw/ Yy4xMC53OjU6MC53amVwL2FyY2hpdmU=, accessed August 28, 2023.

22. Samuel Mendes de Solla to Shearith Israel, 1753, in "Items Relating to Congregation Shearith Israel, New York," *PAJHS* 27 (1920), 6–8.

23. Rock, *Haven of Liberty*, 52–55; Pencak, *Jews & Gentiles*, 56–57.

24. Benjamin L. Carp, *Rebels Rising: Cities and the American Revolution* (New York: Oxford University Press, 2007), 79; Rock, *Haven of Liberty*, 67.

25. Pencak, *Jews & Gentiles*, 46.

26. J. J. Pinto to the Trustees of Shearith Israel, 1759, in "Items Relating to Congregation Shearith Israel, New York," *PAJHS* 27 (1920), 13–17.

27. J. J. Pinto to the Trustees of Shearith Israel, 1759, 13–17; Rock, 309 n26.

28. Pinto to the Trustees of Shearith Israel, 12/22/1765, 24–25. in "Items Relating to Congregation Shearith Israel, New York," *PAJHS* 27 (1920). Pinto did not die in 1766, as was once thought.

29. Rock, *Haven of Liberty*, 76, suggests that Gershom was Pinto's protégé.

30. Shearith Israel to Moses Calo, January 1766, "Items Relating to Congregation Shearith Israel, New York," *PAJHS* 27 (1920), 26.

31. Pencak, *Jews & Gentiles*, 59; Opinion of Whitehead Hicks regarding distribution of synagogue seats, 1770, Jacques Judah Lyons Collection, AJHS.

32. Pencak, *Jews & Gentiles*, 56–60.

33. Naphtali Phillips, *An Eulogium to the Memory of Rev. Gershom Mendes Seixas* (New York: J. H. Sherman, 1816), 11; Gershom Seixas to Sarah Kursheedt, 1/ 29/1814; Papers of the Seixas Family, Series III: Gershom Mendes Seixas and Descendants, Box 1, Folder 12, AJHS.

34. *EAJ*, 2:202–203.

35. Phillips, *Eulogium*, 11.

36. Marcus, *Handsome Priest*, 39.

37. N. Taylor Phillips, "The Levy and Seixas Families of Newport and New York," *PAJHS* 4:204.

38. 1805 Sermon, Unbound Sermons, in Sermons by Gershom Mendes Seixas, AJHS.

39. Gershom Seixas to Sarah Kursheedt, 11/10/1813 and 1/29/1814; Papers of the Seixas Family, Series III: Gershom Mendes Seixas and Descendants, Box 1, Folder 12, AJHS.

40. 1805 Sermon, Sermons by Gershom Mendes Seixas, AJHS.

41. Gershom Seixas to Sarah Kursheedt, 9/24/1814 and 11/4/1813; Papers of the Seixas Family, Series III: Gershom Mendes Seixas and Descendants, Box 1, Folder 12, AJHS.

42. Undated sermon, Sermons by Gershom Mendes Seixas, AJHS.

43. Thomas Jefferson, *Notes on the State of Virginia*, in *The Portable Thomas Jefferson*, Merrill D. Peterson (New York: Penguin, 1975), 210.

44. Gershom Seixas to Sarah Kursheedt, 1/29/1814; Papers of the Seixas Family, Series III: Gershom Mendes Seixas and Descendants, Box 1 Folder 12, AJHS.

45. Carp, *Rebels Rising*, 81–82.

46. Petition signed by Benjamin Seixas 9/21/1775, Seixas Family Papers, Box 1, Folder 16, AJHS.

47. Carp, *Rebels Rising*, 89.

48. George Washington, General Orders, 5/15/1776, https://founders. archives.gov/documents/Washington/03-04-02-0243, accessed August 28, 2023.

49. Spencer McBride, *Pulpit and Nation: Clergymen and the Politics of Revolutionary America* (Charlottesville: University of Virginia Press, 2016), 2.

50. US Congress, "In Congress, March 16, 1776. In Times of Impending Calamity . . ." (Philadelphia: Dunlap, 1776).

51. "Order of Service observed in the Synagogue Shearith Israel, on a day of humiliation, fasting, & prayer, recommended by Congress," in "Items Relating to Congregation Shearith Israel, New York," *PAJHS* 27 (1920), 31.

52. "Prayer for Peace," Gershom Seixas Papers, Folder 6, AJA.

53. 1805 Sermon, Sermons by Gershom Mendes Seixas, AJHS.

54. John Witherspoon, *The Dominion of Providence over the Passions of Men* (Philadelphia, R. Aitken, 1776), 50–51.

55. Thomas Kidd, *God of Liberty: A Religious History of the American Revolution* (New York: Basic Books, 2010), 106. As noted here, it would be accurate to say that Congress and Witherspoon believed that there was a connection between God and good order, but not Christianity specifically. Witherspoon, of course, still thought Christianity was the only true religion—but he did not declare Christianity to be a component of the state, or sole source of moral virtue.

56. Witherspoon, *The Dominion of Providence*, 30, 46, 50–51, 60.

57. Witherspoon, *The Dominion of Providence*, 13; "Order of Service," 31–32.

58. Isaac Franks, "Narrative of the Revolutionary War," SC3672, AJA.

59. Robert Middlekauff, *The Glorious Cause* (New York: Oxford University Press, 1982), 345.

60. N. Taylor Phillips, "Family History of the Reverend David Mendez Machado," *PAJHS* 2:55.

61. N. Taylor Phillips, "The Levy and Seixas Families of Newport and New York," *PAJHS* 4:205; N. Taylor Phillips, "Reverend Gershom Mendes Seixas: The Patriot Jewish Minister of the American Revolution," *American Jewish Year Book*, September 10, 1904–September 29, 1905 (Volume 6), 42; Gershom Seixas, *A Sermon Delivered in the Synagogue in this City*

(New York: Archibald McLean, 1789), 6. Michael Hoberman generously shared a draft paper with me on Seixas and the Enlightenment which helped me sort through what does and does not exist from the flimsy records of Shearith Israel in 1776. I am grateful for his assistance.

62. Jonathan Sarna, *American Judaism: A History* (New Haven, CT: Yale University Press, 2004), 33.

63. Phillips, "Levy and Seixas Families," 205.

64. "Items Relating to Congregation Shearith Israel," *PAJHS* 27:252.

65. Marcus, *Handsome Priest*, 14–15; Phillips, "Levy and Seixas," 206.

66. Edwin Wolf and Maxwell Whiteman, *The History of the Jews of Philadelphia: From Colonial Times to the Age of Jackson* (Philadelphia: Jewish Publication Society of America, 1975), 85; *CAJ*, 1273; David de Sola Pool, *Portraits Etched in Stone: Early Jewish Settlers, 1682–1831* (New York: Columbia, 1952), 47.

67. Rock, *Haven of Liberty*, 79.

68. *CAJ*, 1294.

69. *AJD*, 436–437.

70. Phillips, "Sketch," *PAJHS* 21:216.

71. John Ragosta, *Wellspring of Liberty: How Virginia's Dissenters Helped Win the Revolution and Secured Religious Liberty* (New York: Oxford University Press, 2010), 72; Johann Conrad Döhla, *A Hessian Diary of the American Revolution*, Bruce E. Burgoyne, ed. (Norman: Oklahoma, 1990), 23.

72. Rock, *Haven of Liberty*, 78.

73. Jacob Rader Marcus, "Light on Early Connecticut Jewry," *AJAJ* 1:2 (1949), 26.

74. Phillips, "Sketch," *PAJHS* 2:56.

75. *EAJ*, 1:160

76. Pencak, *Jews & Gentiles*, 62.

77. Rebecca Mendes Seixas to Isaac Seixas, 7/26/1779, "Items Relating to the Seixas Family," *PAJHS* 27: 367–368.

78. Richard J. Purcell, *Connecticut in Transition, 1775–1818* (Middletown, CT: Wesleyan University Press, 1963), 34, 55; *EAJ*, 1:160; *CAJ*, 314.

79. Shalom Goldman, *God's Sacred Tongue: Hebrew and the American Imagination* (Chapel Hill: University of North Carolina Press, 2004), 120.

80. Lopez to Mears, 2/16/1779, in Marcus, "Light on Early Connecticut Jewry," 40.

81. Kenneth Libo and Abigail Kursheedt Hoffman, *The Seixas-Kursheedts and the Rise of Early American Jewry* (New York: Bloch and AJHS, 2001), 30; *CAJ*, 1313.

82. Pencak, *Jews & Gentiles*, 65.

83. Sermon, November 28, 1799, Sermons by Gershom Mendes Seixas, AJHS.

84. Sermon, November 28, 1799, Sermons by Gershom Mendes Seixas, AJHS.

85. April 28, 1779, Aaron Lopez Papers, P–11, Box 14, Folder 34, AJHS; Michael Hoberman, "How It Will End," 297, *EAJ*, 2:170

86. Isaac Seixas to Aaron Lopez, 3/31/1779, Isaac Seixas Letters, SC-11169, AJA.

87. Isaac Seixas to Aaron Lopez, 3/31/1779, quoted in Hoberman, "How It Will End," 284.

88. Richard Buel Jr., *Dear Liberty: Connecticut's Mobilization for the Revolutionary War* (Middletown, CT: Wesleyan University Press, 1980), 190–192.

89. *EAJ*, 1:166.

90. Myers to Lopez, 7/30/1779, in *JITA*, 5. Mears and Myers are the same person. George Washington to Norwalk, CT, officials, 7/11/1779, https://found ers.archives.gov/documents/Washington/03-21-02-0364, accessed August 1, 2023.

91. Mears to Lopez, 7/30/1779, in *JITA*, 5.

92. Jacob Mordecai to Moses, Samuel, Rachel, Ellen, and Caroline Mordecai, 7/20/1796; Myers, Mordecai, and Hays Family Papers, AJA.

93. Buel, *Dear Liberty*, 196. William Samuel Johnson is not the same man as Stratford's religious dissident Samuel Johnson.

94. William Samuel Johnson Papers, Box 4, Folder 2, Connecticut Museum of Culture and History, Hartford, CT.

95. Joseph Plumb Martin, *A Narrative of a Revolutionary Soldier*, ed. Thomas Fleming (New York: Signet Classics, 2010), 49.

96. Buel, *Dear Liberty*, 209.

97. Holger Hoock, *Scars of Independence: America's Violent Birth* (New York: Broadway Books, 2017), 45–50; Christopher French, Orderly Book, Connecticut Historical Society, https://collections.ctdigitalarchive. org/islandora/object/40002%3A5108#page/16/mode/2up, accessed August 8, 2023.

98. Hoock, *Scars of Independence*, 45–49.

99. Affidavit by Myer Myers and Peter Betts against Ralph Isaacs, suspected loyalist, Norwalk, 10/6/76; Myer Myers file, AJA. Thanks to Dana Herman and Julianna Witt for their help in locating this reference.

100. Newell to Trumbull, 11/22/1779, in Louis F. Middlebrook, *A History of Maritime Connecticut During the American Revolution* (Salem, MA: Essex Institute, 1925), 1:206–207; William Samuel Johnson Papers, Box 4, Folder 2, Connecticut Museum of Culture and History, Hartford, CT; Seixas quoted in Hoberman, "How It Will End," 298.

101. Hoock, *Scars of Independence*, 120.

102. M. M. Hays to Aaron Lopez, 6/8/1779, Aaron Lopez Papers, Box 14, Folder 34, AJHS.

103. Hoock, *Scars of Independence*, 45–50; "Items Relating to Congregation Shearith Israel," *PAJHS* 27:252; Wolf and Whiteman, *Jews of Philadelphia*, 98.

Chapter 4

1. Henry Morais, *Jews of Philadelphia* (Philadelphia: Levytype Co., 1894), 456.

2. Solomon Bush to Henry Lazarus, 11/15/1777, *PAJHS* 23 (1915), 177–178.

3. "Examination of Solomon Bush," n8, Armstrong to George Washington, 12/19/1777, https://www.founders.archives.gov/?q=john%20armstrong%20Re

cipient%3A%22Washington%2C%20George%22%20Author%3A%22Armstr
ong%2C%20John%22&s=1111311111&r=13#GEWN-03-12-02-0577-fn-0008,
accessed August 31, 2023.

4. Solomon Bush to Henry Lazarus, 11/15/1777, *PAJHS* 23 (1915), 177–178;
    "List of Monies Received by Mr. Phillips for the Building of the Synagogue,"
    PAJHS 27:462.

5. On the terminology and history of anti-Semitism in America, see Frederic
    Cople Jahrer, *A Scapegoat in the New Wilderness: The Origins and Rise of
    Anti-Semitism in America* (Cambridge, MA: Harvard University Press, 1994),
    and Jonathan Weisman, *(((Semitism))): Being Jewish in America in the Age of
    Trump* (New York: St. Martin's Press, 2018).

6. Edwin Wolf and Maxwell Whiteman, *The History of the Jews of
    Philadelphia: From Colonial Times to the Age of Jackson* (Philadelphia: Jewish
    Publication Society of America, 1975), 147.

7. Arno Penzias, "Foreword," in Laurens R. Schwartz, *Jews and the American
    Revolution: Haym Salomon and Others* (Jefferson, NC: McFarland, 1987),
    xi–xii.

8. The description of anti-Semitism and Jewish military service comes from
    Derek J. Penslar, *Jews and the Military: A History* (Princeton, NJ: Princeton
    University Press, 2013), 4.

9. Adrienne DeArmas, "The Methodology of the Shapell Roster," in
    Adam D. Mendelssohn, *Jewish Soldiers in the Civil War: The Union
    Army* (New York: New York University Press, 2022), 233–236; Marcus
    Rezneck, *Unrecognized Patriots: The Jews in the American Revolution*
    (New York: Greenwood Press, 1975), 22.

10. Lee M. Friedman, "Miscellanea," *PAJHS* 40:1 (September 1950), 76–77.

11. Rezneck, *Unrecognized Patriots*, 51; *USJ*, 1:55.

12. *CAJ*, 1310–1311.

13. Rezneck, *Unrecognized Patriots*, 51.

14. Jonathan Sarna, *Jacksonian Jew: The Two Worlds of Mordecai Noah*
    (New York: Holmes & Meier, 1981), 2.

15. A. J. Messing, "Old Mordecai," *PAJHS* 13 (1905), 71–81.

16. Samson Levy to Moses Levy, 7/16/1776, in *JITA*, 3.

17. Rezneck, *Unrecognized Patriots*, 52–53; *EAJ*, 2:352.

18. "Minutes of the New York Committee of Safety, Jan 22, 1776," *PAJHS* 10
    (1902), 163–166; Harby Family Papers, Box 5, Folder 1, College of Charleston
    Special Collections; Cohen Family of Baltimore and Richmond Papers,
    undated, 1779–1897, AJHS, Box 1, Folder 1.

19. James Hagy, *This Happy Land: The Jews of Colonial and Antebellum
    Charleston* (Tuscaloosa: University of Alabama Press, 1993), 60; *EAJ*, 2:23.

20. "Company of Volunteers formed during the Revolution," Cohen Family of
    Baltimore and Richmond Papers; undated, 1779–1897, Box 1, Folder 1, AJHS;
    "Some Additional Notes on the History of the Jews of South Carolina,"
    PAJHS 19 (1910), 151–156; Michael Hoberman "How It Will End, the Blessed
    God Knows: A Reading of Jewish Correspondence During the Revolutionary

War Era," *American Jewish History* 99:4 (October 2015), 303; Thomas Tobias Papers, Box 5, Folder 1, College of Charleston Special Collections.

21. Penslar, *Jews and the Military*, 20–27, 29, 50, 86.

22. Charles Royster, *A Revolutionary People at War: The Continental Army and American Character, 1775–1783* (Chapel Hill: University of North Carolina Press, 1979), 27.

23. Douglas Egerton, *Death or Liberty: African-Americans and Revolutionary America* (New York: Oxford University Press, 2009), 74–75.

24. George Washington to Tench Tlighman, 3/24/1784, in George Washington, *Writings*, ed. John Rhodehamel (New York: Library Classics of America, 1997), 555–556; George Washington to Patrick Henry quoted in Royster, *A Revolutionary People at War*, 50.

25. Isaac Franks, "Narrative of the Revolutionary War," SC3672, AJA.

26. Franks, "Narrative"; Morris Jastrow, "Documents Relating to the Career of Colonel Isaac Franks," *PAJHS* 4 (1897), 7–34.

27. Isaac Franks to Benedict Arnold, 9/3/1780, *AJD*, 268.

28. Franks described his own career in his pension application. The application and other documentation comes from Jastrow, "Documents Relating to the Career."

29. Fritz Hirschfeld, *George Washington and the Jews* (Newark: University of Delaware Press, 2005), 92; *USJ*, 1:53; William Pencak, *Jews & Gentiles in Early America, 1654–1800* (Ann Arbor: University of Michigan Press, 2005), 124.

30. *Extracts from the Journal of the Provincial Congresses of South Carolina 1775*, ed. William Hemphill (Columbia: South Carolina Archives Department, 1960) 15, 33.

31. John Drayton, *Memoirs of the American Revolution* (Charleston: A. E. Miller, 1821), 1:400.

32. Francis Salvador to William Drayton, 7/18/1776, "Jews and the American Revolution: A Bicentennial Documentary," *AJAJ* 27:2 (1975), 25.

33. Williamson to Rutledge, 8/4/1776, "Jews and the American Revolution," 128–129; Hoberman, "How It Will End," 304.

34. Arthur Middleton to William Henry Drayton, 9/14/1776, Alderman Library Special Collections, University of Virginia.

35. "The Sheftall Diaries: Vital Records of Savannah Jewry (1733–1808)," ed. Malcolm H. Stern, *AJHQ* 54:3 (March 1965), 250.

36. William Few, 1748–1828. "An autobiography of Colonel W[illia]m Few of Georgia, to [a member] of his family in New York," https://dlg.usg.edu/record/dlg_zlna_krc083#item, accessed August 22, 2022.

37. B. H. Levy, *Mordecai Sheftall: Jewish Revolutionary Patriot* (Savannah: Georgia Historical Society, 1999), 51.

38. Pencak, *Jews & Gentiles*, 163; "Sheftall Diaries," 251–252.

39. Hirschfeld, *George Washington and the Jews*, 89.

40. Wright to Germaine, 3/9/1781, *AJD*, 234–235.

41. Levy, *Mordecai Sheftall*, 65–57.

42. "Memoirs of Mordecai Sheftall," in *MAJ*, 1:42.

43. *MAJ*, 1:43–44.

44. Frances Sheftall to Benjamin Lincoln, April (?) 1779, *AJD*, 262–263.

45. Holger Hoock, *Scars of Independence: America's Violent Birth* (New York: Broadway Books, 2017), 212–219.

46. Ebenezer Fox, *The Adventures of Ebenezer Fox, in the Revolutionary War* (Boston: Charles Fox, 1848), 94–95.

47. Mordecai Sheftall to Samuel Elbert, 4/12/1779, *AJD*, 262.

48. Affidavit of Sheftall Sheftall, 1832, *AJD*, 238–239; Mordecai Sheftall to Congress, 12/16/1779, *AJD*, 263.

49. Wright to Germaine, 3/9/1781, *AJD*, 234–235.

50. *Journal of a Lady of Quality*, ed. Evangeline Walker Andrews (New Haven, CT: Yale University Press, 1922), 136–137.

51. Ronald Hurston, *The Golden Rock: An Episode in the American War of Independence, 1775–1783* (Annapolis, MD: Naval Institute Press, 1996), 1.

52. Hurston, *The Golden Rock*, 1–2; Andrew Jackson O'Shaughnessy, *The Men Who Lost America: British Leadership, the American Revolution, and the Fate of the Empire* (New Haven, CT: Yale University Press, 2013), 289.

53. O'Shaughnessy, *The Men Who Lost America*, 295.

54. Barbara Tuchman, *The First Salute* (New York: Knopf, 1988), 16, 20; Mordechai Arbell, *The Jewish Nation of the Caribbean: The Spanish-Portuguese Jewish Settlements in the Caribbean and the Guianas* (Jerusalem: Gefen, 2002), 181.

55. Rock and O'Shaughnessy both identify Mears as a loyalist, but this point is not argued. Mears lived with the other patriot New York Jews in Norwalk, and members of his family petitioned Congress for safety against the British. See also his letter to Lopez that refers to the British as the "savage enemy," 7/30/1779, in *EAJ*, 1:166 and 172. See Rock, *Haven of Liberty*, 60–61 and O'Shaughnessy, *The Men Who Lost America*, 299.

56. *EAJ*, 1:150.

57. Hurston, *The Golden Rock*, 3; Tuchman, *The First Salute*, 90–91.

58. O'Shaughnessy, *The Men Who Lost America*, 292–294, 297, 301, 299.

59. Extract of a letter from St. Eustatius, 3/29/1781, *JITA*, 289; *Parliamentary History of England from the Earliest Period to the Year 1803* (London, 1814), 22: 223–226, 1023; O'Shaughnessy, *The Men Who Lost America*, 297–298; Rock, *Haven of Liberty*, 141–142.

60. Petition, Jews of St. Eustatius to the Commanders in Chief of His Britannic Majesty's Navy and Army in the West Indies, February 16, 1781, *JITA*, 289–290.

61. *JITA*, 289.

62. *JITA*, 286, 289; O'Shaughnessy, *The Men Who Lost America*, 297–298; Rock, *Haven of Liberty*, 141–142.

63. O'Shaughnessy, *The Men Who Lost America*, 305, 292.

64. O'Shaughnessy, *The Men Who Lost America*, 316–318.

65. Katherine Carté, *Religion and the American Revolution: An Imperial History* (Chapel Hill: University of North Carolina Press, 2021), 261–263, 278–279.

66. "Information Given by Two Merchants of Charleston," September 1779, in B. F. Stevens, *Facsimiles of Manuscripts in European Archives Relating to America, 1773–1783*, vol. 23, nos. 1946–2023 (London: "issued only to subscribers at 4 Trafalgar Square," 1895), unpaginated; Saul Jacob Rubin, *Third to None: The Saga of Savannah Jewry, 1733–1983* (Savannah, GA: S.J. Rubin, 1983), 31.

67. Phillipe Séguier de Terson, in *Muskets, Cannon Balls & Bombs: Nine Narratives of the Siege of Savannah*, ed. Benjamin Kennedy (Savannah: Beehive Press, 1974), 15.

68. "Preliminary Facts and Motives—Notes from the Observations of Count d'Estaing," in Stevens, *Facsimiles*.

69. *Revolutionary Records of the State of Georgia*, ed. Allen Candler (Atlanta: Franklin-Turner, 1908), 1:352, 373.

70. Affidavit of Augustine Hobbs, 3/23/1782, filed as "Sheftall, Levi—Indictment as Traitor to the Crown—1782," Keith Read Collection, Box 23, Folder 14, Special Collections Library, University of Georgia.

71. *Revolutionary Records of the State of Georgia*, 1:612, 617. Sheftall's citizenship was restored partially in 1785 and fully in 1787.

72. Rezneck, *Unrecognized Patriots*, 33.

73. David Salisbury Franks, in *MAJ*, 47.

74. David Salisbury Franks, in *MAJ*, 47.

75. Rezneck, *Unrecognized Patriots*, 29–31.

76. *USJ*, 1:74–75.

77. Morris U. Schappes, "Excerpts from Robert Morris' 'Diaries in the Office of Finance, 1781–1784,' Referring to Haym Salomon and Other Jews," *AJHQ* 67:1 (September 1977), 9–49, 10-12.

78. *USJ*, 1:73.

79. Schappes, "Excerpts," 13.

80. Memorial of Haym Salomon to Congress, 8/25/1778, in *PAJHS* 1: 87–88.

81. Memorial, 88.

82. *USJ*, 1:69.

83. Schappes, "Excerpts," 11.

84. *USJ*, 1:68.

85. "A Jew Broker" to Miers Fisher, 3/13/1784, *AJD*, 41–46.

86. *USJ*, 1:72–73.

87. Solomon Solis-Cohen, "Note Concerning David Hays and Esther Etting His Wife," *PAJHS* 2 (1894), 64.

88. Rezneck, *Unrecognized Patriots*, 70, 98, 78.

89. Benjamin Levy to Robert Morris, 12/13/1776, Levy Family Papers, Box 1, Folder 5, AJHS.

90. Abigail Minis et al. to Wright, 10/29/1779, in *Colonial Records of the State of Georgia*, ed. Allen Candler (Atlanta: Franklin-Turner, 1907), 455–456.

91. Frances Sheftall to Mordecai Sheftall, 7/20/1780, *EAJ*, 2:359–361.

92.   Elizabeth Ellet, *Women of the Revolution* (Bedford, MA: Applewood, 2009 [1849]), 163–164.

93.   *DHJUS*, 50.

94.   *CAJ*, 1292.

95.   Cecil Roth, "Some Jewish Loyalists," *PAJHS* 38:2 (December 1948), 91.

96.   *USJ*, 1:55.

97.   Rebecca Franks to Abigail Van Horn, 8/10/1781, *EAJ*, 2:114.

98.   *EAJ*, 2:94–97, 105.

99.   "A Letter of Miss Rebecca Franks, 1778," *PMHB* 16:2 (July 1892), 216–218; Rebecca Franks to Willamina Bond Cadwalader, 2/19/1784, in Mark A. Stern, "Dear Mrs. Cad: A Revolutionary War letter of Rebecca Franks," *AJAJ* 57:1–2 (2005), 15–17.

100.   *EAJ*, 2:116.

101.   Wolf and Whiteman, *Jews of Philadelphia*, 89.

102.   Mordecai Sheftall to Sheftall Sheftall 4/13/1783, *AJAJ* 27:2, 209–210.

Chapter 5

1.   Holger Hoock, *Scars of Independence: America's Violent Birth* (New York: Broadway Books, 2017), 305, 290–291.

2.   William Pencak, *Jews & Gentiles in Early America, 1654–1800* (Ann Arbor: University of Michigan Press, 2005), 211; Eli Faber, *A Time for Planting: The First Migration, 1654–1820* (Baltimore: Johns Hopkins University Press, 1992), 104; Congregation Mikveh Israel, "Minutes and Correspondence of the Congregation, 1782–1790," Robert D. Farber University Archives and Special Collections, Brandeis University, entry for 8/18/1782, 73–74 (hereafter "Minutes and Correspondence"). The congregation dated their minutes inconsistently, sometimes by English calendar, sometimes by Hebrew calendar; the document also has occasional page numbers. I have provided as much information as possible for each citation.

3.   Edwin Wolf and Maxwell Whiteman, *The History of the Jews of Philadelphia: From Colonial Times to the Age of Jackson* (Philadelphia: Jewish Publication Society of America, 1975), 96.

4.   Wolf and Whiteman, *Jews of Philadelphia*, 98–100.

5.   *JITA*, 101.

6.   Marcus Rezneck, *Unrecognized Patriots: The Jews in the American Revolution* (New York: Greenwood Press, 1975), 23.

7.   Benjamin Rush, *The Autobiography of Benjamin Rush* (Princeton, NJ: American Philosophical Society, 1948), 119.

8.   Frame of Government of Pennsylvania, May 5, 1682, https://avalon.law.yale.edu/17th_century/pa04.asp, accessed July 19, 2021.

9.   David Little, "The Pennsylvania Experiment with Freedom of Conscience and Church-State Relations," in in *Disestablishment and Religious Dissent: Church-State Relations in the New American States, 1776–1833*, ed.

Carl H. Esbeck and Jonathan J. Den Hertog, (Columbia: University of Missouri Press, 2019), 73.

10.   Charter of Liberties, 1701, https://avalon.law.yale.edu/18th_century/pa07. asp accessed July 19, 2021; see also Evan Haefeli, "Delaware: Religious Borderland," in *Disestablishment and Religious Dissent,* 38.

11.   Jonathan Derek Awtrey, "Jews and the Sources of Religious Freedom in Pennsylvania," PhD dissertation, Louisiana State University, 2018, 298; William Pencak, *Jews & Gentiles in Early America, 1654–1800* (Ann Arbor: University of Michigan Press, 2005),177–179.

12.   Alexander Hamilton, "Itineratum," in *Colonial American Travel Narratives,* ed. Wendy Martin, 191 (New York: Penguin, 1994), 191.

13.   Hamilton, "Itineratum," 201.

14.   Barnard Gratz and Manuel Josephson to the Jews of Suriname, 1790, *JITA,* 215.

15.   Toni Pitock, "Commerce and Connection: Jewish Merchants, Philadelphia, and the Atlantic World: 1736–1822," PhD Dissertation, University of Delaware, 2016, 271.

16.   Wolf and Whiteman, *Jews of Philadelphia,* 41.

17.   Documents on Newport Slave Trade, *DHJUS,* 38ff.

18.   *PAJHS* 1:60 (1892).

19.   Jonas Phillips to Gumpel Samson, 7/28/1776, *AJAJ* 27:2 (1975), 130-132.

20.   *Journals of Henry Melchior Muhlenberg* [HMM], trans. Theodore G. Tappert and John W. Doberstein (Philadelphia: Evangelical Lutheran Ministerium of Pennsylvania and the United States, 1942), 2:509; 1:4, 263, 25–126.

21.   *Journals of HMM,* 1:332.

22.   Letter of Rev. Henry Melchoir Muhlenberg, 1776, *PMHB* 22:129–131 (1898).

23.   Pencak, *Jews & Gentiles,* 213; Faith E. Rohrbaugh, "The Political Maturation of Henry Melchior Muhlenberg," in *Henry Melchior Muhlenberg: The Roots of 240 Years of Organized Lutheranism in North America,* ed. John W. Kleiner (Lewiston, ME: Edwin Mellon, 1998), 35–59..

24.   *Journals of HMM,* 3:653.

25.   *Philadelphia Evening Post,* 9/24/1776. Emphasis in original.

26.   Franklin to John Calder, 8/21/1784, *The Papers of Benjamin Franklin,* ed. Ellen R. Cohn (New Haven, CT: Yale University Press, 2018), 43:40–42.

27.   Pencak, *Jews & Gentiles,* 213.

28.   Quoted in Owen S. Ireland, *Religion, Ethnicity, and Politics: Ratifying the Constitution in Pennsylvania* (University Park: Pennsylvania State University Press,1995), 245.

29.   Aaron Sullivan, *The Disaffected: Britain's Occupation of Philadelphia During the American Revolution* (Philadelphia: University of Pennsylvania Press, 2019), 140.

30.   Solomon Bush to Henry Lazarus, 11/15/1777, *PAJHS* 23 (1915), 177–178.

31.   Meredith H. Lair, "Redcoat Theater: Negotiating Identity in Occupied Philadelphia, 1777–1778," in *Pennsylvania's Revolution,* ed. William

A. Pencak, (University Park, PA: Pennsylvania State University Press, 2010), 197.

32. B. Gratz and Josephson to the Jews of Suriname, 1790, *JITA*, 215.
33. Pencak, *Jews & Gentiles*, 127.
34. Bennett Muraskin, "Benjamin Nones: Profile of a Jewish Jeffersonian," *American Jewish History*, 83:3 (September 1995), 381–385; *DHJUS* 571, n. 1–4.
35. Pencak, *Jews & Gentiles*, 128.
36. *South Carolina and American Gazette*, 12/3/1778; *DHJUS*, 53–54. Emphasis original.
37. *DHJUS*, 53–54.
38. *DHJUS*, 53–54; *EAJ*, 2:373.
39. On endenization and European Jewry, see David Sorkin, "Is American Jewry Exceptional? Comparing Jewish Emancipation in Europe and America," *American Jewish History* 96:3 (September 2010), 176–184.
40. Pencak, *Jews & Gentiles*, 126; Maya Jasanoff, *Liberty's Exiles: American Loyalists in the Revolutionary World* (New York: Knopf, 2011), 45.
41. "Minutes and Correspondence," 8/18/1782, 73–74. The transformation of the American Jewish community in wartime Philadelphia also suggests a break between United States Jewry and the phenomenon of Atlantic "Port Jews" in the eighteenth century. See Jonathan Sarna, "Port Jews in the Atlantic World: Further Thoughts," *Jewish History* 20 (2006).
42. Most easily found (at least for this date) in *AJD*, 116–117.
43. "Minutes and Correspondence," 3/24/1782.
44. "First Philadelphia Synagogal Constitution, 1770," *AJD*, 95–96.
45. *Charter and Bye-Laws of Kaal Kadosh Mickve Israel of the City of Philadelphia* (n.p., Philadelphia, 1824).
46. "Minutes and Correspondence," 17 Tisra 5543 (9/25/1782).
47. "Minutes and Correspondence," 3/17/1782, 3/25/1782, and 5/29/1782.
48. Documents From Shearith Israel Synagogue, Montreal, 1778–1780, *AJD*, 105–109.
49. "Excerpts, *Hascamoth* of Congregation Mikvé Israel," and "St. Thomas Synagogue Protocols," *JITA*, 195–197, 243.
50. "Constitution and Bylaws of Congregation Shearith Israel, New York, 1790," *AJD*, 150.
51. "Code of Laws of Congregation Mickva Israel, Savannah, 1791–1792," *AJD*, 179–180.
52. "Minutes and Correspondence," 13.
53. Franklin to John Adams, 11/26/1781, *Founders Online*, National Archives, https://founders.archives.gov/documents/Adams/06-12-02-0055, accessed August 18, 2021.
54. Wolf and Whiteman, *Jews of Philadelphia*, 143–144.
55. Thomas Kidd, *God of Liberty: A Religious History of the American Revolution* (New York: Basic Books, 2010), 106.
56. "Minutes and Correspondence," 4/25/1782; Wolf and Whiteman, *Jews of Philadelphia*, 117.

57. Isaac Moses and Adjunta to the President and Vestry of the German Church, 5/1/1782, in "Minutes and Correspondence," following entry for 4/30/1782.

58. Isaac Moses and Adjunta to the President and Vestry of the German Church, 5/1/1782, in "Minutes and Correspondence," following entry for 4/30/1782.

59. Minute Book of Congregation Mikveh Israel, *AJD*, 121.

60. "Minutes and Correspondence," 29–30.

61. "Minutes and Correspondence," 6/2/1782, 42.

62. *EAJ*, 2:129.

63. Congregation of Jews in the City to the President and Council, 9/12/1782; Phillips Family Papers, Box 1, Folder 5, AJHS.

64. Wolf and Whiteman, *Jews of Philadelphia*, 120; "Minutes and Correspondence," 8/12/1782, 65–66.

65. Gottlieb Mittelberger, *Journey to Philadelphia*, trans. Carl Tho. Eben (Philadelphia: John Joseph McVay, 1898), 63.

66. "Prayer for Peace During the American Revolution," *PAJHS* 27:126. See also Jonathan Sarna, "Jewish Prayers for the United States Government: A Study in the Liturgy of Politics and the Politics of Liturgy," in *Liturgy in the Life of the Synagogue: Studies in the History of Jewish Prayer*, ed. Ruth Langer and Steven Fine (Winona Lake, IN: Eisenbrauns, 2005), 208.

67. Wolf and Whiteman, *Jews of Philadelphia*, 100; Emily Bingham, *Mordecai: An Early American Family* (New York: Hill and Wang, 2003), 14; Gustavus Hart, "A Biographical Account of Ephraim Hart and His Son, Dr. Joel Hart, of New York," *PAJHS* 4 (1896), 215–218. The list of subscribers to Mikveh Israel has an even greater geographic diversity. That list included Isaac DaCosta, Simon Nathan, Gershom Seixas, Benjamin Seixas, Solomon Myers Cohen, Haym Solomon, Abraham Levy, Mordecai Sheftall, Hayman Levy, Barnard Gratz, Michael Gratz, Jonas Phillips, Solomon Marache, Jacob Hart, Jacob Mordecai, and Cushman Polack. "Minutes and Correspondence," 3/17/1782, 8.

68. Phillips to Congregation Mikveh Israel, 5/28/1782, in "Minutes and Correspondence." See also "Minutes and Correspondence" 6/13/1782 ("Tuesday Roshodes Tamuz"), 8/12/82 (2 Elul 5542), 8/18/1782 (8 Elul 5542), 49, 63, 70.

69. "Minutes and Correspondence," 5/28/1782, 5/29/1782, 6/2/1782.

70. "Minutes and Correspondence," 6/13/1782 ("Tuesday Roshodes Tamuz"), 49.

71. Aviva Ben-Ur, "The Exceptional and the Mundane: A Biographical Portrait of Rebecca (Machado) Phillips (1746–1831)," in *Women and American Judaism: Historical Perspectives*, ed. Pamela S. Nadell and Jonathan D. Sarna, (Hanover, NH: University Press of New England for Brandeis University), 47, 52, 61.

72. "Minutes and Correspondence," 5/29/1782, 38.

73. "Minutes and Correspondence," 8 Elul 5542 (8/18/82), 70.

74. "Minutes and Correspondence," "Tuesday Roshodes Tamuz" (6/13/1782), 48–49.

75. "Minutes and Correspondence," 17 Tisra 5543 (9/25/1782).

76. "Minutes and Correspondence," 108.

77. "Minutes and Correspondence," 109–110.

78. "Minutes and Correspondence," 25 Tishra 5543 (10/3/82), 19 Hashvan 5543 (10/27/82), 121, 125.

79. "Minutes and Correspondence," 6 Kislev 5543 (10/12/82).

80. "Minutes and Correspondence," 26 Adar II 5543 (3/30/1783).

81. "Minutes and Correspondence," 116.

82. Opinion of Whitehead Hicks regarding distribution of synagogue seats, 1770, Jacques Judah Lyons Collection, AJHS; *AJD*, 111.

83. Minutes of Meeting of Isaac DaCosta, Abisha DaCosta Jr., Isaac DeLeon, and Jacob Tobias, January 25, 1775"; Kahol Kadosh Beth Elohim Records, Box 40, Folder 1, College of Charleston Special Collections.

84. Bingham, *Mordecai*, 15; Jonathan D. Sarna, "The Democratization of American Judaism," in *New Essays in American Jewish History: Commemorating the Sixtieth Anniversary of the Founding of the American Jewish Archives*, ed. Pamela Nadell, Jonathan Sarna, and Lance Sussman (Cincinnati: American Jewish Archives, 2010), 512 n5.

85. Sarna, "Democratization," 512 n11.

86. "Minutes and Correspondence," 6/9/1782.

87. "Minutes and Correspondence," 2 Elul 5542 (8/12/82), 63.

88. Rebecca Samuel to her parents, 1/12/1791, *AJD*, 52.

89. "Minutes and Correspondence," 15 Elul 5542 (8/25/82), 75–77.

90. "Minutes and Correspondence," 15 Elul (8/25/82) 5542, 77.

91. "Minutes and Correspondence," 15 Elul (8/25/82) 5542, 78–79.

92. Sarna, "Democratization," 99; Myron Berman, *Richmond's Jewry, 1769–1976: Shabbat in Shockoe* (Charlottesville: University of Virginia Press, 1979), 7.

93. "Minutes and Correspondence," 11 Tishre 5544 (10/7/83), 144.

94. "Minutes and Correspondence," "Sunday 22d" 11/17/83, 152–153.

95. "Minutes and Correspondence," Gershom Seixas to Parnas and Junta, 2/15/1784.

96. "Minutes and Correspondence," 9/19/1784; 10/10/1784; 11/10/1784; 6/28/1789.

97. "Minutes and Correspondence," "Sunday 22d," 152, 154.

98. 1776 Constitution of the State of Maryland, https://avalon.law.yale.edu/17th_century/ma02.asp, accessed August 8, 2021.

99. Constitution of North Carolina, adopted December 18, 1776, https://avalon.law.yale.edu/18th_century/nc07.asp, accessed August 8, 2021. See also Nicholas P. Miller, "North Carolina: Early Toleration and Disestablishment," in *Disestablishment and Religious Dissent*, 106–107.

100. Spencer McBride, *Pulpit and Nation: Clergymen and the Politics of Revolutionary America* (Charlottesville: University of Virginia Press, 2016), 56–63; Jacob Duché to George Washington, 10/8/1777, https://founders.

archives.gov/?q=duche%20Author%3A%22Duché%2C%20Jacob%22&s=111
1311111&r=2&sr=, accessed August 14, 2021.

101. Madison to Thomas Jefferson, October 24, 1787, *Founders Online* (National Archives), https://founders.archives.gov/?q=inefficacy%20Aut hor%3A%22Madison%2C%20James%22&s=1111311111&r=7&sr=, accessed August 14, 2021.

102. James Ireland, *Life of Rev. James Ireland* (Winchester, VA: J. Foster, 1819), 135, 165–66.

103. John Ragosta, *Wellspring of Liberty: How Virginia's Dissenters Helped Win the Revolution and Secured Religious Liberty* (New York: Oxford University Press, 2010), 174, 172, 176.

104. John Ragosta, *Religious Freedom: Jefferson's Legacy, America's Creed* (Charlottesville: University of Virginia Press, 2013), 70–71.

105. Ragosta, *Wellspring*, 112.

106. Ragosta, *Religious Freedom*, 86.

107. *Journal of the Council of Censors* (Philadelphia: Hall and Sellers, 1783), 20.

108. *The Constitutions of the Several Independent States of America; the Declaration of Independence; the Articles of Confederation Between the Said States; the Treaties Between His Most Christian Majesty and the United States of America,* (Philadelphia: Francis Bailey, 1781), copy purchased by Mikveh Israel, now in the Rosenbach Library, Philadelphia, PA, 62, 77.

109. *Constitutions*, Rosenbach Library, 6, 77.

110. *Constitutions*, Rosenbach Library, 91, 102.

111. *Constitutions*, Rosenbach Library, 1 27.

112. *Constitutions*, Rosenbach Library, 141, 145.

113. *Constitutions*, Rosenbach Library, 164, 173.

114. *Constitutions*, Rosenbach Library, 186.

115. *Constitutions*, Rosenbach Library, 83, 84.

116. "Minutes and Correspondence," 11/20/1783.

117. Constitution of Pennsylvania, September 28, 1776, Section 47. http://avalon. law.yale.edu/18th_century/pa08.asp, accessed August 18, 2021.

118. *EAJ*, 157–158.

119. Benjamin Franklin to London Packet, 6/3/1772, https://press-pubs.uchic ago.edu/founders/documents/amendI_religions14.html, accessed September 20, 2023.

120. *Journal of the Council of Censors* (Philadelphia: Hall and Sellers, 1783), 20.

121. *Philadelphia Independent Gazetteer*, 1/17/1784.

122. Jonas Phillips to the President and Members of the Convention, 9/7/1787, in Max Farrand, *Records of the Federal Convention of 1787* (New Haven, CT: Yale University Press, 1911), 3:78–79. Phillips also wrote a similar letter directly to Washington on the same day. Jonas Phillips to George Washington, 9/7/1787, https://founders.archives.gov/?q=jonas%20phillips&s=1111311111&sa=&r= 1&sr=, accessed September 12, 2021.

123. Hayman Levy, Myer Myers, and Isaac Moses to George Clinton, January 1784, *DHJUS*, 66–67. See also Wolf and Whiteman, *Jews of Philadelphia*, 96, 122, 407 n107.

124. "Minutes and Correspondence," 3/30/1783, 129.

125. *EAJ*, 2:223

126. The Jewish communities in Richmond, Charleston, Savannah, New York, and Philadelphia all had leadership by former KKMI members and a general leadership cadre from KKMI for the 1780s and 1790s. The exception of course was Rhode Island, which had not technically joined the new government in 1789, but their experience has been dealt with in chapter 1.

Chapter 6

1. *DHRC*, 30:409–410.

2. Moses Myers to Samuel Myers, 6/13/1786, and Moses Myers to Marcus Elcan, 6/19/1787, in *EAJ*, 2:207–208, 213; Myron Berman, *Richmond's Jewry, 1769–1976: Shabbat in Shockoe* (Charlottesville: University Press of Virginia, 1979), 90.

3. *EAJ*, 2:195.

4. "Minutes and Correspondence," Gershom Seixas to Parnas and Mahamad of Kahol Kadosh Mikveh Israel, 11/10/1783.

5. "Minutes and Correspondence," 2 Elul 5542 (8/12/1782), 64–66; Gershom Seixas to Shearith Israel, 12/21/1783, Box 1, Folder 10, Seixas Family Papers, AJHS.

6. "Minutes and Correspondence," 67.

7. "Minutes and Correspondence," 109–110.

8. Gershom Seixas to Shearith Israel, 12/21/1783, Box 1, Folder 10, Seixas Family Papers, AJHS.

9. "Minutes and Correspondence," Gershom Seixas to parnas and junta, 2/15/1784.

10. Gershom Seixas to Hayman Levy, 3/15/1784, Box 1, Folder 10, Seixas Family Papers, AJHS.

11. "Items Relating to Gershom M. Seixas," *PAJHS* 27:129–130.

12. Hays to Richea Gratz, 11/27/1793, *AJD*, 63, 67–68.

13. Cecil Roth, "Some Jewish Loyalists," *PAJHS* 38:2 (December 1948), 88–89; Hays quoted in J. Solis-Cohen, "Barrak Hays: Controversial Loyalist," *PAJHS* 45:1 (September 1955), 55.

14. Howard B. Rock, *Haven of Liberty: New York Jews in the New World, 1654–1865* (New York: New York University, 2012), 93–94; "Minutes and Correspondence," 65–66; David de Sola Pool, *Portraits Etched in Stone: Early Jewish Settlers, 1682–1831* (New York: Columbia, 1952), 46.

15. Rock, *Haven of Liberty*, 90–91; "Minutes and Correspondence," 69; "Items Relating to Gershom Seixas," *PAJHS* 27:130–131.

16. Rock, *Haven of Liberty*, 89–90; Constitution and Bylaws of Congregation Shearith Israel, New York—1790, *AJD*, 163–64.

17. Rock, *Haven of Liberty*, 90–91.

18. Rock, *Haven of Liberty*, 91; "From the 2nd Volume of the Minute Books of Congrn: Shearith Israel in New York," *PAJHS* 21:154. Zev Eleff, *Who Rules the Synagogue: Religious Authority and the Formation of American Judaism* (New York: Oxford University Press, 2016), 1–10, argues that this type of raucous, lay-led congregation was the model for American synagogues until Reconstruction.

19. Malcolm H. Stern, "Two Jewish Functionaries in Colonial Pennsylvania," *AJHQ* 57:1 (September 1967), 36, 40–41; "Minutes and Correspondence", 6/9/1782, 8/12/1782. Stern incorrectly identifies Mordecai as a vote against the Cohen-Whitlock wedding.

20. "Minutes and Correspondence," Mordecai to the parnas and junta, 10/30/1784.

21. Stern, "Two Jewish Functionaries," 43.

22. Benjamin Steiner, "Postscript on the Charleston *Shtar Halitzah*," *AJAJ* 73:1 (2021), 66–77.

23. Stern, "Two Jewish Functionaries," 45.

24. Stern, "Two Jewish Functionaries," 46.

25. "Minutes and Correspondence," Jonas Phillips to parnas, 6/5/1786, and Simon Nathan and Michael Gratz to Phillips, 3/17/1784.

26. "Minutes and Correspondence," Michael Gratz et al. to the parnas, 3/15/1784.

27. Benjamin Nones to Congregation Beth Elohim, 9/9/1792, in BB, 584.

28. Edwin Wolf and Maxwell Whiteman, *The History of the Jews of Philadelphia: From Colonial Times to the Age of Jackson* (Philadelphia: Jewish Publication Society of America, 1975), 144.

29. Wolf and Whiteman, *Jews of Philadelphia*, 246.

30. Jacob Cohen to the parnas, 3/15/1802, reprinted in "The Record Book of Reverend Jacob Raphael Cohen," ed. Alan D. Corré and Malcolm H. Stern, *AJHQ* 59:1 (September 1969), 23–82.

31. Jurgen Heideking, *The Constitution Before the Judgment Seat: The Prehistory and Ratification of the American Constitution, 1787–1791* (Charlottesville: University of Virginia Press, 2012), 372.

32. https://www.carpentershall.org/federal-procession, accessed September 25, 2021.

33. Benjamin Rush, "Observations on the Foederal Process," *Pennsylvania Gazette* (Philadelphia), 7/23/1788; Naftali Phillips, "The Federal Parade of 1788," *AJAJ* 7:1 (1955), 65–67.

34. Rush, "Observations on the Foederal Process."

35. "A Jew Broker" to Miers Fisher, 3/13/1784, *AJD*, 40–46.

36. "A Jew Broker" to Miers Fisher, 3/13/1784, *AJD*, 40–46.

37. "A Jew Broker" to Miers Fisher, 3/13/1784, *AJD*, 40–46.

38. Nicole Eustace, *Passion Is the Gale: Emotion, Power and the Coming of the American Revolution* (Chapel Hill: University of North Carolina Press, 2008), 9. Michael Hoberman has demonstrated that Jews also shared in this upwelling and increasing acceptance of emotion as a guide in revolutionary America.

39. Woody Holton, *Unruly Americans and the Origins of the Constitution* (New York: Hill and Wang, 2007), 46ff; Clare A. Lyons, *Sex Among the Rabble: An Intimate History of Gender and Power in the Age of Revolution, Philadelphia, 1730–1830* (Chapel Hill: University of North Carolina Press, 2006), 225; Rosemarie Zagarri, *Revolutionary Backlash: Women and Politics in the Early American Republic* (Philadelphia: University of Pennsylvania Press, 2007), 32–35.

40. James Hagy, "Her Scandalous Behavior: A Jewish Divorce in Charleston, SC, 1788," *AJAJ* 41:2 (1989), 185, 190–191.

41. Hagy, "Her Scandalous Behavior," 185, 192–193.

42. James Hagy, *This Happy Land: The Jews of Colonial and Antebellum Charleston* (Tuscaloosa, AL: University of Alabama Press, 1993), 69.

43. Hagy, *Happy Land*, 43.

44. John L.E.W. Shecut, *Shecut's Medical and Philosophical Essays* (Charleston: A. E. Miller, 1819), 30–32.

45. *Cursory Remarks on Men and Measures in Georgia* [publication data unknown, 1784], 20. Available in Early American Imprints, Series 1, no. 18430.

46. *Cursory Remarks on Men and Measures*, 23, 25–26.

47. *Cursory Remarks on Men and Measures*, 22.

48. *Cursory Remarks on Men and Measures*, 22–26.

49. *Cursory Remarks on Men and Measures*, 25–27.

50. Sheftall Papers, Box 23, Folder 13, Keith Read Collection, University of Georgia.

51. Joel A. Nichols, "Georgia: The Thirteenth Colony," in *Disestablishment and Religious Dissent: Church-State Relations in the New American States, 1776–1833*, ed. Carl H. Esbeck and Jonathan J. Den Hertog (Columbia: University of Missouri Press, 2019); B. H. Levy, *Mordecai Sheftall: Jewish Revolutionary Patriot* (Savannah: Georgia Historical Society, 1999), 99.

52. Affidavit of Moses Nunes, 6/1/1784; Petition of Samuel Nunes to the Hon. George Walton; Nunes-Ribeiro Papers, AJHS.

53. Affidavit of Moses Nunes, June 1, 1784, Legal proceedings against Mordecai Sheftall, 1784; Nunes-Ribeiro Papers, AJHS.

54. William Pencak, *Jews & Gentiles in Early America, 1654–1800* (Ann Arbor: University of Michigan Press, 2005), 158.

55. Affidavit of Moses Nunes, June 1, 1784, Legal proceedings against Mordecai Sheftall, 1784; Nunes-Ribeiro Papers, AJHS.

56. *Cursory Remarks on Men and Measures*, 18–19.

57. Chatham County Superior Court Minutes, 10/5/1784, Georgia State Archives.

58. *Cursory Remarks on Men and Measures*, 20.

59. Chatham County Superior Court Minutes, 10/5/1784, Georgia State Archives.

60. Will of Moses Nunes, October 14, 1785, Manuscript Collection No. 99, Bertram W. Korn Papers, Box 13, folder 1, AJA.

61. Advertisement reprinted in Laurens R. Schwartz, *Jews in the American Revolution: Haym Salomon and Others* (Jefferson, NC: McFarland & Co., 1987), 35.

62. As Rabin notes, "In the eyes of American law . . . Jews have been white from the beginning," that is, their racial classification did not depend on a separate racial category of Jewishness. Shari Rabin, *Jews on the Frontier: Religion and Mobility in Nineteenth-Century America* (New York: New York University Press, 2017), 13–14. The Nunez cases support Rabin against other scholarship that locates Jewish whiteness as a twentieth-century phenomenon, including Eric L. Goldstein, *The Price of Whiteness: Jews, Race, and American Identity* (Princeton, NJ: Princeton University Press, 2006); Matthew Frye Jacobson, *Whiteness of a Different Color: European Immigrants and the Alchemy of Race* (Cambridge, MA: Harvard University Press, 2001).

Chapter 7

1. Ragosta, *Religious Freedom*, 87. On efforts to define the Constitution as explicitly Christian or religious, see Thomas Curry, *The First Freedoms: Church and State in America to the Passage of the First Amendment* (New York: Oxford University Press, 1986), 147; Ellis West, "The Case Against a Right to Religious-Based Exemptions," *Notre Dame Journal of Law, Ethics and Public Policy* 4 (1989–1990); John Fea, *Was America Founded as a Christian Nation? A Historical Introduction* (Louisville, KY: Westminster John Knox Press, 2011), preface and ch. 1, 4.

2. John Ragosta, *Wellspring of Liberty: How Virginia's Dissenters Helped Win the Revolution and Secured Religious Liberty* (New York: Oxford University Press, 2010), 120.

3. Ragosta, *Religious Freedom*, 89.

4. Ragosta, *Religious Freedom*, 55.

5. Ragosta, *Religious Freedom*, 90.

6. Ragosta, *Wellspring*, 56.

7. James Madison to Thomas Jefferson, 1/22/1786, *The Papers of James Madison*, vol. 8, *10 March 1784–28 March 1786*, ed. Robert A. Rutland and William M. E. Rachal (Chicago: University of Chicago Press, 1973), 472–482.

8. John Leland, "The Virginia Chronicle," in *The Writings of the Late Elder John Leland* (New York: G. W. Wood, 1845), 106n.

9. Cohen Family of Baltimore and Richmond Papers, undated, 1779–1897, Box 1, Folder 2, AJHS.

10. Edmund Randolph to James Madison, 5/5/1782, *The Papers of James Madison*, vol. 4, *1 January 1782–31 July 1782*, ed. Robert A. Rutland and William M. E. Rachal (Chicago: University of Chicago Press, 1965), 208–209.

11. On the overlap between Cohen's interactions with Mikveh Israel and his work to support Madison, see Edmund Randolph to James Madison, 8/24/1782, n12, https://founders.archives.gov/documents/Madison/01-05-02-0033, accessed September 30, 2023.

12. James Madison to Edmund Randolph, 8/27/1782, https://founders.archives. gov/documents/Madison/01-05-02-0037 accessed September 30, 2023.

13. Gary Wills, *James Madison* (New York: Henry Holt, 2002), 20.

14. Jones to Madison, 6/25/1782, n2, https://founders.archives.gov/documents/ Madison/01-04-02-0167 accessed September 30, 2023.

15. Fea, "Disestablishment in New Jersey," in *Disestablishment and Religious Dissent: Church-State Relations in the New American States, 1776–1833*, ed. Carl H. Esbeck and Jonathan J. Den Hertog (Columbia: University of Missouri Press, 2019), 26; Nicholas P. Miller, "North Carolina: Early Toleration and Disestablishment," in *Disestablishment and Religious Dissent*, 107.

16. Miles Smith IV, "South Carolina," in *Disestablishment and Religious Dissent*, 183.

17. Stanley Chyet, "The Political Rights of the Jews in the United States: 1776– 1840," *American Jewish Archives* 10:1 (1958), 35.

18. Woody Holton, *Unruly Americans and the Origins of the Constitution* (New York: Hill and Wang, 2007), 4–9.

19. Holton, *Unruly Americans*, 9.

20. *The Records of the Federal Convention of 1787*, ed. Max Farrand (New Haven, CT: Yale University Press, 1966), 1:450–452.

21. *Records of the Federal Convention*, 1:452, 2:364.

22. Edmund S. Morgan, "The Witch and We the People," *American Heritage*, August–September 1983; Philadelphia *Independent Gazetteer*, 5/9/1787, 5/17/ 1787, 7/23/87.

23. *Records of the Federal Convention*, 1:126, see also 1:123.

24. *Records of the Federal Convention*, 2:90.

25. Douglas Bradburn, *The Citizenship Revolution: Politics and the Creation of the American Union, 1774–1804* (Charlottesville: University of Virginia Press, 2009), 49, 52–53.

26. Rosemarie Zagarri, *Revolutionary Backlash: Women and Politics in the Early American Republic* (Philadelphia: University of Pennsylvania Press, 2007), 31; Bradburn, *Citizenship Revolution*, 238.

27. Martha S. Jones, *Birthright Citizens: A History of Race and Rights in Antebellum America* (New York: Cambridge, 2018), 24–26.

28. "Poll Lists Charleston Municipal Elections 1787," *South Carolina Historical Magazine* 56:1 (January 1955), 45–49.

29. *DHRC*, 4:266, 270, 272, 276; 27:308, 311, 394.

30. Pennsylvania *Gazette*, 11/14/1787, *DHRC*, 33:570.

31. Saul Cornell, *The Other Founders: Anti-Federalism and the Dissenting Tradition in America, 1788–1828* (Chapel Hill: University of North Carolina Press, 1999), 20, 25.

32. *Debate on the Constitution*, ed. Bernard Bailyn (New York: Library of America, 2015), 1:902–903; Denise Spellberg, *Thomas Jefferson's Qur'an: Islam and the Founders* (New York: Vintage, 2013), 173.

33. New York *Daily Advertiser*, 1/18/1788, *DHRC*, 3:401.

34. John Sullivan to Jeremy Belknap, 2/26/1788, *DHRC*, 28:240.

35. *DHRC*, 20:627. Natalie Zemon Davis writes that references to Jews in this period are so standard that historians ought to consider such references as likely to be imaginary or hypothetical rather than actual. Davis cited in Pencak, *Jews & Gentiles*, 195, 291 n43.

36. Federalist 43, https://avalon.law.yale.edu/18th_century/fed43.asp, accessed October 1, 2023.

37. "Address and Reasons for Dissent of the Minority of the Convention of Pennsylvania," in *The Anti-Federalist Papers and the Constitutional Convention Debates*, ed. Ralph Ketcham, 239 (New York: Signet, 2003), 239.

38. Leland, "The Virginia Chronicle," 224.

39. *DHRC*, 30:410.

40. Spellberg, *Thomas Jefferson's Qur'an*, 184.

41. *New Hampshire Spy*, 11/20/1787, *DHRC*, 28:51.

42. Abraham Yates to Abraham Lansing, 5/28/88, *DHRC*, 21:1115, emphasis added; *DHRC*, 22:1677.

43. Centinel II, *DHRC*, 1:89.

44. Joseph Spencer, "Ten Objections by a Leading Virginia Baptist," *DHRC*, 2:267.

45. *DHRC*, 5:1055–1057.

46. Cassius, in Massachusetts *Gazette*, 10/2/1787; *DHRC*, 4:30.

47. John Sullivan to Jeremy Belknap, 2/26/1788, *DHRC*, 28:240.

48. Speech of Francis Cummins, 5/20/1788; John Wilson to Samuel Wilson, 7/10/1788, DHRC, 27:359–360, 474–475.

49. *New Hampshire Spy*, 2/15/1788, *DHRC*, 28:123–124.

50. *The Complete Anti-Federalist*, ed. Herbert J. Storing (Chicago: University of Chicago Press, 1981), 3:206.

51. "A Proposal for Reviving Christian Conviction," *Complete Anti-Federalist*, 5:125–126.

52. Federalist 10, https://avalon.law.yale.edu/18th_century/fed10.asp, accessed October 1, 2023; Ellsworth, "Landholder VII," *DHRC*, 3:497–501.

53. *DHRC*, 2:723.

54. Morton Borden, *Jews, Turks, and Infidels* (Chapel Hill: University of North Carolina Press, 1984), 21; George Washington to the Hebrew Congregation of Savannah, 6/14/1790, https://founders.archives.gov/?q=hebrew%20savan nah&s=1111311111&sa=&r=1&sr= , accessed October 1, 2023.

55. Gershom Seixas, *A Sermon Delivered in the Synagogue in this City* (New York: Archibald McLean, 1789), 6.

56. *Cursory Remarks on Men and Measures in Georgia* [publication data unknown, 1784], 19,25. Available in Early American Imprints, Series 1, no. 18430.

57. On theories of the Constitution's written nature as a new development and antidote to common law, see Jonathan Gienapp, *The Second Creation: Fixing*

the Constitution in the Founding Era (Cambridge, MA: Belknap Press, 2018), 10, 86, 108.

58.   Berkin, *Bill of Rights*, 31.

59.   Holton, *Unruly Americans*, x–xi.

60.   The published and suggested proposals can be found most easily here: https://csac.history.wisc.edu/document-collections/constitutional-debates/debate-about-amendments/recommendatory-amendments-from-state-conventions/, accessed September 30, 2023.

61.   Cornell, *Other Founders*, 57.

62.   Carol Berkin, *The Bill of Rights: The Fight to Secure America's Liberties* (New York: Simon & Schuster, 2016), 69, 73, 88, 107.

63.   Gienapp, *Second Creation*, 166–167.

64.   Gienapp, *Second Creation*, 51.

65.   Gienapp, *Second Creation*, 174.

66.   Gershom Seixas, "Sermons, Discourses, and Epistolary Opinions on Religious Matters," 16, 21, Jacques Judah Lyons Collection, AJHS.

67.   *USJ*, 1:82.

68.   Adrian to Evert Bancker, 20 July 1788, *DHRC*, 21:1237; Peter Collin to Nicholas Low, 7/16/1788, *DHRC*, 21:1595; Comte de Moustier to Comte de Montmorin, 8/2/1788, *DHRC*, 21:1628. Note that the fast day was not properly Tish B'Av, but the Fast of Tammuz, a minor fast day related to Tish B'Av. I have used the name of the better-known festival for the sake of clarity. See https://www.commentary.org/articles/michael-schwartz/a-great-compliment-paid-the-jews/, accessed April 15, 2024.

Chapter 8

1.   https://opensiddur.org/prayers/civic-calendar/united-states/washingtons-birthday/prayer-for-george-washington-first-president-of-the-united-states-of-america-by-kahal-kadosh-beit-shalome-1789/, accessed 9/15/2022. The original text is on display at the Weitzman Museum, Philadelphia. Many thanks to Claire Pingel for her help in identifying this artifact.

2.   Moses Gomez to Aaron Lopez, 5/29/1781, Aaron Lopez Papers, Box 14, AJHS.

3.   *Journal of the Constitutional Convention of South Carolina*, ed. Francis Hutson (Columbia, SC: State Commercial Printing, 1946).

4.   Miles Smith IV, "South Carolina," in *Disestablishment and Religious Dissent: Church-State Relations in the New American States, 1776–1833*, ed. Carl H. Esbeck and Jonathan J. Den Hertog (Columbia: University of Missouri Press, 2019), 197.

5.   Nathaniel Levin, "The Jewish Congregation of Charleston," *The Occident* 1.1 (October 1843), http://www.theoccident.com/Occident/volume1/oct1843/charleston.html, accessed September 30, 2023. Christopher Knight does not appear on the list of delegates in the *Journal of the Constitutional Convention of South Carolina*, but the only extant copy has been torn.

6. Andrew Porwancher, *The Jewish World of Alexander Hamilton* (Princeton, NJ: Princeton University Press, 2021), 131–132, 136.

7. Charles Pinckney to George Washington, 11/6/1791, PGW, Presidential Series 9:146–147.

8. Solomon Bush to George Washington, 7/20/1789, PGW, Presidential Series 3:242–244.

9. John Malcolm to Horatio Gates, 3/24/1790, *DHJUS* 73; Porwancher, *Jewish World of Alexander Hamilton,* 126–127.

10. Sheftall Sheftall to Mordecai Sheftall, 11/30/1792, Sheftall Family Letters and Papers, Mordecai Sheftall Papers, AJHS.

11. James Jackson to Mordecai Sheftall, 3/15/1794, AJA; https://elections.lib. tufts.edu/catalog/j9602101m, accessed August 2, 2022.

12. Frances Sheftall to John Milledge, undated, Sheftall Family Letters and Papers, Mordecai Sheftall Papers, AJHS.

13. "Reminiscenes of Mordecai Myers," *DHJUS*, 97.

14. Jacob Henry, "Address to the Committee of the Whole," 1809, *DHJUS*, 124.

15. Morton Borden, *Jews, Turks, and Infidels* (Chapel Hill: University of North Carolina Press, 1984), 25; John Quincy Adams, *Memoirs of John Quincy Adams, Comprising Portions of His Diary from 1795 to 1848*, ed. Charles Francis Adams (Philadelphia: Lippincott, 1874–1877), 304.

16. John Quincy Adams to Thomas Boylston, 7/20/1800, https://founders.archi ves.gov/?q=Jewish%20Period%3A%22Adams%20Presidency%22&s=1111311 111&r=3&sr=, accessed October 1, 2022.

17. J. Q. Adams, *Memoirs*, 155, 164, 502; Diary of John Quincy Adams, 7/11/ 1781, Digital Edition, https://www.masshist.org/publications/adams-papers/ index.php/view/ADMS-03-01-02-0003-0002-0012#sn=2, accessed October 1, 2022.

18. Columbian *Centinel*, 2/5/1794.

19. Terri Diane Halperin, *The Alien and Sedition Acts of 1798: Testing the Constitution* (Baltimore: Johns Hopkins University Press, 2016), 20.

20. *DHJUS*, 571 n1–4.

21. Bennet Muraskin, "Benjamin Nones: Profile of a Jewish Jeffersonian," *American Jewish History* 83:3 (September 1995), 381–385.

22. Halperin, *Alien and Sedition*, 20–23.

23. William Pencak, *Jews & Gentiles in Early America, 1654–1800* (Ann Arbor: University of Michigan Press, 2005), 234–234.

24. Pencak, *Jews & Gentiles*, 234–238.

25. Pencak, *Jews & Gentiles*, 234.

26. BB, 79; *EAJ*, 2:181.

27. Isaac Weld, *Travels Through the United States* (London: John Stockdale, 1807), 1:101–102.

28. Pencak, *Jews & Gentiles*, 241.

29. Pencak, *Jews & Gentiles*, 237–238.

30. Pencak, *Jews & Gentiles*, 241.

31. Pencak, *Jews & Gentiles*, 75–76; Howard B. Rock, *Haven of Liberty: New York Jews in the New World, 1654–1865* (New York: New York University, 2012), 109; James Rivington, "Preface to the American Edition," *DHJUS*, 85; Schappes, "Anti-Semitism and Reaction: 1795–1800," *PAJHS* 38:2 (December 1948), 115; *New York Directory and Register, for the year 1794* (New York: Swords, 1794), 238.

32. *USJ*, 1:85–86.

33. https://loebjewishportraits.com/biography/moses-myers/, accessed September 1, 2023; Myron Berman, *Richmond's Jewry, 1769–1976: Shabbat in Shockoe* (Charlottesville: University Press of Virginia, 1979), 90.

34. *USJ*, 1:87.

35. Halperin, *Alien and Sedition*, 2.

36. Otis in Halperin, *Alien and Sedition*, 44; William Cobbett in Alan Taylor, *Civil War of 1812* (New York: Doubleday, 2011), 84.

37. Halperin, *Alien and Sedition*, 73, 75–77; Wendell Bird, *Criminal Dissent: Prosecutions Under the Alien and Sedition Acts of 1798* (Cambridge, MA: Harvard University Press, 2020), 51, 327.

38. Pencak, *Jews & Gentiles*, 242.

39. *Gazette of the United States*, 7/16/1800.

40. Pencak, *Jews & Gentiles*, 242. Levy was an Episcopalian; see Edwin Wolf and Maxwell Whiteman, *The History of the Jews of Philadelphia: From Colonial Times to the Age of Jackson* (Philadelphia: Jewish Publication Society of America, 1975), 216. See also Hyman Rosenbach, *The Jews of Philadelphia Prior to 1800* (Philadelphia: Edward Stern, 1883), 27.

41. Pencak, *Jews & Gentiles*, 245.

42. "A.W.," *Pittsburgh Gazetteer*, 8/23/1800.

43. Emanuel Milton Altfeld, *The Jew's Struggle for Religious and Civil Liberty in Maryland* (New York: Da Capo [reprint], 1970), 10. *Votes and Proceedings of the House of Delegates of Maryland, November Session, 1797, Being the First Session . . .* (Annapolis, MD: [n.p.], 1798), 69.

44. *Votes and Proceedings of the House of Delegates of Maryland, November Session, 1797, Being the First Session . . .* (Annapolis, MD: [n.p.], 1798), 72.

45. Pencak, *Jews & Gentiles*, 242.

46. Schappes, "Anti-Semitism," 133.

47. New York *Journal*, 2/18/1792.

48. Hugh Henry Brackenridge, *Modern Chivalry* (Richmond: Johnson and Warner, 1815 [1792]), 201. The incident in the novel is not an attack on Jews per se, but a use of dialect intended as a Jewish stereotype.

49. Jonathan J. Den Hertog, *Patriotism and Piety: Federalist Politics and Religious Struggle in the New American Nation* (Charlottesville: University of Virginia Press, 2015), 61.

50. R. S. McDonald, "Was There a Religious Revolution of 1800?," in *The Revolution of 1800: Democracy, Race, and the New Republic*, ed. James Horn, Jan Ellen Lewis, and Peter S. Onuf (Charlottesville: University of Virginia Press, 2002), 173.

51. Den Hertog, *Patriotism and Piety*, 52, 55.

52. *Gazette of the United States*, 8/5/1800; Pencak, *Jews & Gentiles*, 242–243.

53. Nones to the *Gazette of the United States*, 8/11/1800, *DHJUS*, 95. There were American Jews in the Federalist ranks, despite Nones's claim. Ben S. Judah, for example, wrote to Alexander Hamilton from London, asking for permission to purchase weapons for the American cause against France. "Every American," he wrote, "must feel the ardour of aiding his Country to justify her rights." *AJD*, 309.

54. Quoted in Pencak, *Jews & Gentiles*, 245.

55. Gershom Seixas, *A Discourse Delivered in the Synagogue of New York* (New York: William A. Davis, 1798), 19; Jacob Rader Marcus, *The Handsome Priest in the Black Gown: The Personal World of Gershom Seixas* (Cincinnati, OH: American Jewish Archives, 1970), 55.

56. *The Law Practice of Alexander Hamilton: Documents and Commentary*, ed. Julius Goebel Jr. (New York: Columbia University Press, 1969), 2:87.

57. *Law Practice of Alexander Hamilton*, 2:82.

58. Porwancher, *Jewish World of Alexander Hamilton*, 165–172.

59. *The Diaries of Gouverneur Morris*, ed. Melanie Randolph Miller (Charlottesville: University of Virginia Press, 2018), 69, 70.

60. *Law Practice of Alexander Hamilton*, 2:86.

61. John C. Hamilton, *History of the Republic of the United States . . . as Traced in the Writings of Alexander Hamilton and of His Contemporaries* (New York: D. Appleton, 1857–64), 7:711.

62. *Diaries of Gouverneur Morris*, 70.

63. Porwancher, *Jewish World of Alexander Hamilton*, 174.

64. *DHJUS*, 95.

65. *DHJUS*, 98–99.

66. Thomas Jefferson to John Taylor, 6/4/1798, https://founders.archives.gov/?q=Jefferson%20Taylor%201798%20Author%3A%22Jefferson%2C%20Thomas%22%20Recipient%3A%22Taylor%2C%20John%22&s=1111311111&r=5, accessed October 1, 2023.

67. James Monroe to Jacob Cohen, 4/16/1807, Cohen family of Baltimore and Richmond Papers, undated, 1779–1897, Box 1, Folder 1, AJHS.

68. Marcus Rezneck, *Unrecognized Patriots: The Jews in the American Revolution* (New York: Greenwood Press, 1975), 174.

69. James Monroe to Thomas Jefferson, 5/30/1802, https://founders.archives.gov/?q=monroe%20tj%201802%20Author%3A%22Monroe%2C%20James%22%20Recipient%3A%22Jefferson%2C%20Thomas%22&s=1111311111&r=9, accessed October 1, 2023.

70. Rezneck, *Unrecognized Patriots*, 175.

71. Gallatin to Thomas Jefferson, 9/18/1804, https://founders.archives.gov/?q=gallatin%20to%20Jefferson%201804%20Author%3A%22Gallatin%2C%20Albert%22%20Recipient%3A%22Jefferson%2C%20Thomas%22&s=1111311111&sa=&r=76&sr=, accessed October 1, 2023. See also Leon Huhner, "Jefferson's Contemplated Offer of Attorney-General," *PAJHS* 20 (1911),

161–162. Huhner was not sure Gallatin meant Moses Levy, but Levy's prominence in Bache's defense suggests that Gallatin did refer to him.

72.   Thomas Jefferson to William Short, 8/4/1820, https://founders.archives. gov/?q=short%20Author%3A%22Jefferson%2C%20Thomas%22%20Re cipient%3A%22Short%2C%20William%22%20Period%3A%22post-Madi son%20Presidency%22&s=1111311111&r=9, accessed August 12, 2022.

73.   Thomas Jefferson to John Adams, 10/12/1813, https://founders.archives.gov/ documents/Adams/99-02-02-6182, accessed September 30, 2023.

74.   Thomas Jefferson to Ezra Stiles Ely, 6/25/1819, https://founders.archives.gov/ ?q=ezra%20stiles%20ely&s=1111311111&sa=&r=3&sr=, accessed September 29, 2023.

75.   Thomas Jefferson to Joseph Priestley, 4/9/1803, https://founders.archives. gov/?q=priestley%20Author%3A%22Jefferson%2C%20Thomas%22%20Re cipient%3A%22Priestley%2C%20Joseph%22&s=1111311111&r=7, accessed August 12, 2022.

76.   *Jefferson's Extracts from the Gospels*, ed. Dickinson W. Adams (Princeton, NJ: Princeton University Press, 1983), 297.

77.   Abraham Moise, "Memoir," in *A Selection from the Miscellaneous Writings of the Late Isaac Harby* (Charleston, SC: Burges, 1829), 12.

78.   The electoral results of the early republic are much more heavily documented now than in previous decades thanks to the work of Philip Lampi and the New Nation Votes website hosted by Tufts University. See Caroline F. Sloat, "A New Nation Votes and the Study of American Politics, 1789–1824," *JER* 33:2 (Summer 2013), 183–186. Elections results here are from New Nation Votes, https://elections.lib.tufts.edu/catalog/SM0013, accessed August 12, 2022.

79.   New Nation Votes, https://elections.lib.tufts.edu/catalog/bv73c133v#note_ 14, accessed August 12, 2022.

80.   *AJWDH*, 72.

81.   Jonathan Sarna, *Jacksonian Jew: The Two Worlds of Mordecai Noah* (New York: Holmes & Meier, 1981), 15.
       Lawrence A. Peskin, "From Shylocks to Unbelievers: Early National Views of 'Oriental' Jews," *JER* 39:2 (July 2019), 296.

82.   Mordecai Manuel Noah, *Travels in England, France, Spain, and the Barbary States* (New York: Kirk and Mercein, 1819), appendix, ix–x.

83.   Noah, *Travels*, Appendix xv.

84.   Sarna, *Jacksonian Jew*, 17–18, 27–28; Monroe to Noah, 4/25/1815, reprinted in Sarna, *Jacksonian Jew*, 26.

85.   Noah, *Travels*, 378.

86.   Noah, *Travels*, 379.

87.   Noah, *Travels*, 378, 411.

88.   Lawrence A. Peskin, *Captives and Countrymen: Barbary Slavery and the American Public, 1785–1816* (Baltimore: Johns Hopkins University Press, 2009), 198–199, makes the case that Monroe's anti-Semitism was an excuse to cover a secret diplomatic bungle. If so, it was still an anti-Semitic act.

89.   Noah, *Travels*, 380, 379, 381.
90.   Noah, *Travels*, 414–415.
91.   Noah, *Travels*, 379.
92.   BB, 2:323, 320.
93.   *USJ*, 1:91.
94.   Monroe to Mordecai Manuel Noah, 5/15/1818, *Travels*, Appendix xxv–xxvi.
95.   Mordecai Manuel Noah to John Quincy Adams, 7/24/1820, in BB, 3:886–890.
96.   Sheldon and Judy Godfrey, *Search Out the Land: The Jews and the Growth of Equality in British Colonial America, 1740–1867* (Montreal: Queens-McGill University Press, 1995), 171–179. The Godfreys argue that Hart's exclusion probably had as much to do with internal Canadian politics as with anti-Semitism, but the legal and political reality is the same: A Jew won election and was denied the right to sit in a legislature because of his religion.
97.   Ira Rosenwaike, "Further Light on Jacob Henry," *American Jewish Archives* (November 1970), 116–120.
98.   *Journal of the House of Commons of North Carolina, November 1809* (Raleigh: Gales and Seaton, 1809), 27.
99.   *Journal . . . 1809*, 28.
100. Jacob Henry, "Address to the Committee of the Whole," 1809, *DHJUS*, 123.
101. Jacob Henry, "Address to the Committee of the Whole," 1809, *DHJUS*, 124.
102. Jacob Henry, "Address to the Committee of the Whole," 1809, *DHJUS*, 125.
103. BB, 28; Borden, *Jews, Turks, and Infidels*, 49.

Chapter 9

1.   *AJD*, 52. Samuel noted that *galut* [rejection] occurred in New York and Philadelphia, because in those cities "German Gentiles cannot forsake their anti-Jewish prejudice; and the German Jews cannot forsake their disgraceful conduct."
2.   Mordecai Manuel Noah to "Uncle," Charleston, 5/10/1812, in Isaac Goldberg, *Major Noah: American-Jewish Pioneer* (Philadelphia: Jewish Publication Society of America, 1938), 51–52.
3.   Margaret Wilson Gillikin, "Competing Loyalties: Nationality, Church Governance, and the Development of an American Catholic Identity," *Early American Studies* 11:1 (2013), 151.
4.   Peter Cartwright, *Autobiography of Peter Cartwright*, ed. Charles L. Wallis, (Nashville: Abingdon Press, 1956), 101–102.
5.   William McLellin, *Journals of William McLellin, 1831–1836*, ed. Jan Shipps and John W. Welch (Urbana: University of Illinois Press, 1994), 61.
6.   Nathan O. Hatch, *The Democratization of American Christianity* (New Haven, CT: Yale University Press, 1989), 4.
7.   Hatch, *Democratization of American Christianity*, 7; Nancy Towle, *Vicissitudes Illustrated* (Charleston: James L. Burges, 1832), 145.

8. Catherine A. Brekus, *Strangers and Pilgrims: Female Preaching in America, 1740–1845* (Chapel Hill: University of North Carolina Press, 1998), 126–128, 137, 191.

9. Devereux Jarratt to John Coleman, 1/28/1796, in *The Life of the Reverend Devereux Jarratt* (Baltimore: Warner and Hanna, 1806), 181.

10. Anzia Yezierska, *Bread Givers* (New York: Penguin, 2023), 16, emphasis added.

11. For assimilation as the primary challenge for American Jews of the eighteenth and nineteenth centuries, see Jonathan D. Sarna, *American Judaism: A History* (New Haven, CT: Yale University Press, 2004); Emily Bingham, *Mordecai: An Early American Family* (New York: Hill and Wang, 2003); William Pencak, *Jews & Gentiles in Early America, 1654–1800* (Ann Arbor: University of Michigan Press, 2005), 19.

12. Shalom Goldman called the post-revolutionary "fluidity of religious identity" an outgrowth of "a Jewish society which did not yet have an established Rabbinate or religious organizational life," which presupposed the need for clergy and institutions for a valid religious life. Shalom Goldman, "Joshua/James Seixas (1802–1874): Jewish Apostasy and Christian Hebraism in Early Nineteenth-Century America," *Jewish History* 7:1 (Spring 1993), 74. Zev Eleff traces the jeremiads over American assimilation to European rabbis of the 1890s who portrayed America as a religious "wasteland," where laws of *kashrut* and intermarriage were neglected. Zev Eleff, "Rabbi Haym of Volozhin, Rabbi Aharon Kotler, and the Remaking of an American Jewish Prophecy," *AJAJ* 72: 1 and 2 (2020), 88. Such notions of assimilation as betrayal rather than valid religious practice persist in Jewish culture and historiography, but as Eleff points out, they were not the attitudes of early nineteenth-century Jews. The experience of Seixas and the Jewish patriots suggests that assimilation and a loose institutional structure was precisely what American Jews wanted. Shari Rabin makes a similar argument about taking eclectic Jewish practices as a legitimate form of religion in subsequent decades in Shari Rabin, *Jews on the Frontier: Religion and Mobility in Nineteenth-Century America* (New York: New York University Press, 2017).

13. Jonathan D. Sarna, "The Democratization of American Judaism," in *New Essays in American Jewish History: Commemorating the Sixtieth Anniversary of the Founding of the American Jewish Archives*, ed. Pamela Nadell, Jonathan Sarna, and Lance Sussman (Cincinnati: American Jewish Archives, 2010), 99.

14. Howard B. Rock, *Haven of Liberty: New York Jews in the New World, 1654–1865* (New York: New York University, 2012), 114; "Constitution and Bylaws of Congregation Shearith Israel—1790," *AJD*, 149–150, 156. Jonathan Gienapp writes of the correlation between choice as an ideal derived from the revolutionary experience and the rise of written constitutions: "Valorizing constitutional choice focused constitutionalism. As a result of having discrete and identifiable authors, American constitutions themselves became more discrete and identifiable." Though Gienapp is not referring to synagogue

constitutions, the parallel is evident: rules for governing the congregation would not come from vague "tradition," but from a collection of identifiable, American Jews. Gienapp, *The Second Creation: Fixing the Constitution in the Founding Era* (Cambridge, MA: Belknap Press, 2018), 40.

15.   Congregation Shearith Israel Records (microform), reel 1, AJA.

16.   Leibman et al. refer to the Shabbat-observance clause as "the immense level of control that the synagogue board wished to have over the spiritual and social aspects of their congregation's lives," but the constitution also clearly states that membership involved a personal decision to abide by the contract. Leibman et al., "Code of Laws of the Congregation Mickva Israel," *JITA*, 223–226.

17.   "Earliest Record of Our Archives, 12 Iyar 5562 [May 14, 1802]" (mislabeled "Constitution of 1810"), Article 15, Congregation Rodeph Shalom, Early Minutes & Vital Records, 1802–1845, AJA.

18.   Sarna, "Democratization," 99–100; *AJD*, 145ff.

19.   Sarna, "Democratization," 100–102.

20.   Bingham, *Mordecai*, 31.

21.   *AJD*, 180–181.

22.   Robert Cohen, *Jews in Another Environment: Surinam[e] in the Second Half of the Eighteenth Century* (New York: Brill, 1991), 159–172

23.   Signatures of Benjamin Judah and Isaac Gomez, appended to the "Bye-Laws of the Congregation of Shearith Israel, as ratified on the 24 June 1805"; copy microfilmed in Congregation Shearith Israel Records, 1784–1949, AJA.

24.   Memorandum of Emanuel de la Motta on the death of Isaac de la Motta, 1795, transcribed 1796, AJA, SC-2733.

25.   Rabin, *Jews on the Frontier*, 1–3.

26.   Jacob Mordecai to Moses, Samuel, Rachel, Ellen and Caroline Mordecai, 7/20/1796, Myers Mordecai and Hays Family Collection Papers, AJA.

27.   Bingham, *Mordecai*, 95.

28.   Jacob Mordecai to Samuel Mordecai, 11/29/1810, Mordecai Family Papers, Series 1.2, Box 3, Southern Historical Collection, Wilson Library, University of North Carolina, Chapel Hill.

29.   Bingham, *Mordecai*, 110.

30.   Jacob Mordecai to Samuel Mordecai, 11/29/1810, Mordecai Family Papers, Series 1.2, Box 3, Southern Historical Collection, Wilson Library, University of North Carolina, Chapel Hill; Jacob Mordecai to Samuel? Mordecai 9/19/1821, Jacob Mordecai Papers, AJA.

31.   Jacob Mordecai, "Introduction to the New Testament," 236; Jacob Mordecai Papers, AJA.

32.   Ellen Mordecai, *A History of a Heart* (Philadelphia: Stavely & M'Calla, 1845), 7, 9.

33.   Bingham, *Mordecai*, 89, 123.

34.   R. Cantor to Phillips, 7/13/1814, Congregation Mikveh Israel Records, Box 1, Folder 9, AJHS.

35.   Manuel Josephson to Moses Seixas, 2/4/1790, *JITA*, 211.

36. Jonathan Sarna and Dvora E. Weisberg, "A Writ of Release from Levirate Marriage (*Shtar Halitzah*) in 1807 Charleston," *AJAJ* 63:1 (2011), 41, 47. Steiner argues that the *shtar halitzah* was instead an effort to emphasize traditional Jewish law in the face of Solomon Levy's marriage to his sister-in-law. Benjamin Steiner, "Postscript on the Charleston *Shtar Halitzah*," *AJAJ* 73:1 (2021), 76.

37. BB, 533.

38. *AJD*, 182; Rock, *Haven of Liberty*, 119.

39. Rock, *Haven of Liberty*, 120–121.

40. Laura Arnold Leibman, *The Art of the Jewish Family: A History of Women in Early New York in Five Objects* (New York: Bard Graduate Center, 2020), 155, 187; Jacob Mordecai to Moses, Samuel, Rachel, Ellen and Caroline Mordecai, 7/20/1796, Myers Mordecai and Hays Collection Family Papers, AJA.

41. Rock, *Haven of Liberty*, 116.

42. Henry Etting to Ben Etting, 1/8/1826, Etting Family Correspondence, SC-3277, AJA.

43. Solomon Cohen to Joseph Cohen, 6/29/1808, Cohen Family Papers, AJA.

44. Rachel Mordecai to Samuel Mordecai, 4/21/1807, *AJWDH*, 68.

45. Samuel Nunes Carvalho, *Incidents of Travel and Adventure* (New York: Derby and Jackson, 1860), 107, 113.

46. Naphtali Phillips, Bedikah Book, 1798, Box 8, Folder 93, Phillips Family Papers, AJHS.

47. Dianne Ashton, *Hannukah: A History* (New York: New York University Press, 2013), 78–80; Stephen Nissenbaum, *The Battle for Christmas* (New York: Vintage, 1997).

48. Aviva Ben-Ur, "Purim in the Public Eye: Leisure, Violence, and Cultural Convergence in the Dutch Atlantic," *Jewish Social Studies* 20:1 (Fall 2013), 32.

49. Darmstadt, Joseph, "Purim Poem," Richmond, VA, 3/12/1789, AJA.

50. Gershom Seixas to his children, undated; Gershom Seixas to Sarah Kursheedt, 11/10/1813, Papers of the Seixas Family, Series III: Gershom Mendes Seixas and Descendants, Box 1, Folder 12, AJHS.

51. "Committee Report on Choir, 1818," BB, 495.

52. Gershom Cohen to Mordecai Sheftall, 8/29/1791, *AJD*, 183.

53. Rebecca Gratz to Benjamin Gratz, 2/27/1825, *Letters of Rebecca Gratz*, ed. David Philipson, 74–75 (Philadelphia: Jewish Publication Society of America, 1929).

54. Eli Faber, *A Time for Planting: The First Migration, 1654–1820* (Baltimore: Johns Hopkins University Press, 1992), 115.

55. Rebecca Gratz to Benjamin Gratz, 2/27/1825, *Letters,* 74–75.

56. Ketubah for Solomon Etting and Rachel Gratz, 10/9/1791, Solomon Etting Correspondence, Box 1, Folder 6, AJHS.

57. Eleff, *Who Rules*, 17.

58. Bingham, *Mordecai*, 133.

59. E. Lyte to Abraham Pinto, 2/2/1796, *AJD*, 192.

60. BB, 514; Pencak, *Jews & Gentiles*, 243–244.

61. BB, 523.

62. "Earliest Record of Our Archives," Article 13, Congregation Rodeph Shalom, Early Minutes & Vital Records, 1802–1845, AJA; *JITA*, 224–225.

63. 1807 List of Members with Infractions, Kahol Kadosh Beth Elohim Records, Box 19, Folder 1, College of Charleston Special Collections.

64. Rock, *Haven of Liberty*, 122.

65. James Foster to the trustees of Mikveh Israel, 6/5/1788, Jacques Judah Lyons Papers, AJHS.

66. Anna Barrett to the Trustees of Mikveh Israel, 11/13/1794, BB, 701.

67. From the Minutes of the Trustees of Congregation Anshe Chesed, 5/21/1837, BB, 702.

68. Congregation Shearith Israel, "Conversion of Abraham Kirkas, 1848," AJHS.

69. Congregation Mikveh Israel, "Minutes and Correspondence of the Congregation, 1782–1790," Robert D. Farber University Archives and Special Collections, Brandeis University, Tishri 4 5543, 140.

70. *JITA*, 171; https://rodephshalom.org/history, accessed 8/5/2022.

71. Edwin Wolf and Maxwell Whiteman, *The History of the Jews of Philadelphia: From Colonial Times to the Age of Jackson* (Philadelphia: Jewish Publication Society of America, 1975), 226–227.

72. Eleff, *Who Rules*, ch. 1.

73. Rock, *Haven of Liberty*, 122–126; Salomon to Zalegman Phillips, 11/30/1825, BB, 547–548.

74. Rock, *Haven of Liberty*, 126–129.

75. James Hagy, *This Happy Land: The Jews of Colonial and Antebellum Charleston* (Tuscaloosa: University of Alabama Press, 1993), 64–66; Pencak, *Jews & Gentiles*, 134.

76. "Minutes of a Meeting of Isaac DaCosta, Abisha DaCosta, Jr., Jan 25, 1775," KKBE Records, Box 40, Folder 1, College of Charleston Special Collections.

77. Pencak, *Jews & Gentiles*, 135.

78. Isaac Harby, "Discourse Before the Reformed Society of Israelites," in L.C. Moise, *Biography of Isaac Harby with an Account of the Reformed Society of Israelites of Charleston, S.C., 1824–1833* (Columbia, SC: [R.L. Bryan Co.]: 1931), 105.

79. "Selections from the Sabbath Service" in Moise, *Harby*, 77.

80. *DHJUS*, 174.

81. Harby, "Discourse" and "Memorial," in Moise, *Harby*, 103, 54.

82. *DHJUS*, 172.

83. *DHJUS*, 172–173.

84. Gary Phillip Zola, *Isaac Harby of Charleston* (Tuscaloosa: University of Alabama Press, 1994), 114; Sarna, *American Judaism*, 57.

85. Harby, "Discourse," in Moise, *Harby*, 100, 101.

86. "Constitution of the Reformed Society of Israelites," Moise, *Harby*, 62; Sarna, "Democratization," 107.

87. Zev Eleff argues that this model worked well through the Civil War, when again American politics shifted the synagogue. Rabbis took positions as chaplains in the military and used this new legitimacy to secure authority denied to them in previous decades.

88. Leibman, *Art*, 15.

89. Freeman, *Affairs of Honor: National Politics in the New Republic* (New Haven, CT: Yale University Press, 2001), 180.

90. Adam Jortner, *The Gods of Prophetstown: The Battle of Tippecanoe and the Holy War for the American Frontier* (New York: Oxford University Press, 2012), 101–102.

91. Jortner, *Gods of Prophetstown*, 101–102.

92. Goldberg, *Major Noah*, 56–57; Noah to Naphtali Phillips, 6/15/1812, in Goldberg, *Major Noah*, 66–67; Rebecca Gratz to Maria Gist Gratz, 9/2/1832, *Letters of Rebecca Gratz*, 158.

93. BB, 176–181.

94. Michael Hoberman, "'The Confidence Placed in You Is of the *Greatest Magnitude*': Representations of Paternal Authority in Early Jewish American Letters," *Studies in American Jewish Literature* 33:1 (2014), 70–71; Jacob Gratz to John Myers, June 18, 1811, Myers Family Papers, Box 3, Folder 26, AJA.

95. Hoberman, "Confidence," 71; Asher Marx to Moses Myers, 6/10/1811, Myers Family Papers, Box 3, Folder 50, AJA.

96. Rock, *Haven of Liberty*, 116.

97. Gershom Seixas to Chairman and Trustees of Shearith Israel, 9/28/1786, Gershom Mendes Seixas, Typescripts of Correspondence Held by Shearith Israel Congregation, Seixas Family Papers, Box 1, Folder 10, AJHS.

98. Gershom Seixas to Benjamin Seixas, 9/29/1786, Gershom Mendes Seixas Typescripts of Correspondence Held by Shearith Israel Congregation, Seixas Family Papers, Box 1, Folder 10, AJHS.

99. Sarna, *American Judaism*, 50.

100. Rock, *Shearith Israel*, 90–91. Rock gives the date as 1785, but the correspondence is dated to 1786.

101. Dianne Ashton, "The Lessons of the Hebrew Sunday School," in *American Jewish Women's History: A Reader*, ed. Pamela S. Nadell (New York: New York University Press, 2003), 32.

102. Wolf and Whiteman, *Jews of Philadelphia*, 276–277.

103. "Circular by Committee of Hebra Hased V'Amet Regarding Establishment of Women's Hebra," Jacques Judah Lyons Collection, Box 3, Folder 190, AJHS.

104. Rebecca Gratz to Maria Gist Gratz, 6/29/34, *Letters of Rebecca Gratz*, 198–199; Sarna, *American Judaism*, 50.

105. Rebecca Gratz, "Female Hebrew Benevolent Society Annual Report (1835)," in *Four Centuries of Jewish Women's Spirituality*, ed. Ellen M. Umansky and Dianne Ashton (Waltham, MA: Brandeis University Press, 2009), 92–93.

106. Ashton, "Lessons of the Hebrew Sunday School," 32–35.

107. Rachel Mordecai to Maria Edgeworth, 1815, in *JITA*, 58–60.

108. Bingham, *Mordecai*, 66–67.

109. Bingham, *Mordecai*, 195.

110. Rachel Mordecai to Maria Edgeworth, 10/28/1817, in *Education of the Heart: The Correspondence of Rachel Mordecai Lazarus and Maria Edgeworth*, ed. Edgar E. MacDonald (Chapel Hill: University of North Carolina Press, 1977), 24.

111. Bingham, *Mordecai*, 150, 302 n15, 180, 195.

112. Louisa B. Hart, "Address to a Graduating Student of the Hebrew Sunday School," *Four Centuries of Jewish Women's Spirituality*, ed. Ellen M. Umansky and Dianne Ashton (Waltham, MA: Brandeis University Press, 2009), 94

113. *AJWDH*, 78.

114. *AJWDH*, 73–74.

115. "A Jewess," [Emma Mordecai], *The Teachers' and Parents' Assistant* (Philadelphia: C. Sherman, 1845), 3, 35. Emphasis added.

116. Saul Jacob Rubin, *Third to None: The Saga of Savannah Jewry, 1733–1983* (Savannah, GA: S.J. Rubin, 1983), 53.

117. Marriage Contract, Judith Hays and Samuel Myers, 9/20/1796, *JITA*, 137.

118. Rubin, *Third to None*, 53; Wolf and Whiteman, *Jews of Philadelphia*, 127–128.

119. Rebecca Gratz to Maria Gist Gratz, 10/12/1833, *Letters of Rebecca Gratz*, 185.

Chapter 10

1. The story of the Brandon siblings and their African and Jewish ancestors is dealt with beautifully in Laura Arnold Leibman, *Once We Were Slaves* (New York: Oxford University Press, 2021), from which I draw my interpretations. See also Laura Arnold Leibman, *The Art of the Jewish Family: A History of Women in Early New York in Five Objects* (New York: Bard Graduate Center, 2020), 127; "Conversion and Circumcision, Isaac Lopez Brandon," *JITA*, 161.

2. Leibman, *Once We Were Slaves*, 1–18.

3. Adam Jortner, *The Gods of Prophetstown: The Battle of Tippecanoe and the Holy War for the American Frontier* (New York: Oxford University Press, 2012), ch. 6.

4. Leibman, *Art*, 128.

5. Shari Rabin, *Jews on the Frontier: Religion and Mobility in Nineteenth-Century America* (New York: New York University Press, 2017), 13–14.

6. Ralph Austen, "The Uncomfortable Relationship: African Enslavement in the Common History of Blacks and Jews," in *Strangers and Neighbors: Relations Between Blacks and Jews in the United States*, ed. Maurianne Adams and John Bracy (Amherst, MA: University of Massachusetts Press, 1999), 135–136.

7. James Hagy, *This Happy Land: The Jews of Colonial and Antebellum Charleston* (Tuscaloosa: University of Alabama Press, 1993), 91, emphasis added.

8.   Steven R. Weisman, *The Chosen Wars: How Judaism Became an American Religion* (New York: Simon and Schuster, 2018), 20.

9.   William Pencak, *Jews & Gentiles in Early America, 1654–1800* (Ann Arbor: University of Michigan Press, 2005), 89.

10. Sarna's first reference to enslavement is in chapter 3 of *American Judaism*. For a historiographical review of earlier generations of the same error, see Jonathan Schorsch, *Jews and Blacks in the Early Modern World* (New York: Cambridge University Press, 2004), 1–6.

11. Schorsch, *Jews and Blacks in the Early Modern World*, 4.

12. Austen, "The Uncomfortable Relationship," 135–136.

13. A Runaway Slave, "Recollections of Slavery," in *I Belong to South Carolina*, ed. Susanna Ashton (Columbia: University of South Carolina Press, 2010), 67–68.

14. Philip Minis to John Houston, 12/31/1779, Philip Minis Papers, Georgia Historical Society; Aviva Ben-Ur, "Purim in the Public Eye: Leisure, Violence, and Cultural Convergence in the Dutch Atlantic," *Jewish Social Studies* 20:1 (Fall 2013), 36.

15. David Brion Davis, "Jews in the Slave Trade," in *Struggles in the Promised Land: Toward a History of Black-Jewish Relations in the United States*, ed. Jack Salzman and Cornel West (New York: Oxford, 1997), 79.

16. Emily Bingham, *Mordecai: An Early American Family* (New York: Hill and Wang, 2003), 202, 203.

17. Schorsch, *Jews and Blacks in the Early Modern World*, 91–99; Bruce D. Haynes, *The Soul of Judaism: Jews of African Descent in America* (New York: New York University Press, 2018), 68.

18. Albert Raboteau, *Slave Religion: The Invisible Institution in the Antebellum South* (New York: Oxford University Press, 1978), 113; Haynes, *The Soul of Judaism*, 70.

19. Harby's Copy Book, College of Charleston Special Collections; Davis, "Jews in the Slave Trade," 78.

20. Isaac Harby, "No. VII," *Selections from the Miscellaneous Writings*, ed. Henry Pinckney and Abraham Moise (Charleston: James Burges, 1829), 134. Emphasis original.

21. Gary Phillip Zola, *Isaac Harby of Charleston, 1788–1828: Jewish Reformer and Intellectual* (Tuscaloosa: University of Alabama Press, 1994), 94–98; Jonathan D. Sarna, *Jacksonian Jew: The Two Worlds of Mordecai Noah* (New York: Holmes & Meier, 1981), 108–112.

22. Bingham, *Mordecai*, 45; Pencak, *Jews & Gentiles*, 131; Alfred Mordecai, *Life of Alfred Mordecai*, in *MAJ*, 1:68.

23. *AJD*, 145.

24. Haynes, *The Soul of Judaism*, 75–76.

25. *AJD*, 145, 150.

26. L. E. and Polly Miller to the Trustees of Shearith Israel, 2/15/1807, *AJWDH*, 67.

27. Haynes, *The Soul of Judaism*, 81. Emphasis original.

28. Schorsch, *Jews and Blacks in the Early Modern World,* 217–219; Leibman, *Art,* 101, puts the number of biracial Jews at 10 percent of the island's Jewish population.

29. Robert Cohen, *Jews in Another Environment. Surinam[e] in the Second Half of the Eighteenth Century* (Leiden: E. J. Brill, 1991), 159. Clearly, some of these biracial Jews were the children of Black men and European Jewish women, but such encounters were unlikely to be acknowledged by the slave societies of the Caribbean.

30. Cohen, *Jews in Another Environment,* 157–164; *JITA,* 201.

31. Cohen, *Jews in Another Environment,* 159–172.

32. Richard S. Newman, *Freedom's Prophet: Bishop Richard Allen, the AME Church, and the Black Founding Fathers* (New York: New York University Press, 2008), 166–169.

33. Joshua Rothman, *Notorious in the Neighborhood: Sex and Families Across the Color Line in Virginia, 1787–1861* (Chapel Hill: University of North Carolina Press, 2003), ch. 2.

34. Hagy, *Happy Land,* 37–38.

35. Kylie L. McCormick, "Father and Servant, Son and Slave: Judaism and Labor in Georgia, 1732–1809," Master's Thesis, University of Nebraska, 2016, 68.

36. Ben-Ur, "Purim," 42–44.

37. Aviva Ben-Ur, "Jewish Savannah in Atlantic Perspective: A Reconsideration of North America's First Intentional Jewish Community," in *The Sephardic Atlantic,* edited by Sina Rauschenbach and Jonathan Schorsch (Cham, Switzerland: Palgrave Macmillan, 2019), 210–11.

38. Howard B. Rock, *Haven of Liberty: New York Jews in the New World, 1654–1865* (New York: New York University, 2012), 121.

39. Lauren F. Winner, "Taking Up the Cross: Conversion Among Black and White Jews in the Civil War South," in *Southern Families at War: Loyalty and Conflict,* ed. Catherine Clinton (New York: Oxford University Press, 2000).

40. Haynes, *The Soul of Judaism,* 75.

41. Leibman, *Once We Were Slaves,* 132.

42. Winner, "Taking Up the Cross," 199.

43. Ralph Melnick, "Billy Simons, the Black Jew of Charleston," *AJAJ* 32:1 (1980), 3–8.

44. James E. Landing, *Black Judaism: Story of an American Movement* (Durham, NC: Carolina Academic Press, 2001), 119–120; Leibman, *Once We Were Slaves,* 181.

45. *DHJUS,* 118–131.

46. Thomas Tobias Papers, Box 2, Folder 3, College of Charleston Special Collections.

47. Kate E. R. Pickard, "The Kidnapped and the Ransomed (How the Friedman Brothers Liberated an Alabama Slave)," *AJAJ* 9:1 (1957), 3–31.

48. Will of Isaiah Isaacs, 1803, in *Strangers and Neighbors,* 138.

49. Aviva Ben-Ur, "Savannah," 11; McCormick, "Father and Servant," 71.

Chapter 11

1. *Israel's Advocate* (New York: John P. Haven, 1823–26), 61–62.
2. James Morrison Arnell journal, Special Collections, Johns Hopkins University Library, Baltimore, 29ff, 62; Susanna Linsley, "Saving the Jews: Religious Toleration and the American Society for Meliorating the Condition of the Jews," *JER* 34:4 (2014), 625–651; *Israel's Advocate*, 61–62. This claim was not quite true in 1823, as France and a handful of smaller European principalities had emancipated their Jews.
3. Arnell journal, 49, 61, 74.
4. Jacob Mordecai, "Manuscript Vol. 2, New Testament," AJA.
5. Edward Kessler, *An Introduction to Jewish-Christian Relations* (New York: Cambridge University Press, 2010), 5–8; Jacob Rader Marcus, *The Handsome Priest in the Black Gown: The Personal World of Gershom Seixas* (Cincinnati, OH: American Jewish Archives, 1970), 24.
6. BB, 741.
7. Frey initially tried to organize a society to convert the Jews in Britain in 1809. Once he decided that British churches were more interested in sectarian controversies than in upholding Jewish rights or preaching, he abandoned the effort and tried again in America. Linsley, "Saving the Jews," 637; *Israel's Advocate*, 44.
8. Joseph Frey, *The Converted Jew* [Armstrong 2nd ed.] (Boston: Armstrong, 1815), 103; BB, 716.
9. Quoted in Abraham Karp, *Haven to Home: A History of the Jews in America* (New York: Schocken, 1985), 40.
10. Dan Judson, "The Mercies of a Benign Judge: A Letter from Gershom Seixas to Hannah Adams, 1810," *AJAJ* 56: 1 and 2, 179.
11. Judson, "Mercies," 186, 188 n21; George Stanley Faber, *General and Connected View of the Prophecies* (London: F. C. and J. Rivington, 1809), 1:3–4.
12. Hannah Adams, *A History of the Jews* (Boston: John Eliot, 1812), iv.
13. Adams, *A History of the Jews*, 325–326.
14. Sermon, 11/28/1799, Undated Sermon, 1805, Sermons by Gershom Mendes Seixas, AJHS.
15. Gershom Seixas to Sarah Kursheedt, 11/10/1813, 1/23/1814, 4/15/1814; Papers of the Seixas Family, Series III: Gershom Mendes Seixas and Descendants, Box 1, Folder 13, AJHS; Marcus, *Handsome Priest*, 24.
16. Gershom Seixas, 1814 sermon, Seixas Family Papers, Box 1, Folder 14, AJHS. Note that this sermon is appended to a 1939 article on earlier Seixas sermons. Seixas, Undated Sermon, 1805, Sermons by Gershom Mendes Seixas, AJHS, emphasis added.
17. Dianne Ashton, *Rebecca Gratz: Women and Judaism in Antebellum America* (Detroit: Wayne State University Press, 1997), 80.
18. Jacob Nikelsburger, *Koul Jacob* (New York: John Reid, 1816), 8.
19. Salomon Jacob Cohen, *Elements of the Jewish Faith* (Richmond: Gray for Cohen, 1817), 6–7.
20. Shinah Schuyler to Richea Gratz, 12/17/1791, *AJWDH*, 48.

21. Sol Mordecai to Ellen Mordecai, 9/24/1821 (misattributed as Jacob Mordecai to Sol Mordecai), Jacob Mordecai Papers, AJA.

22. Jacob Mordecai to Moses, Samuel, Rachel, Ellen and Caroline Mordecai, 7/20/1796, AJA.

23. Emily Bingham, *Mordecai: An Early American Family* (New York: Hill and Wang, 2003), 150–151; Ellen Mordecai to Sol Mordecai, 9/29/21 (misattributed as written by Jacob Mordecai), Jacob Mordecai Papers, AJA.

24. Bingham, *Mordecai*, 114.

25. Far more Jewish men than women married outside the faith. Laura Arnold Leibman, *The Art of the Jewish Family: A History of Women in Early New York in Five Objects* (New York: Bard Graduate Center, 2020), 79, 17; Jonathan Sarna, *American Judaism: A History* (New Haven, CT: Yale University Press, 2004), 45.

26. *AJWDH*, 103–100.

27. Bingham, *Mordecai*, 168.

28. Slowey Hays to Rebecca Gratz, 8/30/1807, in *JITA*, 49-50.

29. Leibman, *Art*, 77–78.

30. *AJD*, 129.

31. *JITA*, 149.

32. *AJWDH*, 149–150.

33. Ellen Mordecai, *A History of a Heart* (Philadelphia: Stavely & M'Calla, 1845), 14.

34. Bingham, *Mordecai*, 134.

35. Aaron Lazarus to Richard C. Moore [Anglican Bishop of VA], 7/1/1823, AJA.

36. Bingham, *Mordecai*, 134, 137, 150.

37. Bingham, *Mordecai*, 198–199

38. Bingham, *Mordecai*, 154–174.

39. Shalom Goldman, "Joshua/James Seixas (1802–1874): Jewish Apostasy and Christian Hebraism in Early Nineteenth-Century America," *Jewish History* 7:1 (Spring 1993), 68.

40. Walker to Joshua Seixas, 7/20/1832, AJA.

41. Goldman, "Joshua/James Seixas," 73–81.

42. Bingham, *Mordecai*, 197.

43. Jacob Mordecai, "Manuscript Vol. 2, New Testament," AJA.

44. George Bethune English, *Grounds of Christianity Examined* (Boston, 1813), 58.

45. Thomas Paine, *The Age of Reason* (New York: Bennett, 1877), 119.

46. English, *Grounds of Christianity*, 23.

47. English, *Grounds of Christianity*, 6.

48. Paine, *Age of Reason*, 121.

49. Adam Jortner, *Blood from the Sky* (Charlottesville: University of Virginia Press, 2017), chapter 1.

50. Paine, *Age of Reason*, 51.

51. Elihu Palmer, *Principles of Nature* (London: John Cahuac, 1819), 24, 133.

52. Paine, *Age of Reason*, 72.

53. Bingham, *Mordecai*, 111, 292 n5.

54. Jacob Mordecai, Discourse, 9/15/1822, in *The Jew in the American World: A Source Book*, ed. Jacob Rader Marcus (Detroit: Wayne State University Press, 1996), 145.

55. *The Jew*, in BB, 768.

56. "An Israelite," *Israel Vindicated* (New York: Abraham Collins, 1820), 23, 2.

57. *Israel Vindicated*, 6, 10, 67.

58. Jonathan D. Sarna, "The Freethinker, the Jews, and the Missionaries: George Houston and the Mystery of 'Israel Vindicated,'" *AJS Review* 5 (1980), 101–114.

59. BB, 767.

60. BB, 715.

61. BB, 739

62. Will of Elias Boudinot, in BB, 725.

63. BB, 720.

64. Linsley, "Saving the Jews," 721, 739.

65. Linsley, "Saving the Jews," 639.

66. BB, 749.

67. Linsley, "Saving the Jews," 636, 743.

68. "Letter of Protest, May 21, 1825," in BB, 744–476.

69. Linsley, "Saving the Jews," 635, 650.

70. Jonathan Sarna, *Jacksonian Jew: The Two Worlds of Mordecai Noah* (New York: Holmes & Meier, 1981), 44–47.

71. BB, 886–890. The historiography of Ararat is largely concerned with presumed conflicts between Noah's desire for Judaism and his desire to be an American, and therefore falls into the same groove of portraying "Americanism" and Judaism as perpetually separate and incompatible in Jewish life. See Sarna, *Jacksonian Jew*, 61–71; Michael Joseph Schuldiner, "Introduction," *The Selected Writings of Mordecai Noah* (Westport, CT: Greenwood, 1999); and Andrew Porwancher, *The Jewish World of Alexander Hamilton* (Princeton, NJ: Princeton University Press, 2021), 155–162. The other vein of scholarship on Ararat concerns its presumed proto-Zionist status, although if Noah was really trying to draw attention to existing freedoms in America, "Zionism" might not be the best term. Linsley, "Saving the Jews," sets Ararat correctly as a response to missions.

72. G. Herbert Cone, "New Matter Relating to Mordecai M. Noah," *PAJHS*, 11:132.

73. Adam Rovner, *In the Shadow of Zion: Promised Lands Before Israel* (New York: New York University Press, 2014), 26.

74. Rovner, *In the Shadow*, 27.

75. *PAJHS*, 21:230–235.

76. BB, 897.

77. Rovner, *In the Shadow*, 34.

78. *National Advocate*, 1/24/26.

79. BB, 3:903.

80. BB, 3:901–902.

81. Sarna, *Jacksonian Jew*, 44–45.

82. Mordecai Noah to Erasmus Simon, 10/22/1825, AJA, SC-9147.

83. Rovner, *In the Shadow*, 35.

84. Mordecai Noah to Erasmus Simon, 10/22/1825, Mordecai Manuel Noah Documents, AJA.

85. Arnell journal, 38-39; *Israel's Advocate*, 5:39.

86. *PAJHS*, 21:235. Emphasis added.

87. *DHJUS*, 176.

88. *Israel's Advocate*, 3:72.

89. Noah and Mordecai's responses are reprinted in *Modern Orthodox Judaism: A Documentary History*, Zev Eleff, ed. (Lincoln: University of Nebraska Press, 2016), 5–11.

90. Steven R. Weisman, *The Chosen Wars: How Judaism Became an American Religion* (New York: Simon & Schuster, 2018), 40–41.

91. Philadelphia *Gazette*, 2/15/1828; see also C. S. Monaco, *Moses Levy of Florida: Jewish Utopian and Antebellum Reformer* (Baton Rouge: Louisiana State University Press, 2005), 120–123. Monaco's volume is the standard biography of Levy, as most earlier works used the questionable "Diary of Moses Levy" promoted by his converted son. Monaco, *Moses Levy*, 2.

92. Monaco, *Moses Levy*, 57, 66, 1–12.

93. Levy quoted Monaco, *Moses Levy*, 66.

94. Monaco, *Moses Levy*, 98, 102–103, 109.

95. Monaco, *Moses Levy*, 103–112, 151–152.

Chapter 12

1. Maryland *Herald*, 5/18/1823.

2. BB, 15–16.

3. James Kabala, *Church-State Relations in the Early Republic, 1787–1846* (Brookfield, VT: Pickering and Chatto, 2014), 92.

4. Edward Eitches, "Maryland's 'Jew Bill,'" *AJHQ* 60:3 (March 1971), 14.

5. Seth Rockman, *Scraping By: Wage Labor, Slavery, and Survival in Early Baltimore* (Baltimore: Johns Hopkins University Press, 2009), 3.

6. Ira Rosenwaike, "The Jews of Baltimore: 1820–1830," *AJHQ* 67:3 (March 1978), 105–106.

7. Edwin Wolf and Maxwell Whiteman, *The History of the Jews of Philadelphia: From Colonial Times to the Age of Jackson* (Philadelphia: Jewish Publication Society of America, 1975), 125.

8. Rosenwaike, "The Jews of Baltimore," 123; Mikveh Israel Records, Box 1, Folder 4, AJA.

9. *The Occident* 7:4 (July 1849), http://jewish-history.com/occident/volume7/jul1849/obituary.htm, accessed February 6, 2023.

10. Certificate of Naturalization, Etting Family Collection, Box 1, Folder 1, AJHS.

11. Ketubah for the Wedding of Solomon Etting and Rachel Gratz, Etting Family Collection, Box 1, Folder 6, AJHS; Solomon Etting to Barnard Gratz, 11/13/1971, *AJD*, 57.

12. Aaron Baroway, *Solomon Etting: 1764–1847* (Baltimore: Maryland Historical Society, 1920), 10–13.

13. Wolf and Whiteman, *Jews of Philadelphia*, 125; Rosenwaike, "The Jews of Baltimore," 121.

14. Emanuel Milton Altfeld, *The Jew's Struggle for Religious and Civil Liberty in Maryland* (New York: Da Capo [reprint], 1970), 10; *Votes and Proceedings of the House of Delegates of Maryland, November Session, 1797, Being the First Session* . . . (Annapolis, [n.p.], 1798), 69.

15. *Votes and Proceedings of the House of Delegates . . .1797*, 72.

16. *Votes and Proceedings of the House of Delegates of Maryland. . . November Session 1801* (Annapolis: Frederick Green, 1802), 101.

17. *Votes and Proceedings of the House of Representatives of Maryland . . . November Session 1802* (Annapolis: Frederick Green, 1803), 46, 87.

18. *Votes and Proceedings of the House of Delegates of Maryland. . . November Session 1804* (Annapolis: Frederick Green, 1805), 39.

19. Letter to S[olomon?] and Rachel Etting? 7/11/1817, Etting Family Collection, Box 1, folder 6, AJHS; Thomas Kennedy and H. M. Brackenridge, *Sketch of the Proceedings of the Legislature of Maryland . . . on What Is Commonly Called the Jew Bill* (Baltimore: Joseph Robinson, 1819), 14, 21.

20. Joanne B. Freeman, *Affairs of Honor: National Politics in the New Republic* (New Haven, CT: Yale University Press, 2001), 86.

21. Kennedy and Brackenridge, *Sketch*, 20–22

22. Kennedy and Brackenridge, *Sketch*, 13. Emphasis added.

23. Cohen to Thomas, 12/16/1818, BB, 33–36. Thomas is identified as from Baltimore in Kennedy and Brackenridge, *Sketch*, 68.

24. Kennedy and Brackenridge, *Sketch*, 5–9.

25. Kennedy and Brackenridge, *Sketch*, 65, 55–56.

26. Kennedy and Brackenridge, *Sketch*, 56–58.

27. *National Intelligencer*, 9/17/1823.

28. John McMahon, *Remarks of John M'Mahon, in the House of Delegates of Maryland* (Hagerstown, MD: W. D. Bell, 1824), 5; Altfeld, *The Jew's Struggle*, 190.

29. Kabala, *Church-State Relations*, 97.

30. Altfield, *The Jew's Struggle*, 168–172; Easton *Gazette*, 1/25/1823.

31. Easton *Gazette*, 3/1/23.

32. Easton *Gazette*, 3/15/1823.

33. Hagerstown *Torch-Light*, 9/9/1823; Thomas Kennedy, *Civil Rights and Religious Privileges: First Speech of Mr. T. Kennedy . . .* (Annapolis: J. Hughes, 1823), 169.

34. J. M. Young to Brackenridge, 1/13/1819, University of Pittsburgh Library Digital Collections, https://digital.library.pitt.edu/islandora/object/pitt:31735051657983, accessed October 1, 2023; William F. Keller,

The Nation's Advocate: Henry Marie Brackenridge and Young America (Pittsburgh: University of Pittsburgh Press, 1956), 223.

35. Kennedy and Brackenridge, *Sketch*, 52.

36. *National Intelligencer*, 9/10/1823.

37. Baltimore *Morning Chronicle*, quoted in *National Advocate*, 1/29/1823.

38. *Maryland Gazette & Political Intelligencer* (Annapolis), 1/30/1823.

39. BB, 1:45–46; *National Intelligencer*, 1/23/1826.

40. *Votes and Proceedings of the Senate of the State of Maryland, December Session, 1823* (Annapolis: J. Hughes, 1823), 5; H. M. Brackenridge, *Speeches on the Jew Bill* (Dobson: Philadelphia, 1829), 114.

41. James Morrison Arnell journal, Special Collections, Johns Hopkins University Library, Baltimore, 29–30, 58.

42. Hagerstown *Torch-Light*, 9/6/1823.

43. Altfeld, *The Jew's Struggle*, 191.

44. *Maryland Gazette & Political Intelligencer* (Annapolis), 3/4/1819.

45. See Ragosta, *Religious Freedom*, 151–152; Green, *Second Disestablishment*, 195–203.

46. Ragosta, *Religious Freedom*, 150–152. Rehnquist cited Story in his dissent to *Wallace v. Jaffree* (1985), https://supreme.justia.com/cases/federal/us/472/38/, accessed August 8, 2023.

47. Hagerstown *Torch-Light*, 9/23/1823.

48. H. M. Brackenridge to Young, 1/22/1819, University of Pittsburgh Library Digital Collections, https://digital.library.pitt.edu/islandora/object/pitt:317 35051658023, accessed October 1, 2023.

49. Brackenridge, *Speeches*, 116.

50. Kennedy and Brackenridge, *Sketch*, 80–81.

51. *Daily National Intelligencer*, 10/14/1820.

52. Maryland *Herald*, 8/18/1823.

53. *Daily National Intelligencer*, 9/24/1823, identifies the speaker as "A.B." The electoral returns of the early republic are documented thanks to the work of Philip Lampi and the New Nation Votes website hosted by Tufts University. See Caroline F. Sloat, "A New Nation Votes and the Study of American Politics, 1789–1824," *JER* 33:2 (Summer 2013), 183–186. Regarding "A.B.": Of the candidates in Frederick County, New Nation Votes has only one "A.B.": Abraham Blessing. He lost badly, getting only 169 votes (all winners had over 1,600 votes). He would try again in 1824 and finish dead last: See New Nation Votes, https://elections.lib.tufts.edu/catalog/pv63g1907 and https://elections.lib.tufts.edu/catalog/gm8ohw56c, accessed 10/11/2023.

54. *Governor Worthington's Speech om the Maryland Test Act, 1824,* (Baltimore: William Wooddy [sic], 1824), 32; Altfield, *The Jew's Struggle*, 185.

55. https://elections.lib.tufts.edu/catalog/1c18dg55j, accessed 10/11/2023; see also Eitches, "Maryland's 'Jew Bill,'" 277.

56. BB, 1:51.

57. *Worthington's Speech om the Maryland Test Act*, 36; *National Intelligencer*, 1/31/1824.

58. Eitches, "Maryland's 'Jew Bill,' " 272.

59. *Votes and Proceedings of the House of Delegates of Maryland: December Session, 1824.* (Annapolis: Jonas Green, 1825), 163.

60. Mayor and City Council of Baltimore to J. I. Cohen, 1/8/1834, Cohen family of Baltimore and Richmond Papers, undated, 1779–1897, Box 1, Folder 2, AJHS.

61. Brackenridge, *Speeches* (unnumbered).

62. M. S. Polack Collection, AJHS, lists circumcisions in Maryland from 1836 to 1862, and includes ten for Hagerstown.

63. Rosenwaike, "The Jews of Baltimore," 122.

64. J. I. Cohen to John Myers, 6/24/1821, Myers Family Papers, Box 3, Folder 12, AJA.

65. Isaac M. Fein, *The Making of an American Jewish Community: The History of Baltimore Jewry from 1773 to 1920* (Philadelphia: Jewish Publication Society of America, 1971), 43ff.

66. James T. Fisher, *Communion of Immigrants: A History of Catholics in America* (New York: Oxford University Press, 2008), 46–47; Adam Jortner, *No Place for Saints: Mobs and Mormons in Jacksonian America* (Baltimore: Johns Hopkins University Press, 2021).

Conclusion

1. Thomas Jefferson, *The Autobiography of Thomas Jefferson*, ed. Paul Leicester Ford (Philadelphia: University of Pennsylvania Press, 2005 [1914]), 71.

2. Susanna Linsley, "Saving the Jews: Religious Toleration and the American Society for Meliorating the Condition of the Jews," *JER* 34:4 (2014), 639.

3. James Madison to Edward Everett, 3/19/1823, *The Papers of James Madison*, Retirement Series, ed. David B. Mattern, J. C. A. Stagg, Mary Parke Johnson, and Katherine E. Harbury (Charlottesville: University of Virginia Press, 2016), 3:15–18.

4. Jane Kamensky, "Two Cheers for the Nation: An American Revolution for the Revolting United States," *Reviews in American History* 47:3 (September 2019), 309.

5. Thomas Jefferson to James Madison, 1/30/1787, *Papers of Thomas Jefferson*, ed. Julian Boyd (Princeton, NJ: Princeton University Press, 1955), 11:92–97.

6. Gershom Seixas to Sarah Kursheedt, 11/4/1813, Papers of the Seixas Family, Series III: Gershom Mendes Seixas and Descendants, Box 1 Folder 12, AJHS.

INDEX

———

For the benefit of digital users, indexed terms that span two pages (e.g., 52–53) may, on occasion, appear on only one of those pages.